MASS TORT DEALS

Mass tort lawsuits over products like pelvic and hernia mesh, Roundup, opioids, talcum powder, and hip implants consume a substantial part of the federal civil caseload. But multidistrict litigation, which federal courts use to package these individual tort suits into one proceeding, has not been extensively analyzed. In *Mass Tort Deals*, Elizabeth Chamblee Burch marshals a wide array of empirical data to suggest that a systemic lack of checks and balances in our courts may benefit everyone but the plaintiffs – the very people who are often unable to stand up for themselves. Rather than faithfully representing them, plaintiffs' lawyers may sell them out in backroom settlements that compensate lawyers handsomely, pay plaintiffs little, and deny them the justice they seek. From diagnosis to reforms, Burch's goal isn't to eliminate these suits, it's to save them. This book is a must read for concerned citizens, policy makers, lawyers, and judges alike.

ELIZABETH CHAMBLEE BURCH is the Fuller E. Callaway Chair of Law at the University of Georgia School of Law and has been a visiting professor at Harvard Law School. In 2015, she won the American Law Institute's Early Career Scholars Medal. She has published more than 30 articles and essays in journals such as the *New York University Law Review*, *Cornell Law Review*, *Virginia Law Review*, and *Vanderbilt Law Review*. She co-authored a casebook on *The Law of Class Actions and Other Aggregate Litigation* (2009) and is a frequent commentator in various national news media, such as *The New York Times*, *The Wall Street Journal*, *Forbes*, *USA Today*, and *The L.A. Times*. For more information and the book's dataset, please visit www.elizabethchambleeburch.com.

Mass Tort Deals

BACKROOM BARGAINING IN MULTIDISTRICT LITIGATION

ELIZABETH CHAMBLEE BURCH
University of Georgia School of Law

CAMBRIDGE
UNIVERSITY PRESS

CAMBRIDGE
UNIVERSITY PRESS

University Printing House, Cambridge CB2 8BS, United Kingdom

One Liberty Plaza, 20th Floor, New York, NY 10006, USA

477 Williamstown Road, Port Melbourne, VIC 3207, Australia

314–321, 3rd Floor, Plot 3, Splendor Forum, Jasola District Centre, New Delhi – 110025, India

79 Anson Road, #06–04/06, Singapore 079906

Cambridge University Press is part of the University of Cambridge.

It furthers the University's mission by disseminating knowledge in the pursuit of education, learning, and research at the highest international levels of excellence.

www.cambridge.org
Information on this title: www.cambridge.org/9781108416979
DOI: 10.1017/9781108255929

First published 2019

A catalogue record for this publication is available from the British Library.

Library of Congress Cataloging-in-Publication Data
NAMES: Burch, Elizabeth Chamblee, author.
TITLE: Mass tort deals : backroom bargaining in multidistrict litigation / Elizabeth Chamblee Burch, University of Georgia School of Law.
DESCRIPTION: Cambridge, United Kingdom ; New York, NY, USA : Cambridge University Press, 2019. | Includes bibliographical references and index.
IDENTIFIERS: LCCN 2018058436 | ISBN 9781108416979 (hardback) | ISBN 9781108404211 (paperback)
SUBJECTS: LCSH: Complex litigation–United States. | Torts–United States. | Negotiation in business–United States.
CLASSIFICATION: LCC KF8896 .B87 2019 | DDC 346.7303–dc23
LC record available at https://lccn.loc.gov/2018058436

ISBN 978-1-108-41697-9 Hardback
ISBN 978-1-108-40421-1 Paperback

For my family

Contents

Figures

Tables

Acknowledgments

Just as it takes a village to raise a child, this book has been incubating for many years and has been nurtured by many facets of the scholarly community along the way. Various chapters have benefited from the generous comments of Bob Bone, Brannon Denning, Alexandra Lahav, Richard Marcus, Jonathan Nash, Charlie Silver, and faculties at Connecticut School of Law, Elon University School of Law, Emory School of Law, Georgia School of Law, Harvard Law School, Houston Law School, Texas Law School, and UC Hastings College of the Law. A few kind, brave, and loving souls read and commented on the entire manuscript. I'm deeply indebted to them – Thomas Burch, Bearle Chamblee, Peggy Torrey, and Margaret Williams, who is my faithful sounding board.

Conversations and comments from colleagues at various institutions helped improve, shape, and influence the ideas in this book at each stage: Christina Boyd, Andrew Bradt, Howard Erichson, Myriam Gilles, Maria Glover, John Goldberg, Judge Clay Land, Emery Lee, Samuel Issacharoff, David Marcus, Arthur Miller, Judge David Proctor, Morris Ratner, Teddy Rave, Judith Resnik, Bill Rubenstein, Bo Rutledge, Jay Tidmarsh, Tom Tyler, Judge Jack B. Weinstein, Patrick Woolley, and Adam Zimmerman. And though he isn't around to hear it, my thinking on these topics and indeed my entire academic career have been enhanced, sharpened, and forever changed by Richard Nagareda. I will always be in his debt. In the opening chapter of his own book, *Mass Torts in a World of Settlement*, he notes that "innovation by lawyers and judges in the real world of mass tort litigation has driven the academic dialogue on the subject, not vice versa." This book is a testament to those words, for it is a deep study of what happens in the litigation trenches. I wish I could tell him all about it.

Collecting and analyzing data over the course of six years has been possible only through the generosity of my dean, Bo Rutledge, and his predecessor, Dean Rebecca White. Even as schools have tightened their belts nationwide, continuous summer funding from the law school has made it possible for me to conduct my research from a purely academic perspective – without having to rely on external grants or funding that could cast shadows on my conclusions. It's also allowed me to avoid consulting for litigants on either side. Although consulting can be a valuable source of insights, it may also affect one's views and loyalties. So, apart from serving as a class-action notice expert in 2009, I have declined consulting opportunities.

Six years' worth of data collection and analysis couldn't have happened without the help of many student research assistants from Georgia and Harvard: Peyton Bradford, Melissa Conrad-Alam, Ellen Clarke, Lorcan Connick, Lee Deneen, Hayes Dever, David Ehrlich, Ryan Giles, Marcol Harvey, Kyle Hollomon, Richard Liu, David McGee, Savanna Nolan, Michael Nunnally, Sarah Quattrocchi, Charlie Spaulding, and Justin Van Orsdol. I'm also thankful for daily assistance from Nikko Terry, who took pains to help me create the index and proofread the manuscript; T.J. Striepe for being a law librarian extraordinaire and overseeing some of the data collection; and Jim Henneberger and Leslie Grove for turning my private data collection public by designing and breathing life into a searchable website.

A number of attorneys and judges have spoken with me about their experiences in multidistrict proceedings. I promised them anonymity, so I haven't included their names here, but I am appreciative of their trust, our discussions, and their willingness to give me a glimpse into what takes place behind the scenes. In particular, I'm indebted to Lance Cooper, the one attorney who agreed to go on the record; his story enlivens the book tremendously. This book would not be possible without the patience and guidance of Christine Dunn and Matt Gallaway at Cambridge University Press. Most importantly, I'm am thankful each day for my family's love, patience, and support.

Parts of this book draw upon and revise ideas that I first published elsewhere. I'm grateful to those law reviews for their work on *Financiers as Monitors in Aggregate Litigation*, 87 New York University Law Review 1273 (2012); *Disaggregating*, 90 Washington University Law Review 667 (2013); *Remanding Multidistrict Litigation*, 75 Louisiana Law Review 399 (2014); *Judging Multidistrict Litigation*, 90 New York Law University Law Review 71 (2015); *Constructing Issue Classes*, 101 Virginia Law Review 1855 (2015); *Monopolies in Multidistrict Litigation*, 70 Vanderbilt Law Review 67 (2017); and *Repeat Players in Multidistrict Litigation: The Social Network*, 102 Cornell Law Review 1445 (2017) (with Margaret S. Williams).

Introduction

It was her 29th birthday. After ending her shift as a nurse at West Atlanta Pediatrics, Brooke Melton headed out to meet her boyfriend for a celebratory dinner. She was a cautious driver – no speeding tickets, always a seat belt. But as she drove her Chevy Cobalt down the highway, it suddenly cut off. At just before 7:30 P.M. she swerved across the centerline. The oncoming car was unavoidable, it sent her careening into the fast-moving water of Picketts Mill Creek. Twenty minutes later, medics pulled her from the half-submerged Cobalt. And at 10 P.M., the hospital called Brooke's parents and told them about her accident, her broken neck, and how doctors could not save her.

After disbelief gave way to reality, her dad began playing back all the conversations he'd had with Brooke in the weeks before. He remembered how she'd complained that her car sometimes shut off while she was driving it. She had it serviced, fixed, just like he told her to. But as he pored over every detail of her accident and every online discussion board about Cobalts, he found others who'd had the same problems. Brooke was one of many.

The Meltons' subsequent lawsuit uncovered information that sparked a firestorm of suits against General Motors (GM) for ignition-switch defects, which the federal courts corralled before the same judge through a process known as multidistrict litigation, or MDL as it's often called.

In theory, multidistrict proceedings enable many "Davids," like Brooke's family, to pool their resources to efficiently litigate against Goliaths like GM. But, as Brooke's attorney discovered upon entering the inner sanctum of plaintiffs' lawyers who regularly spearhead these suits, there's a significant problem in practice: the system for handling mass torts can fail the very people it was meant to serve. Realizing this, her attorney tried to oust the insiders after learning that they cut a secret deal with GM. But the attempt fell on deaf ears. Why? Backroom deals benefit all the regulars – plaintiffs' lawyers, defendants, and even judges.

These proceedings matter – they involve high-stakes "bet-the-company" litigation and hundreds (sometimes thousands) of plaintiffs. Each proceeding like GM places a single judge in charge of all the similar federal claims filed across the country. Collectively, these proceedings consume more than one-third of the federal courts' pending civil docket and 15–21% of newly filed cases. As the GM litigation suggests, these are not run-of-the-mill disputes; they involve high-profile media magnets like the opioid epidemic, Volkswagen's emissions-cheating software, and Merck's painkiller, Vioxx.

Federal judges certify a few of these proceedings as class actions, which installs the judge as a monitor and paves paths for objecting and appealing – safeguards, in short. But tort-reform efforts have made class certification harder. As the continued suits over defective products suggest, however, those claims haven't gone away. Instead, they proceed as droves of individual suits packaged together by the courts and lawyers into a multidistrict proceeding. The risks for plaintiffs in those proceedings are significant: their lawyer may sell them out and the jury trials they've come to expect are rarer than a Perry Mason rerun.

This book marshals a wide array of empirical data on multidistrict litigation to suggest that the systemic lack of checks and balances for these cases may benefit everyone but the plaintiffs. Analyzing mass-tort proceedings centralized over 22 years and settled over 14, including the deals insiders negotiate, the "common-benefit" attorneys' fees that the lead plaintiffs' attorneys receive to run the litigation, as well as the judicial rulings themselves, reveals a troubling pattern: repeat plaintiff and defense attorneys persistently benefit from the current system. Defense lawyers are able to end sprawling lawsuits on their corporate clients' behalf while lead plaintiffs' lawyers broker deals that reward them handsomely and sometimes pay litigants very little.

For example, in litigation over the acid-reflux medicine Propulsid, only 37 of 6,012 plaintiffs (0.6%) recovered anything through the strict settlement program. Their collective recoveries totaled no more than $6.5 million. Yet, defendant Johnson & Johnson agreed to pay lead lawyers more than $27 million in common-benefit attorneys' fees. In return, what was left of the fund (some $45 million) would go back to Johnson & Johnson.[1] So, it appears that plaintiffs' lawyers profited, Johnson & Johnson paid the equivalent of a regulatory fine, and most plaintiffs were left to puzzle over why they were left empty-handed.

Some cases face even greater risks. Instead of standing as a bulwark against self-dealing, 52.9% of judges not only actively encouraged settlement but also (to varying degrees) approved and enforced the private dispute resolution that resulted. For instance, Judge Susan Wigenton ordered all plaintiffs litigating against Zimmer for faulty hip replacements to participate in the settlement program or face dismissal. The settlement required that participating lawyers (everyone with a case in the federal proceeding) sign up *every* plaintiff they represented, regardless of whether the suit was in state or federal court and regardless of whether the client wanted to

---

[1] Chapter 2 includes further details.

settle. At the same time, Judge Wigenton stayed the multidistrict proceeding, which meant that plaintiffs couldn't continue their discovery efforts or try the slated bellwether cases. And, just in case some attorneys relied solely on state courts, Judge Wigenton sent letters to every state judge with a similar case, urging them to do the same.

As part of that settlement, the lawyers who'd negotiated the federal deal inserted a 4% common-benefit fee to reward themselves for their hard work. Consenting to settle meant consenting to pay leaders 4% of plaintiffs' recoveries – even if the claim wasn't in federal court. The settlement allowed leaders to contract around Judge Wigenton's earlier order forbidding them from taxing state-court cases. Put plainly, the lead lawyers used their official bargaining authority with the defendant to enrich themselves, which Judge Wigenton then approved.

Judge Wigenton's settlement directive bound an elderly plaintiff population to alternative dispute resolution for 18 months. Indeed, most settlements within the dataset included facets of private dispute resolution that you might ordinarily find in a consumer contract for cell phones or credit cards, provisions that evict disputes from court and resolve them before an arbitrator or mediator behind closed doors. In *Vioxx*, for instance, Judge Eldon Fallon, who publicly presided over the multidistrict proceeding, traded his black robe to become the private settlement's chief administrator where he sat not as an appealable Article III judge but as an arbitrator whose ruling was final, binding, and nonappealable.

Arbitration deprives citizens of jury trials and can raise self-dealing concerns as corporate defendants pay their favorite arbitrator to confidentially decide disputes. The *New York Times* recently ran a series on consumer arbitration entitled *Arbitration Everywhere, Stacking the Deck of Justice* that revealed "a far-reaching power play orchestrated by American corporations" to bar people from using the court system.[2] The message was that judges enforce plaintiffs' rights, arbitrators don't.

Because courts appear to remedy all the maladies that arbitration creates, its detractors hail judges as the answer: for both procedural and substantive reasons, litigation is better for consumers, employees, and plaintiffs of most any sort. But it isn't that simple in mass torts. Litigation is not the panacea that arbitration's opponents envision. Empirically analyzing the private, aggregate settlements in the dataset reveals that litigation isn't an antidote to arbitration – it's merely a precursor. Most settlement programs shared a great deal in common with arbitration. Plaintiffs didn't know whether they'd recover when they entered them, claims administrators may tilt justice in favor of the repeat players who pick them, confidential awards make it hard to tell if plaintiffs are treated fairly vis-à-vis one another, and internal "appeals" processes offered little relief.

---

[2]   Jessica Silver-Greenberg & Robert Gebeloff, *Arbitration Everywhere, Stacking the Deck of Justice*, N.Y. TIMES, Oct. 31, 2015, at A1.

All this leaves us with a system in which each of the repeat players appears to benefit from the status quo. For their work on behalf of the plaintiffs, judicially appointed lead lawyers receive hefty common-benefit fees (sometimes upward of $350 million) on top of the attorneys' fees from their own clients. Corporate defendants resolve litigation with what may be relatively minimal expense. Through settlement, judges clear their dockets and often receive favorable press and new high-profile cases. Third-party funders profit, too, by lending money to mass-tort plaintiffs and their law firms with substantial interest. And claims and settlement administrators (who often act a great deal like arbitrators) screen claims and dole out settlement funds – all for a price. The mass-tort system's private underbelly is vast, and the bargains are far-reaching.

By one token, my thesis is quite simple: all is not well in the mass-tort world. Using original empirical research, this book exposes a tight-knit network of repeat players and judges who use government power to push and enforce private deals. In this sense, the book offers what anthropologist Clifford Geertz would call a "thick description."[3] Thick descriptions do more than just crunch numbers and present data, they interpret and ascribe meaning to the practices they observe. As Thoreau put it in *Walden*, going "round the world to count the cats in Zanzibar" wouldn't tell you much else besides how many cats live in East Africa. And I'm afraid it just might put you off our whole endeavor.

Nevertheless, the equivalent of counting the cats in Zanzibar (a thin description) was a necessary predicate to ascribing any meaning to the MDL system as a whole. Gathering data, or counting cats so to speak, took the better part of six years. Here's a thumbnail of an example: I spent weeks just digging up the raw numbers for the *Propulsid* litigation – combing through more than 4,700 docket entries and downloading the relevant ones, reading transcripts, and piecing together the litigation chronology and numbers. It then took several more weeks to assemble the story through news reports, to identify plaintiffs' successes and setbacks, and to layer those data points into the earlier chronology.

From a bird's-eye view, my dataset includes all the products-liability and sales-practice proceedings pending on the MDL docket as of May 14, 2013 – 73 proceedings, centralized over 22 years and settled over 14. Those proceedings collectively included more than 312,500 actions, most of which have now concluded. (An "action," by the way, is a single civil suit, but that one suit may contain many plaintiffs – consolidating claims allows plaintiffs' attorneys to avoid paying hundreds of dollars in filing fees for each person.) Parties settled 34 of those 73 proceedings through nonclass global or inventory settlements, 20 through class-action settlements, 1 through individual settlements, and 1 through bankruptcy. Most class-action settlements involved sales-practice cases without personal injuries, whereas most personal-injury products-liability cases like *Propulsid* settled through private

[3] Clifford Geertz, The Interpretation of Cultures 27 (1973).

global or inventory settlements. For those that weren't settled, defendants successfully used *Daubert* motions on expert evidence, summary judgment, and arbitration
to resolve 12 proceedings, and the remaining 5 proceedings are still being actively
litigated.

This book focuses principally on those mass-tort proceedings that ended in private
settlement. Of those 34 proceedings, private settlements were publicly available in
10. Three of those 10 proceedings contained 2 settlements each for a total of 13
settlements. While 13 deals may not sound like much, collectively they covered
more than 64,000 federal "actions" as well as thousands of uncounted but related
state-court cases. For statistics enthusiasts, the Appendix includes far more details.

Like all data-rich research, moving from tallying cats into broader theories about
how to best interpret those numbers invites controversy. You can construe my
numbers in different ways, and there will certainly be squabbles about what conclusions to draw.

As I wrote this book, for instance, I presented my theories to various audiences
and often incorporated the *Propulsid* data. Sometimes audience members included
Judge Eldon Fallon, who presided over *Propulsid*; Susan Sharko, who represented
Johnson & Johnson; and various involved plaintiffs' attorneys. They lived those
proceedings and would each tell you a very different story. Their understandings
invariably differ from my retrospective view as an outside observer.

In this sense, the book reflects my conscious choices about how to present data
and which case studies to feature based not only on the numbers but also on my
reading of the thousands of motions, arguments, and court transcripts that accom-
pany this raw data. Of course, there may be things that I miss; this area of law is
dynamic and evolving. There is ever so much more to do. In that sense, this book is
meant to provide a portal into this world, to invite discussion, debate, and further
conversations – not to have the last word. To facilitate that discursive process, I have
made all the data that I've collected over the past six years publicly available.[4]

Experts in the field have debated how to handle mass torts for many years now
and I hope that they will discover a new tidbit, perspective, or twist in the pages that
follow. But mass torts aren't just about academics, lawyers, or even judges – they
affect the masses. More specifically, they affect real people like Brooke Melton and
her family, as individuals.

Consequently, to make the entire book more accessible to a diverse audience, I've
tried to tone down the legal and technical jargon and add narrative to the data
through case studies, vignettes, anecdotes, and quotes. And, of course, because my
theories rely on a variety of insights from social psychology, behavioral law and
economics, and complex adaptive systems, some aspects of the material may be new
to most readers. To be sure, case studies and anecdotes cannot substitute for careful

---

[4] You may access and search that data at http://mdldata.law.uga.edu and https://www.elizabeth-
chambleeburch.com/. The password for protected pages is MDLRepeatplay.

evidence. So, for those who would prefer to dive deeper into the technical details, I have included extensive footnotes and appendices.

Before we get on with the book, let me add two caveats. First, despite putting these proceedings under the microscope, some information just isn't publicly available. As the Appendix details, most private aggregate settlements remain private. Even those that are publicly available rarely include information on substantive outcomes – what plaintiffs received, in other words. (Judge Fallon's dockets are usually an exception, and I remain deeply grateful for his commitment to transparency.)

This leaves a big gap and a host of questions: how do outcomes in nonclass multidistrict proceedings compare with those in class actions and those settled outside the centralized proceeding? How much money is paid out and to whom? How long does it take to administer claims? Are like plaintiffs treated equally? How much does it cost to put settlement money in class members' hands versus the costs of paying plaintiffs in private, aggregate settlements? Are plaintiffs treated differently in inventory settlements with a single law firm as opposed to global deals?[5] I could go on. But you get the idea, right? This book is a start, but we're left feeling our way around in the dark on many critical points. And I worry about that.

One more caveat: as Clifford Geertz explains, for thick descriptions, "Behavior must be attended to, and with some exactness, because it is through the flow of behavior – or, more precisely, social action – that cultural forms find articulation."[6] So, I have chosen to use names where exactness is important. The point is not to be salacious, but specific. Divorcing interpretation from what happens "from what, in this time or that place, specific people say, what they do, what is done to them," takes us away from the "heart" of what we're interpreting, Geertz notes.[7]

Still, when people talk about class actions and aggregate litigation, they tend to take cheap shots at the plaintiffs' attorneys who bring them. That's not my aim. In the pages that follow, you will see that I am quite critical of the way attorneys on both sides conduct themselves in this ethical minefield. And it just so happens that ethical obligations are more perilous for plaintiffs' lawyers representing the masses, so my fault finding falls most heavily upon them. But let me make one thing clear: my critique is of the *system as a whole*. Plaintiffs' lawyers do not have a monopoly on systemic failings and misaligned incentives; there is ample blame to go around. Plaintiffs' attorneys must often accept settlement offers as defendants present them, so defendants and their attorneys are on the hook too.

In short, this book aims to shed some light on the high-stakes world of mass torts. It suggests that tunnel vision toward efficiency undermines more than just a

---

5   So-called inventory settlements resolve one law firm's cases. I'm not a fan of the term because it makes people seem like stock, but it is used frequently among courts and attorneys. A "global" settlement, by contrast, resolves most suits brought by many different firms.

6   GEERTZ, *supra* note 3, at 17.

7   *Id.* at 18.

plaintiff's payday. It means fewer jury trials, less transparency, less precedent, and more private dispute resolution (under the guise of Article III courts no less). We seem to have forgotten that legitimate procedures are the skeletal structure that hold the meatier substantive rights and values together. When procedures collapse, so too do communal democratic values, the public's faith in the system's legitimacy, and even the rule of law.

When Mass Torts Meet Multidistrict Litigation

During the fall of her freshman year at Elon University, 18-year-old Michelle Pfleger collapsed while walking to class. "They called me from the hospital," said her mother, "they told me that her heart was not responding and that it wasn't good."[1] The slender, blonde-haired, champion equestrian died from a pulmonary embolism – a blood clot in her lungs that caused her to have a heart attack.[2]

Before she left for college, Michelle asked her doctor to prescribe Yaz, a birth control pill that Bayer advertised as a cure-all for irritability, moodiness, and bloating.[3] She'd seen the commercials: one with Twisted Sister's song "We're Not Gonna Take It" and another with The Veronicas' "Goodbye to You," both showing fashionable young women who are no longer bothered by floating words like *headache, irritability,* and *anxiety.* Voiceovers touted Yaz as a "pill that goes beyond the rest," with enviable side effects like clear skin.[4]

Bayer's marketing campaign skyrocketed Yaz to the best-selling birth control pill in 2008, with sales totaling $781 million in 2009. But the Food and Drug Administration (FDA) warned Bayer that its ads were misleading and requested that the company take the unusual step of airing corrected commercials.[5] Although most birth control pills are considered safe despite a slightly increased risk of developing

---

[1] *New Birth Control Pills: Higher Clotting Risk?*, CBS NEWS (June 2, 2011, 12:35 PM), https://www.cbsnews.com/news/new-birth-control-pills-higher-clotting-risk.

[2] Pamela Sroka-Holzmann, *Mom Blames Yaz for Daughter's Death*, EXPRESS-TIMES (Easton, Pa.), May 11, 2011, at A1.

[3] Susan Todd, *Lawsuits Mounting over Alleged Health Risks of Bayer's Yaz Contraceptive*, STAR-LEDGER (Newark, NJ) (July 11, 2011), https://www.nj.com/business/index.ssf/2011/07/lawsuits_mounting_over_alleged.html. Three studies showed no increased risk.

[4] Natasha Singer, *A Birth Control Pill That Promised Too Much*, N.Y. TIMES, Feb. 10, 2009, at B1.

[5] Julie Deardorff, *Lawsuits Pile Up over Popular Birth Control Pills*, CHI. TRIB. (Sept. 15, 2013), http://www.chicagotribune.com/lifestyles/health/ct-met-birth-control-risks-20130915-story.html.

blood clots, the ingredients in Yasmin and Yaz (a reformulated version of Yasmin) included a new synthetic hormone, Drospirenone.

Seven large studies (including some with FDA-funded research) showed that women taking pills with Drospirenone would have a 1.5 times higher risk of developing blood clots than with other birth control pills.[6] Former FDA commissioner David Kessler, who worked as an expert witness for plaintiffs like Michelle's mom, explained that Bayer's own researchers found increased reports of blood clots among Yasmin users compared with users of other pills. Yet, Bayer didn't tell the FDA.[7]

As more than 11,000 lawsuits nationwide flooded the federal courts claiming that Yaz and Yasmin caused death, strokes, pulmonary embolisms, gallbladder disease, and elevated potassium levels, the Judicial Panel on Multidistrict Litigation (the Panel) centralized them before Judge David Herndon in the Southern District of Illinois. To manage an onslaught of suits like those in *Yaz*, Congress passed the Multidistrict Litigation Act in 1968. The statute authorizes a panel of seven judges selected by the Chief Justice of the U.S. Supreme Court to transfer factually related lawsuits to a single district judge for coordinated pretrial litigation.[8] This prevents corporate employees like those at Bayer from being deposed 11,000 different times, keeps judges from duplicating their efforts and wasting judicial resources, and allows plaintiffs to join forces against a foe with deep pockets. As Professor Arthur Miller once explained, "[L]itigants get more judicial bang for their judicial buck when like things are aggregated and adjudicated together."[9]

Yasmin/Yaz is just one of the hundreds of multidistrict proceedings you're likely to hear about in the news. Perhaps you've read about states' opioid lawsuits against Big Pharma or the $4.69 billion judgment against Johnson & Johnson for failing to warn women about the cancer risks associated with asbestos in talcum baby powder.[10] Or maybe you remember when BP spilled millions of gallons of oil into the Gulf of Mexico in 2010. At the federal level, Yaz, opioid, talc, and the oil spill are each handled using multidistrict litigation (MDL).

Perhaps it's not surprising then that these proceedings have exploded over the past decade. From 2002 to 2017, MDL jumped from 16 to 37% of the federal courts' pending civil caseload.[11] Although the Panel has centralized fewer proceedings in

---

[6] *Id.*

[7] Pam Belluck, *More Detail on Risk Urged for a Contraceptive Label*, N.Y. Times, Dec. 9, 2011, at A20.

[8] 28 U.S.C. § 1407 (2012).

[9] Arthur R. Miller, *What Are Courts For? Have We Forsaken the Procedural Gold Standard?*, 78 La. L. Rev. 739, 740 (2018).

[10] Tiffany Hsu, *Johnson & Johnson Told to Pay $4.7 Billion in Baby Powder Lawsuit*, N.Y. Times, July 12, 2018, at B6; Katie Benner & Jan Hoffman, *Justice Dept. Backs High-Stakes Lawsuit Against Opioid Makers*, N.Y. Times, Feb. 27, 2018, at A10.

[11] Judicial Panel on Multidistrict Litigation, 2017 Year-End Report 1 (2017); Duke Law Center for Judicial Studies, MDL Standards and Best Practices, at x (2014), https://

recent years, it consistently coordinates products-liability cases – "mass torts" or mass harms, in other words.[12] As compared with other types of MDLs such as antitrust, employment practices, or intellectual property, products liability like *Yasmin/Yaz* tend to be the largest type of proceedings on the Panel's docket (comprising a little more than one-third of all the proceedings), but even that number undersells mass torts a bit. Like the mile-long scarf up a magician's bare sleeve, the 11,000 *Yasmin/ Yaz* actions were just *one* proceeding. A look then at all the *actions* on the Panel's docket reveals mass torts' dominance: 95% are products liability.[13] (And remember that a single "action" might contain many individual plaintiffs.)

The popular press often refers to these lawsuits as "class actions," but that's a mistake. Most aren't certified as class actions and that matters. You see, class actions are governed by a special procedural rule, Rule 23, which includes checks and balances and safeguards to make sure that attorneys aren't exploiting people to get rich. You can find plenty of examples suggesting that the rule doesn't always work as planned, but, as we'll see, it may be better than having no buffer at all.

Why then are mass torts so rarely certified as class actions? As this chapter explores, the reasons are multifaceted but one stands out: even though corporations operate nationally (and internationally), their judicial and congressional efforts to cripple nationwide class actions and thereby limit their liability have paid off.[14] Class actions can include people who never file lawsuits, which is good if there are small claims. Otherwise, no lawyer would take on a major bank that charged you $35 in overdraft fees, for instance. Class actions allow attorneys to sue on absent class members' behalf. While you'd be more likely to litigate over a major injury like a pulmonary embolism, not everyone does. For instance, the FDA received reports that 12,600 Yaz users experienced injuries, 8,800 had pulmonary embolisms, and 8,200 had deep vein thrombosis. As you know, however, there were only around

law.duke.edu/sites/default/files/centers/judicialstudies/MDL_Standards_and_Best_Practices_2014-REVISED.pdf.

[12] In 2017, the Panel granted only 48% of parties' requests, a significant decrease from the 10-year average of 64%. JUDICIAL PANEL ON MULTIDISTRICT LITIGATION, 2017 YEAR-END REPORT (2017).

[13] Margaret Williams, Senior Research Associate, Federal Judicial Center, Research Presentation on Multidistrict Litigation at the University of Georgia School of Public & International Affairs (Apr. 14, 2017).

[14] *E.g.*, Class Action Fairness Act of 2005 § 2(a)-(b), Pub. L. No. 109–2, 119 Stat. 4, 4–5 (codified in scattered sections of 28 U.S.C.) (creating federal jurisdiction over class actions, which increases choice-of-law problems and makes certification more difficult); Wal-Mart Stores, Inc. v. Dukes, 564 U.S. 338, 348–66 (2011) (strengthening commonality under Rule 23(a)). For a detailed overview of these changes, see Elizabeth Chamblee Burch, *Constructing Issue Classes*, 101 VA. L. REV. 1855, 1860–66 (2015).

11,000 federal suits. So, eliminating the use of class actions instantly reduces Bayer's potential liability.

Because these changes are "procedural," however, nobody talks about them much. Yet, procedure makes the world turn. It's a fundamental lesson, really. And it's one that corporations have learned all too well: change the rules, change the outcome.

Corporations like Bayer, Merck, and Johnson & Johnson understand that the rules of the game, the procedures in other words, can profoundly impact the result. And so they have used their political heft through the Chamber of Commerce and their advocacy through the defense bar to skew rules or "technicalities," as some say, to their distinct advantage. By exploiting imbalances between a single state's jurisdictional reach and their own nationwide conduct, and shifting attention away from their uniform wrongdoing and toward the way those actions affect people distinctly, corporations frequently dodge class certification.

In its brief opposing class status for the *Yaz* plaintiffs, for instance, Bayer argued, "Overwhelming management problems are clear from a quick reading of the complaint. . . . Individual issues of fact predominate concerning each putative class member's medical history and use of YAZ or Yasmin," plus there are "[i]ndividual issues of law." Bayer then rattled off a litany of differences – all focused on the plaintiffs: specific causation "will require an examination of each person's medical history, including pre-existing conditions and use of other medications," women "ingested different products – YAZ and/or Yasmin – for different periods of time," and the facts will vary depending on "how the doctor balances the risks and benefits of the medicine for that particular patient."[15]

People are unique, yes. But Bayer's conduct was uniform. And adjudicating that conduct will involve common questions about whether its nationwide advertisements were misleading, whether it should have disclosed more information to the FDA, and whether its label failed to warn patients of its risks.

Nevertheless, Judge Herndon sided with Bayer. He declined to certify not only a class of Yaz and Yasmin users who suffered from deep vein thrombosis but also a class alleging that purchasers were economically harmed when Bayer's misleading advertisements (the ones promising to cure a variety of premenstrual symptoms) prompted them to buy Yaz or Yasmin instead of an equally effective, cheaper contraceptive.[16]

---

[15] Bayer's Memorandum in Support of Motion to Strike or Dismiss Class Allegations at 7–8, *In re* Yasmin & Yaz (Drospirenone) Mktg., Sales Practices & Prods. Liab. Litig., No. 09-cv-20108 (S.D. Ill. Sept. 24, 2010).

[16] *In re* Yasmin & Yaz (Drospirenone) Mktg., Sales Practices & Prods. Liab. Litig., No. 09-md-02100, 2012 WL 865041, at *1 (S.D. Ill. Mar. 13, 2012); *In re* Yasmin & Yaz (Drospirenone) Mktg., Sales Practices & Prods. Liab. Litig., 275 F.R.D. 270, 272 (S.D. Ill. 2011).

THE SHIFT AWAY FROM MASS TORT CLASS ACTIONS

To be fair, personal-injury mass tort class actions never stood on very solid ground. Back in the 1960s, as the Civil Rules Advisory Committee considered enacting our modern-day class-action rule to help combat civil-rights abuses, some members worried that the ambitious tort bar might co-opt it to deprive those with personal injuries of their day in court. You see, when a lawyer initiates a class suit, only the named plaintiff participates; others might not even know that someone else is pursuing their claim. That might not bother you much if your bank overcharges you $35, but if you think Yaz killed your daughter, that's a different story.

"[I]t is a drastic thing to cut off the rights of persons who are not parties," reasoned the Civil Rules Advisory Committee reporters in 1962.[17] And in 1963, committee member John Frank announced that he was "unpersuadably opposed to the use of the class action in the mass tort situation" because of people's "loss of individual liberty" and his worries that defendants would take advantage of unscrupulous plaintiffs' attorneys to bind unwitting victims.[18]

Because the class-action rule, Rule 23, allows attorneys to litigate rights belonging to people who aren't present, it includes some protections. Judges must decide if the lawyer and the token plaintiff adequately represent everyone else, and if that plaintiff's claims are like other people's claims such that if the named plaintiff selfishly pursues her own interest, she'll be doing what's best for absent members, too. Nevertheless, the Advisory Committee still worried that a corporate defense attorney might conspire with a plaintiff's lawyer to slyly do away with plaintiffs' rights while making a tidy profit for themselves.

What comforted the Advisory Committee was the ongoing work of a different group, the Coordinating Committee on Multiple Litigation, whose efforts led Congress to enact the MDL statute. Professor Andrew Bradt explains that the two committees began to "liaise." As a result, the Advisory Committee added language to Rule 23's explanatory note stating that a mass accident "is ordinarily not appropriate for a class action because of the likelihood that significant questions, not only of damages but of liability and defenses of liability, would be present, affecting individuals in different ways."[19] Recognizing what would become the MDL statute, the Advisory Committee also added a superiority requirement to Rule 23(b)(3). Class actions had to be "superior to other available methods [like multidistrict litigation] for the fair and efficient adjudication of the controversy."[20]

---

[17] Andrew D. Bradt, *Something Less and Something More: MDL's Roots as a Class Action Alternative*, 165 U. PA. L. REV. 1711, 1721 (2017) (citing a memorandum from the reporters).

[18] *Id.* at 1726 (citing a letter from John Frank to Benjamin Kaplan); *see also* Judith Resnik, *Aggregation, Settlement, and Dismay*, 80 CORNELL L. REV. 915, 923–30 (1995) (describing the advisory committee's history and the evolution of mass torts).

[19] FED. R. CIV. P. 23 advisory committee's notes to 1937 adoption.

[20] Bradt, *supra* note 17, at 1729 (citing a reporter's Dec. 2, 1963, memo).

In class-action lingo, the superiority and predominance requirements aim to ensure that it's worthwhile to use a class action. Predominance asks if the class suit poses more common questions than individual ones and whether those common questions help resolve all the litigation. Otherwise, why bother? Superiority follows up, prompting the judge to make sure that a class action is the best way to handle the suits, not individual litigation or multidistrict litigation, for example. As we saw in *Yaz*, these questions present significant hurdles in personal-injury cases.

Nevertheless, there were a few mass tort class actions during the decades that followed. In the 1980s, judges certified classes over military-contractor defenses in *Agent Orange* and state-of-the-art defenses in *Jenkins v. Raymark Industries*, for instance.[21] But, in the late 1990s, a pair of Supreme Court opinions on the sprawling asbestos cases largely halted this practice and brought the Advisory Committee's concerns about collusion to life.[22]

Much ink has been spilled over those two opinions, *Amchem Products, Inc. v. Windsor* and *Ortiz v. Fibreboard*.[23] Skillful narratives detail how experienced asbestos plaintiffs' lawyers Joe Rice and Ron Motley teamed up with defense lawyer John Aldock (who represented CCR, a consortium of asbestos defendants) to enrich themselves at future asbestos plaintiffs' expense.[24] As Aldock described, "CCR asked us to try to formulate an 'end game,'" so "we secretly began negotiating with the leaders of the plaintiffs' bar (Ron Motley and Joe Rice of South Carolina and Gene Locks of Philadelphia)." "The main antagonist," lamented Aldock, "was Freddie Baron."[25] As we'll see, Fred Baron used Rule 23(e)(5), which allows objectors to raise their concerns to district judges and appellate courts, to halt the asbestos class-action scheme – twice.

In the early 1980s, the asbestos bar was "close-knit," said Baron & Budd attorney Brent Rosenthal. "The attitude of 'mi casa, su casa, my work-product is your work-product' was overwhelmingly prevalent." But in the late 1980s, early 1990s, "the asbestos plaintiffs' bar became increasingly polarized." "From the beginning, Fred [Baron] and Ron Motley had a fierce, sometimes-not-too-friendly rivalry," Rosenthal explained of his partner.

---

[21] *In re* Agent Orange Prod. Liab. Litig., 818 F.2d 145, 166 (2d Cir. 1987); Jenkins v. Raymark Indus., 782 F.2d 468, 470–73 (5th Cir. 1986).

[22] More recently, mass tort settlement class actions have been certified on occasion. *E.g., In re* NFL Players Concussion Injury Litig., 821 F.3d 410, 420 (3d Cir. 2016); *In re* Oil Spill by the Oil Rig "Deepwater Horizon" in the Gulf of Mexico, on April 20, 2010, 295 F.R.D. 112, 161 (E.D. La. 2013) (certifying a class of medical claims).

[23] Ortiz v. Fibreboard Corp., 527 U.S. 815, 852 (1999); Amchem Prods., Inc. v. Windsor, 521 U.S. 591 (1997).

[24] *E.g.,* John C. Coffee, Jr., *Class Wars: The Dilemma of the Mass Tort Class Action*, 95 COLUM. L. REV. 1343 (1995); Susan P. Koniak, *Feasting While the Widow Weeps*: Georgine v. Amchem Products, Inc., 80 CORNELL L. REV. 1045 (1995).

[25] Interview by Judith S. Feigin, Esquire, with John D. Aldock, Esquire, in Wash., D.C., at 137 (Oral History Project of the Historical Society of the District of Columbia Circuit May 11, 2010), http://dcchs.org/JohnDAldock/JohnDAldock_Complete.pdf.

When Ron Motley struck a deal with John Aldock, Fred Baron aimed to derail it. "Opposition appeared to be hopeless to me," Rosenthal wrote, "[b]ut the difficulty of the task only energized Fred."[26] Baron and Rosenthal succeeded, winning the two landmark Supreme Court cases.

In *Amchem*, the Supreme Court explained that "[i]n significant respects, the interests of those within the single class are not aligned." Those with current injuries want "generous immediate payments," but "[t]hat goal tugs against the interest of exposure-only plaintiffs in ensuring an ample, inflation protected fund for the future." In short, the settling parties "achieved a global compromise with no structural assurance of fair and adequate representation for the diverse groups and individuals affected," ruled the Court.[27]

But the key players – John Aldock, Joe Rice, Ron Motley, and Gene Locks – weren't willing to give up so easily. They regrouped and tried to use a different portion of Rule 23, Rule 23(b)(1)(B), which allowed defendants on the brink of bankruptcy to force all their tort plaintiffs into one action so that the court could divide the defendant's assets fairly among them. Otherwise, a big win in one court might mean a payout for that plaintiff, but nothing for the others. Yet, if the more liberal Rule 23(b)(3) was ill-suited to manage mass torts, surely Rule 23(b)(1)(B), which didn't even allow class members to opt out, was even less up to the task. But the dealmakers gave it a shot because, strictly speaking, *Amchem* applied only to Rule 23(b)(3). Fred Baron and Brent Rosenthal began their objection simply this time: "Some people just can't take a hint," they wrote.[28]

The same conflicts pervaded in *Ortiz*. And the Court was dubious about a deal claiming that only "limited funds" were available to divvy up among future asbestos plaintiffs because class counsel settled 45,000 pending claims, claims of current clients in other words, separately but simultaneously. "Class counsel thus had great incentive to reach any agreement in the global settlement negotiations that they thought might survive a Rule 23(e) fairness hearing, rather than the best possible arrangement for the substantially unidentified global settlement class," the Court concluded.[29]

The *Amchem* and *Ortiz* deals weren't just products of an overzealous bar, however. "*Amchem* happened because the federal courts wanted a class action endgame," explains Professor David Marcus. Marcus describes how an "air of judicial desperation" had set in by the late 1980s and how the Federal Judicial Center convened a meeting at the Dolly Madison House in Washington, D.C. Thereafter, judges begged the Panel to coordinate the asbestos cases, which it finally did (despite having denied five previous requests). It sent the cases to Judge Charles

---

[26] Interview by David Marcus with Brent Rosenthal, Esquire, e-mail (Apr. 21, 2016, 2:48 PM).

[27] *Amchem Prods., Inc.*, 521 U.S. at 626–27.

[28] Petition for Writ of Certiorari, Ortiz v. Fibreboard Corp., 1998 WL 34081053, at *1 (Apr. 17, 1998).

[29] Ortiz v. Fibreboard Corp., 527 U.S. 815, 852 (1999).

Weiner, a "master settler." Plaintiffs' lawyers described his chambers as a "dark hole" and a "plaintiffs' Armageddon." As Professor Marcus concludes, focusing on "deal-making attorneys as the prime movers" paints an incomplete picture: "To a significant extent, the lawyers responded to judicial pressure."[30]

Subsequent Supreme Court opinions have made certifying a class in any type of proceeding even tougher.[31] To make a long story short, corporate defendants' efforts to avoid class actions have paid off. Their steady wins convince courts to put plaintiffs under the microscope, spotlighting their uniqueness, while shifting attention away from corporate uniform acts. But this shift from class actions to mass resolution through MDL has served only to exacerbate the issues that began bubbling to the surface in *Amchem* and *Ortiz*. As the coming chapters explore, behind-the-scenes judicial wrangling, settlement cramdowns, conflicts of interest, and attorney-client sellouts flourish. Yet, Fred Baron's remedy – objecting under Rule 23(e)(5) – doesn't exist without the class action.

So, pretend for a moment that you are Michelle Pfleger's mother or father – it might seem safer to bring your own suit. Maybe you'd try to hire a local attorney you've known for years. But that lawyer can't typically afford to take on Bayer. Litigating a single case like *Yaz* can easily cost more than $1 million. So, she might refer your case to a mass-tort specialist like Joe Rice or Gene Locks. Firms like theirs represent hundreds of clients similar to you, which is good for leveling the playing field, but now you're part of their "inventory" of cases – their stock, in other words. Instead of running into your attorney friend around town or calling her for updates, you may be stuck talking with case managers and reading online forums.

Or maybe instead of hiring locally, you search for "Yaz attorney" on the Internet and call one of the many firms that pop up. Those firms are often either the Motley Rice types or will act as a referral service to those firms. If you dial one of those onscreen numbers, chances are your call won't go to that law firm's front desk. Instead, it gets routed to a call center, like the one run by U.S. Legal (a do-it-yourself-type legal website) that's housed behind the late Johnnie Cochran's namesake law office in Dothan, Alabama. An intake operator fills out your chosen firm's form. As these specialized law firms handle hundreds of clients, they aren't well positioned to

---

[30] David Marcus, *The Short Life and Long Afterlife of the Mass Tort Class Action*, 165 U. PA. L. REV. 1565, 1581–89 (2017); *see also* Richard L. Marcus, *They Can't Do That, Can They? Tort Reform via Rule 23*, 80 CORNELL L. REV. 858 (1995) (arguing that federal judges have tackled tort reform through their work under Rule 23).

[31] *Wal-Mart Stores, Inc. v. Dukes* strengthened Rule 23(a)'s commonality standard, requiring plaintiffs not just to come up with common questions but also to pose questions with uniform answers that help resolve the litigation. 564 U.S. 338, 350–51 (2011). *Comcast Corp. v. Behrend*, 569 U.S. 27, 34 (2013), held that plaintiffs' antitrust damages had to be calculable on a classwide basis. Otherwise, divvying up money to individuals might overwhelm predominance, rendering the class noncertifiable. As the dissenters pointed out, before *Comcast*, courts routinely certified classes with individual-damage calculations. *Id.* at 42 (Ginsburg, J., dissenting).

offer you the type of fireside counsel you might want. There is strength in numbers, yes, but also anonymity.

Once you've hired a lawyer, where should you file your lawsuit? Your hometown offers two options: state or federal court. The state court just down the street seems like a good choice, but Bayer will likely remove your suit to federal court (which it can do so long as you don't live in the same state as its headquarters or state of incorporation).[32] As your case moves from state to federal court, it may initially just transition to a different building downtown. But it won't stay there for long. Because other cases across the country present similar factual issues, the Panel will then transfer it to the "transferee judge," who, in *Yaz*, was Judge Herndon. So, regardless of where you live, your case and all the hearings concerning it are now in Illinois.[33] Instead of a grieving parent, you are a number, one of 11,000 others.

While it's true then that you're not an "absent" plaintiff as in a class action, the idea that you'll be able to watch over your attorney's shoulder to ensure she's acting in your best interest or that you can make key decisions about your lawsuit is simply false. You don't have the same kind of control. In theory, individual representation quells the worry that your attorney may sell you out (we think of these as attorney-client "agency problems" because your lawyer is your agent). But, as Stanford Professor Deborah Hensler recognizes, "[I]n practice, individual representation often is provided by plaintiff law firms on a mass basis, with little attention to individual clients." So, she notes, "[T]he same agency problems that bedevil class actions are inherent in multidistrict litigation."[34]

One pelvic-mesh plaintiff described her experience grimly: "I have thought about this whole process with regard to MDLs and had absolutely no idea it would be like this." "I[n] some ways it feels like you are sent to a 'holding jail' while the legal system plays out. You try to get justice in your own area and then your case i[s] moved to another state and it is just 'wait, wait, wait' while your life falls into further destruction." Then, "[a]fter years and years of waiting and being lied to all the while, when the time comes for closure, you are then absolutely blindsided by the treatment by your own attorney. It almost feels like the attorneys are both working for the defendant and themselves."[35]

---

[32] Some suits remain in state court because the plaintiff sues a defendant from the same state where she resides. This destroys what's known as complete diversity. Other suits remain in state court because they're filed in the corporate defendant's home state. The relevant statutes are 28 U.S.C. §§ 1332, 1441, 1446 (2012).

[33] Transferee judges receive cases from the Panel and conduct centralized pretrial litigation. Those cases come from the "transferor judges," the judge that the federal court downtown would assign to your case.

[34] Deborah R. Hensler, *No Need to Panic: The Multi-District Litigation Process Needs Improvement Not Demolition*, 4, https://www.law.gwu.edu/sites/g/files/zaxdzs2351/f/downloads/Deborah-Hensler-MDL-Paper.pdf.

[35] E-mail from Diane Harter (the plaintiff's maiden name) to author (Dec. 4, 2017) (on file with author).

JUDGES' UNENVIABLE TASK

It's not easy or simple for judges to manage the sheer number of cases in a multi-district proceeding, but layering in countless intrinsic human elements makes their jobs that much harder. Just imagine having to juggle attorneys' egos, personal animosities, injured plaintiffs, and defendants with public-relations problems and fickle shareholders on top of addressing the dispute.

Class actions anticipate some of these interpersonal issues by allowing those who don't want to be a part of the proceeding to opt out or object, as Fred Baron did. Certifying a class also gives judges some unique power that they lack in ordinary civil suits. Judges select and formally appoint class counsel, decide whether counsel adequately represents class members, and then determine whether a settlement is fair, reasonable, and adequate. Afterward, they award class counsel's attorney's fee. Unhappy class members can appeal these decisions, which means that appellate law exists to steer judges in the right direction.

As mass tort class actions wane, however, so do all these formal powers. Administratively, nonclass mass torts are even messier: just think of the 11,000 *Yaz* cases. Judges can't pretend these are individual lawsuits. It'd be nearly impossible to hear from 11,000 different attorneys and their clients. So, judges rely on some of the same techniques that helped them manage class actions but with less clear-cut authority and fewer guidelines for doing so.

Appointing Lead Lawyers

To avoid hearing from 11,000 plaintiffs' attorneys, judges appoint a variety of what I collectively call *lead lawyers* or *leaders*. This umbrella term includes lead counsel, plaintiffs' steering committees (PSC) or executive committees (PEC), liaison counsel, and committee chairs. As we'll see in Chapter 3, judges tend to appoint the same people to these positions routinely.

As Figure 1.1 illustrates, if you compare a multidistrict proceeding to a corporation, *lead counsel* would be the litigation's CEOs. Usually limited to a small group of two or three lawyers, lead counsel runs the proceedings and acts on the group's behalf by strategizing, filing key motions, and negotiating settlements, for example. *Steering* or *executive committees* (the terms differ, but the meaning is usually the same) help finance the proceeding, may oversee subcommittees conducting discovery, and might help with strategy, decision making, and settlement. Ideally, they would act as a democratic board of directors that advise and constrain lead counsel, but decision making is as varied as the personalities running the proceeding. *Liaison counsel* disseminates information to other attorneys, calls meetings, and coordinates with counsel in related state (and sometimes bankruptcy) actions. In other words, they act as communication directors and, when the time comes to settle, they rally the troops of lawyers to get them (and their clients) onboard.

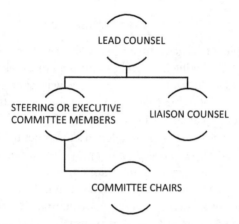

FIGURE 1.1 Leadership hierarchy within multidistrict proceedings

Finally, separate *committee chairs* might head discovery and trial committees or perform specific tasks.

Lead counsel negotiate settlements and dictate trial strategy, but few rules govern this undemocratic process. For example, Judge Susan Wigenton appointed a five-member plaintiffs' liaison counsel (that acted more like a PSC) to head lawsuits against Zimmer over its poorly designed Durom hip cup. Yet, Chris Seeger, one of those five members, quietly joined forces with nonlead lawyer Mark Lanier. Without the other counsel members' knowledge or consent, Lanier and Seeger hashed out a global deal with Zimmer, which they signed on behalf of something they dubbed the "claimants' liaison counsel."[36] Judge Wigenton "approved" their private deal over the real liaison counsel's objections. Seeger later suggested that instituting rules "would take the fun out of mass torts."[37]

Although judges have clear authority to appoint class counsel under Rule 23, that rule requires them to ensure that their picks adequately represent absent class members. But, as Seeger's comment reflects, no rules govern counsel selection in nonclass proceedings. Nevertheless, there tend to be more leaders in nonclass mass-tort proceedings than in class actions. Within the 73 products-liability and sales-practice proceedings in the dataset, certified class actions ranged from 22 lead positions at the high end to 4 at the low end, with an average of 11.5 positions per proceeding, 43.9% of which were filled with repeat players. In the nonclass proceedings concluding in private aggregate settlements, plaintiffs' leadership positions

---

[36] Letter from Gibbs C. Henderson, Plaintiffs' Co-Liaison Counsel, to Judge Susan D. Wigenton at 2, *In re* Zimmer Durom Hip Cup Prods. Liab. Litig., No. 09-cv-04414 (D.N.J. Mar. 21, 2016).

[37] Perry Cooper, *Defendants' Gripes with MDLs, and What to Do About Them*, 18 BNA CLASS ACTION LITIG. REP. 1021 (Oct. 27, 2017).

ranged from 62 in the sprawling pelvic-mesh cases[38] to 3 positions in *Coloplast* or 1 firm in *Mirapex*.[39] These proceedings averaged 21.5 leadership positions a piece (nearly double the class-action positions), 74.6% of which were filled with repeat players.[40]

Although nonclass litigation groups have been around for decades, judges haven't always selected them and they haven't always wielded the power that they do today. Early organizational groups coalesced mainly for attorneys' convenience: lawyers banned together informally to share knowledge and financing, hire experts, create trial handbooks with "hot" documents, and develop "schools" to train lawyers with similar cases.[41] But absent unique financing arrangements, no single committee or attorney's decision bound anyone who hadn't voluntarily consented.[42]

Today's leadership committees differ remarkably: they are judicially appointed, mandatory, and hierarchical. Their raison d'être is judicial – not attorney – convenience. Once appointed, lead lawyers highjack the cockpit and restrict access to the judge. Their duties usurp the traditional attorney's daily responsibilities and, as Judge Herndon did in *Yasmin/Yaz*, some judges funnel all communications through their handpicked leaders.[43]

Evolving from organic, ad hoc groups to mandatory committees has important due process implications for plaintiffs. When ad hoc groups were purely voluntary, attorneys consented to participate. Because that decision fell within her authority as an agent, a lawyer's consent bound her client. But neither clients nor their attorneys freely consent to multidistrict litigation or the judge's choice for lead lawyers. This nonvoluntariness makes the committee appointment more akin to choosing class counsel where absent class members have no say in who represents them. Yet, as we'll see in Chapter 3, few judges consider adequate-representation concerns when selecting leaders in nonclass proceedings.

---

[38] Pelvic-mesh cases refer to those proceedings against *American Medical Systems, Ethicon, Boston Scientific,* and *C.R. Bard*; other proceedings were filed after May of 2013.

[39] The *New England Compounding* litigation was excluded from these calculations given its unique bankruptcy status.

[40] Excluding the unusually high number of pelvic-mesh appointments (in *American Medical Systems, Ethicon, Boston Scientific,* and *C.R. Bard*) lowers the average number of positions to 16.1, with repeat players occupying 61.6%.

[41] Paul D. Rheingold, *The Development of Litigation Groups*, 6 AM. J. TRIAL ADVOC. 1, 5–10 (1982); Byron G. Stier, *Resolving the Class Action Crisis: Mass Tort Litigation as Network*, UTAH L. REV. 863, 899–903 (2005).

[42] *See* Dennis E. Curtis & Judith Resnik, *Contingency Fees in Mass Torts: Access, Risk, and the Provision of Legal Services When Layers of Lawyers Work for Individuals and Collectives of Clients*, 47 DEPAUL L. REV. 425, 443 (1998) (noting that lead lawyers in the *L-Tryptophan* litigation "received no premiums for their group service").

[43] *E.g.*, Minute Order, *In re* Yasmin & Yaz (Drospirenone) Mktg., Sales Practices & Prods. Liab. Litig., No. 09-md-02100 (S.D. Ill. June 19, 2013) (ruling that "only Lead and Liaison Counsel may file pleadings in the Master Docket").

Compensating Lead Lawyers Using Common-Benefit Fees

When lead attorneys take on work that goes beyond what they would do for their own clients and help the plaintiffs (or defendants) as a whole, judges award them what's called a *common-benefit fee*. Common-benefit orders require plaintiffs who settle or win judgments along the way to put some money into a fund to reimburse lead lawyers for fronting litigation costs and compensate them for their beneficial work.

When mass-tort plaintiffs hire an attorney, they sign a retainer agreement that includes a *contingent fee*. Contingent fees are "contingent" on the lawsuit's outcome: if your attorney doesn't recover money for you, then she doesn't get paid either. She also loses the time and money that she invested in the suit. If you do recover money, she is entitled to some percentage of your settlement or judgment – typically in the neighborhood of 33%.[44]

In successful suits, judges set aside some of plaintiffs' *gross settlement proceeds* (the total amount awarded to a plaintiff before she pays her attorneys and her court costs) to pay leaders' common-benefit fees. Common-benefit fees are typically a percentage of the plaintiff's attorney's fee (the 33%). So plaintiffs aren't paying twice for the same services, the fees are just being divided among the lawyers.

Judges' common-benefit-fee orders apply to all cases in the federal proceeding, which means that leaders must pony up a portion of their own clients' recoveries too. But, chances are they will see that money again once the judge awards them their common-benefit fee.

As you might imagine, these common-benefit fees can really add up – 4% of 11,000 plaintiffs' recoveries is likely to be significantly more than 33% of a few clients' awards. To give you a sense of scale, common-benefit fees and costs in *Yasmin/Yaz* exceeded $83 million.

Because common-benefit fees are largely the offspring of creative judges, however, there is no real legal basis for awarding them. Percentages are all over the map – ranging from 4 to 12% of plaintiffs' gross recoveries before costs and fees are subtracted. Judges piece together theories as they go. They have borrowed willy-nilly from the class action's common-fund doctrine, contract principles, ethics, and equity. But, like a hand-me-down sweater, none is a good fit. And when one doctrine's constraints are too snug, judges tend to ignore them.[45] This makes the whole enterprise of awarding common-benefit fees unpredictable. And it leaves disgruntled attorneys grasping for some doctrinal thread to lodge their objections.

---

[44] Herbert M. Kritzer, *The Wages of Risk: The Returns of Contingency Fee Legal Practice*, 47 DePaul L. Rev. 267, 284–86 (1998).

[45] Elizabeth Chamblee Burch, *Judging Multidistrict Litigation*, 90 N.Y.U. L. Rev. 71, 101–9 (2015).

The wiggle room likewise opens the door for leaders to influence both their own and other attorneys' compensation.

Here's how: first, as the proceedings start, lead lawyers try to stabilize their shaky doctrinal existence through judicially ordered participation "agreements." In theory, these documents legitimize leaders' control using consent. The agreements often contain legal jargon to mimic contractual consideration, such as "Participating Attorneys are desirous of acquiring the PSC Work Product and establishing an amicable, working relationship with the PSC," so they intend "to be legally bound" and "agree" to certain assessments.[46]

As in many take-it-or-leave-it contracts, however, there is little actual consent. "The most obvious problem [is] that the exchanges [are] forced," write Professors Charles Silver and Geoffrey Miller.[47] Participation agreements are standardized boilerplate, presented by those with superior bargaining power to lawyers who have no choice but to accept them. Judges forbid attorneys from discovering information from the defendant on their own in the federal proceeding, so they have few options but to rely on the leaders' work.

Judges also tend to rubber stamp leaders' proposed common-benefit orders and defer to their requests to increase fees during the proceeding. When lead lawyers initially ask the judge to create a common-benefit fund, they often suggest modest percentages. But, as the proceedings continue, they want a raise: as Table A.4 shows, at least 26.4% of lead attorneys persuaded judges to boost their common-benefit fees during the proceeding. In *NuvaRing*, for instance, this meant a nearly $14 million fee. The request for a raise escalated one of the highest initial taxes (8%) to 15.5% – the highest common-benefit percentage charged out of all the dataset's proceedings concluding in private settlement. For individually retained attorneys working on a 33% contingent fee, 15.5% nearly halves their paycheck.

Second, leaders perpetuate norms about which kind of common-benefit work is most beneficial and thus most deserving of enhanced compensation. They can then perform that work themselves and pawn less profitable tasks off on others.

Third, some judges ask the lead lawyers to serve on fee-allocation committees. In the *DePuy ASR Hip Implant* litigation, for instance, when Judge David Katz appointed a fee committee comprised in part of several high-level repeat players – Chris Seeger, Pete Flowers, and Steve Skikos – he gave them the power and means to punish, reward, and incentivize other lawyers in five concurrent hip-implant proceedings.[48] If leaders negotiated unfair deals or acted unethically, these carrots

---

[46] *In re* Bextra & Celebrex Mktg. Sales Practices & Prods. Liab. Litig., No. M:05-CV-01699-CRB, 2006 WL 471782, at *8 (N.D. Cal. Feb. 28, 2006) (Exhibit A).

[47] Charles Silver & Geoffrey P. Miller, *The Quasi-Class Action Method of Managing Multi-District Litigations: Problems and a Proposal*, 63 VAND. L. REV. 107, 131 (2010).

[48] *In re* DePuy Orthopaedics, Inc. ASR Hip Implant Prods. Liab. Litig., MDL No. 10-md-2197-DAK (N.D. Ohio Oct. 14, 2015) (case management order no. 25). Contemporaneously pending hip implant cases included *Biomet* (MDL No. 2391), *DePuy ASR* (MDL No. 2197), *Zimmer*

and sticks could dissuade would-be "whistle-blowers" from speaking up, for insiders could hurt them financially.

Finally, as the settlement designers, lead lawyers are positioned to negotiate their common-benefit fees directly with the defendant. As Table A.4 shows, of the proceedings ending in private settlements, 97% taxed state-court attorneys in some form. Eighty percent of the 10 proceedings with publicly available private settlements did so by bargaining with defendants. Consenting to settle meant consenting to fees, even for state-court plaintiffs outside the federal court's reach. In other words, defendants hold a tantalizing carrot. Professors Silver and Miller suggest that by offering lead lawyers "'red-carpet treatment on fees' in return for favorable terms elsewhere," defendants can take advantage of lead attorneys' control over settlement to strike deals that benefit the defendant and the plaintiffs' leaders, but not the plaintiffs.[49]

What this all boils down to is that leaders have enormous power over compensation. They can set their own fees, enrich themselves, and deter and punish dissenters like Fred Baron. For attorneys with cases in the multidistrict proceeding, there is no escaping common-benefit fees or the control that leaders exercise. As Chapter 2 explores further, state-court litigants aren't immune either. Federal judges and their chosen leaders have taxed state-court plaintiffs through a host of creative means.

Nor do appeals offer much relief. Private settlements are consensual and leadership appointments are interim orders that can't typically be appealed. When little appellate guidance exists to constrain or assist transferee judges, errors can persist even as parties push ethical boundaries. Although the same self-serving behaviors judges witnessed in class-action practice linger, instead of wielding Rule 23's weaponry, judges are armed only with the primitive tools carved for ordinary, individual suits.

THE CLAMOR FOR COORDINATION

As they make their way in this brave new world, transferee judges turn to one another for guidance. In *Vioxx*, for instance, state-federal cooperation proved crucial for handling what would balloon to 60,000 personal-injury claims and a federal docket with more than 65,000 entries. After Merck pulled Vioxx off the market in 2004, the initial trickle of lawsuits quickly flooded multiple state and federal jurisdictions. The Panel sent the federal suits to Louisiana, before Judge Eldon Fallon.

Durom (MDL No. 2158), *Wright Medical Technology* (MDL No. 2329), *DePuy Pinnacle* (MDL No. 2391), and *Stryker Rejuvenate and ABG II Hip Implant Products Liability Litigation* (MDL No. 13-2441) (centralized on June 12, 2013).

[49] Silver & Miller, *supra* note 47, at 110.

In early 2005, Judge Fallon invited the judges with the heaviest *Vioxx* dockets to New Orleans for dinner. Reflecting on their first meeting, Judge Carol Higbee noted, "We wanted to get to know one another. We wanted to accommodate each other. The three of us [Judges Fallon, Victoria Chaney, and Carol Higbee] just melded. We got along well, and we respected each other."[50] "I think it's one of the best examples of federal and state court coordination that maybe has happened in a mass tort," she concluded.[51] While each judge decided the issues independently, they used each other as sounding boards, bounced ideas off of one another, and cooperated. As Judge Chaney explained: "We are not reinventing the wheel. We were able to piggyback on each other."[52]

Coordinating can save time, reduce costs, avoid inconsistent rulings, and help stop litigant gamesmanship. "We're doing this on a consolidated basis or a coordinated basis because we recognize the importance of having these cases, both in the State and Federal Court, litigated in more or less the same way," explained Judge Douglas Woodlock in presiding over joint state-federal *Daubert* hearings in the *Fresenius GranuFlo* litigation.[53] As Professor Alexandra Lahav notes, "[C]ommunication between judges avoids a gastonette, where each court waits for the other to decide," and "[c]onsultation allows judges to learn from one another and hopefully produce better decisions." But, she warns, jurisdictional redundancy has perks as well – it can promote "new approaches to social problems" and "correct for systemic errors."[54]

Judges are people, and people are prone to do what others do. Psychologists and behavioral economists label our behavior "herding" because we tend to follow the herd when it comes to deciding what to wear or which products to buy online, for instance. Economics professors Andrew Daughety and Jennifer Reinganum found that judges fall prey to these tendencies too. As appellate judges observe other appellate courts, for example, they "progressively rely more on previous decisions and less on [their own] private information." "[S]ince review of harmonious decisions is rare, ... herding on the wrong decision may remain uncorrected," they observe.[55]

When majorities form a consensus, "our minds go on automatic pilot," explains psychology professor Charlan Nemeth. We consider less information and "turn a

[50] Susan Todd, *Inside the Vioxx Litigation*, THE STAR-LEDGER (Newark, NJ) (Nov. 18, 2007), https://www.nj.com/business/index.ssf/2007/11/inside_the_vioxx_litigation.html.

[51] Robert G. Seidenstein, *Higbee Among Catalysts: How Judges Inspired Vioxx Talks*, N.J. LAW, Nov. 19, 2007, at 5.

[52] Transcript of Proceedings at 37–38, *In re* Vioxx Prods. Liab. Litig., No. 05-md-01657 (E.D. La. Nov. 9, 2007).

[53] Transcript of Day One of Daubert Hearing at 3, *In re* Fresenius Granuflo/Naturalyte Dialysate Prods. Liab. Litig., No. 13-md-02428 (D. Mass. Oct. 14, 2015).

[54] Alexandra D. Lahav, *Recovering the Social Value of Jurisdictional Redundancy*, 82 TUL. L. REV. 2369, 2387, 2394 (2008).

[55] Andrew F. Daughety & Jennifer F. Reinganum, *Stampede to Judgment: Persuasive Influence and Herding Behavior by Courts*, 1 AM. L. & ECON. REV. 158, 158 (1999).

blind eye to bad decisions."[56] A single judge marching to her own drum or a dissenter like Fred Baron can break this spell. But, with the steady cry for coordination and the push for state and federal judges to march in lockstep, conformity and consensus may drown out these checks and balances.

In theory, we might depend on transferor judges and appellate courts as a fail-safe. When cases return to their original federal districts (the federal courthouse downtown in our *Yaz* example), the transferor judge can fix any rulings that mangle state law. But, while multidistrict litigation is ostensibly for pretrial purposes only, in practice, as the old song goes, when you leave that way, you can never go back.[57] Only around 3% of the cases ever return to (or are *remanded* to) the federal courts from whence they came. And, as we've seen, appeals are unlikely too because most mass torts conclude in private settlements. So, while coordination has an upside, judicial errors can persist and practices can become entrenched.

THE PUSH FOR SETTLEMENT AND ITS MANY REWARDS

Like most civil suits, mass torts tend to settle. This helps explain why so few cases return to their original courts, but the pressures prompting these settlements are far from ordinary. Lead plaintiffs' attorneys, defendants, and transferee judges' interests often align in ways that make even a 3% remand rate seem remarkable. Settlement uniformly promotes those insiders' agendas, but each agenda differs.

Lead Plaintiffs' Lawyers Interests

Mass torts are expensive for lead plaintiffs' lawyers, and settlements are often overdue paydays. As contingent-fee lawyers, plaintiffs' attorneys have to front substantial costs (with the risk of not recovering them) to develop both "generic" and "specific" assets.[58]

Generic assets are items that most plaintiffs will need to prove common aspects of their claims. Expert witnesses and documents indicating that a certain product can cause a specific illness are two such examples. But these assets cost money. Hiring experts, reviewing thousands of corporate documents, interviewing and deposing witnesses, and plotting extensive timelines about who knew what and when can run up a tab quickly.

---

[56] CHARLAN NEMETH, IN DEFENSE OF TROUBLEMAKERS: THE POWER OF DISSENT IN LIFE AND BUSINESS 212 (2018).

[57] CONFEDERATE RAILROAD, *When You Leave That Way You Can Never Go Back*, on CONFEDERATE RAILROAD (Atlantic Records 1992); SAM NEELY, *When You Leave That Way You Can Never Go Back* (MCA Records 1983).

[58] RICHARD A. NAGAREDA, MASS TORTS IN A WORLD OF SETTLEMENT 13–14 (2007).

Specific assets include the substantial expense of developing the facts of each client's case as well as proving specific causation – that the product caused *this* plaintiff's injury. In any lawsuit, multidistrict or otherwise, proving specific causation typically falls to the lawyers whom the plaintiff hired to directly represent her. Without a settlement, these costs add up, particularly if attorneys represent hundreds of clients.

Investments may take years to recoup. The parties in *Agent Orange* estimated that trial might take 18 months and appeals could last up to 10 years.[59] To stay afloat in the short term, plaintiffs' law firms might pool their resources, borrow funds from banks, or request financing from third parties. Attorney Michael Pretl, who sued A. H. Robbins in the *Dalkon Shield* litigation, reported: "We handled over 1,000 Dalkon cases, and it took 20 years before we showed a profit .... We borrowed heavily at high interest rates to finance the litigation. Even though we settled $55 million in claims, this will be the first year we'll be in the black."[60] Similarly, one plaintiff's lawyer estimated that a single *Vioxx* case initially cost between $1 million and $1.5 million to develop.[61] So, settlements can save law firms from bankruptcy.

Settlements within centralized proceedings likewise avoid the uncertainty over leaders' fees that could result if the judge remanded cases to their home courts. When judges craft common-benefit orders, they presume that cases will settle and that they will disburse fees. Recovering those fees without a settlement is possible, but tough.

Judges routinely invoke the ill-fitting common-benefit doctrine to pay lead lawyers. It allows attorneys to recover their fees when their efforts confer "a substantial benefit on the members of an ascertainable class, and where the court's jurisdiction" makes it possible "to spread the costs proportionately among them."[62] Setting aside the formidable problem that no class action exists and that judges would need to decide what constitutes a "substantial benefit," there's still the sticky jurisdictional question. If a case did return to its home court, could the transferee judge remand questions about individual issues but retain jurisdiction over common-benefit fees?

On the one hand, under the plain language of the statute that gives life to multidistrict proceedings, § 1407, transferee judges could ask the Panel to separate fees before remanding the rest of the case, which would allow the transferee judge to

---

[59] Kenneth R. Feinberg, *The Dalkon Shield Claimants Trust*, 53 LAW & CONTEMP. PROBS. 79, 80 (1990).

[60] Gregory C. Baumann, *Wanted: Law Firm with Guts; State Makes Casting Call for Counsel to Sue on Tobacco's Medicaid Bill*, DAILY REC. (Wooster, OH), Nov. 17, 1995, at 1.

[61] Joe Nocera, *Forget Fair; It's Litigation as Usual*, N.Y. TIMES (Nov. 17, 2007), http://www.nytimes.com/2007/11/17/business/17nocera.html.

[62] Mills v. Elec. Auto-Lite Co., 396 U.S. 375, 393–94 (1970); *see also* Allen v. Lloyd's of London, 975 F. Supp. 802, 806 (E.D. Va. 1997) (citing *Mills*).

control fees.[63] In practice, the Panel has allowed transferee judges to continue presiding over claims that benefit from uniform and consistent rulings, such as punitive damages.[64]

On the other hand, however, allowing the transferee court to preside over fees postremand (and sometimes posttrial) may run afoul of the Supreme Court's *Lexecon* opinion.[65] As *Lexecon* explains, transferee courts have authority only over "pretrial" proceedings and § 1407 "obligates the Panel to remand any pending case to its originating court when, at the latest, those pretrial proceedings have run their course."[66] Attorneys' fees are postresolution issues, which would leave leaders arguing for their fees before different judges nationwide. Consequently, from the leaders' perspective, settling in the multidistrict proceeding is preferable because it allows them to avoid this uncharted administrative tangle altogether.

Defendants' Interests

Corporate defendants like Bayer are often onboard with centralizing and settling too. Remanding cases to their original federal courts makes it that much harder to corral and extinguish them through a global settlement. Instead of bargaining with a single, unified authority like the plaintiffs' steering committee, defendants must battle with disparate attorneys in piecemeal suits across the country. Those deals would offer all the downsides and none of the finality-related upsides of global settlements.[67]

When Congress originally considered creating multidistrict litigation, corporations opposed it. They thought it robbed them of their ability to divide and conquer, to overwhelm plaintiffs with their resources, and to pick them off one by one.[68] But today, defendants often stand to gain the most. Multidistrict litigation dislodges plaintiffs from their preferred court, forces plaintiffs' lawyers (who have reputations for not hunting well in packs) to battle for lead positions, and renders trials a distant and unlikely threat.

Of course, defendants would prefer to have all the cases against them dismissed. And by using *Daubert* motions to disqualify plaintiffs' experts, summary judgment

---

[63] 28 U.S.C. § 1407(a) (2012) (allowing the Panel to "separate any claim" and "remand any of such claims before the remainder of the action is remanded").

[64] *E.g.*, *In re* Collins, 233 F.3d 809, 810 (3d Cir. 2000) (severing punitive damages); *In re* Roberts, 178 F.3d 181, 184 (3d Cir. 1999) (severing punitive damages); *In re* Asbestos Prods. Liab. Litig. (No. VI), MDL No. 875, 2014 WL 3353044, at *1 n.1 (E.D. Pa. July 9, 2014).

[65] Lexecon, Inc. v. Milberg Weiss Bershad Hynes & Lerach, 523 U.S. 26 (1998).

[66] *Id.* at 34–35.

[67] A small resurgence of the divide-and-conquer-strategy has been apparent in the wake of the Supreme Court's 2017 opinion in *Bristol-Myers Squibb Co. v. Superior Court of California*, 137 S. Ct. 1773 (2017). It remains to be seen how this will continue to play out in mass torts, but I discuss the case briefly in Chapter 5.

[68] Bradt, *supra* note 17, at 1732–35.

motions to show that no genuine factual disputes exist, and arbitration provisions for suits involving contracts (like cellphone sales practices), defendants accomplished uniform dismissal in a little more than 16% of the proceedings within the dataset.

But if they lose dispositive motions and can assess the universe of claims, corporations tend to think about ways to achieve the maximum amount of finality for the lowest possible price. "It's good for the company not to let this [*Prempro*] litigation linger," said one of Pfizer's stockholders, because "[r]esolving these cases gives investors one less thing to worry about."[69] Settlement reassures shareholders, puts public-relations nightmares to rest, and returns focus to a company's primary enterprise.

Judicial Interests

That judges prefer settlements, too, is an open secret. In handling the *Kugel Mesh Hernia Patch* litigation, Judge Mary Lisi sums up what appears to be the prevailing thought: "I view my job in this MDL [a]s to bring every single one of the cases that was transferred here to a resolution."[70]

In his first hearing on the massive opioid lawsuits, Judge Dan Polster made it clear he didn't want "a whole lot of finger-pointing," discovery, or trials. Instead, he said he preferred to "do something meaningful to abate this crisis" by the year's end.[71] The parties proved less pliable, however, and he had to backtrack a bit a month later. He reluctantly scheduled a few trials for the following year to generate information. "It's necessary to do it, and we're doing it, but it's not a substitute or replacement in any way [for settlement]," he said.[72]

Judge Polster took a similar stance when he presided over the *Gadolinium-Based Contrast Agents* proceeding a few years before receiving the opioid suits. "[T]he cases should be settled, all right?" "They can be settled and they should be settled," he declared.[73] So even though plaintiffs wanted to return home with a trial packet in hand, he proposed personally mediating the cases: "if mediation fails, another

[69] Jef Feeley, *Pfizer Paid $896 Million in Prempro Settlements*, BLOOMBERG (June 19, 2012, 4:27 PM), https://www.bloomberg.com/news/articles/2012-06-19/pfizer-paid-896-million-in-prempro-accords-filing-shows-1-.

[70] Transcript of Proceedings at 7, *In re* Kugel Mesh Hernia Patch Prods. Liab. Litig., No. 07-md-1842 (D.R.I. July 29, 2011).

[71] Transcript of Proceedings at 4, *In re* Nat'l Prescription Opiate Litig., No. 17-cv-2804 (E.D. Ohio Jan. 9, 2018).

[72] Daniel Fisher, *Judge Sees Litigation as Only an 'Aid in Settlement Discussions' for Opioid Lawsuits*, LEGAL NEWSLINE – FORBES (May 10, 2018, 11:54 AM), https://www.forbes.com/sites/legalnewsline/2018/05/10/judge-sees-litigation-as-only-an-aid-in-settlement-discussions-for-opioid-lawsuits/#7aa39ce84b99.

[73] Transcript of Pretrial Proceedings at 51–52, *In re* Gadolinium-Based Contrast Agents Prods. Liab. Litig., No. 08-gd-50000 (N.D. Ohio Mar. 18, 2010).

option is baseball-style arbitration with no appeal." It's "a very successful approach" because "it tends to produce a lot of settlements," Judge Polster explained.[74]

A handful of judges think about settlement differently, however. Judge Clay Land, who presided over the *Mentor ObTape* litigation, put it bluntly: "When a transferee judge is assigned an MDL proceeding to manage, the assignment does not elevate him to a wise Solomon-like figure." The goal isn't "to take a 'major policy controversy' and solve it," he said. Instead, "[T]he assignment is to manage the pretrial proceedings as an Article III judge, and when finished, suggest remand to the court of origin for trial."[75]

Settlement wasn't always the endgame in civil suits. As Professor Arthur Miller observes, "Other than a few experiments after the Second World War," judicial management "was virtually non-existent." "Many district judges even believed that involvement in the settlement process was particularly inappropriate."[76]

What changed? In 1983, amendments to Rule 16 (which governs pretrial conferences) expressly authorized judges to facilitate settlement discussions, marking an official end to the purposeful, restrained "hands-off" approach of the 1930s. Back then, the rule makers were reluctant to allow the judge to cajole the parties into settling.[77] Charles Clark, an influential reporter for the Advisory Committee on Civil Rules who helped draft Rule 16 in its original form, noted, "It is no mere chance that no provision is made for settlement negotiations; those are no part of proper pre-trial."[78] He later explained, "[I]t is dangerous to the whole purpose of pretrial to force settlement upon unwilling parties."[79]

By the 1970s and 1980s, however, "managerial judging," which Professor Judith Resnik describes in part as "meeting with parties in chambers to encourage settlement," was gaining steam alongside alternative-dispute-resolution methods like mediation and arbitration.[80] Fueled by perceptions – real or imagined – of increased lawsuits and congested courts, judges began encouraging both settlement and mediation to increase judicial access.[81]

Today, as Judge Jack Weinstein observes, "Federal judges tend to be biased toward settlement. We clean the dishes and cutlery so they can be reused for

---

[74] Transcript of Pretrial Proceedings at 42, *In re* Gadolinium-Based Contrast Agents Prods. Liab. Litig., No. 08-gd-50000 (N.D. Ohio May 2, 2011).

[75] Letter from the Honorable Clay D. Land, Chief U.S. Dist. Judge, Middle Dist. of Ga., to Professor D. Theodore Rave (May 15, 2018) (on file with author).

[76] Miller, *supra* note 9, at 796.

[77] David L. Shapiro, *Federal Rule 16: A Look at the Theory and Practice of Rulemaking*, 137 U. Pa. L. Rev. 1969, 1980 (1989).

[78] Charles E. Clark, *Summary and Conclusion to an Understanding Use of Pre-Trial*, in *Proceedings of the Seminar on Procedures for Effective Judicial Administration*, 29 F.R.D. 454, 456 (1962).

[79] Charles E. Clark, *Objectives of Pre-Trial Procedure*, 17 Ohio St. L.J. 163, 167 (1956).

[80] Judith Resnik, *Managerial Judges*, 96 Harv. L. Rev. 374, 377 (1982).

[81] Ellen E. Deason, *Beyond "Managerial Judges": Appropriate Roles in Settlement*, 78 Ohio St. L.J. 73, 78 (2017).

the long line of incoming customers. Settlements are the courts' automatic washer-dryers."[82]

So, as pretrial judges, transferee judges would be remiss not to encourage settlement conversations. Yet, the "settlement culture," as Judge William Young dubbed it, "is nowhere more prevalent than in MDL practice."[83] As he notes, when *The Manual for Complex Litigation* touts multidistrict proceedings as "a unique opportunity for the negotiation of a global settlement" and instructs transferee judges to "*make the most of this opportunity*," it "seems virtually to command this result."[84]

The judicial report card that the Administrative Office of the Courts issues every March and September only fuels the fire. This "six-month report," as judges call it, publishes data detailing (for each judge) how many motions have been pending for more than six months and how many actions have been pending for more than three years. Efficiently resolving disputes is lauded. But as Professor Harold Koh once quipped, "When you cannot measure what is important, you tend to make important what you can measure."[85]

Perhaps efficiency has lost its equilibrium with fairness. As retired Judge Nancy Gertner reflected, while the six-month reports "were presented to us as efficiency measures, and neutral in their impact, they in fact affected the way the job of judging was done, and advertently or inadvertently, the outcomes."[86] While on the bench, she said she felt pressured to "[v]alue efficiency above all, which meant encouraging parties in a civil case to settle." She explained, "Confidential settlements were always good no matter what the issue; don't look too deeply to see if the issues were fairly litigated. *Any* closing after all is as good as *any other*."[87]

In his remarks to the bar, Judge Clay Land likewise denounced this metric, "Nowhere does it show how much time a judge spent on the bench; how many jurors' hands he shook; how long he listened to lawyers argue their cases in open court; how many jurors he observed expressing pride in having played an indispensable role in their democracy." Instead, "Having been seduced into believing that the focus should be on doing whatever it takes to get the matter resolved, we often defer to the lawyers whenever they agree that a certain course increases the chance of settlement, i.e., allowing us to close the file."[88]

As the six-month report suggests, fears of cost and delay fuel courts' desire for settlement. Yet, for decades now, procedural justice studies conducted on real

---

[82] Jack B. Weinstein, *Comments on Owen M. Fiss, Against Settlement (1984)*, 78 FORDHAM L. REV. 1265, 1265 (2009).

[83] DeLaventura v. Columbia Acorn Tr., 417 F. Supp. 2d 147, 150 (D. Mass. 2006).

[84] *Id.* at 151 (quoting MANUAL FOR COMPLEX LITIGATION (FOURTH) § 20.132 (2004)).

[85] Harold Hongju Koh, *The Just, Speedy, and Inexpensive Determination of Every Action?*, 162 U. PA. L. REV. 1525, 1529 (2014).

[86] Nancy Gertner, *Opinions I Should Have Written*, 110 NW. U. L. REV. 423, 426 (2016).

[87] *Id.* at 428.

[88] Judge Clay D. Land, Lamentations of a Trial Judge, Remarks to the Columbus Inn of Court (Jan. 28, 2015) (on file with author).

people have indicated that cost and delay do not significantly influence litigants' opinions of procedural fairness.[89] To explore corporate defense concerns, however, researchers tested the effects of defendants paying their own costs versus defendants with fees paid by insurance companies. Still they found no relationship between procedural fairness judgments and cost discrepancies.[90] In short, within the realm of traditional tort litigation, cost and delay do not greatly impact how litigants perceive the justice system.

These findings suggest that Herculean efforts to reduce cost and delay should not be shouldered at the expense of voice, dignity, and impartiality in decision making.[91] Nevertheless, cost and delay continue to serve as stalking horses for various political interests on both sides of the aisle.

Directives to reduce cost and delay only partially explain the added settlement push in multidistrict litigation. Transferee judges also receive less obvious, self-interested perks. For example, the Panel views quickly settling a complex case as a hallmark of success that favorably disposes it to reward that judge with a new assignment. As one judge remarked, "Judges aren't created equal. I am doing a good job in my MDL so people will come back to me. Some judges are notoriously slow. This leads to repeat players. You need to assign cases to judges who understand how to move this along."[92]

Multidistrict litigations are plum judicial assignments; they involve interesting facts, media attention, and some of the nation's most talented attorneys. But only around 27% of active judges and 20% of senior judges receive them. Of those chosen few, 80% wanted another one.[93] One transferee judge put it this way, "This is our dessert. This is why we eat our diet. This is our reward for the prisoner cases."[94] The judges who are left out often "campaign" to receive one.[95] And when the Federal Judicial Center asked judges who had never presided over a multidistrict proceeding whether they'd be interested in doing so, 70% said yes. But once they receive one, if they fail to resolve it quickly, they are unlikely to receive another.

---

[89] E. ALLAN LIND ET AL., RAND CORP., THE PERCEPTION OF JUSTICE: TORT LITIGANTS' VIEWS OF TRIAL, COURT-ANNEXED ARBITRATION, AND JUDICIAL SETTLEMENT CONFERENCES, at v, 55–59 (1989), https://www.rand.org/content/dam/rand/pubs/reports/2006/R3708.pdf.

[90] *Id.* at 57; *see also* E. Allan Lind et al., *In the Eye of the Beholder: Tort Litigants' Evaluations of Their Experiences in the Civil Justice System*, 24 LAW & SOC'Y REV. 953, 984 (1990).

[91] LIND ET AL., *supra* note 89, at 78.

[92] Abbe R. Gluck, *Unorthodox Civil Procedure: Modern Multi-District Litigation's Place in the Textbook Understandings of Procedure*, 165 U. PA. L. REV. 1669, 1699 (2017) (interviewing transferee judges).

[93] JUDICIAL PANEL ON MULTIDISTRICT LITIGATION, YEAR-END REPORT 10–11 (2016) (on file with author).

[94] Gluck, *supra* note 92, at 1699 (interviewing transferee judges).

[95] John G. Heyburn II & Francis E. McGovern, *Evaluating and Improving the MDL Process*, 38 LITIG. 26, 30 (Summer/Fall 2012).

WHY LITIGATION MATTERS

When all the consistent stakeholders shift from a trial-oriented view to a settlement-focused one, is anything lost? After all, settlement is efficient, and efficiency increases access to justice for more people.

At the heart of this question lies the thorny matter of what adjudication should accomplish. Looking to statutory and procedural rules for answers tells us that efficiency doesn't stand alone, that it can't be an end in and of itself. Otherwise, we'd be happy enough to settle disputes with a coin flip. Rule 1, for example, tells us that procedures should be construed "to secure the just, speedy, and inexpensive determination of every action," and § 1407 permits MDL transfers to "promote the just and efficient conduct of such actions."[96]

So, the crux of the matter hinges on what "just" means, and for that we have to consider substantive tort law goals. Deterring wrongdoing and compensating victims are important knee-jerk reactions. But are those the only or the most important goals?

To test this question, imagine roads with a toll lane or a red-light camera. These days, if you run the wrong red light or drive in a toll lane without the right permit, no one will pull you over, but a ticket will appear in your mailbox within a few weeks.

What if our justice system became wholly automated too? Would anything be lost? Certainly, it would be efficient, and maybe if everything functioned well then it would deter wrongdoers and compensate victims. But the discovery process would disappear as would the information that process uncovers. Citizens wouldn't have an opportunity to participate in democratic trials where the law views both the weak and the powerful equally. And these public goods matter more in some cases than others.

For instance, remember Brooke Melton who died when her Chevy Cobalt's ignition cut off? Brooke's death in 2010 was far from General Motors's (GM's) first fatality. Four years earlier, 18-year-old Natasha Weigel and her friend Amy Rademaker both died when Natasha's Cobalt did the same thing. Even the police report attributed their deaths to the faulty ignition switch. But when Natasha's family tried to hire an attorney, the lawyer declined to take the case. The economics didn't warrant it, he said. He'd need to "see a potential upside recovery well in excess of $1 million," but, because Wisconsin capped damages at $350,000, litigating against GM was just too expensive for him. Amy's family ran into the same problem. "This is so frustrating to me," said Amy's stepfather. "If we had gone to litigation, this would have gone to the forefront. We could have saved lives."[97]

---

[96] Fed. R. Civ. P. 1; 28 U.S.C. § 1407 (2012).

[97] Barry Meier & Hilary Stout, *Falling Through the Legal Cracks*, N.Y. Times, Dec. 30, 2014, at B1.

By 2014, at least 42 other people died from GM ignition-related defects. Those who sued were silenced by settlements requiring them to keep all discovery information secret. Even once attorney Lance Cooper uncovered the defect while working on Brooke Melton's case, GM offered $5 million to settle, but insisted that the documents remain confidential – at least while the suit against the dealer who'd inspected the car days before the crash continued.

When GM finally recalled the ignition switches, it included only a fraction of the affected cars. Cooper wrote a letter on the Meltons' behalf to the National Highway Traffic Safety Administration explaining that the recall was insufficient and alerted national media outlets. Only then did GM include the full 1.37 million defective vehicles, only then did Congress initiate hearings, and only then did federal regulators fine GM $35 million for its failings. "One of the important issues for the Meltons was accountability," Cooper explained. They "simply wanted the truth and for no one else to suffer a similar loss."[98]

The GM story is one of both corporate malfeasance and government regulatory failure. Tort-reform caps deterred lawyers from investing in early cases and confidential settlements stifled crucial information at great cost. Reflecting on the Wisconsin lawyers' refusal to take Natasha Weigel's case, Cooper said, "Candidly, I think they probably would've discovered what I discovered eight years later." "It would've saved all these people's lives."[99]

As Professor Alexandra Lahav points out, lawsuits can generate public goods. "[L]itigation cannot make up for management dysfunction of the type that was prevalent at GM," but "[w]ithout punitive damages in West Virginia or Georgia [where Cooper sued on the Meltons' behalf], those cases would never have been brought, the plaintiffs' expert who diagnosed the design flaw never hired, and the truth might have taken longer to surface (if it surfaced at all)."[100]

GM illustrates that adjudication values – deterrence, compensation, information production, victim empowerment, public participation in democratic trials, and equality before the law – will inevitably conflict. If the system is principally about empowering victims to vindicate their claims against their wrongdoer, as civil recourse theorists argue, we must then decide what that means for other values.

If plaintiffs settle on the cheap, bring unwinnable lawsuits, or agree to confidential settlements, does that mean the system is performing poorly? Perhaps plaintiffs agree to modest, confidential settlements because that's what they want. And if that's so, then we must decide whether the system is working well despite opaque settlements, information losses, and the lack of public participation. Or, it could be that victims settle cheaply because they're living paycheck to paycheck and can't

[98] Bill Vlasic, *G.M. Settles Switch Suit, Avoiding Depositions*, N.Y. TIMES, Mar. 14, 2015, at B1.
[99] Max Blau, *No Accident: Inside GM's Deadly Ignition Switch Scandal*, ATLANTA MAG. (Jan. 6, 2016), http://www.atlantamagazine.com/great-reads/no-accident-inside-gms-deadly-ignition-switch-scandal/.
[100] ALEXANDRA LAHAV, IN PRAISE OF LITIGATION 49 (2017).

wait for a big payday, or that they're facing procedural hurdles or pressure from their own attorneys.

We began this chapter with the death of 18-year-old Michelle Pfleger, who was taking Yaz when a pulmonary embolism caused her to have two heart attacks. As you might now predict, Bayer began settling cases, though it never admitted any fault. It started with the comparatively less severe gallbladder injuries, setting up a private settlement program just for those 8,800 plaintiffs. It would pay plaintiffs who had gallbladder surgery up to $3,000 and pay those with gallbladder symptoms (but no surgery) up to $2,000. It later brokered a deal for plaintiffs like Michelle who had pulmonary embolisms.

But neither deal left plaintiffs much choice about whether to accept. Despite his earlier ruling that class certification was inappropriate, Judge Herndon automatically enrolled the gallbladder plaintiffs in the private deal just as a Rule 23(b)(3) class action would – but without that rule's protections. Lead lawyers then promised to "use their best efforts" to make sure that 97.5% of all eligible plaintiffs entered the pulmonary embolism settlement and that it would include 100% of those cases set for trial.[101]

Judge Herndon fortified attorneys' efforts to herd plaintiffs into the deal by requiring nonsettling plaintiffs to produce fact sheets, more than three years' worth of pharmacy and medical records, and a case-specific expert report on general and specific causation – all within three months.[102] If they didn't, they'd face dismissal. Although plaintiffs still had to submit pharmacy and medical records as part of the settlement program's claims package, at least no costly experts were required.

Despite the *Yasmin/Yaz* litigation, both birth controls remain on the market. The FDA did require Bayer to change its warning label in 2012.[103] Yaz's label now reads, "Epidemiologic studies that compared the risk of VTE [venous thrombotic event] reported that the risk ranged from no increase to a three-fold increase."[104] For most of us, this new language makes Yaz's risks as clear as mud.

Whether litigation accomplishes all that it should is highly debatable. Goals and values will inevitably conflict, and reasonable people can differ over how to best pursue and prioritize them. As we have seen, when other litigants are similarly injured as in *Yasmin/Yaz* and *GM*, one plaintiff's choices can affect many others. Agreeing to confidential settlements could cover up information that would save

---

[101] ATE Master Settlement Agreement §§ 3.01-.02, *In re* Yasmin & Yaz (Drospirenone) Mktg., Sales Practices & Prods. Liab. Litig., No. 09-md-02100 (S.D. Ill. Aug. 3, 2015).

[102] Case Management Order No. 78 Non-Participating ATE CMO at 5–7, *In re* Yasmin & Yaz (Drospirenone) Mktg., Sales Practices & Prods. Liab. Litig., No. 09-md-02100 (S.D. Ill. Aug. 3, 2015); Case Management Order No. 79 Non-ATE Case Resolution CMO at 3–6, *In re* Yasmin & Yaz (Drospirenone) Mktg., Sales Practices & Prods. Liab. Litig., No. 09-md-02100 (S.D. Ill. Aug. 3, 2015).

[103] Deardorff, *supra* note 5.

[104] Bayer HealthCare Pharm. Inc., Full Prescribing Information 5 (2017), http://labeling.bayer healthcare.com/html/products/pi/fhc/YAZ_PI.pdf.

others' lives, and commanding a disproportionate amount of judicial resources could delay justice and prevent others from participating in their own suits.

But simply prioritizing efficiency as generating the greatest good for the greatest number will run roughshod over individual rights. Like the toll-lane example, a utilitarian bent will weigh preferences without scrutinizing them or judging their value. Justice isn't just about bean counting. As we examine dealmaking in the coming chapters, we cannot fall prey to the same impulse. Looking at cases systematically affords us a unique opportunity to engage the hard question of whether we're making the right trade-offs and to consider what we're losing in the process.

2

Quid Pro Quo Arrangements?

In the 1990s, 30 million people took Propulsid for heartburn. After it was linked to 80 deaths and underwent five label changes, however, Johnson & Johnson agreed to continue marketing it for just a few more months. After that, the company told the FDA that Propulsid would be available only as a last resort for patients who did not respond to safer treatments.[1]

Dr. Sidney Wolfe, who directed the nonprofit consumer-watch group Public Citizen, demanded stronger, more immediate action. Propulsid is "a serious public health hazard," he warned, and the FDA can't "fix the safety problem" through a mere label change.[2] Dr. Alastair Wood, an associate dean at Vanderbilt University Medical Center, echoed Wolfe's sentiment, "The case of Propulsid proves this: When people are falling off a cliff, you don't put up more signs; you put up a fence."[3] Summing up the problem, an FDA official asked, "Is it acceptable for your nighttime heartburn medicine (i.e., something for which you could take Tums) to have the potential to kill you?"[4]

Before Johnson & Johnson eventually withdrew Propulsid from the market in July 2000, patients using the drug reported more than 340 heart-rhythm abnormalities to the FDA, it played a suspected role in 302 deaths, and at least nine children experienced serious heart problems. "If I had known that this drug caused cardiac arrhythmias, I never would have given it to him," said Tina

---

[1] Joseph F. Fried, *Specialty Lawyers Gear Up for Suits over Two Medications*, N.Y. TIMES, July 30, 2000; Sheryl Gay Stolberg, *Heartburn Drug Linked to Deaths to be Withdrawn*, N.Y. TIMES, Mar. 24, 2000, at A15.

[2] Stolberg, *supra* note 1; *Public Citizen Reports 23 New Propulsid Deaths, Calls for Prompt Removal*, 5–8 MEALEY'S EMERG. DRUGS & DEVICES 5 (Apr. 20, 2000).

[3] Gardiner Harris & Eric Koli, *Lucrative Drug, Danger Signals and the F.D.A.*, N.Y. TIMES, June 10, 2005, at A1.

[4] *Id.*

Englebrick, of her three-month-old son Scott who died in 1997.[5] In 1999, a nationally recognized coroner attributed nine-month-old Gage Stevens's Thanksgiving Day death to Propulsid as well.[6] Curiously, the FDA never approved Propulsid for use in children.

Instead in 1997, a top FDA official warned the company that pediatric patients "may be at greater risk" of cardiac problems. And in 1998, the FDA urged Johnson & Johnson to amend the label to warn that "despite more than 20 clinical trials in pediatric patients," Propulsid's "safety and effectiveness ... have not been demonstrated." But the FDA couldn't order the label change (it gained those powers only in late 2007). And Johnson & Johnson's internal memos predicted that the amendment would lead to a $250 million-a-year sales loss. So, it omitted any reference to the clinical trials and watered down the language to read "safety and effectiveness in pediatric patients have not been established."[7]

Meanwhile, Johnson & Johnson brazenly turned Propulsid into a cherry-flavored liquid for its "elderly" patients. Sales showed that 90% went to children. Unbeknownst to the FDA, Johnson & Johnson also financed and promoted a research doctor's book extolling Propulsid's off-label use in children. Capitalizing on peer-to-peer advertising, Johnson & Johnson reached 6,000–8,000 pediatricians and nurses by funding pediatric hospital units that touted Propulsid's benefits during industry conferences.[8] The former deputy director of the FDA's cardiac drugs division put it simply: "It was scandalous that all of these kids were being treated with [Propulsid]" when its safety and effectiveness were never proven.[9]

As droves of people sued, the Panel centralized the federal claims before Judge Eldon Fallon in New Orleans. Initially, the plaintiffs' case looked promising – the first trial in Mississippi state court awarded 10 plaintiffs $100 million.[10] But then came a series of setbacks. A New Jersey state court and Judge Fallon separately denied class certification.[11] Johnson & Johnson won the first federal bellwether trial. Judge Fallon dismissed the second bellwether plaintiff's claims on summary

---

[5] David Willman, *PROPULSID: A Heartburn Drug, Now Linked to Children's Deaths,* L.A. TIMES, Dec. 20, 2000.

[6] *Propulsid Linked to Infant's Death,* 5 MEALEY'S EMERG. DRUGS & DEVICES 18 (May 11, 2000); Harris & Koli, *supra* note 3.

[7] Harris & Koli, *supra* note 3.

[8] *Id.*

[9] Willman, *supra* note 5.

[10] Melody Petersen, *Jury Levies $100 Million Award Against Heartburn Drug Maker,* N.Y. TIMES, Sept. 30, 2001, at A1. The Mississippi Supreme Court later reduced this award and then remanded the cases for a new trial. *Judgment Against Johnson & Johnson Voided,* BLOOMBERG NEWS, May 14, 2004.

[11] *In re Propulsid Prods. Liab. Litig.,* No. 00-md-1355 (E.D. La. June 4, 2002); Shannon P. Duffy, *Class-Action Certification Denied in Suit over Digestive Drug Propulsid,* N.J. L.J., May 6, 2002.

judgment and disqualified the third bellwether plaintiff's experts.[12] Then Johnson & Johnson won a California state-court case.[13]

All the while, however, Johnson & Johnson quietly settled the most threatening lawsuits. In their later common-benefit-fee request, leaders reported that the 4–6% assessment from prior settlements covered almost all the $2 million they fronted for shared costs, meaning that those plaintiffs received an aggregate award of at least $50 million.[14] This seems to contradict the argument that claims over Propulsid were meritless.

Working quietly behind the scenes, in February 2004 the "End Game Committee" announced that they'd successfully negotiated a global settlement, which a unanimous Plaintiffs' Steering Committee approved.[15] Depending on how many of the 4,000 plaintiffs (including 300 death claims) signed up, the fund ranged from $69.5 million to $90 million. Jim Shannon, the plaintiffs' lawyer who initially won $100 million for 10 Propulsid plaintiffs said, "This ain't gonna fly." "We've got people who have been seriously injured and killed by this drug. This is not enough to adequately compensate them."[16]

The form letter that plaintiffs' attorneys sent their clients describing the deal wasn't promising either, but not because leaders thought plaintiffs were entitled to more. It began with the litany of litigation setbacks, warned that the science to date "reveals that most people who took Propulsid suffered no provable injury," and cautioned that most plaintiffs will be unable to prove causation. In lieu of a jury, the "court-approved settlement agreement" (remember, though, it's a private deal, not a class action) would send cases to "a team of court appointed medical experts." So, rather than a jury, plaintiffs would face a panel of doctors who would permit or deny their claims without explaining why. Most clients, advised the letter, "will receive no compensation," but if you don't settle then "you will need to employ other counsel to represent you."[17] In other words, take your chances with the program or find a new lawyer.

---

[12] *Propulsid Didn't Cause Man's Death, Jury Finds in 1st MDL Trial New Orleans*, 8 MEALEY'S EMERG. DRUGS & DEVICES 1 (Apr. 3, 2003); *3rd Bellwether Case Testing Prolonged QT from Propulsid Dismissed for No Causation*, 7 MEALEY'S DAUBERT RPT. 26 (May 2003).

[13] *Johnson & Johnson Not Liable in Propulsid Case*, BLOOMBERG NEWS, May 10, 2003.

[14] *In re* Propulsid Prods. Liab. Litig., No. 00-md-1355 (E.D. La. Sept. 30, 2003) (order on common-benefit cost distribution) ("At some point, a number of cases were amicably resolved."). Dealmakers met their participation threshold in March 2005 for *Propulsid I*, and claims administration was just beginning when lead lawyers first requested common-benefit fees in May 2005. Transcript of Status Conference Proceedings, *In re* Propulsid Prods. Liab. Litig., No. 00-md-1355 (E.D. La. May 25, 2005); Transcript of Proceedings, *In re* Propulsid Prods. Liab. Litig., No. 00-md-1355 (E.D. La. Mar. 24, 2005).

[15] Cites for the *Propulsid* details that follow may be found in Elizabeth Chamblee Burch, *Monopolies in Multidistrict Litigation*, 70 VAND. L. REV. 67, 94–98 (2017).

[16] *J&J Agrees to Propulsid Settlement of $90 Million*, L.A. TIMES, Feb. 6, 2004, at C3.

[17] Form Letter for Claims on Behalf of Decedents, http://propulsid.laed.uscourts.gov/case-information/mdl-mass-class-action/propulsid.

The panel of doctors approved only 32 of 4,245 claims – the confidential payouts remain under seal. Of the remaining funds, $8.3 million went to Canada's Prepulsid Resolution Program and $8.3 million went to charitable organizations, such as the Louisiana Health Public Initiative. Forty million reverted back to Johnson & Johnson, which left $12 million remaining in the fund. So, based on the final fund numbers, as of July 31, 2012, those 32 plaintiffs likely received little more than $3.66 million combined.[18] Yet, the court awarded lead lawyers $22.5 million in attorneys' fees – the precise amount that defendant Johnson & Johnson promised to pay them.

Mixed jury results, adverse summary judgment decisions, and disqualified experts paint a dismal picture of the litigation's merits. But an in-depth investigation by the *New York Times* pieced together corporate and government documents showing that Johnson & Johnson "did not conduct safety studies urged by federal regulators," that "their own consultants could have revealed Propulsid's danger early on," and that their own executive warned, "Do we want to stand in front of [sic] world and admit that we were never able to prove efficacy!"[19]

The article prompted a Senate Finance Committee inquiry into whether Johnson & Johnson misused educational grants to promote Propulsid's use in children despite its own internal concerns. Many of the grants "have no apparent relation to education," the Committee concluded, and could lead recipients to "become so reliant on industry funding that it may compromise their independence."[20] In other words, doctors might recommend it not because they think it's best, but because their institutions need the money.

Senate investigations do not translate into legal liability. They may, however, have some cache with juries and could play a role in increasing settlement values. But two weeks after the Senate began investigating, lead lawyers announced a second *Propulsid* settlement that covered late-filed and state-court cases. This deal mirrored the first and plaintiffs fared no better.

As Table 2.1 summarizes, all told, only 37 of 6,012 plaintiffs (0.6%) ever recovered any money through Propulsid's settlement programs. Collectively, they received little more than $6.5 million.[21] Lead plaintiffs' lawyers negotiated with Johnson &

---

[18] Joint Report No. 97 of Plaintiffs' and Defendants' Liaison Counsel, *In re* Propulsid Prods. Liab. Litig., No. 00-md-1355 (E.D. La. July 31, 2012). The totals added in the text are not, of course, in the Joint Report, but derived from numbers provided in that and previous reports. For details, see Burch, *supra* note 15, at 95–97.

[19] Harris & Koli, *supra* note 3.

[20] Gardiner Harris, *Drug Makers Scrutinized over Grants*, N.Y. TIMES (Jan. 11, 2006), https://www.nytimes.com/2006/01/11/business/drug-makers-scrutinized-over-grants.html.

[21] This number does not include the 2,059 claimants who enrolled in the program, had their claims extinguished, but did not submit claim forms. Memorandum in Support of Motion for Distribution of Attorney's Fees at 5 and Exhibit B (Re: MDL Settlement Program II), *In re* Propulsid Prods. Liab. Litig., No. 00-md-1355 (E.D. La. Aug. 1, 2012). *See* Joint Report No. 97 of Plaintiffs' and Defendants' Liaison Counsel, *In re* Propulsid Prods. Liab. Litig., No. 00-md-1355 (E.D. La. July 31, 2012).

TABLE 2.1 Propulsid *by the numbers*

Total Funds: $84 million to $105 million

- $27 million in common-benefit fees and costs negotiated directly with Johnson & Johnson
- $8.3 million to Canada's Prepulsid Resolution Program
- $8.3 million to Louisiana Health Public Initiative
- $6.5 million to plaintiffs (37 of 6,012 deemed eligible for relief)
- Remainder reverts to defendant Johnson & Johnson (at least $45 million)

Johnson to have it pay them more than $27 million in common-benefit fees and much of the total $84 million to $105 million fund[22] reverted back to Johnson & Johnson.[23]

"[I]n terms of result, we believe that we have performed at levels which justify this fee," boasted plaintiffs' lead lawyer, Russ Herman.[24] Comparing fees to those of big city lawyers, he noted, "the fund is barely adequate to compensate the attorneys," but "we're contingent fee lawyers and contingent fee lawyers always accept the risk that they're not going to be well compensated." "[I]f the only motivation in practicing law is to earn a fee," Herman continued, "then we should become butchers or bakers or candlestick makers. The law is a calling, it's a responsibility. The highest service is to the client, and of course to this court."

Pleased with their achievement, lead plaintiffs' lawyers Russ Herman, Dan Becnel, Jr., James Dugan, Stephen Murray, Chris Seeger, Michael Papantonio, Bob Wright, Charles Zimmerman, and Arnold Levin predicted that *Propulsid* would become a template for all future cases:

> Never before in the history of multidistrict litigation, have counsel achieved a global resolution of this proportion in the unique manner by which this Settlement

---

[22] Funding amounts ranged based on how many claimants enrolled, but those percentages were not disclosed.

[23] Plaintiffs' Liaison Counsel's Memorandum in Support of Motion for Final Distribution of Remaining Funds, *In re* Propulsid Prods. Liab. Litig., No. 00-md-1355 (E.D. La. Jan. 31, 2014); *In re* Propulsid Prods. Liab. Litig., No. 00-md-1355 (E.D. La. Feb. 3, 2014) (order); Memorandum in Support of Motion for Distribution of Attorney's Fees at 5 and Exhibit B (Re: MDL Settlement Program II), *In re* Propulsid Prods. Liab. Litig., No. 00-md-1355 (E.D. La. Aug. 1, 2012); *In re* Propulsid Prods. Liab. Litig., No. 00-md-1355 (E.D. La. Jan. 31, 2014); *In re* Propulsid Prods. Liab. Litig., No. 00-md-1355 (E.D. La. Dec. 15, 2011) (order returning $40,000,000 from *Propulsid I* and $5,000,000 from *Propulsid II* to Johnson & Johnson); *In re* Propulsid Prods. Liab. Litig., No. 00-md-1355 (E.D. La. Nov. 30, 2009) (order granting joint motion for an order authorizing distribution of MDL 1 settlement fund); *In re* Propulsid Prods. Liab. Litig., No. 00-md-1355 (E.D. La. June 2, 2005) (order).

[24] Transcript of Status Conference Proceedings at 4, *In re* Propulsid Prods. Liab. Litig., No. 00-md-1355 (E.D. La. May 25, 2005).

Program resolves the litigation without resort to complex joinder devices or Class Certification. This remarkable approach to resolution of "mass tort" litigation promises to become the template for similar resolution of future litigations of this kind.[25]

They were right. As Figure 2.1 illustrates, those highly connected repeat players replicated and refined some aspect of the *Propulsid* settlements in every subsequent deal within the dataset.[26] This chapter discusses what each settlement provision in Figure 2.1 means, but the bigger question is whether *Propulsid* is something we want lawyers to copy.

DEALMAKERS GERRYMANDER SETTLEMENTS

Propulsid was neither the first nor the last time those plaintiff and defense attorneys faced off against one another. As we will see in Chapter 3, the same counsel work together routinely. In supporting the "consensus" group in a leadership appointment hearing, plaintiff's attorney Francis Scarpulla once noted, "[T]his group works collegially and cooperatively with every single person sitting at that defense table. I've known some of them for 45 years, as long as I've been practicing. And I've probably been lead counsel in more cases than anybody in this courtroom." Defense counsel Jim McGinnis agreed, "I been practicing here for almost 34 years, have known all of the people on that side of the courtroom for most of those years, and I can tell you with the utmost confidence that I've never had a problem with any one of them."[27]

Prominent criminologist Abraham Blumberg once explained that as "lawyer regulars" build their practice through their close relationships with system insiders (judges, clerks, and opposing counsel), the client can become "a secondary figure" who "may present doubts, contingencies, and pressures," yet ultimately "becomes a means to other ends of the organization's incumbents."[28] In other words, our adversarial system can take a backseat to regulars' quid pro quo needs.

To incumbents like lead plaintiff and defense attorneys, multidistrict litigation presents a closed community. And repeat plaintiffs' attorneys may have stronger ties to that community than to their own clients – many of whom they've never met. As Professor Jerome Skolnick observes, working group relationships can become

---

[25] Memorandum in Support of Plaintiffs' Steering Committees' Motion for Award of Attorney's Fees and Reimbursement of Costs, *In re* Propulsid Prods. Liab. Litig., No. oo-md-1355 (E.D. La. May 3, 2005).

[26] In Table A.1, the proceedings in bold are those with the publicly available private settlements.

[27] Transcript of Proceedings at 40, 44–45, *In re* Lithium Ion Batteries Antitrust Litig., No. 13-md-2420 (N.D. Cal. Apr. 16, 2013).

[28] Abraham S. Blumberg, *The Practice of Law as a Confidence Game: Organizational Cooptation of a Profession*, 1 LAW & SOC'Y REV. 15, 20–21, 24 (1967).

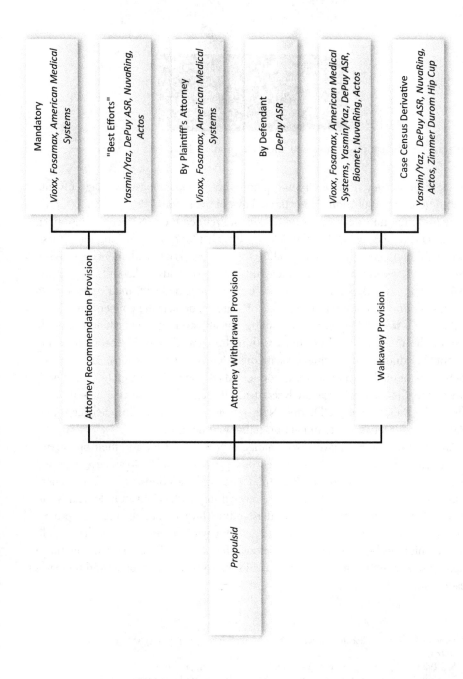

FIGURE 2.1 The evolution of settlement provisions stemming from *Propulsid*

FIGURE 2.2 Repeat players use settlements to promote finality and fees

problematic as they reach a "tipping point where cooperation may shade off into collusion, thereby subverting the ethical basis of the system."[29]

By exploring how dealmakers replicated and refined the settlement provisions in *Propulsid* (the first deal within the dataset), this chapter raises questions about mass-tort deals' reciprocal, quid pro quo-like dimensions. Each settlement featured at least one provision that helped defendants end thousands of lawsuits in one fell swoop, and, in nearly all, lead plaintiffs' lawyers bargained with their opponents to increase their own common-benefit fees. Figure 2.2 depicts the concern simply.

As we will see in Chapter 3, a handful of repeat-player attorneys who consistently occupy the most powerful positions within the dataset's social network have the potential to dramatically influence settlement terms and concessions. As Table A.3 shows, one of the five most centrally connected attorneys did, in fact, help lead each proceeding that produced the analyzed deals. It seems that those lawyers – Richard Arsenault, Dan Becnel Jr., Dianne Nast, Jerrold Parker, and Chris Seeger – may have had a disproportionate impact on settlement design.[30]

Although the central players will change over time, as they and their opponents devise settlement programs, they can massage plaintiffs' choices to achieve a desired result. As behavioral economists Richard Thaler and Cass Sunstein explain, "There is no such thing as a 'neutral' design; ... everything matters." Even little details can affect what people choose.[31] By understanding human nature and our proven tendencies to act in predictable ways (to go along with the status quo or the default, for example), dealmakers can self-consciously frame plaintiffs' choices to encourage them to settle. Getting to "yes" ends lawsuits for corporate defendants and increases leaders' fees.

---

[29] Jerome H. Skolnick, *Social Control in the Adversary System*, 11 J. CONFLICT RESOL. 52, 69 (1967).

[30] *See* Table A.1 (providing percentages of repeat players in each proceeding).

[31] RICHARD H. THALER & CASS R. SUNSTEIN, NUDGE: IMPROVING DECISIONS ABOUT HEALTH, WEALTH, AND HAPPINESS 3 (2009).

By deploying incentives and nudges, while steadfastly maintaining that plaintiffs can freely choose whether to settle, negotiators consciously influence plaintiffs' choices – for better or worse. As it turns out, a number of settlement terms arguably benefit the lead plaintiffs' lawyers or the defendant, but not necessarily the plaintiffs. Some nudge plaintiffs to enter into a settlement program and dismiss their lawsuit before they know whether they'll recover anything. These provisions provide defendants with closure. Others help end lawsuits by deterring additional people from suing either by restricting attorney advertisements or reducing payouts to those who haven't hired an attorney before the settlement is announced. And then there are those provisions that reward the dealmakers by increasing lead plaintiffs' lawyers' common-benefit fees and allowing leftover settlement money to revert to the defendant.

DEFENDANTS NEGOTIATE TO END ALL LAWSUITS

When you think about settling a lawsuit, you probably envision a defendant offering a plaintiff money in exchange for dismissing her claims. The lawyers, like real estate agents, broker the deal, but don't live in the house or sign the documents. In *Propulsid* and all subsequent deals within this book's dataset, however, the lead lawyers didn't just broker the settlement, they became parties to it. And the "settlements" didn't offer plaintiffs a fixed amount, but a chance to recover through a program that may or may not compensate them.

This new and unusual state of affairs was born from corporate defendants' desire to end bet-the-company litigation. They wanted to reassure shareholders that, despite an onslaught of lawsuits, the company wasn't headed for bankruptcy. With class actions off the table, however, lawyers had to get more creative to end the suits and combat what's known in economic circles as the holdout problem.

Holdout problems arise when a defendant's offer to fund a settlement depends on having enough plaintiffs participate to make it worthwhile. If too few sign on, the deal is off. The temptation, then, is for a few plaintiffs to balk at their amount, demand more, and thereby imperil the deal for everyone else, including the lawyers who get paid only if the deal goes through. Similarly, a lawyer might be tempted to settle most of her cases but continue litigating those with the strongest claims or most sympathetic facts – a practice known as "cherry picking."

Curbing these problems took a little doing and fundamentally shifted settlement design: unlike traditional settlements between plaintiffs and defendants, all 13 deals in the dataset are agreements between lead lawyers and defendants.[32] If a client wants to settle, then her individual attorney must typically sign the agreement too.

---

[32] As the Appendix details, in 10 of the 34 proceedings concluding in private aggregate settlements, the deals were publicly available. The proceedings in which those settlements occurred collectively included 64,107 federal actions. This number does not include the thousands of related state-court cases resolved through the same settlements.

By aiming some terms at the lawyers, such as requiring them to recommend the deal to all their clients and withdraw from representing those who won't settle, settlement architects nudge plaintiffs toward a defendant's closure goal – and pave the way for ethical conundrums. Ethics rules require a client to give informed consent when an attorney's duties to that client might conflict with the attorney's duties to someone else. These rules likewise demand that lawyers act in each client's best interest and prohibit attorneys from using settlements to promise not to represent future clients with cases against the same defendant.[33] Often known as lockout agreements or lawyer buyout agreements, these new-suit deterrence provisions hope to prevent more lawsuits by dissuading plaintiffs' attorneys from seeking and accepting new clients. They effectively pull the most talented and most knowledgeable lawyers off the market.

As Table 2.2 illustrates, despite the inherent tension between defendants' closure goals and lawyers' ethics, a look at the settlements within the dataset shows that:

- 100% included *walkaway, withdrawal, or "blow"* provisions: should fewer than the desired percentage of plaintiffs enter the settlement program, the defendant may call the deal off;
- 61% included *case-census* provisions: dealmakers jointly petition the judge to issue a census that requires all attorneys with a case in the multidistrict proceeding to register all their clients' state and federal claims, whether filed or unfiled, so that the defendant can use that number as the denominator for calculating compliance with the walk-away percentage;
- 53% included *attorney-withdrawal* provisions: lawyers must no longer represent clients who refuse to settle;
- 84% included *attorney-recommendation* provisions: all participating attorneys must recommend that all their clients enter the settlement program;
- 38% included *new-suit deterrence* provisions: by aiming to prevent new lawsuits from being filed once a settlement is announced, these provisions take various forms, such as reducing payouts to those without counsel on the settlement date, restricting lawyer advertising, or affirming that participating lawyers have no intent to solicit new clients; and
- 30% included *reverter* clauses: whatever money is left in a settlement fund after the program doles it out then reverts to the defendant, which can incentivize defendants to craft strict recovery criteria.

Corporate defendants can and do manipulate settlement offers to force plaintiffs' lawyers to think of their clients as a group – not as individuals. There are, however, some ethical principles that restrict their unbridled freedom. Model Rule of

---

[33] MODEL RULES OF PROF'L CONDUCT r. 1.7(a), 2.1, 5.6(b) (AM. BAR ASS'N 2016).

TABLE 2.2 *Provisions benefiting defendants within the analyzed settlements*

Settlement provision	Included in the following settlements	Deviations and notes	Percentage of settlements including the provision (of 13)
Walkaway provision	All	Range in plaintiff participation requirement from 85 to 100%	100%
Case-census provision	*Yasmin/Yaz I & II, DePuy ASR I & II, Vioxx, NuvaRing, Actos, Zimmer Durom Hip Cup*	Case-census provisions provide a denominator for the walkaway provision	61%
Attorney-withdrawal provision	By plaintiffs' attorney: *Propulsid I & II, Vioxx, Fosamax, American Medical Systems* By defendant: *DePuy ASR I & II*	*DePuy ASR* allowed the defendant to expel noncompliant law firms	53%
Attorney-recommendation provision	Mandatory: *Propulsid I & II, Vioxx, Fosamax, American Medical Systems* "Best efforts": *Yasmin/Yaz I & II, DePuy ASR I & II, NuvaRing, Actos*	"Best efforts" required participating lawyers to use their best efforts to convince clients to settle	84%
New-suit deterrence provisions	*DePuy ASR I & II, Zimmer Durom Hip Cup, Fosamax, American Medical Systems*		38%
Reverter clauses	*Propulsid I & II, DePuy ASR I & II*		30%

Professional Conduct 8.4(a) states: "It is professional misconduct for a lawyer to violate or attempt to violate the Rules of Professional Conduct, knowingly assist or induce another to do so, or do so through the acts of another."[34]

When plaintiffs' lawyers receive an "aggregate settlement" offer,[35] Rule 1.8(g) requires them to "inform each [client] about all the material terms of the settlement,

---

[34] MODEL RULES OF PROF'L CONDUCT r. 8.4(a) (AM. BAR ASS'N 2016).

[35] An aggregate settlement settles "the claims of two or more individual claimants" with interdependent claims, meaning that "the value of each claimant's claim is not based solely on individual case-by-case facts and negotiations." PRINCIPLES OF THE LAW OF AGGREGATE LITIGATION § 3.16 (AM. LAW INST. 2010) (citing Howard M. Erichson, *A Typology of Aggregate Settlements*, 80 NOTRE DAME L. REV. 1769 (2005)).

including what the other clients will receive."[36] According to the American Bar Association's ethics opinion, this means that clients must learn about the total settlement amount, whether other clients are participating (and, if so, how much they will get), the attorney's fees and costs, and how those costs will be shared.[37]

As this chapter describes, however, these rules have done little to help navigate the ethical quandaries in mass torts. They've proven too flimsy to be of much use. Courts and commentators have divided over how they apply to aggregate settlements, which dampens the threat of potential disciplinary repercussions. As it stands, defendants exploit plaintiffs' attorneys' financial self-interest and loyalty to certain clients to get them thinking that what's good for the goose must be good for the gander. But when clients' needs and circumstances vary drastically, that's unlikely to be true.

Agree to Settle or Call the Deal Off

Defense-friendly settlement provisions form a menu of options that complement one another. In *Propulsid*, for example, dealmakers combined walkaway provisions, settlement bonuses, and a hybrid recommendation-withdrawal provision to convince plaintiffs to dismiss their suit and enter the program. Here's how it worked: first, unless 85% of the death claims and 75% of the injury claims enrolled, then Johnson & Johnson could exit, or "walk away" from, the deal.[38] This created "something of a risk," defense counsel conceded, but he was so "confident in the plaintiffs committee to reach the enrollment level," he said that he started hiring fund administrators.[39]

Second, if 100% of nondeath plaintiffs enrolled, Johnson & Johnson would add a $4 million "bonus" to the available settlement funds.[40] Of course, for plaintiffs, the fund's size ended up mattering little. Remember that the panel of doctors and strict claims criteria prevented more than 99% of them from recovering anything at all. What the bonus could do, however, was bloat the size of the fund so that when leaders later tethered their common-benefit-fee request to it, their request wouldn't raise eyebrows by appearing out of line with plaintiffs' "recoveries." (We will explore this issue more in the coming pages.)

---

[36] MODEL RULES OF PROF'L CONDUCT r. 1.8(g) cmt. 13 (AM. BAR ASS'N 2016).

[37] ABA Comm'n on Ethics & Prof'l Responsibility, Formal Op. 06–438 (2006).

[38] MDL-1355 Term Sheet at § 1.B, *In re* Propulsid Prods. Liab. Litig., No. 00-md-1355 (E.D. La. Apr. 30, 2004) [hereinafter Propulsid I Settlement]. The plaintiffs' steering committee represented about 4,000 people, 300 of whom allegedly died from using Propulsid. *Johnson & Johnson Unit in Legal Settlement Over Propulsid Suit*, DATAMONITOR INDUSTRY NEWSWIRE, Feb. 10, 2004.

[39] Transcript of Status Conference at 11, *In re* Propulsid Prods. Liab. Litig., No. 00-md-1355 (E.D. La. Aug. 6, 2004).

[40] Propulsid I Settlement, *supra* note 38, at § 3.B.

Third, an "opt-out" form accompanied the agreement. But the form wasn't for opting out of the settlement, as you might think. Instead, it allowed counsel to withdraw, meaning that nonsettling plaintiffs opted out of their attorney-client relationship. This form later became the template for more sophisticated attorney recommendation and withdrawal provisions.

Two months after the second *Propulsid* settlement, the Panel centralized suits over Merck's painkiller, Vioxx, before the same judge, Judge Eldon Fallon. Despite having a new foe, *Vioxx* and *Propulsid* included many of the same lead plaintiffs' lawyers – Richard Arsenault, Dawn Barrios, Russ Herman, Arnold Levin, and Chris Seeger.[41] Adapting lessons from *Propulsid*, the *Vioxx* deal demanded that a lawyer certify that she had put all her clients into the settlement program and withdrawn from representing those who refused. If fewer than 85% of plaintiffs signed up, then Merck could walk away and neither plaintiffs nor their attorneys would receive a dime.[42]

The massive nature of the *Vioxx* proceeding (more than 105 million prescriptions and eventually more than 60,000 suits), the size of the settlement fund ($4.85 billion), and the resulting media attention put these mandatory recommendation and withdrawal provisions under the microscope as never before. As one plaintiffs' attorney said, "Maybe the settlement is worthwhile for some people, and maybe others are in for a rude awakening." He continued, "You make a lot of money as an attorney but the plaintiffs are really being trounced on."[43]

Plaintiff Gene Weeks, for instance, worked as a front-end maintainer for Ball Corporation (a glass-jar manufacturer) until a fall at work damaged his spine. After neck surgery, he took one Vioxx a day for two years and had a heart attack two years later. The *Vioxx* settlement required plaintiffs to have taken 30 pills within 60 days of a heart attack. So, Weeks didn't seem to qualify. Despite explaining this to his attorney, he received a letter from her stating that "we have carefully reviewed the details of the Settlement Program" and we "strongly recommend that you agree to participate." Confused, he called her and explained his ineligibility again. "She seemed to ignore this fact and continued to demand that I accept the terms of the settlement," Mr. Weeks said. She advised me "that I would never get to go to trial if I did not participate" and "if I did not agree to the terms of the settlement the firm

---

[41] *In re* Propulsid Prods. Liab. Litig., No. 00-md-1355 (E.D. La. June 2, 2005) (order); *In re* Propulsid Prods. Liab. Litig., No. 00-md-1355 (E.D. La. Oct. 23, 2000) (pretrial order no. 3); *In re* Vioxx Prods. Liab. Litig., No. 05-md-01657 (E.D. La. Apr. 8, 2005) (pretrial order no. 6); *In re* Vioxx Prods. Liab. Litig., No. 05-md-01657 (E.D. La. May 19, 2009) (pretrial order no. 41) (appointment of private third-party payor bellwether trial committee).

[42] Master Settlement Agreement § 1.2.8.1, 11.1, *In re* Vioxx Prods. Liab. Litig., No. 05-md-1657 (E.D. La. Nov. 9, 2007) [hereinafter Vioxx Settlement].

[43] Ron Zapata, *Critics Say Lawyer Provision of Vioxx Deal Is Unethical*, LAW360 (Mar. 25, 2008, 12:00 AM), https://www.law360.com/articles/51064/critics-say-lawyer-provision-of-vioxx-deal-is-unethical.

would not represent me." Although settlement administrators eventually accepted his claim and awarded him a confidential sum, he lamented, "I was browbeaten by counsel."[44]

As ethics professors Howard Erichson and Benjamin Zipursky argue, the *Vioxx* deal ran afoul of numerous rules requiring independent and loyal advice, informed client consent, and the need to abide by a client's settlement choice. "A lawyer who tells the client, 'Settle or you're fired!,'" they explain, "is hardly abiding by the client's decision."[45]

In response to these ethics questions, *Vioxx's* dealmakers amended the settlement slightly to say, "[e]ach enrolling counsel is expected to exercise his or her independent judgment in the best interest of each client individually before determining whether to recommend enrollment in the program."[46] Commenting on the change, Judge Fallon said, "I do feel that nothing in the settlement agreement, including the amendment, contemplates or even requires the attorney to undertake any action that would violate the Rules of Professional Conduct."[47]

Erichson and Zipursky disagreed. "Of course, every lawyer should exercise independent judgment," but "[m]erely saying so," without altering the substance of either the mandatory-recommendation clause or the mandatory-withdrawal clause "hardly eliminates the ethical concerns." Their conclusion? "Too little, too late, too boilerplate."[48]

Asked to opine on the settlement, the Connecticut Bar Association agreed with Professors Erichson and Zipursky. The deal "would compel plaintiffs' counsel to do the impossible," it found. "It would require her to provide 'independent professional judgment' to each client." But it then "restricts the advice she can give: either recommend that all clients accept the settlement or that none of them accept it."[49]

These red flags did little to dampen lawyers' enthusiasm for mandatory recommendation and withdrawal provisions, however. Just three years after the controversial *Vioxx* deal, some of the same lawyers upped the ante in litigation over Merck's osteoporosis drug, Fosamax, which plaintiffs claimed made their jawbones degenerate. Ted Mayer of Hughes, Hubbard & Reed and Bruce Kuhlik, Merck's general counsel appeared again for the defense, and Chris Seeger, James Dugan II, and Shelly Sanford served as lead lawyers as they had in *Vioxx*. This time, however, these dealmakers came armed with an ethics advisor and included a severability provision

---

[44] Plaintiffs' Motion to Vacate, Rescind or Declare the Release of All Claims, *In re* Vioxx Prods. Liab. Litig., No. 05-md-01657 (E.D. La. Apr. 22, 2009) (Exhibit A).

[45] Howard M. Erichson & Benjamin C. Zipursky, *Consent Versus Closure*, 96 CORNELL L. REV. 265, 283 (2010).

[46] Amendment to Settlement Agreement § 1.2.2 (Jan. 17, 2008), Vioxx Settlement, *supra* note 42.

[47] Transcript of Status Conference at 12–13, *In re* Vioxx Prods. Liab. Litig., 05-md-1657 (E.D. La. Jan. 18, 2008).

[48] Erichson & Zipursky, *supra* note 45, at 291.

[49] Connecticut Bar Ass'n, Informal Ethics Op. 08–01 (Feb. 20, 2008).

to ensure that the rest of the settlement would remain intact even if one clause violated "the applicable state(s)' rules of legal ethics."[50]

Here's why they were cautious: like its predecessors, the *Fosamax* deal required attorneys to recommend it to all their clients and withdraw from representing those who refused.[51] But this time Merck demanded *all* plaintiffs participate – 100%. Barring that, Merck could exercise a nuclear option and blow the deal up, or it could reduce the settlement amount by however much the allocation committee determined would have been paid to nonparticipating claimants and their counsel.[52] Happy enough with the eventual 95% acceptance rate, Merck did not walk away, but the judge allowed numerous attorneys to withdraw from representing nonsettling clients.[53]

By now, you get the idea. Just within the dataset, 7 of the 13 settlements required that attorneys withdraw from representing nonsettling clients, and 11 of the 13 either required attorneys to recommend the deal unanimously or certify that the lead lawyers would "use their best efforts to achieve sufficient participation."

Attorneys get paid only if the deal sticks, which creates a crablike mentality. A few clients could avoid the settlement's centripetal forces. But their lawyers pull them into the settlement, like crabs in a fishing bucket who haul one another back in should one scramble toward freedom. The financial incentives for dragging plaintiffs into the program, especially after many years of investing in the lawsuit, are overpowering.

Each new deal provides high-level repeat players on both sides an opportunity to tweak their strategy. They'll cast a broader participation net or invent new bait to induce plaintiffs to settle. Oftentimes, the change will push the ethical boundaries just a little further. The next one will do the same, and so on. Ethics slip away one deal at a time.

Consequently, to help insulate them from a "clear and serious" ethical breach that would require them to forfeit their common-benefit fees, lead plaintiffs' lawyers hired Professor Lynn Baker as the ethics advisor in *Fosamax*, *Vioxx*, *NuvaRing*, and some of the pelvic-mesh litigation.[54] Defending the use of mandatory recommendation provisions, she notes that they do "require that the plaintiffs' attorney give the same *bottom-line recommendation* to each client: that the client participate in

---

[50] Master Settlement Agreement ¶ 1–2, 5, Exhibit C at C-15 (certification and joinder of counsel, claimant's counsel), *In re* Fosamax Prods. Liab. Litig., No. 06-md-1789 (S.D.N.Y. Mar. 24, 2014) [hereinafter Fosamax Settlement].

[51] *Id.*

[52] *Id.* at ¶ 11.

[53] *E.g.*, *In re* Fosamax Prods. Liab. Litig., No. 06-md-1789 (S.D.N.Y. Sept. 22, 2014) (order).

[54] Restatement (Third) of the Law Governing Lawyers § 37 (Am. Law Inst. 2000) ("A lawyer engaging in clear and serious violation of duty to a client may be required to forfeit some or all of the lawyer's compensation for the matter.").

the settlement," but reasons that an attorney can still provide "candid advice." Maybe the lawyer doesn't think that the settlement treats some clients fairly, but that participating "is nonetheless the client's best path."[55] Moreover, to lawyers working on a contingent fee, the withdrawal provisions, she suggests, likewise make sense: "[C]ontinuing to represent a nonsettling claimant may well impose an 'unreasonable financial burden'" that would justify withdrawing under the relevant ethics rule.[56]

Professors Zipursky and Erichson disagree: "A lawyer may not drop one client like a 'hot potato'" just because it is financially more lucrative to do so.[57] Some judges have begun to accept this argument as well.[58] In litigation over the hypertension drug Benicar, lawyers from Wagstaff & Cartmell wanted to withdraw from representing Terry McDaniel because it would be financially burdensome to go to trial. McDaniel was one of only five out of 2,000 plaintiffs who didn't want to settle. As Magistrate Judge Joel Schnider admonished in denying lawyers' request to withdraw, the fact that trial would be expensive "is not a surprise to counsel," who "knew this when they undertook to represent [the] plaintiff." "If counsel is now 'scared off by the prospect of paying for trial," they shouldn't have represented McDaniel in the first place. Moreover, "that hundreds of counsel's clients settled is undoubtedly lucrative," so "[c]ounsel must accept the good with the bad." In short, "The Court will not countenance a situation where a lawyer is permitted to abandon a client who chooses not to settle," Judge Schnider wrote.[59]

Thwarting New Claims: Advertising Prohibitions and Discounts

Controversial though they are, uniform recommendation provisions persist and have been around for a while. Even lead counsel in the asbestos inventory settlements (negotiated alongside the *Amchem* class that the Supreme Court eventually overturned) agreed "to recommend that its clients seriously consider" and use their "best efforts to encourage" clients to take the deal.[60] And even back then some ethics scholars argued that it restricted the lawyer's right to practice and violated Model

[55] Lynn A. Baker, *Mass Torts and the Pursuit of Ethical Finality*, 85 FORDHAM L. REV. 1943, 1954–55 (2017).

[56] *Id.* (discussing MODEL RULES OF PROF'L CONDUCT r. 1.16(b)(6) (AM. BAR ASS'N 2016)).

[57] Erichson & Zipursky, *supra* note 45, at 286.

[58] *E.g., In re* FEMA Trailer Formaldehyde Prods. Liab. Litig., No. 07-md-01873, 2011 WL 4368719, at *2 (E.D. La. Sept. 16, 2011) ("Not only would the burden of locating and communicating with these plaintiffs be shifted from plaintiffs' counsel to the Court and defendants' counsel (which is unfair given that it was plaintiffs' counsel who brought them into this matter), but the penalty for these attorneys' withdrawal would be borne largely by the legions of plaintiffs who are actively cooperating in the prosecution [of] their claims and waiting for the resolution of a matter which has already taken years to litigate.").

[59] McDaniel v. Daiichi Sankyo, Inc., No. 17-cv-3495-RBK-JS (D.N.J. Aug. 15, 2018) (memorandum opinion and order).

[60] Georgene v. Amchem Prods., Inc., 157 F.R.D. 246, 301 (E.D. Pa. 1994).

Rule 5.6. That rule aims to ensure that those who "by virtue of their background and experience, might be the very best available talent" remain open for business.[61] Put differently, corporate defendants shouldn't be able to eliminate lawsuits by paying the attorneys who bring them to stop suing. The rule remains the same, but lawyers have invented new ways to shutter their doors.

In both *Fosamax* and *American Medical Systems* (one of the pelvic-mesh proceedings), plaintiffs' lawyers had to represent that they had no intent to solicit or accept new clients. In the same breath, the deals claimed that nothing within them intended to improperly restrict lawyers' ability to practice law.[62] Surely this wouldn't make it difficult to hire experienced counsel or violate Rule 5.6, argue Professors Stephen Gillers and Richard Painter, for "[m]arket forces should assure that as some lawyers retire from suing certain defendants, others will replace them."[63] Yet, as we'll see in Chapter 3, the mass-torts legal-services market may not be efficient. Cases are expensive to develop and the market is saturated with insiders and lawyers who would face financial and social sanctions if they crossed those insiders. After all, leaders can furnish them with lucrative common-benefit work – or not.

Citing two class-action cases, however, Professor Lynn Baker argues that courts find these nonsolicitation provisions unproblematic.[64] But class actions are the wrong comparison. Class counsel is ethically obligated to the class as a whole. Promising not to represent future cases only makes sense: the class settlement extinguishes the claims of all absent class members who don't opt out – all counsel's current "clients," in other words. When inserted in nonclass settlements and coupled with repeat players' need to preserve a reputation for not unraveling deals, the picture looks different. A lawyer's intent not to represent new clients makes it harder for prospective plaintiffs (and those whose counsel drops them unceremoniously for refusing to settle) to find competent counsel. That's the precise concern behind Model Rule 5.6.[65]

Refining things a bit in *DePuy ASR* and *Zimmer Durom Hip Cup*, leaders who helped run both proceedings, like Chris Seeger and Wendy Fleishman, experimented with a clause to discourage would-be plaintiffs from coming out of the

[61] ABA Comm'n on Ethics & Prof'l Responsibility, Formal Op. 93–371, at 2 (1993); Carrie Menkel-Meadow, *Ethics and the Settlements of Mass Torts: When the Rules Meet the Road*, 80 CORNELL L. REV. 1159, 1199–1200 (1995).

[62] Fosamax Settlement, *supra* note 50, at ¶ 77; Master Settlement Agreement § IV.S, *In re* American Medical Sys., Inc. Pelvic Repair Sys. Prods. Liab. Litig., No. 12-md-02325 (S.D.W. Va. June 14, 2013).

[63] Stephen Gillers & Richard W. Painter, *Free the Lawyers: A Proposal to Permit No-Sue Promises in Settlement Agreements*, 18 GEO. J. LEGAL ETHICS 291, 308 (2005).

[64] Baker, *supra* note 55, at 1959–60 (citing Desantis v. Snap-On Tools Co., 2006 WL 3068584, at *12 (D.N.J. Oct. 27, 2006) and La. Mun. Police Emps.' Ret. Sys. v. Black, C.A. No. 9410-VCN, 2016 WL 790898, at *5 & n.37 (Del. Ch. Feb. 19, 2016)).

[65] ABA Comm'n on Ethics & Prof'l Responsibility, Formal Op. 93–371, at 2 (1993).

woodwork to sue after they'd announced a settlement. This "latecomer provision" immediately reduced the awards of those who had no lawyer as of the settlement date by 29%. It affected two groups of people: (1) pro se litigants (plaintiffs who choose to represent themselves) and (2) those who hired attorneys and sued after the settlement date.[66]

Just as some settlements aim to deter prospective plaintiffs by making lawyers promise that they don't intend to represent new clients, latecomer provisions discourage attorneys from accepting new business by decreasing would-be clients' awards (and their attorney's contingent fees). They thus run up against the same ethical rules that prohibit counsel from restricting their own right to practice through a settlement. But, because everyone they represent is automatically excluded, they cleverly deter other lawyers from entering the market instead of limiting their own practice. They thereby impair the value of nonclients' claims while preserving funds for their own clients – and their own attorneys' fees.[67]

Latecomer provisions are troubling for yet another reason: they unfairly tax pro se litigants for representing themselves. *DePuy ASR*'s dealmakers claimed that the 29% tax discounted pro se payouts to the same amount they would've received if they'd had to pay attorneys' fees.[68] But there's no evidence they would've fared any better with counsel. And those who hired lawyers later were essentially taxed twice: once for being "unrepresented" and then again in paying their new attorney's contingent fee.

On top of the 29% reduction, plaintiffs' leaders took a cut of pro se litigants' awards to pay their common-benefit fees and expenses. That aspect makes some sense. By negotiating a deal that pro se plaintiffs wanted to accept, leaders conferred a benefit. At the same time, however, leaders attempted to keep pro se plaintiffs at arm's length. According to the settlement, they "remain Unrepresented Claimants" even if they "obtain assistance" from the lead lawyers.[69] Although leaders don't represent pro se litigants in a conventional sense, they are obligated to act in their (and all plaintiffs in the proceeding's) best interest by virtue of controlling the litigation.

---

[66] Settlement Agreement, art. 3, § 4.4, *In re* DePuy Orthopaedics, Inc. Hip Implant Prods. Liab. Litig., No. 10-md-2197 (N.D. Ohio Nov. 9, 2013) [hereinafter 2013 DePuy ASR Settlement]; 2015 ASR Settlement Agreement, art. 3, § 4.4, *In re* DePuy Orthopaedics, Inc. Hip Implant Prods. Liab. Litig., No. 10-md-2197 (N.D. Ohio Mar. 2, 2015) [hereinafter 2015 DePuy ASR Settlement]; U.S. Durom Cup Settlement Program Agreement § II.A.2.e, *In re* Zimmer Durom Hip Cup Prods. Liab. Litig., No. 2:09-cv-04414-SDW-SCM (D.N.J. Feb. 11, 2016) [hereinafter Zimmer Durom Settlement].

[67] MODEL RULES PROF'L CONDUCT r. 5.6(b) (AM. BAR ASS'N 2016).

[68] ASR Settlement – Benefits Overview at 4, *In re* DePuy Orthopaedics, Inc. ASR Hip Implant Prods. Liab. Litig., No. 10-md-2197 (N.D. Ohio Mar. 20, 2015), https://www.usasrhipsettlement.com/Un-Secure/WebNews.aspx.

[69] 2013 DePuy Settlement, *supra* note 66, at art. 3, § 4.4; 2015 DePuy ASR Settlement, *supra* note 66, at art. 3, § 4.4.

Leaders lobby for the right to manage others' lawsuits. Allowing them to do so without incurring any duty of loyalty would invite leaders to exploit plaintiffs while avoiding any liability for doing so. By reducing pro se plaintiffs' recoveries by an additional 29%, leaders favored clients over nonclients – a move that the Supreme Court explicitly forbid class counsel from making.[70]

As you may recall from Chapter 1, in *Ortiz*, asbestos defendants offered to settle plaintiffs' attorneys' client inventories on favorable terms. But there was a catch: those lawyers also had to agree to appear as class counsel in a limited-fund class that resolved future plaintiffs' claims. That group didn't fare as well. As the Supreme Court admonished in reversing the deal, assuming "that plaintiffs' counsel could be of a mind to do their simple best in bargaining for the benefit of the settlement class is patently at odds with the fact that at least some ... also negotiated the separate settlement of 45,000 pending claims" that would not be paid in full without a "successful Global Settlement Agreement."[71]

In other words, if a corporation offered to settle an attorney's "inventory" of cases (thereby netting her substantial attorney's fees), but demanded that she represent future plaintiffs' cases in return, that attorney can't be trusted to do right by those future plaintiffs. She's never met them. And the financial incentives to sell them down the river to maximize her current clients' awards and her own fees is overpowering. This is what we think of as a structural problem – the lawyer is in a naturally conflicted position. Faithfully representing both groups would test even the most loyal Atticus Finch types. The sellout may occur quietly with no overt collusion, but the temptations will shade an attorney's loyalties toward her own self-interest and her current clients nevertheless.

As *DePuy ASR* illustrates, leaders face the same conflicts as they negotiate global settlements outside of class actions. Without obligating them to act in the plaintiffs' best interests or appointing attorneys whose economic interests are tied to each group, it's like asking the fox to guard the henhouse. If leaders strike side deals or better deals for their own clients (or those with counsel) while bargaining on the group's behalf, we cannot feign surprise when they favor their and their clients' interests at others' expense. Nevertheless, *DePuy ASR*'s leaders can't have it both ways. Either they fulfilled their fiduciary obligations to unrepresented plaintiffs by protecting their financial interests and should be paid for any benefit they conferred on them, or they sold them out and should receive nothing.

---

[70] Ortiz v. Fibreboard Corp., 527 U.S. 815, 852 (1999); John C. Coffee, Jr., *Class Action Accountability: Reconciling Exit, Voice, and Loyalty in Representative Litigation*, 100 COLUM. L. REV. 370, 388 (2008) ("After *Ortiz*, such 'side settlements' now seem to represent a per se 'impermissible conflict of interest.'"); Roger C. Cramton, *Individualized Justice, Mass Torts, and "Settlement Class Actions": An Introduction*, 80 CORNELL L. REV. 811, 832 (1995).

[71] *Ortiz*, 527 U.S. at 852.

Reclaiming Remaining Funds

The *DePuy* ASR settlement didn't just deter new plaintiffs from suing – the 29% went back into the defendant's coffers.[72] Reverter clauses are classic red flags in class actions: they can indicate collusion, incentivize strict claims-filing criteria, and undermine tort law's deterrent effect.[73] Yet, because nonclass deals aren't subject to the same judicial and appellate scrutiny, settlement designers in both *DePuy* ASR and *Propulsid* used them.

As we saw, *Propulsid* paired its reversion clauses with stringent recovery criteria and leaders tied their fee request to the fund's initial size – not plaintiffs' actual benefit. As Justice O'Connor recognized in class actions, allowing judges to base attorneys' fees on a fund's sticker price would "decouple class counsel's financial incentives from those of the class, increasing the risk that the actual distribution will be misallocated between attorney's fees and the plaintiffs' recovery." This can, she warned, "undermine the underlying purposes of class actions by providing defendants with a powerful means to entic[e] class counsel to settle lawsuits in a manner detrimental to the class."[74]

* * *

When it comes to corporate defendants' closure goals, veteran plaintiffs' attorney Paul Rheingold aptly sums up the current state of affairs: "[T]here is a lot of client coerciveness in seeking a high level of participation." Counsel "insinuate to clients that it is for the common good that all participate," which courts reinforce by placing "great burdens" on any plaintiff who wants to proceed to trial, he explained. Lawyers then point to "a report by an 'ethicist' that the plan is not unethical."[75] "Where," he writes, "is the line between convincing the client that this is proper, and coercion, which we can assume is unethical?"[76]

LEAD PLAINTIFFS' ATTORNEYS BARGAIN FOR THEIR FEES

Just as corporations crave closure, lead plaintiffs' lawyers want common-benefit fees. Whether one is tendered in exchange for the other is impossible to say with any certainty because all bargaining occurs behind closed doors.

---

[72] 2015 DePuy ASR Settlement, *supra* note 66, at §§ 7.1.3.1, 7.1.7; 2013 DePuy ASR Settlement, *supra* note 66, at §§ 7.1.3.1, 7.1.7.

[73] Sylvester v. CIGNA Corp., 369 F. Supp. 2d 34, 47 (D. Me. 2005) (noting "the reverter clause and clear sailing clause raise a presumption of unfairness"); BARBARA J. ROTHSTEIN & THOMAS E. WILLGING, MANAGING CLASS ACTION LITIGATION: A POCKET GUIDE FOR JUDGES 13 (2005).

[74] Int'l Precious Metals Corp. v. Walters, 530 U.S. 1223, 1223 (2000) (O'Connor, J., statement respecting the denial of the petition for a writ of certiorari).

[75] Paul D. Rheingold, *Mass Torts – Maturation of Law and Practice*, 37 PACE L. REV. 617, 633–34 (2017).

[76] Paul D. Rheingold, *Ethical Constraints on Aggregated Settlements of Mass-Tort Cases*, 31 LOY. L.A. L. REV. 395, 404 (1998).

Still, quid pro quo arrangements aren't necessarily illicit deals secretly negotiated in seedy hotel rooms. Thinking exclusively in those terms is a red herring.[77] Most quid pro quos evolve from mutual trust, shared understandings, and bargaining norms. They may stem from self-interest, but they are woven into the litigation culture through expectations and reciprocity.

Nevertheless, sometimes obvious warning signs exist. In open court, *Propulsid*'s lead plaintiffs' lawyer Russ Herman remarked, "Johnson & Johnson's express wish was to have all cases resolved." "In the negotiation for Propulsid II," he went on, "there were certain *quid pro quos* that were not involved in Propulsid I. One of the issues was that Johnson & Johnson insisted that unused funds would have 100 percent reversion to J&J." Consequently, Herman continued, "[T]he [plaintiffs' steering committee] and the state liaison folks who negotiated Propulsid II insisted that ... J&J should pay a reasonable attorney's fee, which was agreed to."[78]

Dawn Barrios, plaintiffs' state liaison counsel, then described how she and fellow leader Arnold Levin "went out and negotiated with Johnson & Johnson, particularly on the reversionary interest." "The last meeting we had [with defense counsel Tom Campion]," she continued, "confected the exact numbers of the settlement, as well as the attorney's fees."[79] In other words, they gave Johnson & Johnson closure and returned most of the settlement money to it in exchange for their common-benefit fees – a "quid pro quo," in Herman's words.

As Herman and Barrios's comments reflect, any lawyer working on a contingent fee wears two hats: as a self-interested investor who bankrolls the proceeding, and as an other-regarding agent who develops claims, negotiates deals, and advises clients. As financiers, leaders and non-leaders alike invest substantial resources. In *Propulsid*, for instance, lead attorneys spent more than $2 million on depositions, experts, personnel, and copying costs as well as more than $2.4 million on flights and hotels.[80] Nonlead attorneys in the Vioxx Litigation Consortium considered 30,000 potential clients and accepted only 2,000, but that process alone took a combined 1,601,150 hours by staff, paralegals, attorneys, nurse practitioners, and medical experts at a cost of $13.5 million.[81]

Litigation expenses like these could easily bankrupt a law firm, and leaders must frequently respond to capital calls to invest more resources as proceedings continue. But, as *Propulsid* demonstrates, acting as both an investor and an agent can tempt

---

[77] Howard M. Erichson, *The Problem of Settlement Class Actions*, 82 GEO. WASH. L. REV. 951, 963 (2014).

[78] Transcript of Proceedings at 7–8, *In re* Propulsid Prods. Liab. Litig., No. 00-md-1355 (E.D. La. Aug. 22, 2012).

[79] *Id.* at 17.

[80] Transcript of Status Conference Proceedings at 5, *In re* Propulsid Prods. Liab. Litig., No. 00-md-1355 (E.D. La. May 25, 2005).

[81] Charles Silver & Geoffrey P. Miller, *The Quasi-Class Action Method of Managing Multi-District Litigations: Problems and a Proposal*, 63 VAND. L. REV. 107, 128 (2010).

the purest of hearts: a lawyer's monetary self-interest as an investor in a joint venture with her clients may be at odds with her duty of loyalty to those same people.[82]

As Judge Hellerstein witnessed in handling the suits brought by the cleanup workers from the World Trade Center disaster on September 11, 2001, the bigger the investment and the more cash-strapped the law firm becomes, the more tempting it may be accept a deal that requires lawyers to strong arm clients into settling. In that proceeding, if more than 525 eligible cleanup workers declined to settle, then lead lawyers would fall short of the deal's 95% participation demand. Noticing that attorneys filed a slew of voluntary dismissals right before the settlement's deadline, Judge Hellerstein convened counsel and their clients only to learn that the clients never gave their attorneys explicit authority to dismiss their cases.[83]

To further complicate matters, some of these cleanup workers qualified for a legislative program: if they gave up their right to sue, they could enter into an alternative victim compensation fund. Fifty-nine plaintiffs chose this option, but plaintiffs' firm Napoli Bern, which also happened to be liaison counsel and represent 10,000 other plaintiffs, agreed to represent them anyway. To squeak by the 95% threshold, however, Napoli Bern simply removed those 59 plaintiffs from the settlement's eligibility list.

As Judge Hellerstein saw it, Napoli Bern was deeply conflicted on multiple fronts: litigating the 59 plaintiffs' eligibility would delay justice for the firm's other clients and dilute the money awarded to the most severely injured plaintiffs. Plus, the firm was deeply in debt. Meeting the 95% rate, however, would net it about $150 million in attorneys' fees. To remedy the conflict, Judge Hellerstein appointed those 59 plaintiffs new, conflict-free counsel. Napoli Bern refused to cooperate, however. So, Judge Hellerstein ordered the firm to send his order on the conflicts question to each affected plaintiff and to give plaintiffs' contact information to new counsel.[84]

Of course, conflicts are inherent to some degree in every billing arrangement. Hourly billing incentivizes defense counsel to work slowly and prolong lawsuits by filing unnecessary motions. And pro bono services may encourage lawyers to skimp on research, revisions, and strategy sessions so that they can return to paying clients. No fee system is perfect.

Efforts to align the interests of lawyers with their clients have plagued class actions since their inception and, as the next two sections explore, similar concerns spill over to their nonclass brethren. For instance, some class-action attorneys aim to exaggerate a settlement's value to justify hefty attorneys' fees by settling for coupons, sending money to a third-party charity ("cy pres"), using reversion provisions that return "unclaimed" funds to the defendant, and agreeing to onerous claims-filing

---

[82] John C. Coffee, Jr., *Kutak Symposium*, 13 Geo. J. Legal Ethics 331, 341 (2000).
[83] *In re* World Trade Ctr. Disaster Site Litig., 754 F.3d 114, 119 (2d Cir. 2014).
[84] *In re* World Trade Ctr. Disaster Site Litig., 769 F. Supp. 2d 650 (E.D.N.Y. 2011).

procedures that make it hard for plaintiffs to recover anything.[85] As *Propulsid* illustrated, nonclass settlements employ nearly identical settlement terms. And leaders, like class counsel, sometimes rely on smoke and mirrors to justify their fees – they anchor requests to a fund's sticker price rather than plaintiffs' actual payout.

Other class settlement provisions act like sticky fly paper, aspiring to capture as many members as possible. By including broad claim releases and sprawling class definitions, defendants achieve greater closure and class counsel expands their "franchise" and fees, as Professor Howard Erichson puts it.[86] Once again, these translate into nonclass deals as leaders use private settlements to attract and tax state-court plaintiffs that are otherwise beyond the federal court's reach.

Bargaining with Defendants for Common-Benefit Fees

If you were selling your house, you'd probably worry if you discovered that the buyer was paying your real estate agent. You might wonder if all those repairs were necessary and why you were paying all the closing costs. In short, you'd have little confidence that your agent faithfully represented your best interests.

Lawyers are agents too. When they negotiate aspects of their fees with the defendant, they raise concerns over self-dealing.[87] Yet, as Table A.4 shows, lead plaintiffs' lawyers in 90% of the proceedings with publicly available settlements in the dataset did just that. Corporate defendants don't pay plaintiffs' lawyers out of the goodness of their hearts – they want something in return.

Contingent fees are designed to increase as a plaintiff's recovery increases. They thereby tie attorneys' fates to their clients' outcomes. But when corporations pay leaders' common-benefit fees directly instead, as they did in *Propulsid, Tylenol,*[88] and *Biomet,*[89] they sever that tie. Fees don't rise with clients' recoveries. Instead, they may be linked to things defendants want. So, plaintiffs' leadership might negotiate settlement funds with flashy amounts and use that inflated number to justify their fees to the judge, but capitulate to a defendant's demands for high participation thresholds, stringent claims-resolution criteria, cy pres relief (like money to third-party charities), reverter clauses, or all the preceding – as *Propulsid* did.

Arguing for part of his fees in *Propulsid*, plaintiffs' lead attorney Russ Herman, began: "Your Honor, we're here to confirm a $22,500,000 legal fee that was

---

[85] Howard M. Erichson, *Aggregation as Disempowerment: Red Flags in Class Action Settlements,* 92 Notre Dame L. Rev. 859, 864 (2016).

[86] *Id.*

[87] Silver & Miller, *supra* note 81, at 134.

[88] *In re* Tylenol (Acetaminophen) Mktg., Sales Practices, & Prods. Liab. Litig., No. 13-md-2436 (E.D. Pa. Feb. 21, 2007) (order granting the PSC's motion to modify CMO 12 to increase the percentage holdback).

[89] Biomet Common Benefit Settlement Agreement, *In re* Biomet M2a Magnum Hip Implant Prods. Liab. Litig., No. 12-md-2391 (N.D. Ind. Jan. 31, 2014).

negotiated [with defendant Johnson & Johnson] in connection with the MDL 1355 settlement."[90] Then, adding weight to Justice O'Connor's worries, he tethered his fee request to the settlement's sticker price: "The $70 million plus available for claimants has been placed already in the fund with Deutsche's [*sic*] Bank and the claims procedure is ongoing."[91] Of course, as you now know, the claims procedure didn't do much for plaintiffs: Only 37 of 6,012 of them appeared to recover anything, and collectively they received less than $6.5 million.

Unfortunately, some of *Propulsid*'s fee practices have become commonplace. Consider, for example, how common-benefit fees unfolded in lawsuits over Biomet's hip replacements. In October 2012, the Panel sent suits to Biomet's home state of Indiana before Judge Robert Miller. He allowed the plaintiffs' lawyers to organize themselves,[92] then appointed their consensus picks to leadership positions.[93] Less than a year and a half later, co-leaders Mark Lanier and Tom Anapol announced that they'd negotiated a private aggregate settlement. At that point, Judge Miller had issued several case management orders and denied Biomet's motion to dismiss based on federal preemption,[94] but hadn't ruled on any other merits-based motions.

As part of their deal, Lanier and Anapol convinced Biomet to pay the steering committee $6 million in common-benefit fees.[95] In return, plaintiffs' lawyers had to shepherd roughly 90% of their clients into the settlement program.[96] At that point, leaders had both the $6 million plus a 5% court-ordered common-benefit fee. But Judge Miller required them to accept the lesser of the two – not both.[97]

In their fee request, leaders appeared to graciously accept the lesser award of $6 million (the gross settlement amount was $144.3 million, 5% of which made the common-benefit set aside $7.2 million).[98] They pointed out that $6 million was only 3.99% of the total settlement value – a figure "many objective parties" would cite as

---

[90] Transcript of Status Conference Proceedings at 3, *In re* Propulsid Prods. Liab. Litig., No. 00-md-1355 (E.D. La. May 25, 2005).

[91] *Id.* at 4.

[92] Transcript of Proceedings at 15, *In re* Biomet M2a Magnum Hip Implant Prods. Liab. Litig., No. 12-md-02391 (N.D. Ind. Nov. 16, 2012).

[93] *In re* Biomet M2a Magnum Hip Implant Prods. Liab. Litig., No. 12-md-2391 (N.D. Ind. Nov. 16, 2012) (plaintiffs' proposed counsel organizational structure).

[94] *In re* Biomet M2a Magnum Hip Implant Prods. Liab. Litig., No. 12-md-2391 (N.D. Ind. Aug. 21, 2013) (opinion and order).

[95] Biomet Common Benefit Settlement Agreement, *In re* Biomet M2a Magnum Hip Implant Prods. Liab. Litig., No. 12-md-2391 (N.D. Ind. Jan. 31, 2014).

[96] *Id.* at ¶ 2 (noting that Biomet's funding obligation kicked in once the settlement "vests" according to the walkaway provision).

[97] Case Management Order Establishing Common Benefit Fee and Expense Funds at § 2(c), *In re* Biomet M2a Magnum Hip Implant Prods. Liab. Litig., No. 12-md-2391 (N.D. Ind. Feb. 3, 2014).

[98] Motion for Payment of Common Benefit Attorneys' Fees and Expenses from the Biomet Common Benefit MDL Assessment Fund at ¶ 10, *In re* Biomet M2a Magnum Hip Implant Prods. Liab. Litig., No. 12-md-2391 (N.D. Ind. Aug. 7, 2015).

"being underpaid." Leadership, however, "agree[d] that this amount is reasonable" because it allowed "for 100% return of the provisional 5% assessment to counsel and claimants alike."[99]

Although charitable on the surface, the $6 million seems like double dipping, like they're paid twice to do the same work. Here's why: they represented so many of the settling plaintiffs that they had no pending cases left and Judge Miller had to appoint a new steering committee.[100] If the original committee had taken the 5% court-ordered assessment, they'd have to put 5% of their own contingent fees into the fund too. That same money would then come back to them in the form of common-benefit fees. So, they'd earn a bit from nonclients' cases, but because most plaintiffs were clients, presumably leaders wouldn't receive much more than their prenegotiated contingency fees.

Accepting $6 million directly from the defendant, however, was a bonus – money leaders couldn't have gotten otherwise. And yet, it seemed to compensate them again for work they'd already promised to do under their clients' initial retainer, hence the double dipping. Common-benefit fees are supposed to compensate attorneys for the benefit they confer on *others* – not for work on their own cases.[101]

What's more, the settlement happened quickly, without much discovery. "I think there were some 30(b)(6) depositions that were done. I think that's it," lamented nonlead attorney Kyle Bachus.[102] "The fact is that the group of people who have been ordered to pay a common benefit cost, that money hasn't been used," he explained. It's "odd in and of itself," he concluded, that "there was an agreement put in place to say that that common benefit was only going to benefit those that resolved the case and not benefit those that continued [to litigate]."[103]

After objectors proposed that some of the $6 million provide seed money for a new steering committee to develop the nonsettled cases, Biomet's attorney John Winter flatly refused: "[T]hat money can only go to the current PSC [plaintiffs steering committee]. That was the deal that was negotiated. It was created, in part, for multiple different reasons, to make this work, so Biomet believes the order requires that $6 million to only go to the PSC."[104] Winter never explained what those "multiple different reasons" were.

Allowing lead plaintiffs' lawyers to negotiate their fees with corporate defendants – either by inserting fee-related provisions within the settlement or by having the defendant pay their fees directly – violates basic agency law. Side payments

[99] *Id.* at ¶ 18.
[100] *In re* Biomet M2a Magnum Hip Implant Prods. Liab. Litig., No. 12-md-2391 (N.D. Ind. Apr. 28, 2015) (order).
[101] *Id.*
[102] Transcript of Proceedings at 28, 30, *In re* Biomet M2a Magnum Hip Implant Prods. Liab. Litig., No. 12-md-2391 (N.D. Ind. May 18, 2015).
[103] *Id.* at 28–29.
[104] *Id.* at 30, 57.

negotiated without client consent should be given directly to clients. Agency law makes it plain that agents have "a duty not to acquire a material benefit from a third party" when they're doing business "on behalf of the principal."[105]

Negotiating fees with one's opponent likewise gives defendants a powerful bargaining chip that they might exchange for things like lower settlement awards, higher participation rates, or rigorous claims criteria.[106] After all, common-benefit fees are big business: using a settlement agreement to contract around the initial judicial fee award in litigation over Guidant's defibrillators, for instance, boosted leaders' fees by $29.7 million.[107] The worry then is that leaders' financial self-interest may no longer be linked to their clients' outcome, but to corporate defendants' desires.

Enticing the State-Court Lawyers

Naturally, some attorneys will prefer state court. "My firm avoids getting involved in the cesspool of MDLs," says Pennsylvania plaintiffs' attorney Donald Haviland, because "you have a core group of lawyers who live and die by this practice." "They love to aggregate, and they love to sell their clients down the river for pennies on the dollar."[108] The Havilands of the world want to control their own suits. But federal leaders have long tentacles and lots of latitude. They've used their bargaining authority with defendants to extract wealth from state-court plaintiffs and their lawyers.

State-court lawyers pose a conundrum to federal leadership: from leaders' perspective, those attorneys may simply sit back, wait for them to negotiate a deal, and then swoop in to capitalize on the settlement. In this picture, state-court plaintiffs and their lawyers are free riders who, without paying, are unjustly enriched at the leadership's expense.

But depicting state litigants as free riders isn't always right. Taxing hard working state lawyers and free riders uniformly makes little sense from a restitutionary perspective. It also undermines industrious counsel's potential to act as a competitive check on the federal proceeding.

To deal with their free-rider "problem," however, plaintiffs' leadership committees came up with two ideas. Both rely on the veneer of consent: (1) judicially ordered "voluntary" participation agreements, and (2) clauses within a global settlement stating that anyone (state-court plaintiffs included) who accepts the deal likewise consents to leaders' common-benefit fees.

---

[105] RESTATEMENT (THIRD) OF AGENCY §§ 8.02, 8.03 (AM. LAW INST. 2006).

[106] Silver & Miller, *supra* note 81, at 134.

[107] *In re* Guidant Corp. Implantable Defibrillators Prods. Liab. Litig., MDL No. 05–1708, 2008 WL 682174, at *2–4, 16 (D. Minn. Mar. 7, 2008).

[108] Daniel Fisher, *Opioid Lawyer Trying to Avoid "Cesspool" Asked for by National Plaintiffs Firm*, FORBES (Aug. 8, 2018, 6:00 AM), https://www.forbes.com/sites/legalnewsline/2018/08/08/opioid-lawyer-trying-to-avoid-cesspool-created-by-colleagues/#5f647c7e6b85.

First, as Table A.4 shows, in 85% of the 34 proceedings concluding in private aggregate settlements within the dataset, transferee judges ordered common-benefit assessments long before settlements occurred. Most used voluntary participation agreements. As Chapter 1 explained, however, these aren't voluntary. They're take-it-or-leave-it contracts of adhesion – lawyers have no choice but to accept whatever work product the leaders generate. Signing the agreement also means that attorneys with a single case in the federal proceeding must consent to having all her clients' cases taxed regardless of whether the case is pending in state or federal court or how much work she's done on her own.

Some judges have seen through the ruse. In handling claims over tainted ConAgra Peanut Butter, Judge Thomas Thrash tied his order to common benefit's origins in restitution theory. He assessed only those state plaintiffs who consented or who "received a tangible benefit" from leaders' efforts.[109] And, in presiding over the *Kugel Mesh Hernia Patch* proceeding, Judge Mary Lisi recognized that she could not tax would-be plaintiffs who hadn't sued or state-court plaintiffs who weren't before her.[110]

Other courts embrace "voluntary" participation agreements. In suits over the diabetes drug, Avandia, Judge Cynthia Rufe assessed fees for all claims in which an attorney who signed a participation agreement had a fee interest, "regardless of whether those claims are subject to the jurisdiction of [MDL 1871]."[111] Plaintiffs' lawyer Tom Girardi, who'd been handling state-court cases for six years, objected: "[W]e made 105 [state] court appearances," "we advanced $14 million in costs," "we paid our own experts," and "we totally prepared these cases outside of any influence of the MDL," he explained.[112] "I personally negotiated the settlement," and "we got four times as much money for heart attacks as the MDL, because of the preparation and work we did."[113]

Girardi represented around 25 federal plaintiffs and roughly 4,000 in state court, but the common-benefit assessment taxed them all uniformly. He appealed Judge Rufe's order to the Third Circuit, which held that district courts can't require attorneys who litigate solely in state court to pay federal leadership fees, but they can enforce participation agreements.[114] So, Girardi had to pay common-benefit fees

---

[109] *In re* ConAgra Peanut Butter Prods. Liab. Litig., No. 07-md-1845 (N.D. Ga. Apr. 6, 2009) (order granting in part and denying in part plaintiffs' motion for the establishment of a common-benefit fund).

[110] *In re* Kugel Mesh Hernia Patch Prods. Liab. Litig., No. 07-md-01842 (D.R.I. Nov. 19, 2009) (memorandum and order).

[111] *In re* Avandia Mktg., Sales Practice & Prods. Liab. Litig., 617 Fed. App'x. 136, 139 (3d Cir. 2015).

[112] Transcript of Hearing at 12, *In re* Avandia Mktg. Sales Practice & Prods. Liab. Litig., No. 07-md-1871 (E.D. Pa. Mar. 26, 2014).

[113] *Id.* at 14.

[114] *In re Avandia*, 617 F. App'x at 141. For the total fees and costs awarded, see *In re* Avandia Mktg., Sales Practice & Prods. Liab. Litig., No. 07-md-01871, 2012 WL 6923367, at *1 (E.D. Pa. Oct. 19, 2002) (awarding $143,750,000 as 6.25% of the estimated value of the settlements and $10,050,000 for future administrative fees and expenses).

for *all* 4,025 some-odd clients. As you might imagine, this discourages law firms from investing in and developing competing state-court suits.

Second, in lieu of, or sometimes in addition to a participation agreement, leaders in 80% (8 of 10) of the proceedings with publicly available nonclass settlements used those agreements to entice state-court plaintiffs into paying their fees. Accept the settlement, accept our fees. Either by including fees directly within the deal or inserting provisions requiring all settling plaintiffs to consent to the transferee judge's orders, any state-court plaintiff who wanted to take the global deal had to consent to common-benefit fees too. With the defendant's blessing, leaders rope in settling state-court plaintiffs who would otherwise fall outside of the federal court's jurisdiction.

In *Zimmer Durom Hip Cup*, for example, Judge Susan Wigenton initially pro-hibited language in leaders' proposed common-benefit order that taxed state-court litigants.[115] And when a series of nonlead attorneys independently argued that they hadn't benefitted from leaders' work, the magistrate judge reduced the assessment from 4 to 1%.[116] Leaders appealed to Judge Wigenton, who provided no relief.[117] Instead, on February 22, 2016, she sent their request back to the same magistrate judge who reduced their fee.[118] A few weeks later, on March 11, 2016, Zimmer sent Judge Wigneton a letter announcing a settlement program.[119]

By negotiating directly with Zimmer, Chris Seeger and Mark Lanier bargained away the common-benefit-fee problems. They included a provision that taxed all settling plaintiffs 4%.[120] By settling, a state or federal plaintiff and her attorney also consented to the leaders' fee. With plaintiffs' "consent," leaders worked around the jurisdictional problem that prevented Judge Wigenton from taxing state-court plain-tiffs directly and eliminated objections about how much plaintiffs had or hadn't benefitted from leaders' efforts. Judge Wigenton then blessed this backdoor solution by ordering all lawyers with a case before her to enroll *all* their clients into the settlement, regardless of whether their cases were pending in state or federal court, or whether they'd even filed them at all.[121]

---

[115] *In re* Zimmer Durom Hip Cup Prods. Liab. Litig., No. 09-cv-04414 (D.N.J. Jan. 21, 2011) (case management order 3).

[116] *E.g., In re* Zimmer Durom Hip Cup Prods. Liab. Litig., No. 09-cv-04414 (D.N.J. Dec. 22, 2011) (order).

[117] Plaintiffs' Liaison Counsel's Notice of Appeal of Magistrate Judge's Dec. 2, 2015 Order on Motion to Reduce Assessment, *In re* Zimmer Durom Hip Cup Prods. Liab. Litig., No. 09-cv-04414 (D.N.J. Dec. 11, 2015).

[118] *In re* Zimmer Durom Hip Cup Prods. Liab. Litig., No. 09-cv-04414 (D.N.J. Feb. 22, 2016) (order).

[119] Letter to Judge Susan D. Wigenton from Andrew Campbell, *In re* Zimmer Durom Hip Cup Prods. Liab. Litig., No. 09-cv-04414 (D.N.J. Mar. 11, 2016).

[120] Zimmer Durom Settlement, *supra* note 66, at § V.C.

[121] *Id.* at § I.B.

WHAT DO PLAINTIFFS RECEIVE?

The status quo consistently benefits the same insiders: lead plaintiffs' lawyers broker deals that increase their own common-benefit fees and corporations end lawsuits. For corporate defendants, it seems like striking a deal with plaintiffs' lawyers might be a cheaper alternative to pulling products off the market or being upfront about a device or drug's side effects and risks. As we have seen, the practices and procedures leading up to the private settlements in the dataset and, where available, the settlement programs themselves – the procedural "inputs," in other words – have raised the specter of quid pro quo deals. As Table A.4 shows, however, little is known about plaintiffs' actual recoveries – the "outputs."

We know, of course, that *Propulsid* plaintiffs fared poorly because only 0.6% recovered anything. From what little data is available, the low claimant-compensation rate in *NuvaRing* (42%) is alarming when you consider the $13.9 million in common-benefit fees and costs.[122] And in *Ortho Evra*, lawyers received $41 million in common-benefit fees and costs while plaintiffs' recoveries totaled only $68 million.[123] The percentage of enrolled plaintiffs who recovered anything appears higher in *Vioxx* (65.9%),[124] *Biomet* (66%),[125] *Pradaxa* (96.8%),[126] and per-

[122] For information on fees and costs, see Special Master's Supplemental Report and Recommendation, and Ex. A, *In re* NuvaRing Prods. Liab. Litig., No. 08-md-1964 (E.D. Mo. Sept. 2, 2015); Special Master's Report and Recommendation Regarding the Allocation and Distribution of Common Benefit Fees and Expenses, *In re* NuvaRing Prods. Liab. Litig., No. 08-md-1964 (E.D. Mo. Dec. 16, 2014); *In re* NuvaRing Prods. Liab. Litig., 08-md-1964 (E.D. Mo. Dec. 18, 2014) (order approving special master's report); *In re* NuvaRing Prods. Liab. Litig., No. 08-md-1964 (E.D. Mo. Sept. 15, 2015) (order granting special master's supplemental recommendation). For claims rates, see Transcript of Status Hearing at 7, *In re* NuvaRing Prods. Liab. Litig., No. 08-md-1964, (E.D. Mo. Sept. 9, 2015) (noting that 424 out of 3,704 claims had been denied, and 473 [based on numbers given] were still in the claims review process).
[123] Transcript of Proceedings, *In re* Ortho Evra Prods. Liab. Litig., No. 06-cv-40000 (N.D. Ohio Jan. 15, 2009). As of March 31, 2008, the court assessed a 3% award of $2,061,535.29 based on settlements to date, which means plaintiffs recovered $68,717,843.00. Memorandum in Support of PSC's Motion for Reimbursement of Certain Advanced Costs, *In re* Ortho Evra Prods. Liab. Litig., No. 06-cv-40000 (N.D. Ohio Apr. 17, 2008). No updates are available after 2008.
[124] *In re* Vioxx Prods. Liab. Litig., No. 05-md-01657 (E.D. La. Jan. 3, 2014) (order and reasons, at 8).
[125] *In re* Biomet M2a Magnum Hip Implant Prods. Liab. Litig., No. 12-md-2391 (N.D. Ind. Aug. 26, 2015) (order); Motion for Payment of Common Benefit Attorneys' Fees and Expenses from the Biomet Common Benefit Assessment Fund at 4, *In re* Biomet M2a Magnum Hip Implant Prods. Liab. Litig., No. 12-md-2391 (N.D. Ind. Aug. 7, 2015).
[126] For fees and costs see Special Master's Report & Recommendation on the Distribution of Common Benefit Fees & Expenses, *In re* Pradaxa (Dabigatran Etexilate) Prods. Liab. Litig., No. 12-md-2385 (S.D. Ill. Dec. 4, 2014). For claimant recovery see *In re* Pradaxa (Dabigatran Etexilate) Prods. Liab. Litig., No. 12-md-2385 (S.D. Ill. Dec. 29, 2014) (case management order no. 88, at 7).

haps *Yaz/Yasmin* (59% of gallbladder claims).[127] But the dearth of information for the remaining 93% of the dataset's proceedings ending in private settlement is what concerns me most. If information that lead lawyers are willing to make public already appears to favor them and benefit defendants – what's being concealed in the truly private aspects of the deals?

Some academics have argued that creating finality for defendants through class and mass actions can unlock a "peace premium" and generate funds that might not otherwise exist.[128] Bundling claims and thereby reducing transaction costs can benefit plaintiffs by reducing expenses. And if corporate defendants can save on legal fees and reassure their stockholders by ending the majority of the lawsuits through a global deal, they might be willing to pay a premium to do so. But the limited evidence available suggests that if these premiums exist, the gains unlocked in exchange for delivering peace may be common-benefit fees – not bigger plaintiff awards.

Inadequate Representation

Although outsiders know very little about what plaintiffs receive even in the publicly available private deals, we know more about the *procedures* used to generate those outcomes. If procedures include built-in fairness protections, then they might give us confidence in the outcomes – even if we can't lift the curtain and judge those results for ourselves. Conversely, if those procedures don't exist (and they don't), then outcomes shrouded in secrecy should trouble us even more.

Class actions provide a useful baseline here, for they offer a smorgasbord of procedural safeguards even though those safeguards don't always perform optimally. In the *Sulzer Inter-Op Hip Prosthesis* litigation, for example, provisional lead lawyers struck an eyebrow-raising deal with Sulzer less than two months after the Panel sent the cases to Judge Kathleen O'Malley. *Defendant* Sulzer hired Dickie Scruggs, a noted *plaintiffs'* attorney, to design a Rule 23(b)(3) class settlement that minimized

---

[127] *In re* Yasmin & Yaz (Drospirenone) Mktg., Sales Practices & Prods. Liab. Litig., No. 09-md-2100 (S.D. Ill. Nov. 20, 2015) (order); Special Master's Report and Recommendation Regarding the Allocation & Distribution of Common Benefit Fees & Expenses, *In re* Yasmin & Yaz (Drospirenone) Mktg., Sales Practices & Prods. Liab. Litig., No. 09-md-2100 (S.D. Ill. Nov. 6, 2015); Transcript of Status Conference at 2–3, 7b, *In re* Yasmin & Yaz (Drospirenone) Mktg., Sales Practices & Prods. Liab. Litig., No. 09-md-2100 (S.D. Ill. Sept. 29, 2014) (providing information on claimants' recovery rates). Further information on recovery rates was made available only to the court and parties. Transcript of Status Conference at 2, *In re* Yasmin & Yaz (Drospirenone) Mktg., Sales Practices & Prods. Liab. Litig., No. 09-md-2100 (S.D. Ill. Apr. 8, 2016).

[128] Samuel Issacharoff & D. Theodore Rave, *The BP Oil Spill Settlement and the Paradox of Public Litigation*, 74 LA. L. REV. 397, 414–15 (2014); Richard A. Nagareda, *The Preexistence Principle and the Structure of the Class Action*, 103 COLUM. L. REV. 149, 162 (2003); D. Theodore Rave, *Governing the Anticommons in Aggregate Litigation*, 66 VAND. L. REV. 1183, 1192–98 (2013).

opt outs. In return, it promised to pay him a "low seven-figure number" plus a "success fee" of $20 million if the judge approved the deal.[129]

The settlement placed liens on virtually all Sulzer's assets in favor of settling class members. Anyone opting out would have to wait at least six years before getting paid. If Sulzer settled with an opt-out claimant on more favorable terms, it would have to pay all the class members too.[130] Generous? No. Instead, it functioned a bit like a doomsday device. The idea wasn't to detonate it, but to deter class members from opting out, to signal that they weren't going to get a better deal. This was their one chance.

As Scruggs put it, I gave "a lien on the company, lock stock and barrel, to the class to secure payments to the class plaintiffs. That presented a dilemma to anyone who opted out."[131] "[I]f anybody opts out, they still have to try their case, win their case, win their appeal, and then there would be no assets to satisfy their judgment, because they are all pledged to the class."[132] "The flaw here," chided Professor John Coffee, "may be that [the deal] is too clever by half."[133]

A parade of objections followed, the most significant of which was that the provision essentially turned a Rule 23(b)(3) opt-out class into a non-opt-out, limited fund class.[134] "It's ridiculous," said Andres Pereira, who filed 23 cases against Sulzer – class lawyers "have cut a deal with the company that is to the company's benefit and probably will be to their benefit, but won't be to the benefit of the putative class members."[135] Two weeks later, however, Judge O'Malley conditionally certified two subclasses, one for those who had the hip revision surgery and one for those who hadn't (but might).[136]

Appealing to the Sixth Circuit, objectors forced the settlement designers to tweak the deal. Class counsel bargained for greater benefits to class members, changed its questionable provisions, and removed the lien – all before the Sixth Circuit could rule on the original settlement.[137] As Professor Richard Nagareda explained, in

---

[129] Jess Bravin, *Sulzer Medica Reaches Novel Class-Action Pact,* WALL ST. J., Aug. 16, 2001, at A1. For a riveting look at Scruggs's career, see CURTIS WILKIE, THE FALL OF THE HOUSE OF ZEUS: THE RISE AND RUIN OF AMERICA'S MOST POWERFUL TRIAL LAWYER (2010).

[130] *In re* Inter-Op Hip Prosthesis Liab. Litig., 204 F.R.D. 330, 354 (E.D. Ohio 2001). This is similar to what's known as a "most-favored nation" clause, which prevents a contracting party from reaching a better deal with a third party. It signals to plaintiffs that a company will treat subsequent plaintiffs similarly and that there's no benefit in delaying settlement.

[131] Symposium, *A Novel Approach to Mass Tort Class Actions: The Billion Dollar Settlement in the Sulzer Artificial Hip and Knee Litigation,* 16 J.L. & HEALTH 169, 192 (2001).

[132] Bravin, *supra* note 129.

[133] *Id.*

[134] RICHARD A. NAGAREDA, MASS TORTS IN A WORLD OF SETTLEMENT 156–57 (2007).

[135] Bravin, *supra* note 129.

[136] *In re* Inter-Op Hip Prosthesis Liab. Litig., 204 F.R.D. 330, 338–39 (N.D. Ohio Aug. 31, 2001).

[137] Nagareda, *supra* note 128, at 205 n.240 (2003) ("A preliminary ruling by the Sixth Circuit did not bode well for that court's ultimate disposition of the settlement and, as such, spurred negotiations that ultimately recast the deal.").

approving the new settlement, Judge O'Malley got it right: removing the lien and the trust fund, which overreached by altering opt outs' preexisting rights to sue, "purchased rather than simply appropriated" those rights and thereby kept "with their status as a form of property."[138]

Objectors entered the picture again when it came time to award common-benefit fees. This time, Judge O'Malley withheld payments from 10 law firms that represented both class members and nonclass plaintiffs. "[C]ounsel must now argue that, contrary to their earlier representations to the Court, they did not maximize the common benefit in this class action," she wrote. Class members' primary interest "was to maximize their compensation," but opt-outs "necessarily sought compensation that would not be available to the class, an interest in direct conflict with that of class members." These attorneys, she warned, "are continuing to put at risk Sulzer's ability to make all promised payments to the class."[139]

To be sure, judges can fall down on the job in class actions; conflicts can escape scrutiny and collusive deals can persist. But, as *Sulzer* illustrates, unlike in nonclass mass torts, there are checks on judges and counsel. Because class counsel may be the only one who will receive an attorney's fee, competing lawyers have every incentive to encourage class members to object or opt out. And, if objectors face a chilly reception before the district court, then they can appeal. Appellate courts are further removed from the district court's close working relationship with leaders and may be more willing to reverse collusive settlements and chastise self-dealing attorneys. But none of those measures are currently available when mass torts aren't certified as classes. So, although substantive outcomes in class actions are hard to measure (and may be no better), the procedural checks are more robust.

Intragroup Conflicts

Nonclass multidistrict proceedings that end in private deals can't be appealed when things go sour. Entering into the settlement program means waiving any objections participants might have and refusing to settle means that a plaintiff has no standing to challenge the deal. Put simply, there's no way to object.

As Chapter 1 explained, multidistrict litigation is designed for administrative ease – plaintiffs agree neither to it nor the judge's leadership picks. That makes installing leaders more like appointing class counsel. But as Chapter 3 will describe in more detail, judges pay little attention to adequate representation on the front end – often selecting leaders before conflicts arise. And though plaintiffs have their own lawyers (unlike all but the named plaintiff in class actions), that attorney is powerless. She cannot fire the lead lawyers even when she feels they are not acting in her clients'

---

[138] NAGAREDA, *supra* note 134, at 159.
[139] *In re* Sulzer Inter-Op Hip Prosthesis & Knee Prosthesis Liab. Litig., 268 F. Supp. 2d 907, 928–29 (N.D. Ohio June 12, 2003).

best interest, and she regains control of her clients' suits only in the unlikely event of remand. Often, the most she can do is complain that the leaders have violated their fiduciary obligations to the whole group – a move that risks alienating her from them and the judge who handpicked them.

No checks and balances ensure adequate representation at the back end, either. Without a class action, judges lack the overt authority to ensure private nonclass settlements are "fair, reasonable, and adequate."[140] And, unlike class objectors who get paid only by improving the settlement, lead lawyers have no reason to raise conflicts. They profit from representing as many people as possible – not from acknowledging differences.

Perhaps it's not surprising then that some lead plaintiffs' attorneys prefer the freedom of nonclass mass torts. When Judge Douglas Woodlock initially balked at the parties' request to approve their private settlement in the *Fresenius GranuFlo/ Naturalyte* dialysis litigation and suggested that a class action might be a clearer way for him to get involved, lead plaintiffs' lawyer Anthony Tarricone demurred, "that requires all kinds of additional procedures and perplexities." So, while Tarricone acknowledged that there would be disputes as to how to handle cases under the private settlement, opting for a class action was undesirable: "[W]e would have to have probably multiple class representatives in different categories of cases, and the notice requirements are arduous and costly, and then the time factor is one that is extraordinary. I mean, the NFL case was settled almost two years ago. We're still in the Appeals Court."[141] Stripping away adequate-representation protections seems faster and cheaper for lawyers.

In class actions, the Supreme Court has interpreted the Constitution's Due Process Clauses to require separate representation as soon as a structural conflict of interest arises.[142] Structural conflicts are those that present a significant danger that plaintiffs' lawyers might put their own self-interest above plaintiffs' best interest or skew the way they handle the suits such that some plaintiffs are favored over others for reasons having little to do with their claims.[143]

Although nonclass proceedings give lawyers room to wheel and deal and may speed up the process, they can spell trouble for plaintiffs. After all, multidistrict transfer requires one common factual question. And that question needn't unite plaintiffs in any meaningful way. Without guarantees that lead lawyers are adequately representing them, one plaintiff's gain may spell another's loss. Why might that be?

---

[140] FED. R. CIV. P. 23(e).

[141] Transcript of Status Conference at 7–8, *In re* Fresenius Granuflo/Naturalyte Dialysate Prods. Liab. Litig., No. 13-md-02428 (D. Mass. Apr. 29, 2016).

[142] Amchem Prods., Inc. v. Windsor, 521 U.S. 591, 625–26 (1997); Hansberry v. Lee, 311 U.S. 32, 45 (1940). As Professor Morris Ratner has explained, this now means different things in different circuits. Morris A. Ratner, *Class Conflicts*, 92 WASH. L. REV. 785, 803–25 (2017).

[143] PRINCIPLES OF THE LAW OF AGGREGATE LITIGATION § 2.07(a) (AM. LAW INST. 2010).

Lead counsel not only sits at the negotiation table but also chooses which claims to develop. Without separate representation, plaintiffs who are fewer in number, such as those who are too frail to undergo revision surgery or who have less lucrative claims, may find their interests overshadowed and undermined by the majority. In the pelvic-mesh cases, for example, nearly half of the plaintiffs did not have removal or revision surgery, but those suits were worth only 10% of the litigation's overall value.[144] Although judicially appointed leaders controlled their claims, those leaders had no particular reason to invest in or litigate them. Instead, they had every incentive to direct their resources and settlement efforts toward the more profitable revision plaintiffs.[145] Judge Joseph Goodwin ultimately dismissed the nonrevision mesh cases against Johnson & Johnson's medical-device unit Ethicon without prejudice, opening the door to the possibility of a future suit if the plaintiff underwent revision surgery, but foreclosing recovery until then.[146]

Claims will inevitably vary in value. "Defendants have offered next to nothing to settle cases involving mesh products that have not been removed," wrote one plaintiff's lawyer to his clients.[147] In lawsuits over pelvic mesh and defective hip implants (such as those against Sulzer, DePuy ASR, Biomet, Zimmer, Wright Medical Technology, DePuy Pinnacle, and Stryker), some plaintiffs will simply need a doctor to confirm that the replacement works properly. Others will have high-value claims from undergoing revision surgery, and still others may need revision surgery but are medically ineligible for some reason.

Judge O'Malley, who certified *Sulzer* as a class action, recognized that those plaintiffs who would not have revision surgery needed separate counsel.[148] Those who underwent revision surgery had no self-interested reason to make sure that funds remained to compensate those who might need surgery in the future. Attorneys seeking to maximize their profits would likewise focus on the revised group. Because the proposed settlement included both groups and the groups could be antagonistic to one another, counsel "cured this conflict by the use of separately represented classes."[149]

But these safeguards don't exist in the nonclass mesh and hip implant proceedings. *Biomet's* leadership roster – engineered by a consensus of attorneys who,

---

[144] Alison Frankel & Jessica Dye, *New Breed of Investor Profits by Financing Surgeries for Desperate Women Patients*, REUTERS (Aug. 18, 2015, 4:00 PM), https://www.reuters.com/investigates/special-report/usa-litigation-mesh/.

[145] Robert G. Bone, *Agreeing to Fair Process: The Problem with Contractarian Theories of Procedural Fairness*, 83 B.U. L. REV. 485, 549 (2003).

[146] *In re* Ethicon, Inc. Pelvic Repair Sys. Prods. Liab. Litig., No. 12-md-02327 (S.D. W. Va. Apr. 11, 2018) (pretrial order no. 293 regarding disposition of nonrevision Gynecare TVT products cases).

[147] Matthew Goldstein & Jessica Silver-Greenberg, *How Profiteers Lure Women into Often-Unneeded Surgery*, N.Y. TIMES, Apr. 14, 2018, at A1.

[148] *In re* Inter-Op Hip Prosthesis Liab. Litig., 204 F.R.D. 330, 335–36 (N.D. Ohio 2001).

[149] *Id.*

according to Mark Lanier "all play well together in the sandbox" – was unified.[150] The settlement program they negotiated covered only those plaintiffs who had revision surgery.[151] So, too, did the *DePuy ASR* settlement program.[152] *DePuy ASR*'s leaders, like *Biomet*'s, represented everyone.[153] In *Biomet*, Judge Miller appointed a new plaintiffs' steering committee to continue litigating on behalf of nonsettling plaintiffs.[154] But that's not the norm.

In *DePuy ASR*, for example, after leaders negotiated two settlements for those who had their hips revised, they left some 4,000 unrevisables to their own devices. "If you're medically unrevisable, then you fill out your plaintiff fact sheet, you – you can open up discovery, and you can move forward with your case," explained plaintiffs' executive committee member Steven Skikos. But plaintiffs couldn't return to their home courts. Instead of asking for a remand, attorneys "need to reach out to DePuy counsel and advise they want to pursue discovery, offer their clients up for depositions," clarified Ellen Relkin, another executive committee member.[155]

Multidistrict litigation produces efficiencies by collectively developing the common aspects of plaintiffs' claims. When team efforts dissolve into solo efforts to unearth plaintiff-specific facts, coordination has outlived its utility. Cases should return home.

Forced coordination – be it a class action or multidistrict proceeding – warrants adequate representation. When leaders have no economic incentive to develop minority or outlier claims, those plaintiffs have no seat at the decision-making table. After leaders settle, they have no incentive to continue developing cases. When a deal doesn't include plaintiffs' claims or they don't want to settle, plaintiffs must often go it alone – without counsel (who has withdrawn), in a forum they didn't choose. In the *Sulzer* class, by contrast, unrevisables at least had a representative at the table. And in the spirit of Fred Baron, who successfully derailed the asbestos cases before the Supreme Court, objectors raised a host of concerns over arm's-length bargaining

---

[150] Transcript of Proceedings at 15, *In re* Biomet M2a Magnum Hip Implant Prods. Liab. Litig., No. 12-md-2391 (N.D. Ind. Nov. 16, 2012); *In re* Biomet M2a Magnum Hip Implant Prods. Liab. Litig., No. 12-md-2391 (N.D. Ind. Dec. 5, 2012) (order concerning plaintiffs' counsel organizational structure).

[151] Settlement Agreement at § 2, *In re* Biomet M2a Magnum Hip Implant Prods. Liab. Litig., No. 12-md-2391 (N.D. Ind. Jan. 31, 2014).

[152] 2013 DePuy ASR Settlement, *supra* note 66, at Recitals § D; 2015 DePuy ASR Settlement, *supra* note 66, at Recitals § F.

[153] *In re* DePuy Orthopaedics, Inc., ASR Hip Implant Prods. Liab. Litig., No. 10-md-2197 (N.D. Ohio Jan. 26, 2011).

[154] *In re* Biomet M2a Magnum Hip Implant Prods. Liab. Litig., No. 12-md-2391 (N.D. Ind. May 27, 2015) (case management order no. 3, at 6).

[155] Transcript of Open Court Conference Proceedings at 11, 15, *In re* DePuy Orthopaedics, Inc., ASR Hip Implant Prods. Liab. Litig., No. 10-md-2129 (N.D. Ohio Nov. 10, 2016); Barry Meier, *Frustration from a Deal on Flawed Hip Implants*, N.Y. TIMES, Nov. 25, 2013, at B1 (noting that 4,000 plaintiffs were not covered by the deal).

and the settlement's terms. If they really wanted to, class members could also opt out and pursue their suit closer to home.

Attorney Conflicts

When leaders settle on terms that are likely to benefit their own clients and advance the claims that promise them the highest rate of return, rifts can arise between them and other attorneys. Dealmakers design the settlement matrix and hammer out the confidential guidance documents. These documents spell out the recovery criteria and point values. In what feels a bit like insider trading, this knowledge allows leaders to tailor their own clients' submissions to maximize their payout (and their own contingent fees).

In *Biomet*, for instance, nonlead plaintiffs' counsel noticed a disturbing pattern: each time a plaintiff sought an "enhanced" award (rather than taking the presumptive $200,000), Biomet sought to mediate for less money. While the settlement allowed Biomet to do so for "good cause," contesting every single case where plaintiffs wanted an enhancement suggested something other than good faith.[156] So, nonleaders demanded answers.

The settlement's architects explained that they understood that if a plaintiff thought she was entitled to more than the presumptive award, she could indeed seek an enhancement, but, after opening the file, Biomet could likewise seek a reduction.[157] The agreement spelled out none of this. But it didn't contradict it either.

Weighing in, Judge Miller ruled, "What Biomet was accused of having done – what Biomet concedes it did – was permissible under the Master Settlement Agreement and was no surprise to the Plaintiffs' Steering Committee with which it was negotiated. There is no basis for me to say Biomet has acted in bad faith."[158]

To be fair, plopping a pot of money in front of any group can prompt a pirate-like mentality. Disagreements about who should get what and why will inevitably surface in any form of aggregate litigation.

But aggregative mechanisms do not abide by the law of the sword and plank. Instead, they incorporate different procedural protections. Class actions demand that named plaintiffs and class counsel adequately represent warring subgroups, provide opportunities for dissent, and allow objectors to appeal. Judges must certify settlements as fair, reasonable, and adequate. Plus, ethics rules declare that class counsel must act in class members' best interest.

---

[156] Letter from Gregg Borri to Judge Miller, *In re* Biomet M2a Magnum Hip Implant Prods. Liab. Litig., No. 12-md-2391 (N.D. Ind. Apr. 27, 2015).

[157] *In re* Biomet M2a Magnum Hip Implant Prods. Liab. Litig., No. 12-md-2391 (N.D. Ind. May 27, 2015) (case management order no. 3, at 2–3).

[158] *Id.* at 4.

Nonclass aggregation, however, requires that individual counsel advise clients about the risks of representing multiple clients up front, and then act in each client's best interest by providing informed advice on whether to settle.[159] But the integrity of that individual attorney-client relationship declines as an attorney's client "inventory" swells. And we cannot rely solely on an attorney to give faithful advice to her clients as settlements place conditions on that advice, tie the attorney's fees to plaintiffs' participation rate, and demand that lawyers withdraw from representing clients who won't settle. As we're about to see, that settlement advice may be even more complicated than these pulls suggest – attorneys' close ties with one another can also shade their judgment in ways that prioritize communal interests over clients' interests.

[159] MODEL RULES OF PROF'L CONDUCT r. 1.7, 1.8, cmt. 13 (AM. BAR ASS'N 2016).

3

The Rise of Repeat Players

Plaintiff's attorney Lance Cooper is no stranger to products-liability cases – he litigated a Ford Bronco II rollover back in the 1990s. But he's not among the usual suspects that judges appoint to lead multidistrict proceedings. After his investigation into Brooke Melton's case led GM to double its car recall, however, he started getting calls from lawyers in Louisiana, Mississippi, and California – all wanting him to join their "team." "They're all MDL lawyers," Cooper said, "but they know nothing about this litigation." He eventually agreed to work with Roland Tellis of Baron & Budd and Adam Levitt of DiCello Levitt. Thereafter, Cooper quickly found himself "sucked up" in the mass-tort world. "I flew up to the Panel hearings in Illinois," he explained, and it was "surreal." "All these vendors were there catering to lawyers – claims administrators, document discovery folks, all up there wining and dining everyone."[1]

The Panel sent the proceedings to Judge Jesse Furman in New York and he appointed Steve Berman, Elizabeth Cabraser, and Mark Robinson to lead the cases temporarily. But Cooper wanted that position on a more permanent basis. "No," his new teammates told him, "it wouldn't be good to challenge them. This is the way the game is played and they won this round. We need to ingratiate ourselves with them so we can get on the executive committee." So Cooper attended the meeting before the meeting. "It was all about coalitions, who's going to get on the exec committee, who's going to support who," Cooper explained. "It reminded me of a scene out of an old mafia movie," he said.[2]

Lance Cooper did land a spot on the executive committee. But he quickly realized that Steve Berman "was going to control everything." Still, Cooper continued to press forward with Brooke Melton's case in state court. "I had a

---

[1] Telephone Interview with Lance Cooper, Founding Partner, The Cooper Law Firm (May 8, 2018).
[2] *Id.*

tremendous opportunity to proceed with aggressive discovery" in her case, he said, but "I got pushback from Berman and [co-lead Bob] Hilliard." They wanted all the discovery to go through the multidistrict proceeding.

The state court judge set a trial date for the Meltons, but it was delayed "because of the MDL co-leads and GM," Cooper explained. So, the multidistrict proceeding's discovery bottleneck waylaid the very case that helped give it life. Nor could Cooper control most depositions. "We need to take a tight trial deposition, 30 minutes, so when the jury's watching, it's interesting," he said. But he felt like the leaders' depositions were long and rambling. It was "lawyers just wanting to bill time." The entourage that appeared for every deposition was "plaintiffs' lawyers acting like defense lawyers," Cooper lamented. "My clients are harmed because they're having to pay for people to be there who don't need to be." "It was a disaster," Cooper concluded, "not a single deposition that was taken in the MDL was useful for trial." Yet, Judge Furman declared the depositions finished, so "I was hamstrung from taking any more."[3]

Lance Cooper resigned from the executive committee in April 2015.[4] E-mail exchanges between him and Bob Hilliard show increasing acrimony. "[Y]ou suggest that it is a conflict if I sit on the EC and also advocate on behalf of my clients in state court cases," Cooper wrote.[5]

Cooper also thought that Hilliard and Steve Berman put their own self-interest first, particularly when it came to selecting cases for bellwether trials. If bellwether trials represent the remaining cases in a proceeding, they can provide a yardstick for the proceeding's strengths and weaknesses and help set settlement values for all the plaintiffs. So Cooper worried that a weak case would affect his clients. He told Hilliard, "We also received a phone call from one of the lawyers in the MDL who had a potential bellwether case. The lawyer told me that your partner ... told him that the case would have a better chance of being picked as a bellwether case if he agreed to pay your law firm 50% of the attorneys' fees." "Although I have never been involved in an MDL before, that is just simply wrong," Cooper wrote.[6]

The initial bellwether trial plan was to try a strong, sympathetic case first – one where James Yingling, a young father of five, died in a single-vehicle crash. But, as Cooper's e-mail suggested, Steve Berman and Bob Hilliard seemingly wanted a portion of the attorneys' fee for that case. And Yingling's family's lawyer didn't want to hand the reins (and half of his fees) over to them. So, they moved Yingling's case

[3] *Id.*

[4] Declaration of Robert C. Hilliard in Support of Co-Lead Counsel's Memorandum in Opposition to Lance Cooper's Motion to Remove Co-Lead Counsel for Reconsideration of the Order Approving the Qualified Settlement Fund, Exhibit 1, at 1, *In re* Gen. Motors LLC Ignition Switch Litig., No. 14-md-2543 (S.D.N.Y. Feb. 2, 2016); Declaration of Lance A. Cooper, Exhibit 4, at 1–2, *In re* Gen. Motors LLC Ignition Switch Litig., No. 14-md-2543 (S.D.N.Y. Feb. 5, 2016).

[5] Declaration of Lance A. Cooper, *supra* note 4, Exhibit 4, at 2.

[6] *Id.*

from first to fifth and put one of Bob Hilliard's cases first. As Hilliard explained, after Yingling's lawyer "declined Co-Lead Counsel's participation, ... Co-Lead Counsel determined that it would be in the best interests of all MDL plaintiffs if Co-Lead Counsel adjusted the order of trials so that Co-Lead Counsel could try the first bellwether case."[7]

"Your intentions are obvious," Yingling's lawyer wrote to Hilliard, "You want to control this litigation and maximize the fees earned by your law firm regardless of the harm your actions may cause the MDL plaintiffs." The case that Hilliard placed first, explained Yingling's lawyer, involved a plaintiff with soft-tissue injuries who was out of work for only a few months, whereas "Mr. Yingling was a 35 year old father who lingered 17 days with a profound brain injury." When he died, he "left behind a wife and five children."[8] After receiving this objection, the leaders relented slightly, moving Yingling from fifth to third – but not first.[9]

Bad bellwether trials can hurt all plaintiffs' settlement prospects. And the bellwethers in *GM* went south as soon as they began: Bob Hilliard withdrew the first suit after his soft-tissue-injury client committed perjury and fraud at trial, GM won the second, the *Yingling* case then settled, leaders voluntarily dismissed the fourth, and then leaders settled the last two.

After Hilliard's client perjured himself in the first bellwether, Lance Cooper made national headlines by suggesting that the court remove Hilliard from his leadership role.[10] Cooper claimed that Hilliard put himself first. "If he is permitted to continue in his role as a co-lead, it will only get worse," Cooper wrote. In addition to the bellwether issues, Cooper alleged that Hilliard "cut a secret deal with GM," which settled 1,385 plaintiffs' claims (all Hilliard's cases except those slated as bellwethers) in exchange for a "high-low deal." High-low agreements set the range for a jury's award: if a plaintiff wins a big verdict, the arrangement would lower it to a prenegotiated amount, thereby limiting GM's financial exposure. Conversely, if GM wins, under the deal the plaintiff would still receive a nominal "low-end" award. But the high-low deal that Hilliard divulged to the court in chambers applied not just to one case but to all the remaining bellwether trials.[11]

"[W]hen a lead attorney negotiates a side-settlement of his firm's inventory of cases while retaining control of an MDL," wrote Professor Charles Silver in

[7] Declaration of Robert C. Hilliard, *supra* note 4, at ¶ 20.
[8] Declaration of Victor H. Pribanic, Exhibits 3 & 4, *In re* Gen. Motors LLC Ignition Switch Litig., No. 14-md-2543 (S.D.N.Y. Feb. 5, 2016).
[9] Plaintiffs' Reply Brief in Response to Co-Lead Counsel's Memorandum in Opposition to Lance Cooper's Motion to Remove Co-Lead Counsel & for Reconsideration of the Order Approving the Qualified Settlement Fund at 7–8, *In re* Gen. Motors LLC Ignition Switch Litig., No. 14-md-2543 (S.D.N.Y. Feb. 5, 2016).
[10] Barry Meier, *Lawyers Suing G.M. over Defect Are Now Fighting Each Other*, N.Y. TIMES (Feb. 5, 2016), https://www.nytimes.com/2016/02/06/business/lawyers-suing-gm-over-defect-are-now-fighting-each-other.html; Barry Meier, *Lawyer for Plaintiffs Suing G.M. Steps Up Criticism of Another*, N.Y. TIMES (Feb. 7, 2016), https://www.nytimes.com/2016/02/08/business/lawyer-for-plaintiffs-suing-gm-steps-up-criticism-of-another.html.
[11] Declaration of Robert C. Hilliard, *supra* note 4, at ¶ 37.

supporting Cooper's motion, there's "a clear and well-recognized potential for a serious conflict of interest." Why? "[T]he parties who *are* at the bargaining table can expropriate wealth from the parties who *are not*, and share it between themselves." There needn't be any underhanded deal or conscious collusion. It's a structural conflict. "[T]he structure – negotiating a side-settlement while also controlling a separate aggregate proceeding," Silver explained, "creates incentives and opportunities to help one group of people at the expense of another." Those "opportunities cannot be policed."[12]

When Lance Cooper sought to remove Bob Hilliard, GM – the defendant – hired an ethics expert to defend Hilliard. Professor Geoffrey Miller argued that lawyers' "duty to protect and advance the interests of their own clients is not limited by any obligations owed to clients of other attorneys."[13] "[W]hat struck me first," responded Professor Silver, "was that General Motors LLC, the Defendant, retained [Miller]." If Hilliard was doing a bang-up job, GM should want to get rid of him. "GM's hope that he will retain control of the MDL is a bad sign," Silver concluded.[14]

The two debates introduced in this vignette summarize the last chapter and frame this one. Chapter 2 introduced the debate over whether dueling sides are somehow in cahoots and how their working relationships might affect their clients. In this chapter, Lance Cooper, an outsider, gives us a glimpse into the world behind that debate, a world with tight-knit, sharp-elbowed cliques where high stakes and the fear of being blackballed usually means that even disgruntled lawyers don't break rank publicly. The existence of that coterie, how judges enable it, whether (and how) it envelops defense attorneys, and the nature of leaders' ethical obligations to non-clients is the subject of this chapter.

REPEAT PLAYERS

Most attorneys specialize, of course. In mass-tort proceedings, however, specialization seems to have given way to an inner circle of favorites. "[T]he 'good ol' boy' network of intertwined law firms has sought to capture the case and exclude all but the usual cast of characters," wrote plaintiffs' attorney Wayne Travell as he pled for a leadership role in litigation over the level of formaldehyde in wood floors.[15] His entreaty fell on deaf ears. As so often happens, the judge tapped the "regulars."

Most people rarely encounter the justice system. When they do, it's sporadic: marriage licenses, divorces, traffic tickets, and wills. But some encounter the judicial

[12] Declaration of Charles Silver at 6–7, 10, *In re* Gen. Motors LLC Ignition Switch Litig., No. 14-md-2543 (S.D.N.Y. Feb. 5, 2016).
[13] Declaration of Geoffrey Parsons Miller at ¶ 10, *In re* Gen. Motors LLC Ignition Switch Litig., No. 14-md-2543 (S.D.N.Y. Feb. 2, 2016).
[14] Declaration of Charles Silver, *supra* note 12, at 3.
[15] The Williams Plaintiffs' Group's Response to Other Parties' Application to Serve on Plaintiffs Steering Committee at 1, *In re* Lumber Liquidators Chinese-Manufactured Flooring Prods. Mktg., Sales Practices & Prods. Liab. Litig., No. 15-md-02627 (E.D. Va. Aug. 3, 2015).

system regularly – think Johnson & Johnson, Google, or attorneys, for example. At one end of the spectrum lie extensive repeat players like Johnson & Johnson. Infrequent participants ("one-shotters"), like most people, lie at the other. Many of us may fall somewhere in between. But it's not these casual encounters that I'm referring to, it's those repeat players with substantial experience across many multidistrict proceedings.

Professor Marc Galanter's renowned work suggests that high-level repeat players – whether plaintiffs' attorneys or corporate defense lawyers – can have different goals than the one-shot clients they represent. Insiders develop expertise, have a stable of go-to specialists, cultivate relationships with institutional incumbents like judges and special masters, and enjoy economies of scale with low start-up costs for any given case.[16] Because they encounter the system's inhabitants frequently, their reputation is important: attorneys might become known as masterful trial lawyers or settlement artists, and corporations may have a reputation for vigorously defending every case.

The point is that repeat players have more in mind than just that one lawsuit – they play the long game. They may act strategically to maximize gains over a series of cases, and play for "rules," the shorthand term for standard practices and norms that will favorably tip the scales their way in future cases.

In multidistrict proceedings, institutional incumbents can organize quickly, save costs, and use their expertise to generate better outcomes. These cases are complex. It takes know-how to understand the science behind injuries, evaluate the risks of various strategies, effectively manage other lawyers, and build the personnel that these proceedings demand. When insiders invest, it signals to others that it's a high-stakes case. Because certain firms are known to intensively vet cases with experts long before filing a complaint, suing can act like a neon sign. Other firms will advertise and recruit clients, and cases may settle faster than they otherwise might. But incumbents may also develop mutually beneficial relationships with their opponents in which one-shot clients become pawns.

To see whether Travell and Cooper's intuition about repeat players was accurate, I collected data on all of the judicially appointed lead plaintiff and defense attorneys in all products-liability and sales-practice MDLs pending as of May 14, 2013. Table A.1 lists those 73 proceedings, Table A.2 lists the high-level defense firms, and Table A.3 includes the high-level plaintiffs' lawyers. As Figure 3.1 illustrates, I found that multidistrict litigation is rife with repeat players.[17]

On the defense side, pharmaceutical companies like Bayer and Merck frequently battle multiple products-liability proceedings simultaneously. And they turn to the

---

[16] Marc Galanter, *Why the "Haves" Come Out Ahead: Speculations on the Limits of Legal Change*, in In Litigation: Do the "Haves" Still Come Out Ahead? 13, 14 (Herbert M. Kritzer & Susan S. Silbey eds., 2003).

[17] For more information on these numbers and on repeat players, see Elizabeth Chamblee Burch & Margaret S. Williams, *Repeat Players in Multidistrict Litigation: The Social Network*, 102 Cornell L. Rev. 1445 (2017).

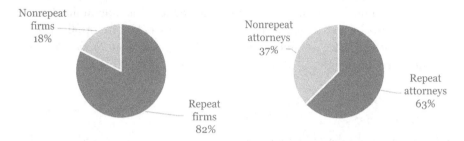

Defense-Side Repeat Play   Plaintiff-Side Repeat Play

Nonrepeat firms 18%

Repeat firms 82%

Nonrepeat attorneys 37%

Repeat attorneys 63%

FIGURE 3.1 Repeat players judicially appointed within the MDL dataset

same lawyers and law firms to defend them. Of course, defense lawyers are rarely judicially appointed to leadership positions; the defendant hires the law firm directly and different partners may spearhead distinct matters. So, evidence of repeat play by attorneys' law firms was more indicative: of the 414 available leadership positions, attorneys from repeat-player defense firms occupied 341, or 82.3%, of those leadership roles.[18] The 19 defense firms whose attorneys occupied five or more leadership positions claimed 41.5% of all lead roles.

In these same proceedings on the plaintiffs' side, repeat attorneys held the most powerful leadership positions 62.8% of the time (in 767 of 1,221 available positions). Influential positions and who makes key decisions vary by proceeding. For instance, in *GM*, Lance Cooper was on the executive committee, but he claimed that "EC members were more or less 'siloed' and asked to review documents and take depositions without any real understanding of the big picture."[19] And in the *NFL Concussion* litigation, plaintiffs' steering committee member Mike McGlamry argued that co-lead counsel Chris Seeger "bypassed his own Co-Lead Plaintiffs' Counsel ... and the Court-appointed PSC and PEC" to allocate "the vast majority of work for himself and his firm." "Mr. Seeger effectively became a solitary dictator over MDL-2323," McGlamry concluded.[20]

---

[18] Of the individual defense lawyers that were judicially appointed to lead positions, 17.6% were repeat players, and of the 414 available leadership roles, attorneys from repeat-player defense firms occupied 341 positions.

[19] Plaintiffs' Motion to Remove the Co-Leads & Reconsider the Bellwether Trial Schedule at 7, *In re* Gen. Motors LLC Ignition Switch Litig., No. 14-md-2543 (S.D.N.Y. Jan. 25, 2016).

[20] Declaration of Michael L. McGlamry Responding in Opposition to Christopher A. Seeger's Proposed Allocation of Common Benefit Attorneys' Fees, Payment of Common Benefit Expenses, & Payment of Case Contribution Awards to Class Representatives at 13–14, *In re* NFL Players' Concussion Injury Litig., No. 12-md-2323 (E.D. Pa. Oct. 27, 2017).

The same decision makers tend to occupy these pivotal roles time and again: 50 lawyers occupied 30% of all plaintiff-side leadership positions. Broken down by firm, even though only 40.7% of the plaintiffs' law firms were repeat players (e.g., had more than one lawyer from that firm appointed to a lead role in the dataset), attorneys from the top 70 repeat plaintiffs' law firms held 78% of all available positions. Put starkly, lawyers from a mere 16% of the involved law firms held nearly 54% of all leadership roles.

THE SOCIAL NETWORK

What this means is that, like high school in-groups, the mass-tort world is insular. Using this book's dataset, Dr. Margaret Williams, a talented statistician, conducted a social network analysis to see whether connections existed between proceedings, lead plaintiffs' attorneys, and defense lawyers. In other words, she graphed the relationships between the same lawyers identified in the preceding statistics.

Network analysis reveals ties the naked eye cannot see and thus enabled us to generate hypotheses about leaders' influence on legal norms. Graphing the data in this way shows whether connections exist within data and highlight which actors are the most important and powerful within the group.

A snapshot of the social network appears in Figure 3.2. It factors in data about all plaintiff and defense attorneys appointed to leadership roles, the type of leadership positions those lawyers held, how many total appearances they made in the data, the size of the proceeding, and how many appearances each attorney's firm made. We then built an adjacency matrix and employed a two-mode (actors and events) projection of a bipartite network to graph the ties between lawyers judicially appointed to leadership positions (the actors) in multidistrict proceedings (the events).[21]

If that sounds like mumbo jumbo and if looking at the network just reminds you of a kaleidoscope, don't worry. Networks simply show whether connections exist between objects, or, in this case, between various attorneys and multidistrict proceedings. Zooming in on each dot (or *node*) would reveal a name or the number of an MDL proceeding, as Figure 3.3 shows.[22] And while networks don't allow us to identify friends, enemies, or dissenters, they do let us look at agents' ties to one another. From there we can formulate theories about what flows through

---

[21] *See* M. E. J. Newman, *The Structure and Function of Complex Networks*, 45 SOC'Y FOR INDUS. & APPLIED MATHEMATICS REV. 167, 174, 204 (2003) (discussing the use of bipartite graphs for mapping social networks). For more on our social network, including graphs and analysis, see Burch & Williams, *supra* note 17.

[22] You can do this by going to https://works.bepress.com/elizabeth_burch/29/, downloading, and then enlarging the figure.

FIGURE 3.2 Network of lead lawyers in products-liability and sales-practice multidistrict proceedings

those ties – control, influence, resources, information, settlement practices, culture, and norms, for instance.

To analyze multidistrict attorneys and proceedings, we used several different statistical measures. *Degree centrality* indicates the number of ties one attorney or proceeding (a "node") has to other lawyers or proceedings within the data. High-degree centrality tends to indicate a node that others might identify as being integral to the suit. Think of *betweenness centrality* as a bridge. It shows how often one node is on the shortest path to other nodes. Just as bridges make it easy to travel from point A to point B, these "bridgers" are well positioned to play a gatekeeping or toll-collecting role. Their power comes from the ability to filter, distort, or threaten to stop communicating information. Finally, *eigen values* demonstrate how close one

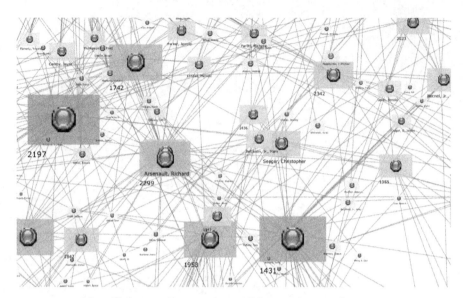

FIGURE 3.3 Magnified view of one segment of the social network

powerful node is to another. In other words, popularity. High eigen values show how connected a node is to well-connected others.[23]

No matter what measure of centrality we used, however, the same five attorneys maintained their elite network position: Richard Arsenault, Daniel Becnel, Jr., Dianne Nast, Jerrold Parker, and Chris Seeger. By consistently occupying the most central positions, these plaintiffs' lawyers are powerful not only because they led the proceedings and brokered deals but also because they are connected.[24]

Network insights are particularly important in multidistrict litigation where repeat players are prevalent. The more often a lawyer appears in proceedings, the more likely she is to be appointed to a leadership position, and the more power she has, the more opportunities she has to play for rules. As Chapter 2 illustrated, there are advantages and disadvantages to repeat play. Repeat players are a known entity. They offer consistency and expertise, which can be particularly helpful to new transferee judges as they navigate their first multidistrict proceeding.

But repeat players' informational advantage may have downsides too. Less high-profile attorneys who have extensive experience in the trenches of discovery or trial committees may be locked out of leadership opportunities. The same leaders may approach problems in the same old ways even though fresh insights and different perspectives from other lawyers could pose novel and creative solutions. And, even

---

[23] STEPHEN P. BORGATTI ET AL., ANALYZING SOCIAL NETWORKS 163–75 (2013).

[24] A list of the top 25 high-level repeat-plaintiffs' counsel appears in the Appendix, as does a list of the defense firms with the most leadership experience.

when privy to unique information that others lack, attorneys may not share it for fear the dominant group member will disapprove.[25]

SOCIAL NETWORKS, GROUP DECISIONS, AND AMPLIFIED ERROR

As Figures 3.2 and 3.3 show, attorneys and judges who regularly participate in multidistrict proceedings form a strong, cohesive network. All kinds of things can flow through a network – money, trust, influence, information, reputations, and even emotions.[26] Each and every tie provides leaders with opportunities to influence and be influenced. As Professors Nicholas Christakis and James Fowler explain, all social networks "tend to magnify whatever they are seeded with."[27] As they demonstrate, networks can spread things like joy and health, but they can also spread unethical behavior and selfish norms.

Think of it this way: social influencers with many friends are likely to impact others' clothing choices and spawn (and terminate) trends. Similarly, attorneys' connectedness in the network may allow them to diffuse, adapt, and replicate beneficial norms and practices – trends, in other words. It also positions them to rebuke or sanction rogue, nonconforming attorneys, like Lance Cooper, and to stop or distort information. Elite repeat players may enjoy preferential treatment, too; the more connected they are, the more influential and connected they become. Put simply, the "rich get richer," but for reasons that may have little to do with talent and much to do with culture and reputation.[28]

The social network may also affect decision making. Unlike most decisions in ordinary litigation, well-connected MDL leaders tend to decide strategy in groups. Decades of research shows that as individuals, we suffer from predictable biases and errors when choosing. Others can influence our choices by the way they pose a problem or a solution. When groups decide, they tend to amplify – not correct – these problems. And, while any group can succumb to the blunders I'll identify, repeat play among plaintiff and defense attorneys can exacerbate them even further.

Insiders versus Outsiders

The mass-torts plaintiffs' bar is small, and the same people work together frequently. As plaintiffs' lawyers collaborate and trumpet the rights of "the little guys," they form

---

[25] *See* CASS R. SUNSTEIN, GOING TO EXTREMES: HOW LIKE MINDS UNITE AND DIVIDE, 28–29 (2009).

[26] CHARLES KADUSHIN, UNDERSTANDING SOCIAL NETWORKS: THEORIES, CONCEPTS, AND FINDINGS 125–26 (2013).

[27] NICHOLAS A. CHRISTAKIS & JAMES H. FOWLER, CONNECTED: THE SURPRISING POWER OF OUR SOCIAL NETWORKS AND HOW THEY SHAPE OUR LIVES 31 (2009).

[28] PAUL MCLEAN, CULTURE IN NETWORKS 32 (2017); Arnout van de Rijt et al., *Field Experiments of Success-Breeds-Success Dynamics*, 111 PROC. NAT'L ACAD. SCI. 6934, 6935–36 (2014).

a group – though not necessarily one predicated on friendship. Groups form as people work toward a common goal, share physical and social immediacy, and have overlapping norms.[29] Once they consider themselves a group, members tend to look out for each other; they exhibit trust, reciprocity, and altruism toward other members.[30]

In-groups exist on both sides of the mass-torts bar. The roster changes from time to time depending on social and litigation conditions, but its members meet routinely – sometimes informally, before the Panel convenes every other month, and sometimes formally. On September 12, 2016, for instance, plaintiffs' lawyers kicked off a confidential, invitation-only Mass Tort Leaders Strategy Summit at the W Hotel in New York. By including only "the most seasoned mass tort leaders" and refusing to permit invitees to send substitutes or extend additional invitations, organizers maintained exclusivity.[31]

Summit leaders' principal goal was to prevent irreparable damage to their future practice. So, their detailed agenda ranged from creating more efficient settlement processes "after the handshake," to "managing rogue lawyers," to "balancing diversity of leadership vs[.] experience needed for mass tort success."[32] By selectively curating their members to include enough experts "to contribute different perspectives," or so they claimed, summit members mapped "recommended solutions or best practices." Only after hammering out their action plan did they welcome "the kind of inclusion and diversity ... necessary to maximize the success of what comes out of September 12."[33]

On the defense side, both formal and informal coordination exists among seasoned litigators, the U.S. Chamber of Commerce, and a regular slate of lobbyists pushing tort-reform agendas. Defense attorney John Beisner often sits at the helm

[29] Albert A. Cota et al., *The Structure of Group Cohesion*, 21 PERSONALITY & SOC. PSYCHOL. BULL. 572, 574, 577 (1995); R. Scott Tindale et al., *Shared Cognition in Small Groups*, in BLACKWELL HANDBOOK ON SOCIAL PSYCHOLOGY: GROUP PROCESSES 1, 5 (Michael A. Hoagg & R. Scott Tindale eds., 2001).
[30] *See* Nancy R. Buchan et al., *Let's Get Personal: An International Examination of the Influence of Communication, Culture and Social Distance on Other Regarding Preferences*, 60 J. ECON. BEHAV. & ORG. 373, 374–75 (2006) (reviewing the literature on other-regarding preferences).
[31] Organizers included James Gotz, Rob Jenner, Tobi Millrood, and Michelle Parfitt.
[32] E-mail from Robert Jenner, James Gotz, Tobi Millrood & Michelle Parfitt to Andy Birchfield, Sharon Booth, Dave Buchanan, Mike Berg, Elizabeth Cabraser, Russ Herman, Steve Herman, Ron Johnson, Seth Katz, Mike London, Dianne Nast, Mike Papantonio, Troy Rafferty, Chris Seeger, Aimee Wagstaff, Mike Weinkowitz, Sol Weiss (Aug. 13, 2016, 1:51 PM EST) (on file with author).
[33] E-mail from Robert Jenner, James Gotz, Tobi Millrood & Michelle Parfitt to Andy Birchfield, Sharon Booth, Dave Buchanan, Mike Berg, Elizabeth Cabraser, Russ Herman, Steve Herman, Ron Johnson, Seth Katz, Mike London, Dianne Nast, Mike Papantonio, Troy Rafferty, Chris Seeger, Aimee Wagstaff, Mike Weinkowitz, & Sol Weiss (Aug. 27, 2016, 10:34 AM EST) (on file with author).

of these intersections. As one plaintiffs' attorney put it, Beisner is the "common denominator"; "you'll see consistent arguments from the Chamber or other tort reform groups he's involved with and J&J."[34] Beisner frequently represents Johnson & Johnson as it (and its many subsidiaries) battle thousands of lawsuits over the risks of talcum powder, transvaginal mesh, hip implants, and prescription medicines such as antipsychotic Risperdal and blood thinner Zarelto. Legislative reform proposals – from the Class Action Fairness Act, which passed in 2005, to the Fairness in Class Action Act, proposed in 2017 – can often be traced back to Johnson & Johnson's legal frustrations.[35]

In groups where members are long-term friends, colleagues, or business associates (as in the tort-reform movement or the Mass Tort Leaders Strategy Summit), members tend to cooperate to achieve the best collective outcome for the group.[36] Group identity leads to favoritism and trust, and trust enables members to work together for their mutual gain.[37] Substantial research demonstrates that members' views about what's fair change depending on whether the situation involves another group member (someone else in the Summit or the Chamber) or someone outside the group, such as one-time clients or nonrepeat attorneys.[38] As we'll see, these in-group implications can spell trouble.

Group Deliberation Can Be Myopic

Like high-school cliques, in-groups have members who are in the thick of things and others on the outskirts hoping to move up a rung on the status ladder. As the social network illustrated, the most central attorneys are also likely to be those perched at the top of that ladder and to be the most *cognitively central*, meaning that most of what they know, other people know too. Others on the group's periphery, however, may have information that no one else knows – and it may be critically important. Yet, when a group deliberates, its cognitively central members – the high-level repeat players – tend to talk more. Although they may know only what everyone

---

[34] Amanda Bronstad, *For Plaintiffs Bar, Taking on J&J Means Battling a Shadow Foe*, Nat'l L.J., Aug. 18, 2017 (quoting plaintiffs' attorney Leigh O'Dell).

[35] *Id.*

[36] Robert C. Ellickson, Order without Law 167 (1991) ("[M]embers of a close-knit group develop and maintain norms whose content serves to maximize the aggregate welfare that members obtain in their workaday affairs with one another."); Leigh Thompson et al., *Cohesion and Respect: An Examination of Group Decision Making in Social and Escalation Dilemmas*, 34 J. Exper. Soc. Psychol. 289, 291–92 (1998).

[37] Charlan Nemeth, In Defense of Troublemakers 167 (2018); Carol M. Rose, *Giving, Trading, Thieving, and Trusting: How and Why Gifts Become Exchanges, and (More Importantly) Vice Versa*, 44 Fla. L. Rev. 295, 311–12 (1992).

[38] E.g., Tom R. Tyler & E. Allan Lind, *Intrinsic Versus Community-Based Justice Models: When Does Group Membership Matter?*, 46 J. Soc. Issues 83, 84–86 (1990).

else knows, they're viewed as more credible and what they say disproportionately influences the outcome.[39]

To see how this might work, imagine a lawsuit over defective hip implants where lead plaintiffs' counsel have negotiated a tentative settlement with the defendant and are presenting it to the remaining steering committee members. Many variables exist: plaintiffs have multiple injuries, their claims arise under different state laws, and they allege various causes of action. Steering committee members meet in person or through conference calls. Because each member's client portfolio differs, each has some information that others lack.

The two-lead counsel, let's call them Abe and Bo, are well-connected, central players. Speaking first, Abe suggests that they should accept the deal, even though it requires them to recommend that each one of their clients settle. Bo then agrees, mentioning that the settlement increases their common-benefit fees.

Ellen, however, is less sure that settling is the best option. She has some clients with very strong cases that the deal seems to undervalue and others for whom it would be fair. But this is the first steering committee she's served on and she is nervous about appearing disagreeable and naïve. Accordingly, she publicly agrees with Abe and Bo.

Tom is likewise new. He has several "nonrevisables," clients whose health is too poor to have the faulty hip implant removed. He knows the settlement doesn't cover them and is worried about their plight once leaders turn their efforts toward administering a settlement rather than continuing discovery. But he weighs Abe, Bo, and Ellen's views against his and defers to their judgment – they have litigated these kinds of cases before, he thinks.

Tom and Ellen are in a *cascade*. Cascades can occur when a few well-connected insiders signal that a particular position on a fact or a value judgment is correct and, instead of relying on their own information to the contrary, others fall in line.[40] Tom and Ellen's privately held knowledge suggests that settling may not be the best bet for their clients, or at least not some of them. They nevertheless keep their opinions and knowledge to themselves.

Why? Studies from social psychology suggest several possibilities. First, Tom and Ellen's reputations are on the line. They hope to work with these incumbents again and aspire to climb the leadership ranks within an entrepreneurial, risk-taking group. As veteran plaintiffs' lawyer Elizabeth Cabraser explained, attorneys like Tom and Ellen should build their reputations by "becoming known not only to

[39] Tatsuya Kameda, Yohsuke Ohtsubo & Masanori Takezawa, *Centrality in Sociocognitive Networks and Social Influence: An Illustration in a Group Decision-Making Context*, 73 J. PERSONALITY & SOC. PSYCHOL. 296, 305–6 (1997).

[40] CASS R. SUNSTEIN, WHY SOCIETIES NEED DISSENT 55–56, 74–75 (2003) [hereinafter SUNSTEIN, DISSENT].

fellow steering committee members but even opposing counsel."[41] So, even when peripheral group members are privy to unique information that others lack, as Ellen and Tom are, they tend not to voice it for fear of disapproval.[42] Discussing shared information is safer; it leads others to view them as more competent, credible, knowledgeable, and even more likeable.[43] So, these members will often bite their tongues and adjust their positions to tilt toward whatever the dominant member believes.[44] They are conforming, not disclosing their privately held information or disagreeing.[45]

Cascades and reputational concerns arise in leadership selection too. When judges require attorneys to openly object to proposed leaders as Judge Carl Barbier did in *Deepwater Horizon*,[46] they are unlikely to receive candid comments. The conditions are ripe for conformity. Passing a microphone in open court to solicit information (or requiring written objections) is unlikely to extricate new information; others will simply echo the sentiment of those asked first.[47]

Second, even if Tom and Ellen are somehow immune to peer pressure and have nerves of steel, they might believe that Abe and Bo know best. After all, they have more experience. Groups tend to systematically disregard and underestimate their lower status members while overestimating the brilliance and performance of their high-status members.[48]

Abe and Bo – experienced and respected mass-tort attorneys who are highly connected – may likewise experience a boost from their *halo effect*. When any of us likes (or dislikes) a person, we tend to assume that we like everything about that person, even if we haven't ever witnessed a particular trait in action.[49] Leaders often benefit from this halo effect – their opinions seem wiser, their questions appear

---

[41] Brandon Lowrey, *How to Land a Leadership Role in Multidistrict Litigation*, Law360 (Apr. 4, 2016, 5:35 PM), https://www.law360.com/articles/779730/how-to-land-a-leadership-role-in-mul tidistrict-litigation.

[42] Reciprocity and reputational concerns, along with trustworthiness, are most robust when people cooperate with one another over time in repeated interactions. Frans van Dijk et al., *Social Ties in a Public Good Experiment*, 85 J. Pub. Econ. 275, 291–92 (2002).

[43] Robert B. Cialdiani, Influence: The Psychology of Persuasion 176–77 (2007); Cass R. Sunstein, Going to Extremes: How Like Minds Unite and Divide, 27–29 (2009) [hereinafter Sunstein, Going to Extremes].

[44] Sunstein, Going to Extremes, *supra* note 43, at 26–27.

[45] Stefan Schulz-Hardt et al., *Productive Conflict in Group Decision Making: Genuine and Contrived Dissent as Strategies to Counteract Biased Information Seeking*, 88 Organizational Behav. & Hum. Decision Processes 563, 564 (2002).

[46] *In re* Oil Spill by the Oil Rig "Deepwater Horizon" in the Gulf of Mexico, on Apr. 20, 2010, MDL No. 10–2179 (E.D. La. Aug. 10, 2010) (pretrial order no. 1, setting initial conference at 14).

[47] Sunstein, Dissent, *supra* note 40, at 23–24, 68–69; Sunstein, Going to Extremes, *supra* note 43, at 90–93.

[48] Sunstein, Going to Extremes, *supra* note 43, at 27–29.

[49] Daniel Kahneman, Thinking Fast and Slow 82–83 (2011); Cass R. Sunstein & Reid Hastie, Wiser: Getting Beyond Groupthink to Make Groups Smarter 22–23 (2015).

more intellectual, and people defer to them. But this deference can lead groups astray, particularly when other members are unwilling to speak up and act as a corrective.

Abe and Bo's initial signal might be uninformed or misinformed. They might have only clients for whom the settlement would be great. So, if Tom or Ellen mentioned their concerns, they could have changed the outcome. But, when people deliberate in a group with others that they admire (especially when their own reputation is important), lower-status group members tend to stay silent.[50] The group focuses solely on the shared information and fails to extract Ellen and Tom's beneficial insights.

Third, money matters. The only way that Abe, Bo, Tom, Ellen, and the other steering committee members will get paid is to settle their cases. The proposed deal requires that each of them treat their clients in the same way – recommend that they settle. If some defect and counsel their clients otherwise, the settlement might fail to reach the corporate defendant's required participation threshold. Thus, attorneys' financial fates are intertwined. Injecting information that could endanger the consensus toward settling would jeopardize not only Tom and Ellen's reputation but also their pocketbook – and everyone else's, too. Psychological tugs pull in this direction as well; recall that group members slant their fairness considerations toward others in the group, not outsiders.

Studies also demonstrate that when groups with like-minded members discuss a position they can *polarize*, or move toward an extreme version of what their individual members thought before they deliberated. Polarization occurs with greater frequency and intensity when group members are connected through friendship, mutual affection, or solidarity, as members of the Summit or the Chamber of Commerce might be.[51] Confident experts like successful repeat players are even more likely to polarize groups.[52] So, when insiders like Abe and Bo speak first, others defer to them and voice arguments that merely support – not contradict – what influencers have already said. And once lower-status group members hear what the Abes and Bos of the group think, they may skew their own positions toward those higher-status members in hopes of fitting in.[53]

All these influences can tempt high-status members to rely on what they already know – to confirm their original beliefs – in lieu of seeking new information held by a few. But attorneys and businesses have different expertise and diverse consumers. When that information remains hidden, how can groups decide what's best?

---

[50] SUNSTEIN & HASTIE, *supra* note 49, at 37–42.

[51] Michael A. Hogg & Sarah C. Hains, *Friendship and Group Identification: A New Look at the Role of Cohesiveness in Groupthink*, 28 EUR. J. SOC. PSYCHOL. 323, 323–35 (1998).

[52] SUNSTEIN & HASTIE, *supra* note 49, at 22–23.

[53] Michael A. Hogg, *Social Identity, Self-Categorization, and the Small Group*, in UNDERSTANDING GROUP BEHAVIOR: SMALL GROUP PROCESSES AND INTERPERSONAL RELATIONS 227, 234 (Erich Witte & James H. Davis eds., 1996).

Sanctions Silence Dissent

If Tom and Ellen raised the concerns of a minority of plaintiffs (particularly without being delegated that task) they could become outcasts. That is why, for example, Lance Cooper's motion to remove leaders in GM was a surprise: to openly accuse the leaders of sidelining and "siloing" other executive committee members amounted to heresy. Groups like the Summit, in-groups comprised of highly connected actors, tend to police their members (or their want-to-be members) internally through social and financial sanctions. If it sounds a little like a cartel, it's for good reason.

Cartels punish defectors by imposing costs on them and denying them access to meetings, other group members, and financial opportunities; lead lawyers can do the same thing. When attorneys become leaders, they have the power to control access to the judge and swiftly inflict financial costs on troublemakers. Leaders can distribute work to their allies as a reward.[54] They also sit on fee-allocation committees, which divvy up common-benefit fees, and use settlements to restrict attorney advertising and reduce client demand. Because judges value cooperation and talk with one another, insiders could always report rogue behavior to the judge, thereby blocking the objector from future leadership roles.

In the *NFL Concussion* litigation, Chris Seeger served as a one-man fee-allocation committee. As steering committee member Mike McGlamry explained, Seeger "not only decided who would be permitted to perform tasks, he then decided that those he selected would be awarded above and beyond by his application of a [fee] multiplier." "Likewise, he penalized those firms that he did not select," said McGlamry.[55]

As the social network suggests, repeat players' relationships not only allow knowledge of things like common settlement practices to flow freely between them but also information about attorneys' reputations. That makes it possible to credibly punish and reward others. It also decreases the likelihood that information about tacit or explicit collusion would surface or that members would raise ethical concerns about settlement practices on their client's behalf.

What little evidence exists bears this out. As Table A.4 illustrates, in only 38% of the proceedings concluding in private settlements did rivals object to common-benefit fee assessments that diminished their paychecks. Most of those were lawyers complaining about their own common-benefit allocation – not the assessment. The attorneys who spoke freely with me only on the condition of anonymity explained

---

[54] Myriam Gilles, *Tribal Rituals of the MDL: A Comment on Williams, Lee, and Borden, Repeat Players in Multidistrict Litigation*, 5 J. TORT L. 173, 177 (2012) ("[L]oyalty will ensure friendly firms get plenty of work (and lodestar) on the case – and that their future motions for transfer will be reciprocally supported by other, powerful lawyers.").

[55] Declaration of Michael L. McGlamry, *In re* NFL Players' Concussion Injury Litig. No. 12-md-2323 (E.D. Pa. Oct. 27, 2017).

that objecting to fees or leadership picks would mean that they'd be "blackballed" in future proceedings.

Sanctions are nevertheless difficult to assess quantitatively. The best evidence is silence. In rejecting Lance Cooper's motion to remove the leaders in GM, however, Judge Furman noted that "the Cooper Plaintiffs provide no evidence other than Cooper's own say-so." "Tellingly," writes Furman, "not one of the hundreds of other lawyers representing plaintiffs in the MDL or in parallel state proceedings – and none of the other nine members of the Executive Committee – joined Cooper in making his motions." "That silence," Furman claims, "is deafening."[56] But that silence isn't deafening – it's expected.[57]

Norm Entrenchment

Without dissent, plaintiffs' lawyers and defendants are likely to replicate actions that lead to financial gains. The more a behavior occurs, the more likely it is to stick and become acceptable. Economics professors Ernst Fehr and Simon Gächter define a social norm as a "behavioral regularity ... based on a socially shared belief of how one ought to behave" that in turn prompts the use of informal social sanctions to enforce the prescribed behavior.[58] Sound familiar?

As Professor Stanley Milgram demonstrated with his crowd experiment where research assistants stared up at a city window, the more people who exhibit a particular behavior, the more others are likely to copy it.[59] Add in the fact that insiders can demonstrate complicated, shared behavior without explicitly coordinating with each other and hypotheses about the potential for norm development and entrenchment can be extensive.

If members lower on the totem pole observe higher-ups acting unethically, then that behavior may become the descriptive norm. We're all prey to what Harvard Business School Professor Max Bazerman calls "ethical fading." "If we're busy and life is good and we're making money ourselves," Bazerman observes, "we act like we

[56] *In re* Gen. Motors LLC Ignition Switch Litig., No. 14-MD-2543 (S.D.N.Y. Apr. 12, 2016) (order at 17–18).

[57] For instance, research shows that in workplaces around 70% of employees don't speak up even when they spot problems because they fear repercussions or assume that what they say won't matter. KATHLEEN D. RYAN & DANIEL K. OESTREICH, DRIVING FEAR OUT OF THE WORKPLACE (1993).

[58] Ernst Fehr & Simon Gächter, *Fairness and Retaliation: The Economics of Reciprocity*, 14 J. ECON. PERSP. 159, 166 (2000).

[59] Stanley Milgram, Leonard Bickman & Lawrence Berkowitz, *Note on the Drawing Power of Crowds of Difference Size*, 13 J. PERSONALITY & SOC. PSYCHOL. 79 (1969); *see* NICHOLAS A. CHRISTAKIS & JAMES H. FOWLER, CONNECTED: THE SURPRISING POWER FOR OUR SOCIAL NETWORKS 24 (2009).

don't notice something is wrong – but at the same time we're exposing our clients to this enormous risk."[60]

Questionable tactics, particularly among in-group members, can be contagious. Rather than speaking out when settlement practices disserve their clients, nonlead attorneys may assume it's okay because everyone else is doing it. Psychologist Robert Cialdini explains, "As slaughterhouse operators have long known, the mentality of a herd makes it easy to manage. Simply get some members moving in the desired direction and the others – responding not so much to the lead animal as to those immediately surrounding them – will peacefully and mechanically go along."[61] So, questionable practices may be entrenched and replicated not only because they benefit repeat actors but also because they get woven into the legal, social, and ethical culture.

Connected attorneys have ample opportunity to disseminate and enshrine practices that favor them. For example, Duke Law Center for Judicial Studies appointed an editorial board of six, high-level repeat players to create an *MDL Standards and Best Practices* guide. As the guide's introductory remarks explain, some of the "best practices ... reflect ideas that the Board has noted have become increasingly common," while others "focus upon new, innovative approaches by particular transferee judges that the Board felt were outstanding" and should be adopted by "other transferee judges going forward."[62]

Some of the "best practices" favor the incumbents who penned them. In selecting lead lawyers, for instance, the guide suggests that judges look for those with a "demonstrated track record of successfully working with others, building consensus, and amicably managing disagreements," and seek "lawyers who have worked together previously" who can "vouch" for one another.[63]

Once norms take root, several factors shelter them from appellate review. First, because most mass torts result in private settlements, outcomes are inoculated from appeal. Second, even though final orders for a single case within a proceeding are immediately appealable,[64] most interim rulings don't end the lawsuit. So, they are reviewable only if the attorney can convince the court that the issue is so compelling that it must be heard immediately through what's called an *extraordinary writ of mandamus*. Third, even if the appellate court grants mandamus or considers a dismissed case, it tends to do so using the highly deferential abuse-of-discretion standard. In reviewing asbestos orders, for example, the Third Circuit noted that it

---

[60] Dina Gerdeman, *Why Ethical People Become Unethical Negotiators*, WORKING KNOWLEDGE (Harvard Bus. Sch., Bos., Mass.), July 30, 2018; McKenzie Rees, Ann Tenbrunsel & Max Bazerman, *Bounded Ethicality and Ethical Fading in Negotiations*, 32 ACAD. OF MGMT. PERS. (Mar. 16, 2018).

[61] ROBERT B. CIALDINI, INFLUENCE: THE PSYCHOLOGY OF PERSUASION 156 (2007).

[62] DUKE LAW CENTER FOR JUDICIAL STUDIES, STANDARDS AND BEST PRACTICES FOR LARGE AND MASS-TORT MDLs, i–ii (2014), https://judicialstudies.duke.edu/sites/default/files/centers/judi cialstudies/standards_and_best_practices_for_large_and_mass-tort_mdls.pdf.

[63] *Id.* at 55.

[64] Gelboim v. Bank of Am. Corp., 135 S. Ct. 897 (2015).

did so "with deference, particularly in the MDL context," for "[d]istrict judges must have authority to manage their dockets."[65] Vague initial standards, subjective decisions about which attorneys would best serve the plaintiffs, and the lack of precedent make this standard a formidable hurdle.

As Professors Charles Silver and Geoffrey Miller explain, the "dearth of challenges" isn't because lawyers are happy with the status quo. Instead, "they do not wish to alienate MDL trial judges, who have considerable power to make life unpleasant for them," and "as a practical matter, the option of appealing is closed."[66] In short, norms become embedded not because they are best practices, but because they benefit powerful interests and cannot be weeded out.

CHOOSING LEAD LAWYERS

So, how is it that a handful of well-connected lawyers have come to dominate the multi-billion-dollar mass-tort industry? As a formal matter, the transferee judge appoints them to a coveted leadership position. But as Lance Cooper's comments about the meeting before the meeting suggested, much behind-the-scenes wrangling takes place first. Attorney David Berg likened the process to "the mob on Black Friday who rush into Walmart on the day after Thanksgiving."[67] Formally, judges tend to use one of several methods to select leaders – consensus selection, competitive selection, or a hybrid of the two. Unfortunately, judges rarely explain their methodology or reasoning.

The *consensus method* lets lawyers hash out leadership slates among themselves. Because the real fights occur outside of court, consensus picks are simpler for judges. But there is a direct link between this method and what plaintiffs' lawyers have dubbed the "club" and the "good ol' boy network."[68] Private ordering favors attorneys with long-standing business relationships, encourages backscratching, and condones behind-the-scenes politicking. As Judge Fallon once quipped, allowing attorneys to select one another "would involve intrigue and side agreements which would make Macbeth appear to be a juvenile manipulator."[69]

In angling for a position in *Vioxx*, attorney Daniel Becnel writes, "I personally called a meeting at Antoine's Restaurant in New Orleans, at my expense, and invited every lawyer who had a filed case or was interested in the litigation to meet and confirm leadership. At this meeting I made a motion that the group unanimously

[65] *In re* Asbestos Prods. Liab. Litig. (No. VI), 718 F.3d 236, 243 (3d Cir. 2013).

[66] Charles Silver & Geoffrey P. Miller, *The Quasi-Class Action Method of Managing Multi-District Litigations: Problems and a Proposal*, 63 VAND. L. REV. 107, 119 (2010).

[67] Jonas Karlsson & Marie Brenner, *Danger in the Ring*, VANITY FAIR'S HIVE (Dec. 12, 2013, 8:03 PM), https://www.vanityfair.com/news/politics/2014/01/nuvaring-lethal-contraceptive-trial.

[68] Amanda Bronstad, *'Good Ol' Boys Club' in MDL: Same Plaintiffs Firms Repeatedly Lead Suits*, NAT'L L.J. (Sept. 28, 2015, 12:00 AM), https://www.law.com/nationallawjournal/almID/1202738239700/Good-Ol-Boys-Club-In-MDL/.

[69] *In re* Vioxx Prods. Liab. Litig., 760 F. Supp. 2d 640, 643 n.4 (E.D. La. 2010).

ask Judge Fallon to appoint Chris Seeger and Andy Birchfield as Lead Counsel."[70] By the time Judge Fallon formally appointed them, their leadership was a foregone conclusion.[71]

As Becnel's remark reflects, players make backroom deals as to how many positions to create and who will occupy them long before the judge acts. In the *Power Morcellator* cases, one of the lead lawyers noted, "The leadership team was created before we even applied for an MDL."[72] So, although that judge appeared to use a competitive-selection process with open applications, one competing attorney withdrew and another joined the consensus slate, prompting co-lead counsel to remark, "Part of our effort over the last year was to get the team together . . . [so] that we wouldn't have to worry about competition. It worked."[73]

The upside is that attorneys who have previously labored in the trenches together will know more about one another's work habits and expertise than the judge. They'll be able to design a team that maximizes their strengths. And working together frequently makes them accountable to one another. They can ostracize unorganized attorneys with poor work product, those who are inefficient time managers with inflated billable hours, and those who cannot complete assignments on time. But indebtedness might likewise mean that lawyers who would otherwise be excluded may nevertheless remain if lead or liaison counsel owes them.

As this suggests, consensus arrangements can result in bloated committees. Large leadership structures tempt lawyers to duplicate work to inflate their fees. As Judge Lucy Koh admonished in the *Anthem Data Breach* proceeding, "I rejected your eight firm structure, . . . and I see that the law firms, the four law firms that I rejected have billed $3,624,920." "If I didn't want eight," she continued, "why would I want 53 to work on this case? What justification do you have for 53 law firms working on this case? I would never have appointed you . . . had I known you were going to pile on 53 law firms on this case. I never would have."[74]

A substantial body of scholarship suggests that well-functioning decision-making groups tend to have only five to six members who are not like-minded.[75] Yet judges often appoint groups more than twice that size: Judge Jesse Furman appointed

---

[70] Application of the Becnel Law Firm, LLC as Per Order No. 6(D), *In re* Vioxx Prods. Liab. Litig., No. 05-md-1657 (E.D. La. Jan. 26, 2011).

[71] SNIGDHA PRAKASH, ALL THE JUSTICE MONEY CAN BUY: CORPORATE GREED ON TRIAL 13–14 (2011).

[72] Amanda Bronstad, *In a First, Women Compose Majority of MDL Committee*, NAT'L L.J. (Nov. 19, 2015), https://www.law.com/nationallawjournal/almID/1202742961283/In-a-First-Women-Compose-Majority-of-MDL-Committee/.

[73] *Id.*

[74] Transcript of Proceedings at 19, *In re* Anthem, Inc. Data Breach Litig., No. 15-md-02617 (N.D. Cal. Feb. 1, 2018).

[75] While financing the suit may require leaders and steering committees to get buy in from additional attorneys, empirical research suggests that "[g]roups containing 3 to 8 members [are] significantly more productive and more developmentally advanced than groups with 9 members or more," and productivity further increases in groups with only five to six

15 leaders in GM, Judge Carl Barbier appointed 15 in the *Deepwater Horizon* litigation, and Judge Eldon Fallon typically appoints 12 because, as he often says, there were 12 apostles.

"Is it the usual suspects?" asked plaintiffs' attorney James Young, "If that is true, there are good reasons for it."[76] Insiders like Richard Arsenault argue that large committees are necessary for "an extraordinary David versus Goliath dynamic," and that "deference should be given to experienced plaintiffs counsel who have been in these wars and understand what kinds of teams they need to put together."[77] Although litigation funding needs may legitimately swell leadership ranks, when repeat players fulfill past favors and promises to one another, they may needlessly deplete plaintiffs' recoveries as Lance Cooper alleged in GM.

Unfortunately, current competitive selection and hybrid processes may do little to improve the status quo. *Hybrid* methods allow interim lead counsel (who was initially selected by the judge) to apply, nominate executive committee members, and appoint subcommittees while permitting those who weren't initially chosen to apply. As two objectors in GM complained, however, this process "effectively self-appoints [temporary lead counsel] as permanent Lead Counsel" and then "empowers them to handpick the majority of the Executive Committee."[78]

In theory, a *competitive selection* process that allows anyone to apply should overcome backroom deals. Using an application process, explains insider Elizabeth Cabraser, "promotes diversity naturally, without discounting merit, because it simply eliminates the barriers to entry that a slate system can subconsciously impose."[79] Noting the way in which Judge Charles Breyer competitively selected leaders in the *Volkswagen "Clean Diesel"* litigation, Cabraser remarked, "I have seen a definite trend away from slates and toward public application procedures."[80]

Selection Criteria

But when judges select lawyers using any method, they stress applicants' cooperative tendencies, ability to finance the litigation, and experience – factors that all sound good in theory but favor repeat players and discourage lawyers from raising

members. Susan A. Wheelan, *Group Size, Group Development, and Group Productivity*, 40 Small Group Res. 247, 257–58 (2009).
[76] Daniel Fisher, *Usual Suspects: Lawyers Used to Getting Their Way in MDL Process to Lead Opioid Litigation*, Forbes (Jan. 23, 2018, 10:03 AM), https://www.forbes.com/sites/legalnews line/2018/01/23/usual-suspects-lawyers-used-to-getting-their-way-in-mdl-process-to-lead-opioid-litigation/#571798254de6.
[77] Bronstad, *supra* note 68.
[78] Letter to Judge Jesse M. Furman from Steve W. Berman, Elizabeth J. Cabraser, & Mark P. Robinson Jr. at 4, *In re* Gen. Motors LLC Ignition Switch Litig., No. 14-md-02543 (S.D.N.Y. July 7, 2014).
[79] Julie A. Steinberg, *More Women Plaintiffs' Lawyers Becoming Complex Litigation Leaders*, Bloomberg BNA (Feb. 3, 2017), https://www.bna.com/women-plaintiffs-lawyers-n57982083338/.
[80] *Id.*

legitimate concerns in practice. "I have already articulated some of the criteria," explained Judge Jesse Furman in picking GM's leaders, "but let me just underscore and note among the more important is the demonstrated ability and resources to handle litigation of this nature and complexity, [and] the demonstrated ability to cooperate and work well with other counsel."[81] Judge Stanwood Duval, who presided over the *Hurricane Katrina* litigation, suggested that finding "team players" should be "the primary factor in choosing" leaders.[82]

How do judges know who'll play together nicely? They call each other. For instance, in picking attorneys to handle the *Biomet Magnum Hip Implant* proceedings, Judge Robert Miller, a former Panel member, said, "one of the advantages of having been on the MDL panel is I know most of the judges who have your MDLs, and so I emailed them this week, gave them a list of names that had been submitted, and said 'Tell me anybody who I should not appoint.'"[83] This, too, advantages incumbents.

When judges rely on experience, financing, and cooperative tendencies to competitively select leaders, they open the door for influencers in the plaintiffs' bar to play a substantial role. As Elizabeth Cabraser's comment suggested, in *Volkswagen*, Judge Breyer used a formal application process that requested the traditional criteria. But if other lawyers in the proceeding supported a particular applicant, then that applicant could indicate the support in her submission.[84] Listing the backing of 67 lawyers, Cabraser won *Volkswagen*'s popularity contest.[85] Two other attorneys received a surfeit of 60 endorsements.

As is often the case with group action, after the initial applications appeared on the *Volkswagen* docket, more than a dozen lawyers scrambled to realign themselves behind the emerging winner, positioning themselves to receive lucrative common-benefit work. In appointing Cabraser as lead counsel, Judge Breyer cited her groundswell of support as a factor along with his own "first-hand knowledge" from having worked with her before.[86] Also appearing on his list? The two other consensus picks.

Experience requirements and financing concerns likewise contribute to the repeat-player phenomenon. High-level repeat players, by their very nature, have

---

[81] Transcript of Proceedings at 119, *In re* Gen. Motors Ignition Switch Litig., No. 14-md-2543 (S.D.N.Y. Aug. 11, 2014).

[82] Stanwood R. Duval Jr., *Considerations in Choosing Counsel for Multidistrict Litigation Cases and Mass Tort Cases*, 74 LA. L. REV. 391, 393 (2014).

[83] Transcript of Proceedings on November 16, 2012, at 16–17, *In re* Biomet M2a Magnum Hip Implant Prods. Liab. Litig., No. 12-md-2391 (N.D. Ind. Nov. 21, 2012).

[84] *In re* Volkswagen "Clean Diesel" Mktg., Sales Practices & Prods. Liab. Litig., MDL No. 15-md-02672-CRB (N.D. Cal. Dec. 22, 2015) (pretrial order no. 2).

[85] Alison Frankel, *Judge Charles Breyer, MDL Disruptor?*, REUTERS (Jan. 21, 2016), https://www.reuters.com/article/idUS180571388320160121.

[86] *In re* Volkswagen "Clean Diesel" Mktg., Sales Practices & Prods. Liab. Litig., No. 15-md-02672-CRB (N.D. Cal. Jan. 21, 2016) (pretrial order no. 7).

the most experience. A mere 16% of the involved plaintiffs' law firms occupied nearly 54% of all leadership roles in the dataset, but many lawyers and law firms have experience with these cases. In *Vioxx* alone, for example, 92 law firms received common-benefit fees but most were not in a leadership position.[87]

Financing may thus pose a more substantial hurdle than experience. "Look, we spend millions on this," said plaintiffs' lawyer Hunter Shkolnik, "and none of this can be taken as a tax loss if [the cases] don't work."[88] Firms must often pool their assets to foot the bill. Yet, attorneys are most likely to partner with those they trust. Consequently, when judges want experienced attorneys who can afford to finance not only their own clients' claims but discovery for *all* the plaintiffs as well, the pool of "qualified" candidates is shallow.

Adequate Representation?

What judges tend not to focus on is adequate representation. They know that plaintiffs lose some of their autonomy and decision-making control, of course. But because each plaintiff has her own counsel, they might not think that appointing leaders would implicate due process concerns. It does, though. Here's why:

Multidistrict proceedings require only a common factual question, which means that plaintiffs' claims, injuries, and representational needs vary long before settlement. Differences can arise at every turn, risking inadequate representation at each step in the deal-making process. Leaders get to choose which claims to invest in – and which ones to ignore. Not all claims get "worked up." Yet plaintiffs whose claims are overlooked are straightjacketed: they can't conduct their own discovery or return to their original federal court.

In the *Biomet* litigation over defective hip implants, defense lawyers pointed out a host of variables: did a plaintiff have surgery to revise the implant, if so, is the explanted device available to analyze, and if not, is the patient eligible for surgery or considered a "nonrevisable" (ineligible for revision surgery); did the implant occur after 2011 when the ability of alternative designs could change state-of-the-art defenses; are there statute of limitations issues; and what are the plaintiffs' causes of action – some claimed cobalt and chromium poisoning in addition to device loosening?[89] Nevertheless, no one on the 22-person steering committee was tasked with representing specific interests; they were unified even as plaintiffs' needs differed.

---

[87] *In re* Vioxx Prods. Liab. Litig., No. 05-md-01657 (E.D. La. Sept. 27, 2011) (awarding 92 of 108 law firms common-benefit fees).

[88] Jonas Karlsson & Marie Brenner, *Danger in the Ring*, VANITY FAIR (Dec. 12, 2013), https://www .vanityfair.com/news/politics/2014/01/nuvaring-lethal-contraceptive-trial.

[89] *E.g.*, Transcript of Proceedings on November 16, 2012, at 27–29, *In re* Biomet M2a Magnum Hip Implant Prods. Liab. Litig., No. 12-md-2391 (N.D. Ind. Nov. 21, 2012).

Leaders have no incentive to raise these distinctions on their own and it may not be profitable to develop each aspect of the case. If only a handful of plaintiffs suffered cobalt and chromium poisoning, for example, it might not be financially savvy to invest in the expensive studies and expert reports needed to prove a causal link. In short, pointing out conflicts and developing the tentacles of ancillary claims may not be lucrative for leaders and may siphon their time and resources away from the heart of most claims. Whether they're paid a contingency fee for each client or a common-benefit fee for their work on behalf of all plaintiffs, attorneys profit from representing as many people as possible – not from pointing out their idiosyncrasies.

That doesn't mean that those differences aren't important, though. The Federal Judicial Center's *Manual for Complex Litigation*, which suggests case-management techniques for lawyers and judges, makes two key – but often overlooked – points about adequate representation. First, it recognizes that "[c]ommittees are most commonly needed when group members' interests and positions are sufficiently dissimilar to justify giving them representation in decision making."[90] Second, it suggests courts consider "whether designated counsel fairly represent the various interests in the litigation" and, "where diverse interests exist, ... designate a committee of counsel representing different interests."[91]

Some judges, like Judge Catherine Perry (who sits on the MDL Panel), take measures to ensure that leaders will properly represent potentially warring factions. In the *Genetically Modified Rice* litigation, for instance, she adjusted the attorneys' consensus picks to include separate counsel for Mississippi farmers who might become class members and farmers who would prefer to litigate their cases individually in state court.[92]

But most judges take no such precautions. Instead, they focus on the *Manual's* other criteria – experience, financial resources, and cooperative tendencies. Recognizing a conflict would mean appointing separate counsel. And separate counsel could waylay settlement negotiations.

By exalting cooperation and team play when appointing leaders, transferee judges signal that squeaky wheels are unwelcome. In *GM*, dissent and adequate representation seemed to take a backseat to other values. "If you are a dissenting voice, you should make yourself heard, but at the same time the ability to work together and work through agreements is absolutely important and essential," Judge Furman told the leaders. So, even though he wanted to ensure that the leadership team represented plaintiffs' geographic and claim diversity, he agreed with temporary lead

[90] MANUAL FOR COMPLEX LITIGATION (FOURTH) §§ 10.221, 10.224 (2004) ("[B]ecause appointment of designated counsel will alter the usual dynamics of client representation in important ways, attorneys will have legitimate concerns that their clients' interests be adequately represented.").

[91] *Id.* at § 10.224.

[92] *In re* Genetically Modified Rice Litig., No. 06-md-1811 (E.D. Mo. Apr. 18, 2007) (order appointing leadership counsel).

counsel, ruling that a "flexible committee structure" would be "adequate to deal with [any] issues as they arise."[93]

Here's the rub: even though plaintiffs' attorneys are known to be an opinionated, aggressive group, in the mass-tort world they must go along to get along. One insider wishing to remain anonymous told me, "[N]o one will [speak out] because it's suicide." By silencing their discord, representing as many plaintiffs as possible, staying on good terms, and working "well" with others – even when it disadvantages their current clients – plaintiffs' attorneys can thrive.

DO LEADERS OWE DUTIES TO NONCLIENTS?

Given what we now know about the pressure, temptation, and settlement pushes lawyers face in multidistrict proceedings, we can't expect individual representation to promise a fair process. As dealmakers negotiate and formulate settlements, plaintiffs with structurally conflicting interests need someone to advocate for them. But that someone rarely exists.

Malpractice claims afterward don't help either. A search in Bloomberg Law for each plaintiff's firm involved in three or more proceedings in the dataset turned up only a handful of malpractice cases.[94] Why? I don't think it's because plaintiffs are exuberant about the status quo. Instead, malpractice claims run into procedural and substantive hurdles.

Procedurally, most begin in state court where the plaintiff lives. But leaders quickly remove those cases under diversity jurisdiction and request that the Panel transfer them to the same transferee judge who chose them for leadership roles. Once they wind up back in the multidistrict proceeding, most disappear into the sea of other cases. It's difficult to follow what happens to them from looking at the master multidistrict docket. Those that could be tracked were either mired in arbitration or dismissed.

Substantively, unlike class counsel's duties, the question of whether leaders owe fiduciary obligations to nonclients (and if so, what those obligations are) is a murky and undeveloped area of law. Think about it pragmatically, though. When agents handle movie stars' careers or someone in real estate helps you buy a home, they must be loyal to you and put your interests before theirs.[95] Unless you say it's okay, those agents can't use their position to benefit themselves or someone else. By hiring them, you consent to be bound to actions they take on your behalf (so long as those acts fall within the scope of the relationship, of course – your real estate agent couldn't book you an acting gig). The same goes for lawyers, who are agents for their clients.

---

[93] Transcript of Proceedings at 119, *In re* Gen. Motors Ignition Switch Litig., No. 14-md-2543 (S.D.N.Y. Aug. 11, 2014).

[94] Coverage of state court dockets is spotty, at best. So, it is possible that there could be malpractice claims in state court that would not turn up from this search.

[95] RESTATEMENT (THIRD) OF AGENCY § 8.01 cmt. b (AM. LAW INST. 2006).

The quandary, however, is that neither individuals nor their chosen counsel hire leaders to act on their behalves – leaders are judicially selected. Do those lawyers owe nonclients similar duties of loyalty? The *Manual for Complex Litigation*, which judges rely upon to appoint leaders, thinks so: lead attorneys must "act fairly, efficiently, and economically in the interests of all parties and parties' counsel."[96] Interpreting this, the drafters of the American Law Institute's *Principles of the Law of Aggregate Litigation* explain, "Because 'parties' counsel' are fiduciaries of the clients they directly represent, in multidistrict litigations a double layer of fiduciary relationships also obtains."[97] In other words, yes. Leaders are agents' agent.

Some leaders agree. As Howard Nations observed in the *Gadolinium* litigation before Judge Dan Polster, "As members of the Plaintiffs Steering Committee, we owe a duty to everyone who is paying money into the common benefit fund."[98]

This remark may have you thinking back to this chapter's opening pages and Lance Cooper's motion to remove Bob Hilliard as a leader in *GM* – and rightly so. Cooper squarely teed up the issue. But the outcome is confusing. Judge Jesse Furman began by observing that Cooper's motion cited "no legal authority" for the idea that "Hilliard owes all plaintiffs in the MDL fiduciary duties." But he conceded, "[T]he Court has not found ... any legal authority" either. Fair enough, none exists.

In denying Cooper's motion, however, Judge Furman noted, "That is not to say that Hilliard does not have significant authority vis-à-vis all personal injury and wrongful death plaintiffs. He plainly does, as he speaks on their behalf (to both New GM and the Court) and has the authority to make any number of decisions that are binding [on them]." Nevertheless, the onus of protecting clients fell on individual counsel because even though Hilliard owed "significant" duties to nonclients in the proceeding, those obligations weren't "as strong" as those class counsel owes to a class.[99]

This is curious. How can Hilliard bind nonclient plaintiffs? They didn't hire him as their agent, so there is no consent. Judge Furman did not appoint Hilliard to adequately represent the group as he would class counsel. Even if he had, but then declined to certify the class, the Supreme Court has made it plain that uncertified classes have no binding effect on would-be class members.[100] Finally, there is no such thing as virtual representation. As the Supreme Court explained in *Taylor v. Sturgell*, virtual representation would "recogniz[e], in effect, a common-law kind of class action" that's "shorn of [Rule 23]'s procedural protections."[101] So, there is no

[96] MANUAL FOR COMPLEX LITIGATION (FOURTH) § 10.22 (2004).

[97] PRINCIPLES OF THE LAW OF AGGREGATE LITIGATION § 1.04 reporter's notes on cmt. a (AM. LAW INST. 2010).

[98] Transcript of Proceedings at 15, *In re* Gadolinium-Based Contrast Agents Prods. Liab. Litig., No. 08-gd-50000 (N.D. Ohio May 2, 2011).

[99] *In re* Gen. Motors LLC Ignition Switch Litig., No 14-md-2543 (S.D.N.Y. Apr. 12, 2016) (order at 14).

[100] Smith v. Bayer, 564 U.S. 299, 314 (2011).

[101] 553 U.S. 880, 901 (2008).

consent or adequate representation and virtual representation doesn't exist. We are out of options. Without more, Hilliard's actions cannot bind nonclient plaintiffs.

Leaders' fiduciary obligations aren't just academic questions. Nor are they limited to once-in-a-blue-moon motions to remove leaders. In *Yasmin/Yaz*, leaders' fiduciary duties arose as part of a malpractice claim: when neither lead nor individual counsel responded to Bayer's motion to dismiss their claims, three women sued their various lawyers in state court. The leaders then removed the case to federal court and the Panel transferred it to Judge Herndon (who'd appointed leaders to their roles). Alleging that the leaders breached their fiduciary obligations toward them, the women requested class certification.[102]

Judge Herndon dismissed their complaint for failing to state a claim. In so doing, he reasoned that leaders' responsibilities were limited to those that he spelled out in the case management order appointing them. Nothing in that order required them to respond to his Lone Pine order on individual plaintiffs' behalf, particularly when they had individual counsel. He noted, however, that "lead and liaison counsel should put the common and collective interests of all plaintiffs first" and cited Professor Charles Silver in suggesting that in pursuing "the good of all," leaders must make "tradeoffs that are reasonably 'likely to maximize the value of all claims in the group.'"[103]

Professor Silver explains that when leaders displace individual counsel and control the proceedings, they assume those lawyers' duties, "including the fiduciary duty to refrain from exploiting clients." "Otherwise," he reasons, "MDL procedures would alter plaintiffs' substantive rights by allowing lead attorneys to take advantage of them."[104] This makes sense intuitively. Allowing leaders to bind nonclient plaintiffs without any responsibility to act in their best interest could cause much mischief.

Construing these duties differently would also violate the Rules Enabling Act, which prohibits procedural rules from abridging, enlarging, or modifying substantive rights.[105] Procedurally appointing leaders would divest represented plaintiffs of substantive, contractual rights that they would have had if their own attorneys retained control – namely the ability to sue their lawyer for breaching a fiduciary duty. If fiduciary obligations vanish, so do plaintiffs' substantive rights. As I suggest in Chapter 6, appointing leaders according to Rule 23(g)'s class-counsel requirements and periodically remanding plaintiffs whose claims fall outside the scope of those that leaders choose to pursue can clarify leaders' obligations and alleviate conflicts.

---

[102] Casey v. Roger Denton, No. 17-cv-521-DRH (S.D. Ill. Aug. 11, 2017).

[103] Casey v. Roger Denton, No. 17-cv-521-DRH (S.D. Ill. Sept. 4, 2018) (memorandum & order at 12–13).

[104] Charles Silver, *The Responsibilities of Lead Lawyers and Judges in Multidistrict Litigations*, 79 FORDHAM L. REV. 1985, 1989–90 (2011).

[105] 28 U.S.C. § 2072 (2012).

4

Judges as Bulwarks and Nudgers

Plaintiffs' lawyers – the very people that plaintiffs hire to advise them – may be the ones who leave them with little choice but to settle. Between clauses that require lawyers to recommend the deal to all their clients and withdraw from representing nonsettling clients, settlement offers might feel a bit like *The Godfather*'s Don Corleone: "I'm gonna make him an offer he can't refuse."[1] Explaining this pressure, Judge Jack B. Weinstein once quipped, "Theoretically, each client has the option of rejecting his share of a settlement .... In practice, the attorney almost always can make a global settlement and convince the clients to accept it."[2]

That said, as Harvard professor Cass Sunstein and Nobel Prize winner Richard Thaler note in their popular book, *Nudge*, people often "need nudges for decisions that are difficult and rare, for which they do not get prompt feedback, and when they have trouble translating aspects of the situation into terms that they can easily understand."[3] Deciding whether to settle in the MDL context certainly fits the bill. But if attorneys' settlement advice is salted with self-interest, who else might push plaintiffs in the right direction?

Judges are innate authority figures who seem well positioned to nudge plaintiffs – as the growing literature (and controversy) over so-called managerial judges reflects.[4] Litigants respect and defer to judges. Renowned psychologist Robert Cialdini observed that these kinds of authority figures can give us "a valuable shortcut for deciding how to act in a situation." "Because their positions speak of superior access

---

[1] THE GODFATHER (Paramount Pictures 1972). Richard Nagareda has written about class-action settlements extensively in these terms. Richard A. Nagareda, *Closure in Damage Class Settlements: The Godfather Guide to Opt-Out Rights*, 2003 U. CHI. LEGAL F. 141 (2003).

[2] Jack B. Weinstein, *Ethical Dilemmas in Mass Tort Litigation*, 88 Nw. U. L. REV. 469, 521 n.212 (1994).

[3] RICHARD H. THALER & CASS R. SUNSTEIN, NUDGE: IMPROVING DECISIONS ABOUT HEALTH, WEALTH, AND HAPPINESS 74 (2009).

[4] Alvin K. Hellerstein et al., *Managerial Judging: The 9/11 Responders' Tort Litigation*, 98 CORNELL L. REV. 127 (2012); Judith Resnik, *Managerial Judges*, 96 HARV. L. REV. 374 (1982).

to information and power," he explains, "it makes great sense to comply with the wishes of properly constituted authorities." "It makes so much sense, in fact," he warned, "that we often do so when it makes no sense at all."[5]

In one of the highest profile nudges to date, Judge Alvin Hellerstein acted against his own self-interest in promoting settlement by rejecting a deal between New York City and its workers who developed a variety of cancers and life-threatening diseases while cleaning up Ground Zero. He was a uniquely situated contrarian: he not only presided over these suits, but also over all the lawsuits arising out of the September 11 World Trade Center attacks.

After spending eight years on the *World Trade Center* suits, Judge Hellerstein stunned plaintiff and defense attorneys when he rejected a $657.5 million settlement offer to more than 10,000 rescue and cleanup workers. The offer attempted to use group cohesion to promote closure in a close-knit community of firefighters and police officers by adding $82.5 million to the $575 million offer if 100% rather than just 95% of the plaintiffs signed up.[6]

Speaking directly to the plaintiffs about their free will, Judge Hellerstein assured them, "No one is going to twist your arms and no one is going to add to the complexities and no one's going to make you feel afraid to exercise the right choice." Elaborating, he said:

> Most settlements are private; a plaintiff and defendant come together, shake hands, and it's done with. Although the judge may look and see if there's some infant or some compromise or something else, basically it's the parties that decide. It's the parties that grant the fee. The judge has no part in it.
>
> This is different. This is 9/11. This is a special law of the commons. This is a case that's dominated my docket, and because of that, I have the power of review. If I don't think it is fair, I'm going to tell you that, and you will make the judgment how to deal with it.[7]

Making himself available in union meetings, police precincts, and fire departments, he likewise appealed to their collective nature: "I'll come and I'll talk to you just as you have talked to me. And let's decide, is it good or is it not good?" He called for transparency: "I want accountability. I want judicial control over this process,

---

[5] ROBERT B. CIALDINI, INFLUENCE: THE PSYCHOLOGY OF PERSUASION 218 (2007).

[6] Mireya Navarro, *Federal Judge Orders More Talks on 9/11 Deal*, N.Y. TIMES (Mar. 19, 2010), https://www.nytimes.com/2010/03/20/nyregion/20zero.html; *see also* Hellerstein et al., *supra* note 4, at 157.

[7] Transcript of Status Conference at 54:14–24, 62:24, 63:8–12, *In re* World Trade Ctr. Disaster Site Litig., No. 21-mc-00100 (S.D.N.Y. Mar. 19, 2010). Professor Tobias Wolff has argued that the underlying substantive law in Congress's statutory scheme authorized Judge Hellerstein's actions. Tobias Barrington Wolff, *Managerial Judging and Substantive Law*, 90 WASH. U. L. REV. 1027, 1052–53 (2013).

because that's what's fair. If I'm the judge, I can be reversed. If the parties appoint someone, he's the dictator. We don't have dictators."[8]

The lawyers were devastated. One noted that Judge Hellerstein was "guided by a concept of fairness that's not in the law."[9] After working toward a deal for more than two years only to see it upended, attorneys were quick to question Hellerstein's authority to approve, reject, or modify a deal that both sides agreed to. Appealing to the Second Circuit, defendants explained they were "deeply troubled" by the effect that "judicial interference may have on the ability of individual plaintiffs to consult with their lawyers [and] make their own decisions." "Plaintiffs who wish to partici- pate in the settlement process must be given the opportunity to do so free from Court interference or influence," defendants argued.[10] Of course, whether Judge Hellerstein had formal authority mattered little. Simply pronouncing the deal unfair would deter most plaintiffs from accepting it.

But what about the flip side? If the negotiating lawyers could convince a judge to intervene in their private deal in some explicit or implicit way, might that judicial imprimatur persuade nonlead lawyers and plaintiffs alike to take it? Leaders hope so. In requesting that Judge Douglas Woodlock appoint a special settlement master to preside over a private settlement in the *Fresenius GranuFlo* litigation, lead plaintiffs' lawyer Anthony Tarricone conceded as much, "having the imprimatur of the Court on this settlement, especially given the large number of claims," will make things "go more smoothly."[11]

Robert Cialdini's work suggests this is true. As authority figures, judges' endorse- ment can seal the deal. Denouncing and approving private settlements are, after all, but two sides of the same coin. As we will see, however, there are differences. When judges take steps to limit plaintiffs' ability to freely choose whether to settle, their actions are paternalistic. By contrast, judges who make additional information and arguments available to plaintiffs engage plaintiffs' capacity for reason and appeal to them to exercise their choice in a different way. They don't supplant their ability to decide for themselves.

In this sense, Judge Susan Wigenton's role in presiding over the *Zimmer Durom Hip Cup* litigation is the flip side of Judge Hellerstein's role in the *World Trade Center* litigation. Zimmer began marketing its novel hip implant in 2006 only to suspend sales two years later because the cup often failed prematurely. Instead of the bone growing into the cup to secure it as designed, X-rays showed that that implant frequently loosened, causing pain and swelling as the metal cup rubbed

---

[8] Transcript of Status Conference at 54:14–24, 62:24, 63:8–12, *In re* World Trade Ctr. Disaster Site Litig., No. 21-mc-00100 (S.D.N.Y. Mar. 19, 2010).

[9] Navarro, *supra* note 6.

[10] Memorandum in Support of Motion on Short Notice for Stay Pending Appeal at 4, *In re* World Trade Ctr. Disaster Site Litig., No. 21-mc-00100 (S.D.N.Y. Apr. 15, 2010).

[11] Transcript of Status Conference at 6, *In re* Fresenius Granuflo/Naturalyte Dialysate Prods. Liab. Litig. No. 13-md-02428 (D. Mass. Apr. 29, 2016).

against bone. This led Zimmer's own highly paid consultant, nationally known orthopedic surgeon Dr. Lawrence Dorr, to put it simply: "It's a bad design."[12] But instead of recalling the hip or fixing the flaws, Zimmer temporarily suspended sales only to return the product to surgeons' shelves with new instructions for how to use it.

Judge Susan Wigenton actively ruled on a number of merits-related motions. But after deciding whether conflicting facts warranted trial, whether the experts were qualified, and even presiding over bellwether trials, Judge Wigenton took a highly unusual step: she ordered plaintiffs to settle or face dismissal. Her order required that plaintiffs enter into a private settlement program that entailed at least 18 months of mediation unless they settled sooner.[13]

She likewise stayed the multidistrict proceeding, which meant that plaintiffs couldn't continue their discovery efforts, try more of the slated bellwether cases, or return to their original courts for trial. In excess of 30 law firms representing more than 200 plaintiffs objected.

Objectors first questioned how Chris Seeger, one member of a five-member plaintiffs' liaison counsel (the only lead lawyers in the proceeding), who teamed up with nonlead lawyer Mark Lanier to negotiate the deal with Zimmer, could bind all the plaintiffs when even the entire counsel lacked that authority.[14] Any lead lawyer's power is necessarily hemmed in by the order authorizing it (as well as due process constraints). And Judge Wigenton's order included no such authority.[15] "[E]ssentially it's a cram down on the rest of the plaintiffs," complained objectors, "we must participate or our cases will be dismissed."[16]

Objectors likewise challenged Judge Wigenton's authority – what gave her the ability to force their clients to settle? The lawsuit was not a class action, and, while New Jersey's local rules allowed her to refer cases to mediation over the parties' objection, those rules capped any stay of the proceedings at 90 days.[17] Forcing nonconsenting plaintiffs into the settlement program, however, meant instituting an 18-month delay.[18]

---

[12] Barry Meier, *Complaints Undermine Hip Device*, N.Y. TIMES, July 24, 2008, at C1; Barry Meier, *A Call for a Warning System on Artificial Joints*, N.Y. TIMES, July 29, 2008, at A1.

[13] *In re* Zimmer Durom Hip Cup Prods. Liab. Litig., No. 09-cv-04414 (D.N.J. May 13, 2016) (case management order regarding settlement agreement).

[14] Letter from Gibbs C. Henderson to the Honorable Susan D. Wigenton, *In re* Zimmer Durom Hip Cup Prods. Liab. Litig., No. 09-cv-04414 (D.N.J. Mar. 21, 2016).

[15] *In re* Zimmer Durom Hip Cup Prods. Liab. Litig., No. 09-cv-04414 (D.N.J. Sept. 23, 2010) (case management order no. 1, at 7–9).

[16] Transcript of Proceedings at 22, *In re* Zimmer Durom Hip Cup Prods. Liab. Litig., No. 09-cv-04414 (D.N.J. May 9, 2016).

[17] Local Civil and Criminal Rules of the United States District Court for the District of New Jersey, § 301.1(e)(6) (staying proceedings for "a period of 90 days" and requiring any extension requests to be made jointly by the parties and the mediator).

[18] Transcript of Proceedings at 22, 24, *In re* Zimmer Durom Hip Cup Prods. Liab. Litig., No. 09-cv-04414 (D.N.J. May 9, 2016).

Chris Seeger, however, argued that Judge Wigenton's "inherent authority" to manage her docket empowered her to send an elderly plaintiff population into a private settlement program without their consent.[19] She agreed.

Judge Wigenton's hearing on the matter – 10 days after the required settlement registration deadline – did little to appease objectors' concerns. Responding to them, she said, "you're saying that as a District Judge handling a case in this court that I do not have the authority to manage a case the way I see fit? That's your position. Fair?"[20] Clarifying her own position, she stated, "I completely, totally and whole heartily disagree with this notion and concept that I do not have the authority to manage a case in the manner that I feel is appropriate. I think that strains logic."[21]

Objectors' ethical concerns fell flat too. The settlement program required any lawyer with a single client who wished to enroll to then enroll *all* her clients – regardless of a client's desires, regardless of whether the case was pending in state or federal court (or even filed at all), and regardless of whether a client even qualified to settle under the deal's terms. The program didn't cover plaintiffs with "unrevised" hips (those with the hip cup still implanted). Still, their lawyers had to place them in the program to avoid dismissal.

Those who qualified to settle may not have fared much better. For example, a lawyer with one client who wanted to settle and another dead set on following through with her scheduled state-court trial (that already comes on the heels of a failed mediation) must enroll that state-court client in another 18-month mediation before she can have her day in court.

From an ethical standpoint, the settlement program put plaintiffs' lawyers in a pickle. Attorneys must advise individual clients about the pros and cons of settling such that each client can make an informed choice. A lawyer who tells a client, "you're in the settlement program, period," is not providing her with independent and loyal advice.[22] Clients decide whether to settle – not their attorneys.[23] Moreover, conflict-of-interest rules forbid attorneys from representing clients (absent consent) where there's a "significant risk" that the attorney's duty to someone else such as another client, the defendant, or other plaintiffs' counsel will materially limit her advice to that client.[24] Put simply, clients deserve faithful representation, not advice that's tainted by obligations to the defendant or to other plaintiffs – unless a client consents.

---

[19] Letter from Christopher A. Seeger to the Honorable Susan D. Wigenton at 2, *In re* Zimmer Durom Hip Cup Prods. Liab. Litig., No. 09-cv-04414 (D.N.J. Mar. 31, 2016).

[20] Transcript of Proceedings at 68, *In re* Zimmer Durom Hip Cup Prods. Liab. Litig., No. 09-cv-04414 (D.N.J. May 9, 2016).

[21] *Id.*

[22] MODEL RULES OF PROF'L CONDUCT r. 1.4(b), 2.1 (AM. BAR ASS'N 2016) ("A lawyer shall explain a matter to the extent reasonably necessary to permit the client to make informed decisions regarding the representation.").

[23] *Id.* at r. 1.2 ("A lawyer shall abide by a client's decision whether to settle a matter.").

[24] *Id.* at r. 1.7(a).

Judge Wigenton, however, appeared to set these concerns aside in favor of expediency: "And while I appreciate plaintiffs' counsel making the arguments of ethical concerns, . . . the course that we're on is such that this will take another five to ten years."[25] "And the only arguments I hear are arguments: One, I don't have the authority; two, there's an ethical dilemma that will exist; which makes no sense to me, whatsoever."[26]

So, instead of remanding cases to their courts of origin for trial as objectors requested, she entered Seeger and Lanier's proposed order – verbatim.[27] Her order stayed the litigation so long as the settlement agreement remained in effect. It required all plaintiffs in the multidistrict proceeding to participate, which, in turn, dictated that all their lawyers enroll their state-court clients and those who had not yet sued. Just in case some attorneys litigated solely in state courts, Judge Wigenton sent letters to every state judge with a similar case, urging them to issue the same orders.[28] "You see a lot of people who, with a gun to their head, felt like they were between a rock and a hard place," objectors said.[29]

JUDGES NUDGE

As the proceedings before Judges Hellerstein and Wigenton convey, this chapter narrates some of the judicial nudges lurking behind the data in Table A.5. A mere 8% of judges in the dataset took no steps whatsoever to endorse, promote, or enforce private deals. Instead, as that table highlights, 64.7% of judges presiding over private aggregate settlements formally appointed the private claims administrator or settlement master. And, to varying degrees, 52.9% of federal judges "approved" private settlements, blurring conventional wisdom that private settlements are just that – private.

Yet, these nudges may not be as informed as we would hope. Nearly a third of the judges presiding over those deals hadn't ruled on the merits before the settlements occurred. Even when they had, some of their nudges may feel more like shoves because they are laced with the threat of dismissal. Judicial pushes may thus be an added source of coercion, not relief, for plaintiffs.

Once the lead lawyers negotiate a private deal, some judges not only exalt the settlement program but also receive regular settlement updates and comment on the adequacy of settlement amounts. Challenging Judge Hellerstein's vision of the

---

[25] Transcript of Proceedings at 71, *In re* Zimmer Durom Hip Cup Prods. Liab. Litig., No. 09-cv-04414 (D.N.J. May 9, 2016).

[26] *Id.* at 68.

[27] *In re* Zimmer Durom Hip Cup Prods. Liab. Litig., No. 09-cv-04414 (D.N.J. May 13, 2016) (case management order regarding settlement agreement).

[28] Letter from the Honorable Susan D. Wigenton to State Court Judges, *In re* Zimmer Durom Hip Cup Prods. Liab. Litig., No. 09-cv-04414 (D.N.J. May 17, 2016).

[29] Transcript of Proceedings at 21, *In re* Zimmer Durom Hip Cup Prods. Liab. Litig., No. 09-cv-04414 (D.N.J. May 9, 2016).

nondictatorial judicial role, some preside over settlements as arbitrators, hear "appeals" from the settlement using a clear-error standard (which heavily defers to the claims administrator's decision), stay litigation until the settlement process concludes, automatically enroll plaintiffs in the settlement program, and order all challenges to the deal into binding arbitration.

As the *Zimmer* and *World Trade Center* objectors noted, whether judges have the actual authority to do some of these things is uncertain at best. Some judges invoke their general equitable authority, while others claim power under Rule 16, which allows judges to facilitate settlement and adopt special procedures for managing difficult actions involving complex issues or multiple parties. And still others cite no explicit authority at all.

In certified class actions, Rule 23(e) demands judicial involvement. Judges must consider whether a settlement is fair, reasonable, and adequate before formally approving it. That approval is what legitimizes the deal. So long as class counsel adequately represented the absent class members and the member doesn't opt out, preclusion doctrines bind them to the settlement – whether they recover anything or not.

But nonclass multidistrict proceedings that settle like the *Zimmer* litigation are technically just larger versions of one-on-one settlements. As with traditional contracts, the legitimacy of these deals has little to do with the judge and everything to do with whether the parties consent. Settlements are private agreements. Rule 41(a) says as much by allowing plaintiffs to dismiss their actions without a court order.

Nevertheless, as Judge Hellerstein illustrated, when settlements depend on plaintiffs' consent, it's easy for judges to signal their views. Settlement designers count on it, aiming to invoke the mantle of judicial authority and incite what psychologist Robert Cialdini dubs the automated, "click, whirr" response in plaintiffs – the signal to stop thinking for themselves and defer to an authority figure. Judges not only know the law but also how they plan to respond if no settlement occurs. They can provide superior knowledge and inside information.

So, it's tempting to think that judicial nudges might be just the thing to send plaintiffs reliable signals about a settlement's merits. Professors Andrew Bradt and Theodore Rave argue strongly in favor of this view: just as a political candidate's party affiliation sends easy signals to voters on election day, "the MDL judge can provide critical information to individual claimants in easily digestible form at the moment they most need it."[30]

As we shall see, however, judges may lack the information they need to send these signals reliably. Because discovery is conducted between the litigants, judges are not immediately privy to the documents, experts, medical records, and strategy that lie at the parties' fingertips. Unless judges rule on the merits through the adversarial

---

[30] Andrew D. Bradt & D. Theodore Rave, *The Information-Forcing Role of the Judge in Multi-district Litigation*, 105 CAL. L. REV. 1259, 1284 (2017).

process, they may know only what the plaintiffs' leadership and defendants want them to know.[31] This is a sobering thought, for once a judge decides a deal is fair, her subsequent orders can send a firm message: settle or I'll dismiss your case.

Judges try hard to remain objective. But neither they nor their nudges are consistently neutral. Recall Chapter 1's discussion of the near universal push for settlement. Although settlements can play a crucial role in ensuring court access, global settlements are worn like badges of honor in the multidistrict litigation community and six-month reports try to shame judges with a lengthy backlog.[32] If you heap a burgeoning caseload on top of this already established norm, few judges can resist the siren's call of a settlement.

When judges tie themselves to the mast and act against that self-interest as Judge Hellerstein initially did in rejecting the prepackaged settlement, there is added reason to trust them. As dealmakers request judicial assistance in fulfilling a private settlement's terms, judges may legitimately decline to issue these rulings out of a self-regarding concern to avoid promoting deals that seem unfair. Those decisions are not paternalistic, particularly when judges explain why they refused. Justifying their reasoning in writing appeals to plaintiffs' agency and allows them to decide for themselves.

When judges use their power to approve, enforce, and push plaintiffs into private settlements, however, they not only appear to exceed the authority that rightly belongs to them, they may impinge on plaintiffs' free will to consent. My aim here isn't to castigate judges who have developed and adhered to this prevailing norm, however. Promoting settlement is now firmly woven into judicial culture. Transferee judges voluntarily assume an enormous burden when they tackle complex cases, and it can seem counterintuitive to resist entering orders that all the leaders agree upon.

But what may seem uncontroversial can have serious costs. My goal then is twofold: to expose those costs by identifying areas where judicial activity intrudes on plaintiffs' settlement autonomy, and, ultimately, to improve our adversarial system's functionality. As I suggest in Chapter 6, judges stand on firmer footing when it comes to nudging lawyers, for they are officers of the court. So, it's not that judges should stand by in the face of attorneys' shenanigans. Instead, they should send valid signals by issuing reasoned opinions on motions that delve into the claims' strengths and weaknesses and adjust leaders' common-benefit fees to rise and fall with how well the plaintiffs fare. But judges shouldn't nudge the plaintiffs – they're often already bruised from their own counsel's prodding.

---

[31] David M. Jaros & Adam S. Zimmerman, *Judging Aggregate Settlement*, 94 WASH. U. L. REV. 545, 589 (2017).

[32] Miguel de Figueiredo, Alexandra D. Lahav & Peter Siegelman, *Against Judicial Accountability: The Effects of the Six Month List* (Feb. 20, 2018), https://ssrn.com/abstract=2989777.

JUDICIAL SIGNALS ABOUT THE MERITS

Once parties hash out a deal, there's no incentive to air their dirty laundry. The push and pull of the adversarial system – and the information that it dredges up – collapses. Class actions confront this conundrum routinely: once class counsel settles with the defendant, it's hard for judges steeped in an adversarial culture to discern whether the settlement is fair, reasonable, and adequate. For American judges, playing an inquisitorial role may feel as unnatural as wearing a British powdered wig. And why should the settling parties imperil their détente by pointing out its flaws?

These problems plague transferee judges who preside over nonclass mass torts, particularly when the dealmakers plead for their help in forming, condoning, or enforcing some aspect of their "private" settlement. Still, the prelude to settlement may give judges glimpses into the merits. Adversaries are likely to hash out their differences during pivotal merits-related inquiries: summary judgment motions, *Daubert* motions on proposed expert testimony, class certification motions, and bellwether trials. These flashpoints illustrate the traditional judging model at work and give judges a chance to indicate a case's strengths and weaknesses.

Pretrial motions send simple, red-light green-light signals about whether the proceedings should continue the march toward the proverbial trial. (Or, more likely the bellwether trial.) Unless those signals are red, then they should help inform how much a claim is worth.

Granted, pretrial opinions inform the settlement's terms only indirectly. Pressing this point, Professor Geoffrey Miller has argued that these signals should be far more explicit, something along the lines of a "preliminary judgment" instead.[33] Imperfect though they are, these pretrial opinions are all we currently have. And they can serve as a barometer of the judge's view. Indeed, defense-side lore suggests always moving for summary judgment just to force judges to get their feet wet.

Bellwether trials aren't a magical elixir for ferreting out a proceeding's strength either, but trying representative cases surely helps set settlement prices for the remaining cases. Trials expose strengths and weakness among competing factual accounts and identify which legal roadblocks will prove most problematic. But some plans to select bellwether cases suffer from preventable problems. For example, judges may let the parties pick a handful of their own cases and then toss in a few judicially selected suits for good measure. Parties are likely to choose their strongest cases. So litigant-driven sampling skews toward the outliers, not the average.[34] Other methods, such as "first in first out," where lawsuits filed first are tried first, fare no better. Generating reliable information about the remaining suits is a gamble at best – not a statistical certainty as it might be.

---

[33] Geoffrey P. Miller, *Preliminary Judgments*, 2010 U. ILL. L. REV. 165, 167–68.
[34] Alexandra D. Lahav, *The Case for "Trial by Formula,"* 90 TEX. L. REV. 630, 571 (2012).

Even if bellwether cases are properly stratified and randomly selected, the sample size must be large enough to produce reliable results.[35] "[B]ellwether trials give us some information, but they don't give us much," lamented plaintiffs' attorney Roger Denton, "the defendants have figured out a way to eliminate all my cases."[36] As Denton's comment suggests, when defendants strategically settle the strongest cases, they can purposefully distort the sample population.[37] And when cases earmarked as bellwethers settle, fewer cases tend to be tried.

As Professors Amos Tversky and Daniel Kahneman's famous work on the law of small numbers suggests,[38] parties and the judge are likely to put exaggerated faith in the handful of bellwethers that do occur, regardless of how they were selected. Despite looking through a keyhole, what they see they may nevertheless afford inordinate weight, using the scant information that emerges to price the full array of remaining claims. Lavishing attention on the case-specific content revealed during trial, they forget about its generalizability.[39] When the sample size is too small, that information deserves far less trust, for it may not reflect the remaining cases' characteristics well at all.

To be sure, testing the merits through some bellwether trials is better than not testing them at all. But bellwether trials can give judges an imperfect glimpse into a proceeding's overall strengths and weaknesses.

Still, bellwether trials and pretrial previews occur less often than we might hope or expect. Before the first reported private aggregate settlements in the dataset occurred, 38% of transferee judges had not ruled on summary judgment motions, 32% had not decided *Daubert* motions, and 55.8% had not presided over bellwether trials. Perhaps less surprisingly given that the cases are products-liability proceedings and that fewer parties requested class certification, 76.4% had not considered certifying a class.

When judges don't engage with the merits through pretrial motions and trials, the relative strength of plaintiffs' cases may matter little in settlement negotiations. As Professor Janet Alexander explains, "Because the safety valve of adjudication is

---

[35] The sample size will differ depending on how homogenous the group or subgroup is. As Professor Robert Bone has recognized, heterogeneity can affect reliability, which, in turn, can affect sampling's cost-benefit calculus. Robert G. Bone, *Tyson Foods and the Future of Statistical Adjudication*, 95 N.C. L. REV. 607, 642–43 (2017).

[36] Transcript of Motion and Status Hearing at 40–41, *In re* NuvaRing Prods. Liab. Litig., No. 08-md-01964 (E.D. Mo. Jan. 26, 2012).

[37] Michael J. Saks & Peter David Blanck, *Justice Improved: The Unrecognized Benefits of Aggregation and Sampling in the Trial of Mass Torts*, 44 STAN. L. REV. 815, 841–42 (1992).

[38] Amos Tversky & Daniel Kahneman, *Belief in the Law of Small Numbers*, 76 PSYCHOL. BULL. 105 (1971).

[39] For a thorough treatment of these biases, see Amos Tversky & Daniel Kahneman, *Judgment Under Uncertainty: Heuristics and Biases*, 185 SCI. 1124 (1974).

not available, the strength of the case on the merits simply drops out of the settlement calculus."[40]

Of course, in multidistrict proceedings there may be other information sources. State courts may conduct trials or issue merits-related opinions, for example. But those judges are typically not the ones who provoke and endorse aggregate settlements. And that makes a difference. Think of it this way – would watching baseball on television prepare you to hit a fast pitch? I suspect not. Likewise, reading opinions and observing other judges' proceedings from afar doesn't involve the same information-gathering and decision-making functions as presiding over a case first hand.[41]

Writing opinions can inform and transform one's thinking. As Judge Richard Posner observes, "[T]he process of writing, which means searching for words, for sentences, in which to express meaning, is a process of discovery rather than just of expressing preformed ideas."[42] Others note, "Writing is 'thinking in ink.' The actual process of writing helps the writer analyze the subject at hand and draw conclusions. Thus, as you write, new ideas will bubble up that you should incorporate into the analysis."[43]

Deciding whether factual questions exist through summary judgment, engaging with the science behind the tort, and wrestling with whether an expert is truly qualified all force judges to grapple with a case. That is, after all, why most judges agree to take on multidistrict proceedings – they say that they are "immensely satisfying, 'roll up one's sleeves' work."[44]

Presiding over bellwether trials brings judges closer to the merits still. Remarking on her experience with the *Vioxx* trials, Judge Carol Higbee lamented, "The attorneys learned what the strengths were of their cases; they learned what the weaknesses were of their cases. Going through that, whether you want to call it *drama* or *combat* or whatever term you want to use for a trial, it's still the best way of getting at the truth."[45] Judge Clay Land, who presided over several bellwether jury trials in the *Mentor Corp. ObTape* litigation, echoed this message:

---

[40] Janet Cooper Alexander, *Do the Merits Matter? A Study of Settlements in Securities Class Actions*, 43 STAN. L. REV. 497, 524 (1991).

[41] This can also present a problem for transferor judges who receive cases when remanded from transferee judges; they are far less familiar with the ins and outs of the case. As Chapter 6 notes, however, there may be other compelling reasons that weigh in favor of sending nonsettled cases back to their original courts.

[42] RICHARD A. POSNER, REFLECTIONS ON JUDGING 240 (2013).

[43] MARY L. DUNNEWOLD, BETH A. HONETSCHLAGER & BRENDA L. TOFTE, JUDICIAL CLERKSHIPS: A PRACTICAL GUIDE 216 (2010).

[44] Abbe R. Gluck, *Unorthodox Civil Procedure: Modern Multidistrict Litigation's Place in the Textbook Understandings of Procedure*, 165 U. PA. L. REV. 1669, 1675 (2017) (interviewing transferee judges).

[45] Transcript of Status Conference at 32–33, *In re* Vioxx Prods. Liab. Litig., No. 05-md-01657 (E.D. La. Nov. 9, 2007) (order, at 1) (emphasis in original).

A jury does not read selective portions of a sterile transcript to discern what happened. A jury sees evidence and hears evidence. They observe body language and interpret sighs, pauses, "uh ohs," and "uh huhs." They notice eye contact and furtive glances. They not only hear the "what" but also evaluate the "how" and the "why." What they do can only be done live and in person.[46]

The same can be said for the presiding judge. Judges can see witnesses' demeanors up close; they must make evidentiary rulings in the heat of battle. Nowhere else is the adversarial nature of our system more fully displayed than in trial.

THE MISSING MERITS

Nevertheless, some judges have no engagement with the merits through these traditional flashpoints. Within the dataset of proceedings ending in aggregate settlements, in nearly one-third (10 of 34), the transferee judge had not conducted bellwether trials nor ruled on summary judgment, *Daubert*, or class certification motions before the first private settlement occurred.[47] Yet, those judges approved and oversaw the private settlements that resulted. When combined with the settle-or-I-won't-represent-you push that plaintiffs sometimes receive from their own lawyers, plaintiffs' backs are against the wall. How can they freely choose between litigating and settling, especially when they lack any impartial information about their suit's worth?

Granted, not all the judges in those 10 proceedings rubber-stamped the settlement without merits-related information. Judge Joseph Goodwin, whose *American Medical Systems Pelvic Repair* and *Coloplast Corp. Pelvic Repair* proceedings fall into this statistic, presided over seven pelvic-mesh MDLs simultaneously (some of which included bellwether trials and merits-related rulings). Those other cases may have given him insight before he appointed special settlement masters to administer settlements and allocate payments in *American Medical Systems* and *Coloplast*. And the judges in *Avandia*, *Baycol*, *Biomet*, *Ortho Evra*, and *Gadolinium Contrast Dyes* issued merits-related pretrial rulings *after* the first wave of settlements. None of the judges in these 10 proceedings held bellwether trials before the first settlement, but some did schedule trials that never occurred.

Three of the 10 proceedings within this category had even less conventional engagement with the merits. The judges overseeing *Pradaxa*, *DePuy ASR*, and *Watson Fentanyl Patch Litigation* never presided over a bellwether trial or issued summary judgment, *Daubert*, or class certification rulings. Yet, each made his views about the settlement known. To be sure, these proceedings lie at one end of the

---

[46] *In re* Mentor Corp. ObTape Transobturator Sling Prods. Liab. Litig., MDL No. 08-md-2004, No. 12-cv-176 (M.D. Ga. Oct. 20, 2016) (order, at 1).

[47] A table of these proceedings and the judicial actions within each proceeding appears in Table A.4.

spectrum. Still, examining some of these judicial case-management techniques allows us to consider whether concerns arise as judges expand prosettlement norms.

Take *Pradaxa*, for example. In its first four years on the market, Pradaxa became a best-selling drug, generating more than $2 billion in sales for its private German manufacturer, Boehringer Ingelheim. Advertised as a safe alternative to Coumadin, which helps prevent blood clot-induced strokes, Pradaxa nevertheless suffered from a glaring flaw: unlike its predecessors, it had no antidote – doctors couldn't stop the bleeding when they needed to do so. In 2011 alone, four short years after the FDA approved it, doctors prescribed Pradaxa to 850,000 patients but also linked it to 1,000 deaths and 3,781 side-effect incidents.[48]

None of this was news to Boehringer. Its own internal research papers fretted over how patients would react to the drug – some would absorb too little and be prone to strokes while others would absorb so much that they would risk bleeding to death.[49] But instead of airing and investigating these worries, company leaders warned that making the research public would make it "extremely difficult" to defend its long-held position that users did not need blood tests. Responding to the push to publicize the research, one insider wrote, "I would like to ask you to check again whether this is really wanted."[50] Reflecting on the company's self-interest when making these safety-related decisions, Dr. Lisa M. Schwartz, a professor of medicine at the Dartmouth Institute, asked, "In these situations, where the stakes are really high, how crazy is it that it's in the hands of people who are so conflicted?"[51]

As lawsuits mounted in 2012, the Panel transferred them to East St. Louis, Illinois, before Judge David Herndon. Over the next two years, Judge Herndon grew increasingly frustrated by Boehringer's failure to respond to discovery requests and litigation holds. He sanctioned the company twice, adding up to nearly a million dollars in fines, and moved employee depositions from Amsterdam to the United States. After the Seventh Circuit reversed the move to the United States (but not the fines), Judge Herndon issued a warning: "The wrongs here are egregious in the eyes of the Court." "[T]here may be more orders yet to come."[52] That was in March 2014, a month after he made Boehringer's internal research papers and e-mail responses public.

Judge Herndon scheduled bellwether trials for the following September, which meant that he would consider pretrial matters in May. But then, on May 20, he wanted to know why the proceeding hadn't yet settled and ordered lawyers with

[48] Katie Thomas, *New Emails in Pradaxa Case Show Concern Over Profit*, N.Y. Times (Feb. 7, 2014), https://www.nytimes.com/2014/02/08/business/new-emails-in-pradaxa-case-show-concern-over-profit.html.

[49] Katie Thomas, *Study of Drug for Blood Clots Caused a Stir, Records Show*, N.Y. Times, Feb. 5, 2014, at B1.

[50] *Id.*

[51] *Id.*

[52] *In re* Pradaxa (Dabigatran Etexilate) Prods. Liab. Litig., No. 3:12-md-02385-DRH-SCW (S.D. Ill. Mar. 12, 2014) (case management order no. 62).

settlement authority to appear before him the next day.[53] A few days later, he appointed a negotiating committee and personally supervised an "extensive mediation process."[54] The very next day, news outlets reported that Boehringer would pay $650 million to settle suits in state and federal court (an average award of $162,500).[55]

The private settlement program exists nowhere in the public domain. Yet, Judge Herndon issued a slew of accompanying orders. He stayed the litigation indefinitely, which meant that nonsettling plaintiffs could not conduct further discovery or have their cases remanded.[56] He called for a census of claimants: all attorneys with a case before him had to include 11 categories of information for all their clients (regardless of where or even whether they'd filed suit) to estimate which settlement tier the client might fall into – regardless of whether the client wanted to settle.[57] He ordered the private claims administrator to attend his status conferences and update him on the program's payouts until those payouts concluded.[58]

When the parties wanted to change aspects of their private deal, such as the funding date, they had Judge Herndon order it.[59] When they wanted nonsettling plaintiffs to face additional discovery burdens, Judge Herndon instituted them.

Plaintiffs who refused to settle had approximately 15 days after the settlement's opt-in deadline to produce fact sheets, affidavits, and pharmacy and medical records dating back to five years before their alleged injury occurred. In total, plaintiffs had a little more than two months to produce an expert report on both general and specific causation. If they failed, they had just 20 days to fix the deficiency – a deadline that could not be extended.[60] All these demands on nonsettling plaintiffs, Judge Herndon explained, stemmed from lead lawyers' private settlement negotiations.[61]

Yet, when the private settlement ran out of money before the first phase of payouts had concluded, the burden of excusing the shortfall (and payout reductions) fell

[53] *In re* Pradaxa (Dabigatran Etexilate) Prods. Liab. Litig., No. 3:12-md-02385-DRH-SCW (S.D. Ill. May 20, 2014) (case management order no. 73).

[54] *In re* Pradaxa (Dabigatran Etexilate) Prods. Liab. Litig., No. 3:12-md-02385-DRH-SCW (S.D. Ill. Dec. 29, 2014) (case management order no. 88).

[55] Jef Feeley, *Boehringer Pays $650 Million to End Blood-Thinner Cases*, BLOOMBERG (May 28, 2014, 11:40 AM), https://www.bloomberg.com/news/articles/2014-05-28/boehringer-pays-650-million-to-end-blood-thinner-cases.

[56] *In re* Pradaxa (Dabigatran Etexilate) Prods. Liab. Litig., No. 3:12-md-02385-DRH-SCW (S.D. Ill. May 28, 2014) (minute order).

[57] *In re* Pradaxa (Dabigatran Etexilate) Prods. Liab. Litig., No. 3:12-md-02385-DRH-SCW (S.D. Ill. May 29, 2014) (case management order no. 76).

[58] *In re* Pradaxa (Dabigatran Etexilate) Prods. Liab. Litig., No. 3:12-md-02385-DRH-SCW (S.D. Ill. May 29, 2014) (case management order no. 77).

[59] *In re* Pradaxa (Dabigatran Etexilate) Prods. Liab. Litig., No. 3:12-md-02385-DRH-SCW (S.D. Ill. Aug. 26, 2014) (case management order no. 83).

[60] *In re* Pradaxa (Dabigatran Etexilate) Prods. Liab. Litig., No. 3:12-md-02385-DRH-SCW (S.D. Ill. May 29, 2014) (case management order no. 78). Table A.6 includes the time frame that other courts have used for issuing similar orders.

[61] *In re* Pradaxa (Dabigatran Etexilate) Prods. Liab. Litig., No. 3:12-md-02385-DRH-SCW, 2015 WL 1500230, at *1 (S.D. Ill. Mar. 27, 2015).

not to the contracting parties, but to Judge Herndon. In a case management order, he described the foresight with which the parties had bargained, noting that "based on [his] own participation, it is quite clear that the defendant was simply at the point where it would pay no additional money to settle the cases globally." Still, he continued, "the tendered offer represented an excellent compensation package for the global inventory."[62] That more plaintiffs took the deal than the lead lawyers anticipated was heartening – not shortsighted. "The participation rate was higher than 98%," he wrote, which "demonstrate[s] the value that the settlement is providing to the claimants."[63] Perhaps. Or it may reflect the burden that plaintiffs needed to satisfy if they didn't settle.

Courts typically interpret contractual provisions only *after* the parties breach their deal; judges are a last resort, not a first line of defense. And though judges are increasingly active in promoting settlement discussions in all civil cases, unless parties reserve jurisdiction through a consent order, a court's role concludes shortly after the parties settle.

Judges' active role in administering and interpreting private settlement programs departs from what we expect in ordinary, bipolar cases. Nevertheless, their engagement with and sometimes outright endorsement of these private agreements proves integral to achieving closure. Judicial involvement may be the most effective tool that settlement architects wield.

THE SETTLEMENT SHOVE

Even if you're skeptical about judges facilitating, endorsing, interpreting, and subsequently enforcing private settlements without first digging into the merits through traditional veins, the question still remains as to whether judges who have made many merits-related rulings should make their views on private settlements known. Having a knowledgeable judge send signals is, in fact, what many scholars depict as the ideal. As Chapters 2 and 3 described, repeat players' ongoing relationships raise the worry that the adversarial features of our system may be overshadowed by insiders' quid pro quo needs.[64] Accordingly, a judge who is a well-informed neutral seems to be a natural police officer.

Turning to the data in Table A.5, however, judges in only 50% of the 34 proceedings ending in private aggregate settlement made at least three merits-related rulings (summary judgment, *Daubert* motions, class certification, or presiding over a

---

[62] *In re* Pradaxa (Dabigatran Etexilate) Prods. Liab. Litig., No. 3:12-md-02385-DRH-SCW (S.D. Ill. Dec. 29, 2014) (case management order no. 88).

[63] *Id.*

[64] Abraham S. Blumberg, *The Practice of Law as a Confidence Game: Organizational Cooptation of a Profession*, 1 LAW & SOC'Y REV. 15, 20–21, 24 (1967).

bellwether trial) before that settlement occurred.[65] Of the 18 proceedings in which judges approved private deals, only 50% ruled on at least three merits-related motions before endorsing those deals.

As the objections from the lawyers in the *World Trade Center* litigation reflected when Judge Hellerstein rejected their private agreement, whether rulings endorsing (or rejecting) a private settlement are welcome nudges or heavy-handed shoves can depend on one's vantage point. We already considered one example from this group – Judge Wigenton's handling of the *Zimmer Durom Hip Cup* proceeding. But examining one more, the *Yasmin/Yaz* proceeding, may shed some additional light on how strong judicial settlement signals and subsequent rulings may affect plaintiffs' choices.

Unlike his role in presiding over *Pradaxa*, in the *Yasmin/Yaz* birth control litigation, Judge David Herndon decided both *Daubert* and class certification motions. He also appointed a committee to "negotiate terms of a voluntary Gallbladder Resolution Program" on the same day that the parties announced they'd reached a deal.[66] Although the mechanism for including qualifying plaintiffs was novel and unorthodox, it was not exactly voluntary. The settlement automatically enrolled plaintiffs with gallbladder injuries and required nonparticipating plaintiffs to affirmatively opt out – not in.[67] Remember, however, that this was not a class action; Judge Herndon had already decided that the litigation failed to meet Rule 23's criteria.

Citing debatable authority and precedent under Rules 16(a)(5), 16(d), *Vioxx*, and *Propulsid*, Judge Herndon ruled, "This Court has authority to preside over and manage various aspects of the Agreement and the Gallbladder Resolution Program."[68] He then notified plaintiffs and ordered that "all MDL Gallbladder Plaintiffs ... are automatically enrolled in, and bound by the terms of, the Gallbladder Resolution Program unless such Plaintiff submits a 'Notice of Intent to Opt Out Form' ... by the 'Opt-Out Deadline.'"[69] If plaintiffs did not "opt out" before the deadline or complete a claims-compensation package, then Judge Herndon would dismiss their suit with prejudice.[70]

---

[65] It is possible that merits-related rulings appeared on individual case dockets, but they did not appear on the MDL master docket. Thus, all the attorneys in the centralized proceeding would not have received notice.

[66] *In re* Yasmin & Yaz (Drospirenone) Mktg., Sales Practices Prods. Liab. Litig., No. 09-md-2100 (S.D. Ill., Mar. 15, 2013) (case management order no. 59).

[67] Settlement Agreement, §1.01(A), *In re* Yasmin & Yaz (Drospirenone) Mktg., Sales Practices & Prods. Liab Litig., No. 09-md-02100-DRH-PMF (S.D. Ill., Mar. 15, 2013) [hereinafter Yaz Gallbladder Settlement].

[68] *In re* Yasmin and Yaz (Drospirenone) Mktg., Sales Practices Prods. Liab. Litig., No. 09-md-2100 (S.D. Ill., Mar. 15, 2013) (case management order no. 60, at 2).

[69] *Id.*

[70] *Id.*

Yaz's settlement designers seized the pull of default rules. As Professors Richard Thaler and Cass Sunstein explain, "[D]efaults are ubiquitous and powerful," for "many people will take whatever option requires the least effort, or the path of least resistance."[71] By changing the default from opting in to opting out (as in a class action), both Judge Herndon and the dealmakers relied on plaintiffs' behavioral tendencies not to act.

Curiously, the subsequent *Yaz* settlement for arterial thromboembolism (ATE) claims, which would have covered the death of 18-year-old Michelle Pfleger from Chapter 1, contained no automatic enrollment provision. It's impossible to know why. Perhaps the easy categorization of gallbladder injuries made dealmakers think that few would balk, whereas blood clots leading to significant events like heart attacks, strokes, and death merited more thought. Alternatively, it could be that a different judge played a signature role.

This other judge, Judge Arnold New, presided over the *Yasmin/Yaz* lawsuits in Philadelphia state court. His hand in provoking the ATE settlement is reminiscent of Judge Jack Weinstein's role in prompting the *Agent Orange* settlement. Just as Judge Weinstein did in *Agent Orange*, Judge New personally appeared when the *Yaz* negotiations hit a roadblock. With jury selection scheduled to begin the next day, "Judge New was here until about 4:45 in the morning," remarked plaintiffs' attorney Michael Weinkowitz.[72]

In describing Judge Weinstein's similar tactics in *Agent Orange*, one plaintiffs' lawyer bemoaned the toll that those round-the-clock negotiations took the weekend before trial:

> I could see how psychologically it was affecting all the members of the [plaintiffs' steering] committee, particularly the ones who were going to have to try the case, to get to be ready to go on Monday. So many things that we had to do, and here we were down at the courthouse negotiating this settlement . . . the judge wore us all down with that tactic . . . the judge made us negotiate around the clock knowing that we had a difficult time being ready for trial, we were thin on manpower, and we were working night and day to get ready . . . . Plus the fact that it tired us and made us less resistant to pressure, and he knew that, I think.[73]

Given this, one might read between the lines in *Yaz* when attorney Weinkowitz continued, "Judge New, Special Master Ellis, and Judge Herndon were all instrumental in the parties reaching the agreement."[74]

---

[71] THALER & SUNSTEIN, *supra* note 3, at 85.

[72] Matt Fair, *Philly Court Proves Its Mettle Crafting Nationwide Yaz Deal*, LAW360 (Aug. 4, 2015, 8:50 PM), https://www.law360.com/articles/687336/philly-court-proves-its-mettle-crafting-nationwide-yaz-deal.

[73] PETER H. SCHUCK, AGENT ORANGE ON TRIAL 161 (1986) (quoting Benton Musslewhite).

[74] Fair, *supra* note 72.

Even though Judge Herndon did not broker the ATE deal, he played a pivotal role in promoting it, shepherding plaintiffs into the program, and ensuring that the deal stuck. Beforehand, he'd gotten exasperated with defendants: "[E]ven though an MDL judge certainly can and should be helpful to the litigation ... by facilitating settlement," he explained, "when that settlement posture must come from wearing everyone down over time or expecting an entire group of catastrophically injured women, for the most part, to simply drop their claims, the MDL judge is not properly exercising his duties by simply standing by or dragging the pretrial proceedings out."[75]

When the parties trumpeted the ATE deal six months later, Judge Herndon helped make it work. He included the settlement's enrollment deadlines in a judicial order and appointed two special masters who would preside over the agreement and issue final, binding, and nonappealable decisions.[76] He issued a census to count every plaintiff.[77] He entered a Lone Pine order that required only nonsettling plaintiffs to produce fact sheets, more than three years' worth of pharmacy and medical records, and a case-specific expert report on general and specific causation – all within three months.[78] Although plaintiffs had to submit pharmacy and medical records as part of the settlement program's claims package, no experts were required. Once again, Judge Herndon (and the other judges in this category) sent a message: settle.

SETTLEMENTS' HANDMAIDENS

Not all judges are as overt about endorsing a private settlement program. But some nevertheless signal their views by acquiescing to dealmakers' request to issue orders that further a settlement's goals. Each entreaty is designed to nudge plaintiffs toward settling.[79] Orders that promote and enforce private settlements may be just as effective as open endorsement, for, as communication theorist Marshall McLuhan explained, "The *medium* is the message."[80] Put simply, the communication

---

[75] *In re* Yasmin & Yaz (Drospirenone) Mktg., Sales Practices Prods. Liab. Litig., No. 09-md-2100 (S.D. Ill., Feb. 13, 2015) (case management order no. 70).

[76] *In re* Yasmin & Yaz (Drospirenone) Mktg., Sales Practices Prods. Liab. Litig., No. 09-md-2100 (S.D. Ill., Aug. 3, 2015) (case management order no. 76).

[77] *In re* Yasmin & Yaz (Drospirenone) Mktg., Sales Pract. Prod. Liab. Litig., No. 09-md-2100 (S.D. Ill., Aug. 3, 2015) (case management order no. 77, census of claims).

[78] *In re* Yasmin & Yaz (Drospirenone) Mktg., Sales Pract. Prod. Liab. Litig., No. 09-md-2100 (S.D. Ill., Aug. 3, 2015) (case management order no. 78, nonparticipating ATE CMO); *In re* Yasmin & Yaz (Drospirenone) Mktg., Sales Pract. Prod. Liab. Litig., No. 09-md-2100 (S.D. Ill., Aug. 3, 2015) (case management order no. 79, non-ATE case resolution CMO).

[79] For a helpful account of the different ways that action or inaction may qualify as paternalistic, see Seana Valentine Shiffrin, *Paternalism, Unconscionability Doctrine, and Accommodation,* 29 PHIL. & PUB. AFF. 205, 211–21 (2000).

[80] MARSHALL McLUHAN, THE MEDIUM IS THE MASSAGE (1967). The word "massage" in the title was a mistake, but apparently, Marshall liked it so much, he instructed the typesetter to leave it alone.

channel – the judge – is a form of consequential messaging.[81] And the message is typically either: "settle" or "the settlement is good."

These messages aren't easy to ignore. In a typical proceeding, the lead lawyers will hammer out a deal with the defendant. Remember, though, that deal is between the leaders and the defendant, not between the plaintiffs and the defendant as you might think – at least not initially. Once the lead plaintiffs' lawyers explain why the settlement offer is good, many will consent. At that point, plaintiffs have the capacity and freedom to decide for themselves. They can exercise their own agency, though, as Chapter 5 explains, they may lack the details and payment amounts that the ethics rules require for informed consent.

Others need cajoling. Some nonlead lawyers might prefer to withhold their strongest cases – to "cherry pick" and "hold out," so to speak. Accordingly, leaders make a series of judicial requests that push reluctant plaintiffs or their counsel to conform. Lead lawyers might ask the judge to appoint the settlement's claims administrator or a settlement master, thereby lending a judicial imprimatur to the deal. Of the 34 proceedings that concluded in private aggregate settlements within the dataset, 64.7% of judges formally appointed claims administrators or settlement masters.[82] In the eyes of many nonlegally sophisticated plaintiffs, this legitimizes the deal. Yet, because the settlement is private, judges don't scrutinize its terms; there is no transparent, adversarial airing of its pros and cons, nor a reasoned opinion as to whether lead lawyers adequately represented plaintiffs with conflicting interests.

Most judges understand how this looks. In questioning leaders' request to appoint a settlement special master in the *Fresenius GranuFlo* litigation, Judge Douglas Woodlock observed, "[I]t is nice to be asked to provide an imprimatur," but "[it's] not my responsibility to provide imprimaturs to various kinds of things." Without a role in reviewing or administering the deal – as he would have in a class action – Judge Woodlock demurred, "I try not to exercise my jurisdiction when ... it is the judicial equivalent of a blurb on the back of a new best seller."[83] Yet, once the parties created a marginal role for him – to review the settlement master's determinations on "only the most limited basis" for "clear error" – he agreed.[84]

Next, to enable corporate defendants to decide whether enough plaintiffs signed up to reassure their shareholders, some leaders request a census order. Although lead lawyers could count heads on their own, it's difficult for them to determine how

---

[81] Robert Cialdini, Pre-suasion: A Revolutionary Way to Influence and Persuade 184 (2016).

[82] All subsequent percentages in this section reflect the numbers for this subset of data – the 34 proceedings that concluded in private, nonclass aggregate settlements.

[83] Transcript of Status Conference at 6, *In re* Fresenius GranuFlo/Naturalyte Dialysate Prods. Liab. Litig. No. 13-md-02428 (D. Mass. Apr. 29, 2016).

[84] *In re* Fresenius GranuFlo/Naturalyte Dialysate Prods. Liab. Liti. No. 13-md-02428 (D. Mass. June 27, 2016) (memorandum and order appointing Eric D. Green as Settlement Special Master).

many unfiled claims or state-court plaintiffs exist. So, they again enlist the transferee judge's help. And judges in 35% of the dataset's proceedings concluding in private settlements required the attorneys to register all their clients – whether pending in state or federal court, and whether the claims are filed or unfiled.

Although the judge plays no role in enforcing provisions that prompt lawyers to recommend that all their clients settle, when settlements go one step further and require that all participating attorneys stop representing nonsettling clients, lawyers must ask the judge to relieve them of their obligations.[85] From a client's perspective, these are among the most ethically troubling orders. They allow her lawyer to abandon her if she refuses to settle. Nevertheless, of the dataset's proceedings concluding in private settlements, 35% of those judges allowed attorneys to withdraw, while others like Judge Woodlock in *Fresenius GranuFlo* noted that they were "systematic in not permitting withdrawal."[86] Anecdotally at least, refusing to allow withdrawals may prompt individual lawyers to engage more; a host of plaintiffs' attorneys objected to Fresenius's proposed Lone Pine order even though plaintiffs' leaders acquiesced.

For those who still won't settle, leaders often ask judges to issue Lone Pine orders that require nonsettling plaintiffs to provide proof of their injuries and supporting expert opinions. Within the dataset, 67.6% of judges presiding over proceedings that concluded in private aggregate settlements issued these orders.[87] Colorfully described by plaintiffs' leadership as "a post-settlement mop-up procedure," and by defendants as "put up or shut up," both sides use Lone Pine orders to send a pointed message to nonsettling plaintiffs: accept the deal or prepare for what may be a short-fused evidentiary burden that could require experts to testify as to the link between the defendant's product and your injury.[88]

For multiyear proceedings where lead lawyers share discovery and deposition testimony with nonlead attorneys, these evidentiary burdens might not be so bad. But information doesn't always trickle down. As Lance Cooper alleged in *GM*, some leaders huddle amongst themselves, siloing nonleaders (and sometimes even those on the executive committee) such that they are privy neither to decision making nor developing the claims nor choosing which claims to develop.

---

[85] Of the private settlements that were publicly available (13 settlements resulting from 10 multi-district proceedings), 53% contained withdrawal provisions and 61% included census orders.

[86] Transcript of Status Conference at 16, *In re* Fresenius GranuFlo/Naturalyte Dialysate Prods. Liab. Litig. No. 13-md-02428 (D. Mass. Dec. 14, 2016).

[87] Table A.5 includes more information on these orders, such as when they were issued, and how many days plaintiffs had to comply.

[88] *In re* Fosamax Prods. Liab. Litig., No. 06-md-1789 (S.D.N.Y. July 30, 2014) (order) (quoting Plaintiffs Steering Committee's Memorandum of Points & Authorities in Opposition to Defendant Merck's Motion for Entry of Lone Pine Order at 7, *In re* Fosamax Prods. Liab. Litig., No. 06-md-1789 (S.D.N.Y. Oct. 29, 2012)); Transcript of Proceedings at 59, *In re* Biomet M2a Magnum Hip Implant Prods. Liab. Litig., No. 12-md-2391 (N.D. Ind. May 18, 2015) (quoting defense attorney John Winter).

Once leaders negotiate a settlement, they no longer continue their discovery efforts. And, with the stay in place, an iron-willed client would have to produce her own evidence then wait for the settlement program to run its course before continuing discovery. As Judge Nancy Gertner once quipped, "If you don't enable those without access to the evidence time to get it, they will lose. Judicial shortcuts, procedural rules, affected not just the speed of justice, but the quality."[89]

JUDICIAL CULTURE AND MOTIVATIONS

Table A.5 shows that judges in only 3 of 34 proceedings (8%) chose not to further private agreements in any way whatsoever. These three judges, Judges Bill Wilson (*Prempro*), James Rosenbaum (*Mirapex*), and Clay Land (*Mentor ObTape*) did not approve private deals or appoint claims administrators or special masters to preside over them, nor did they issue Lone Pine orders and case census orders or allow attorneys to withdraw from nonsettling plaintiffs. They are the outliers.

Why do the other 92% of judges take steps – large or small – to usher plaintiffs into, "legitimize," and enforce private deals? As Chapter 1 explained, most federal judges openly favor settlement. Sometimes, this prosettlement stance may be justified. As Professors Samuel Issacharoff and Robert Klonoff argue, "[T]he ability of a legal system to resolve the repeat harms associated with mass society is itself an important justice value, one that brings recompense to the many, deters untoward behavior, and provides a critical lever to prevent state regulatory monopoly."[90]

Yet, some judges may feel pressured into this prosettlement norm: the six-month report attempts to publicly shame judges with the longest backlogs. And the Panel has exhibited a historic commitment to awarding new proceedings to active case managers with a proven ability to resolve them.[91]

So, on one hand, the prosettlement norms embedded in Federal Rule of Civil Procedure 16 are ubiquitous and one might say that the practices discussed in this chapter fit well within this frame. On the other hand, these practices extend significantly beyond encouraging parties to settle. Some judges seem to become private deal brokers and enforcers, while wielding the public power of staying and dismissing plaintiffs' claims. As this chapter has described, this norm can have real costs to transparency, ethics, information development, plaintiffs' faith in the litigation process, and victim empowerment. As Judge Jack Weinstein acknowledged, "Even though bulk settlements may technically violate ethical rules, judges often encourage their acceptance to terminate a large number of cases."[92]

---

[89] Judge Nancy Gertner (Ret.), *Opinions I Should Have Written*, 110 Nw. L. Rev. 423, 431 (2016).

[90] Samuel Issacharoff & Robert H. Klonoff, *The Public Value of Settlement*, 78 Fordham L. Rev. 1177, 1179 (2009).

[91] Andrew D. Bradt, *"A Radical Proposal": The Multidistrict Litigation Act of 1968*, 165 U. Pa. L. Rev. 831, 907 (2017); de Figueiredo, Lahav & Siegelman, *supra* note 32.

[92] Jack B. Weinstein, Individual Justice in Mass Tort Litigation 74 (1995).

Most judges concede that they would never use the same tactics in a typical civil suit. The "singular theme" that emerged from Yale professor Abbe Gluck's interviews with 20 experienced multidistrict litigation judges was "MDL exceptionalism." "This," she concluded "is a type of litigation that judges insist is unique, too different from case to case to be managed by the transsubstantive values that form the very soul of the FRCP [Federal Rules of Civil Procedure]."[93] In other words, the regular rules and practices developed for run-of-the-mill disputes simply won't cut it when it comes to multidistrict litigation.

If judges view these cases as a whole different species, it makes sense that their responses to similar requests would change as well. Framing a situation in a certain way, for example, can dictate how we react: if you thought a social engagement was a date as opposed to a business meeting, you'd act differently, I suspect. Framing multidistrict proceedings as distinct from more routine single-plaintiff-versus-single-defendant lawsuits can do the same.

Ample evidence exists that judges do indeed frame these proceedings differently. One judge who sat on the Panel put it starkly:

> [W]hen we grant an MDL, we look to whether a judge has a particular experience; we are telling the judge this is a different kind of case because we are giving it to *you*. We are asking them to bring their experience to bear and figure out what remedy and procedure to use.[94]

Gluck concluded that when judges receive a proceeding from the Panel, they join an elite cadre of judges who view themselves as more qualified than others.[95]

Adopting a multidistrict litigation frame also seems to mean that creativity is warranted and accepted; functioning outside the dictates of the Federal Rules of Civil Procedure and crafting "MDL common law" is expected, if not encouraged.[96] These norms can be readily transmitted through social networks. As Chapter 3 illustrated, the actors in multidistrict proceedings form a highly cohesive network, meaning that the culture of these proceedings – ideas, practices, norms, schemas, frames, innovations, and values (culture, for short) – may be readily diffused to judges and lawyers alike. Consider two examples.

First, judicial case-management techniques can influence other judges. As sociologist Ronald Burt suggests, diffusion can occur not only when people are directly connected but also when they share social structural positions and emulate what others are doing, as new transferee judges might.[97] Prestige breeds imitation, with

---

[93] Gluck, *supra* note 44, at 1674.

[94] *Id.* at 1693.

[95] *Id.* at 1698.

[96] *Id.* at 1679; Pamela K. Bookman & David L. Noll, *Ad Hoc Procedure*, 92 N.Y.U. L. Rev. 767, 786–87 (2017).

[97] Ronald S. Burt, *Social Contagion and Innovation: Cohesion versus Structural Equivalence*, 92 Am. J. Soc'y 349 (1987).

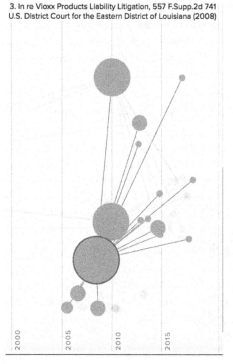

3. In re Vioxx Products Liability Litigation, 557 F.Supp.2d 741
U.S. District Court for the Eastern District of Louisiana (2008)

FIGURE 4.1 Diffusion of Lone Pine orders post-*Vioxx*

people often imitating those with a higher status even on matters that lie outside
of that person's expertise.[98] Take Lone Pine orders, for example.

Figure 4.1[99] highlights Judge Fallon's Lone Pine order in *Vioxx*, which kickstarted
a trend. As the figure shows by linking his initial order (the large circle in the bottom
center) to subsequent opinions citing him (indicated by links to the smaller
circles), when judges impose these evidentiary burdens, they frequently cite *Vioxx*
for support. Similarly, judicial inventions may spread through the annual Transferee
Judges' Conference where MDL judges discuss and showcase their case-
management efforts.

Second, highly specialized repeat players can use their own influence to design,
implement, and refine settlement practices that work to their advantage. Remember

[98] Joseph Henrich & Francisco J. Gil-White, *The Evolution of Prestige: Freely Conferred Deference as a Mechanism for Enhancing the Benefits of Cultural Transmission*, 22 EVOLUTION &
HUM. BEHAV. 165, 184 (2001).

[99] This is an image taken from a search for the term "Lone Pine order" in Ravel Law, which was
then further refined to focus on district courts. Ravel Law, http://www.ravellaw.com (Sept. 16,
2018). Note that the other large circle in the top middle of the graph is Judge Goodwin's
opposing order in *In re* Digitek Prods. Liab. Litig., 264 F.R.D. 249 (S.D. W. Va. 2010), which
I discuss later in this chapter.

Duke's *MDL Standards and Best Practices* guide for judges? Its editorial board consisted of six highly connected, repeat-player attorneys.[100] To disseminate the board's recommendations, Duke held a series of invitation-only conferences for "seasoned MDL judges" and "distinguished lawyers well experienced in handling large mass-tort MDLs."[101]

When it comes to private settlement, the guide suggests that, if the parties request it, "the court should be prepared to take an ongoing role in implementing and enforcing the settlement agreement."[102] (Of course, the requesting "parties" are the lead lawyers who negotiated the deal – not the plaintiffs or necessarily those whom they hired to represent them.) The drafters hope that active involvement "will remove some or even many cases from the dockets." Thus, the guide argues that judges should "play some role in resolving disputes that arise with respect to the enforcement of the settlements."[103] Yet, as the editorial board's composition suggests and as one transferee judge quipped, "[I]t's less judges making up procedures than good lawyers making them up and bringing them to judges."[104]

As judges innovate, frame multidistrict litigation distinctly, and work closely with lead lawyers to resolve a proceeding over several years, those leaders have an extraordinary opportunity to shape judicial perspectives. Like everyone else, the people judges work and associate with influence them both directly and indirectly. Commenting on this unique relationship, one anonymous transferee judge explained:

> Most MDL judges are involved more personally in these cases than other cases .... I had a conference in person, it was off the record, roll-up-sleeves work. I don't usually do this at all in civil cases, usually the [magistrate judges] do the pretrial management. This creates wonderful relationships and is very satisfying. It's problem solving together.[105]

As another judge observed, "You have to work as a team, it's less adversarial. You need to discuss it and ... get along."[106] Indeed, in Professor Gluck's interviews with transferee judges, they all described their relationships with the attorneys as "unusually collaborative."[107]

---

[100] DUKE LAW CENTER FOR JUDICIAL STUDIES, MDL STANDARDS AND BEST PRACTICES (2014), https://law.duke.edu/sites/default/files/centers/judicialstudies/MDL_Standards_and_Best_Prac tices_2014-REVISED.pdf.

[101] *Second Multidistrict Litigation Institute*, DUKE LAW SCHOOL https://law.duke.edu/judicialstu dies/conferences/november2015/.

[102] DUKE LAW CENTER FOR JUDICIAL STUDIES, STANDARDS AND BEST PRACTICES FOR LARGE AND MASS-TORT MDLS, 122–23 (2014), https://judicialstudies.duke.edu/sites/default/files/centers/ judicialstudies/standards_and_best_practices_for_large_and_mass-tort_mdls.pdf.

[103] *Id.* at 123.

[104] Gluck, *supra* note 44, at 1691.

[105] *Id.* at 1700–1.

[106] *Id.* at 1701.

[107] *Id.* at 1700.

When lawyers and judges engage in collaborative, multiyear endeavors, working groups can form.[108] Once a group forms, research shows that members tend to exhibit other-regarding preferences – trust, reciprocity, and altruism – toward other members.[109] Members' fairness considerations can change based on whether the situation involves another group member (inclusionary concerns for the regulars) or individuals outside the group (exclusionary concerns for one-time plaintiffs).[110] Although these studies were conducted outside mass torts, they do raise questions about whether the close relationships that judges develop with leaders – combined with the breakdown of the adversarial process in a settlement's wake – could eclipse the caution lights that might ordinarily flash when judges receive requests to nudge unwilling plaintiffs into a settlement program.

Inclusionary concerns for working group members likewise align with self-interest. Case-management practices that help form and enforce settlements benefit the key stakeholders: lead plaintiffs' attorneys, defendants and their attorneys, and, yes, the judges.

Self-interest combined with social network ties, collaborative working group relationships, and other-regarding preferences for fellow group members can play a significant role in shaping transferee judges' settlement decisions. Professor James Kwak identifies each as a symptom of what he labels "cultural capture."[111] Of course, "capture" is a loaded term that can denote payoffs or overly cozy relationships between a regulator and the regulated entity – often without nuance or supporting evidence. But, while cultural capture is inherently insidious, it is neither nefarious nor necessarily based on material self-interest.

Stripped of its more sinister connotations, cultural capture's descriptive power is quite useful.[112] Kwak explains the term like this: "cultural because it operates through a set of shared but not explicitly stated understandings about the world"

---

[108] *See* R. Scott Tindale et al., *Shared Cognition in Small Groups, in* BLACKWELL HANDBOOK ON SOCIAL PSYCHOLOGY: GROUP PROCESSES 5 (Michael A. Hoagg & R. Scott Tindale eds., 2001) (demonstrating that groups can form when would-be members are physically proximate, when they share experiences or historic events, and when they have unified or overlapping goals, values, and intentions).

[109] *See* Nancy R. Buchan et al., *Let's Get Personal: An International Examination of the Influence of Communication, Culture and Social Distance on Other Regarding Preferences*, 60 J. ECON. BEHAV. & ORG. 373, 374–75 (2006) (reviewing the literature on other-regarding preferences).

[110] Tom R. Tyler & E. Allan Lind, *Intrinsic Versus Community-Based Justice Models: When Does Group Membership Matter?*, 46 J. SOC. ISSUES 83, 84–86 (1990).

[111] James Kwak, *Cultural Capture and the Financial Crisis, in* PREVENTING REGULATORY CAPTURE 71, 80–93 (Daniel Carpenter & David A. Moss eds., 2014).

[112] Elite repeat players' influence on transferee judges may have co-opted plaintiffs' ability to freely and voluntarily consent to settle, but, relative to a system devoid of coordinated proceedings, the net social benefits remain positive.

and "capture because it can produce the same outcome as traditional capture – regulatory actions that serve the ends of industry [or insiders]."[113]

To be sure, cultural capture cannot completely explain why judges acquiesce to leaders' settlement-related requests. And, as Kwak acknowledges, "Cultural capture, if anything, is even harder to identify empirically [than traditional capture], because there are always multiple explanations for why someone forms the beliefs she has."[114] Yet, if the company we keep can shape our mind-sets, then surely engaging in a collective endeavor with lead plaintiff and defense attorneys can influence judges.

Symptoms of judicial capture in multidistrict proceedings are not limited to cultural and sociological influences. Judges depend on lead lawyers for information and expertise in the same way regulators depend on a regulated industry.[115] Elite repeat plaintiff and defense attorneys are, after all, the industry experts. At the height of their careers, these actors may have handled 20–50 proceedings, sometimes more. In contrast, some of the most experienced mass-tort transferee judges have presided over five proceedings.[116] Given that judges have few independent information sources and must be generalists, it is natural for them to defer to experts across a variety of subject matters.

But as the adversarial process breaks down in a settlement's wake and settlement architects request orders furthering their private agreement, those experts become less trustworthy. Judges need information from fresh sources. As Chapter 6 explores, if given the right incentives, nonlead attorneys could fill this void and loosen leaders' stranglehold on information and expertise. Yet, as it stands, some judges channel all communication through the leaders. This leaves no outlet for dissenting perspectives and allows lead lawyers to act as information gatekeepers.

DISSECTING JUDICIAL PATERNALISM

It's helpful to remember that plaintiffs don't typically choose multidistrict litigation. They select a lawyer and a forum, but like Dorothy in the *Wizard of Oz*, they may quickly find themselves on unfamiliar turf. After a whirlwind, they're "represented" by a lawyer they have never met who litigates their case in a place that would ordinarily lack personal jurisdiction over them.

Nothing about multidistrict coordination preserves the fundamental tenets of self-determination or consent in liberal theory, nor does it reflect the control that we

---

[113] Kwak, *supra* note 111, at 79.
[114] *Id.*
[115] Nolan McCarty, *Complexity, Capacity, and Capture, in* Preventing Regulatory Capture 99, 102–3, 119 (Daniel Carpenter & David A. Moss eds., 2014).
[116] Judge Eldon Fallon, for instance, has presided over *Propulsid,* the *Murphy Oil* class action litigation, *Vioxx, Chinese Drywall,* and *Xarelto.*

usually associate with being a party to a suit.[117] Following the yellow brick road doesn't lead plaintiffs home, or to trial. The only control they have is over their consent to settle. And so, even when judges are fully informed, the steps they take to usher plaintiffs into a settlement program may undermine both plaintiffs' primary mechanism for expressing their autonomy and the legitimacy of the outcome.

We often think of the judiciary as *enabling* autonomy. The state, through the judiciary, enforces contracts and protects rights. This furthers our independence, for it gives us the freedom to enter an agreement with a stranger and know that its terms will be enforced – if not by the stranger, then by the state. So, the state creates a supportive infrastructure for contracting parties. But its support is not limitless.

Just as if I asked you to help me con someone else, you could (as could the state) refuse to help me perform or enforce my immoral deal – even if the person I conned freely (but unwittingly) consented.[118] You would, in short, need to exercise your own moral judgment and rebuff me. Similarly, the state can decline to enforce agreements that are oppressive or unfair on substantive unconscionability grounds. The focus would be on the agreement's content – its substance.

Other legal doctrines such as duress, fraud, and procedural unconscionability capture the idea that the state should not assist the Don Corleones of the world in enforcing Godfather-esque deals – those consented to while a gun's pressed to the temple. Though extreme, this vividly illustrates procedural unconscionability's concern with the agreement process: did overreaching occur in forming the contract? Was there undue pressure, missing information or misinformation, or inadequate representation? Questions here center on the conditions under which plaintiffs consented.[119]

If plaintiffs were trying to prevent courts from enforcing an agreement for the sale of goods, they would have to demonstrate both a defect in the bargaining process (procedural unconscionability) and a lopsided, unfair contract term (something that is substantively unconscionable). Accordingly, most work on judicial paternalism examines the role that judges should play in enforcing or voiding contracts that the law deems unconscionable. If a judge decides that an agreement is immoral or unfair, then, like the con artist example, she has a legitimate self-regarding reason to refrain from imposing its terms.[120]

---

[117] *See* JOHN RAWLS, A THEORY OF JUSTICE 108–17 (1971) (explaining that obligations can arise through voluntary acts such as promises and agreements, and natural duties).

[118] Shiffrin, *supra* note 79, at 223–24.

[119] This inquiry is analogous to procedural unconscionability in contract law. *See* U.C.C. 2.302 (AM. LAW INST. & UNIF. LAW COM'N 1977); RESTATEMENT (SECOND) OF CONTRACTS § 208 (AM. LAW INST. 1981); *see also* Ingle v. Circuit City Stores, Inc. 328 F.3d 1165, 1170–73 (9th Cir. 2003) (distinguishing between procedural and substantive unconscionability and suggesting a sliding-scale approach); Harris v. Green Tree Fin. Corp., 183 F.3d 173, 181 (3d Cir. 1999) ("Procedural unconscionability pertains to the process by which an agreement is reached and the form of an agreement including the use therein of fine print and convoluted or unclear language.").

[120] Shiffrin, *supra* note 79, at 224.

For instance, after the negotiating parties in the *World Trade Center* litigation hammered out the logistics of their deal, they jointly asked Judge Hellerstein for a stay.[121] They asked him to get involved; they *wanted* his help in making the settlement stick. They just didn't predict his response: he scheduled a show-cause hearing, listened to not only the lawyers but also to the plaintiffs, and then said, "In my judgment, this settlement is not enough."[122] In thinking through whether this response was paternalistic, consider two hypothetical scenarios:[123]

> 1. *Intervention or Refusal for Plaintiffs' Benefit.* The dealmakers ask Judge Hellerstein to assist them in carrying out their private settlement by staying the proceedings (or allowing them to withdraw from representing plaintiffs who refuse to settle, issuing a census order, or entering a Lone Pine order). Thinking that the deal would (or would not) be good for the plaintiffs to accept, Judge Hellerstein enters (or refuses to enter) orders that promote the deal (such as a stay or census) or that place burdens and costs on those who refuse (such as Lone Pine orders or attorney requests to withdraw).

These tactics are paternalistic. Judge Hellerstein is inhibiting the plaintiffs' freedom and choice to settle – their agency, in other words. Although leaders have requested his assistance, Judge Hellerstein is not only substituting his judgment for the plaintiffs' judgment but also working around plaintiffs' agency to get them to behave as he believes they should.[124] Promoting the settlement for plaintiffs' benefit would likewise benefit him, for it shrinks his docket and may favorably dispose the Panel to send complex cases his way.

> 2. *Self-Regarding Refusal.* The dealmakers ask Judge Hellerstein to assist them in carrying out their deal by staying the proceedings (or allowing them to withdraw from representing plaintiffs who refuse to settle, issuing a census order, or entering a Lone Pine order). Judge Hellerstein refuses to help because he believes that assisting would implicate him in an exploitative relationship, and that the endeavor is unworthy of his time and energy given his other commitments and ideals.

Scenario 2 would not be paternalistic. Rather, it would reflect Judge Hellerstein's unwillingness to lend his support – and the authority of his office – to a settlement

---

[121] Memorandum of Law in Support of Plaintiffs' and Defendants' Joint Application for an Order to Show Cause for a Stay, *In re* World Trade Ctr. Disaster Site Litig., No. 1:21-mc-00100-KH (S.D.N.Y. Mar. 12, 2010).

[122] Transcript of Proceedings at 54, *In re* World Trade Ctr. Disaster Site Litig., No. 1:21-mc-00100-KH (S.D.N.Y. Mar. 19, 2010).

[123] Each example is adapted from Shiffrin, *supra* note 79, at 225–26.

[124] On the importance of motives, see generally David L. Shapiro, *Courts, Legislatures, and Paternalism*, 74 VA. L. REV. 519 (1988); Shiffrin, *supra* note 79, at 205.

he cannot defend.[125] As political and legal philosopher Seana Shiffrin explains, "Although judicial opinions reflect a range of concerns, sometimes including pure concern for the position of the disadvantaged party, a dominant concern of judges is self-regarding: it is to avoid facilitating the actions of an exploiter rather than to act to protect the disadvantaged party."[126]

Judges may go one step further, not only refusing to act to avoid complicity, but explaining the reasons for their refusal. They thereby engage plaintiffs' capacity for reason. Again, this is not paternalistic. It appeals to plaintiffs to exercise their agency in another way; it does not supplant their agency as in Scenario 1.

In Scenario 1, judicial orders paternalistically tinker with plaintiffs' independent agency to bring the proceedings to a close. It bears particular scrutiny for it best captures what occurred within the dataset when 64.7% of judges appointed claims administrators or settlement masters to formally preside over private settlements,[127] 67.6% issued Lone Pine orders, 35% issued census orders, and 35% allowed attorneys to withdraw from representing nonsettling clients.

Little has been said about the judge's role in nudging contractual consent in the first place. In one respect, issuing orders like these is not so different than deciding whether a contract is unconscionable.[128] Each scenario involves the state inserting itself in private, contractual affairs at the parties' request. Like the judge who declines to enforce a contract because of her own self-regarding desire not to facilitate others' exploitative actions (to help with the "con," in other words), a judge faced with a request for census, withdrawals, or Lone Pine orders might refuse to assist with what she views as coercive or unfair settlements (Scenario 2).

By contrast, the decision to affirmatively assist, to *issue* a bevy of orders promoting a private settlement (Scenario 1) is different. Orders that further the deal invoke the mantle of judicial authority to nudge noncompliant plaintiffs toward consent. This is troubling for libertarians, but likewise raises interesting questions for non-libertarian, liberal autonomy advocates.[129] Even if we are comfortable taking on certain other-regarding (and freedom-limiting) constraints that make it possible for members of society to cooperate with each other, there is still a question about

---

[125] Shiffrin, *supra* note 79, at 227–28.

[126] *Id.* at 229.

[127] All subsequent percentages in this section reflect the numbers for this subset of data – the 34 proceedings that concluded in private, nonclass aggregate settlements.

[128] Much ink has been spilled over paternalism in contract. *See, e.g.*, Duncan Kennedy, *Distributive and Paternalist Motives in Contract and Tort Law, with Special Reference to Compulsory Terms and Unequal Bargaining Power*, 41 MD. L. REV. 563, 563 (1982); Anthony T. Kronman, *Paternalism and the Law of Contracts*, 92 YALE L.J. 763 (1983).

[129] John Stuart Mill's essay, *On Liberty*, raised a number of questions about paternalism and its uses when he contended that "the only purpose for which power can be rightfully exercised over any member of a civilized community, against his will, is to prevent harm to others." JOHN STUART MILL, ON LIBERTY 68 (G. Himmelfarb ed., Penguin Books 1982) (1859). This has been debated at length. *E.g.*, H.L.A. HART, LAW, LIBERTY AND MORALITY (1963).

where judicial intervention (state action) in *forming* a private deal falls within these accommodations.

It is one thing, for instance, for the state to support and enforce the institution of contract, and even for judges to invoke a self-regarding refusal to enforce unconscionable contracts. It is quite another to use the state to help form and perform a private agreement, as dealmakers do when requesting judicial assistance with private settlements. In short, judicial action here operates not as a shield as in unconscionability doctrines, but as a sword.

By viewing state action through this lens, judicial nudging can be an added source of procedural coercion – not relief – for plaintiffs. Sure, there is cause for concern as lead plaintiffs' lawyers reach what may be quid pro quo deals with defendants. Those arrangements give rise to substantive concerns about the agreement's content – is what they agreed to fair? They should also prompt us to question whether plaintiffs' consent was truly informed, for plaintiffs' attorneys may have ample self-interested incentives to skew the information they provide. But focusing solely on these questions ignores a related one about the procedural conditions that judges create.

Unlike Scenario 2, most judges within the dataset were not a liberating force for substantively unfair terms; instead, they may be an overbearing source of procedural pressure. Consider smoking for example. Insurance premiums and privacy practices allow us to decide whether to smoke based on risks and rewards that closely surround that activity: social and sensory desires versus health risks – not job or insurance-coverage losses.

In highly personal decisions, like whether to smoke or settle a lawsuit involving bodily harm, our choices should center on factors closely related to the activity – the merits of our suit and the risks of trial, for example.[130] Plaintiffs' choices shouldn't be hemmed in by short-fused evidentiary production orders, constrained by an inability to conduct discovery, or obstructed by an attorney's threat to withdraw.

Plaintiffs already experience plenty of prosettlement pushes from their own lawyers that undermine their autonomy and independent agency. And, because the settlement is "private," few relief valves exist – there are no formal paths for objecting or appealing. When judges then intervene, it may seem as though dismissal is plaintiffs only alternative to settling.

JUDICIAL AUTHORITY TO INTERVENE?

If you believe that you can freely choose something only once you know enough about it and when no one is twisting your arm, then judicial nudges might not be the elixir we seek. Of course, judicial actions in this arena are far from uniform. Thus far we've witnessed a spectrum for judicial approval, with judges picking and

[130] Shiffrin, *supra* note 79, at 247–48.

choosing tools from an eclectic workbench. At the "hard shoves" end lie cases like *Zimmer Durom Hip Cup* and *Yaz/Yasmin*, where judges expressly approve and directly enforce private settlements. At the gentler end, some judges embrace a smattering of orders that help facilitate or enforce private settlements, such as allowing attorneys to withdraw from representing nonsettling clients or issuing census orders, Lone Pine orders, or stays. And then, somewhere in the middle, lie techniques such as appointing the private claims administrator or settlement master, enforcing private settlement deadlines through judicial dismissals, and championing the settlement on the record.

Census and Lone Pine Orders

Unlike summary judgment, where plaintiffs must show that important factual disputes warrant a jury's time and attention, or even Rule 11 motions to sanction attorneys for bringing a frivolous case, census and Lone Pine orders demand little engagement with a case's merits. In their attempt to gain a decisive headcount through a census, judges invoke their authority over the lawyers appearing before them; they require those attorneys to divulge information about all their clients – regardless of where (or even whether) those claims are pending. But federal courts should not bootstrap their jurisdiction onto the backs of the attorneys who practice before them. Jurisdiction attaches to claims – not lawyers. Nor does supplemental jurisdiction allow lawyers to serve as a conduit to clients who have no business pending before the court.

Lone Pine orders stand on slightly firmer footing, at least jurisdictionally. These orders aim to combat what's known as the "field of dreams" problem. That is, as soon as the Panel centralizes a proceeding, some lawyers may flood it with dubious claims – build it and they will come. By requiring case-specific proof, the thinking is that Lone Pine orders (and plaintiffs' fact sheets as less onerous versions are called presettlement) will help screen weak cases.

Some courts, however, worry that Lone Pine orders are illegitimate end runs around the federal rules – rules that are tested through approximately 30 months of committee debate for even minor changes.[131] For instance, the Ohio Court of Appeals reasoned, "It gives courts the means to ignore existing procedural rules and safeguards. When the Lone Pine order cuts off or severely limits the litigant's right to discovery, the order closely resembles summary judgment, albeit without the safeguards that the Civil Rules of Procedure supply."[132]

In presiding over the *Digitek* multidistrict proceedings, Judge Joseph Goodwin concluded, "Given a choice between a 'Lone Pine Order' created under the court's

---

[131] Peter G. McCabe, *Renewal of the Federal Rulemaking Process*, 44 Am. U. L. Rev. 1655, 1671–72 (1995).

[132] Simone v. Girard City Bd. of Educ., 872 N.E.2d 344, 350 (Ohio Ct. App. 2007).

inherent case management authority and available procedural devices such as summary judgment, motions to dismiss, motions for sanctions and similar rules, I believe it more prudent to yield to the consistency and safeguards of the mandated rules."[133] Consequently, he issued no Lone Pine orders in *Digitek* proceedings.[134]

Even the relatively conservative Eleventh Circuit agrees, "[W]e do not think that it is legally appropriate (or for that matter wise) for a district court to issue a *Lone Pine* order requiring factual support of the plaintiffs' claims before it has determined that those claims survive a motion to dismiss under *Twombly*."[135] Although courts are free to use partial summary-judgment motions (where no factual disputes exist on a particular element of the plaintiff's claim or the defendant's defense) during discovery and Rule 12(b)(6) motions to dismiss for failing to state a claim even sooner, they shouldn't use Lone Pine orders as "platforms for pseudo-summary judgment motions," warned the court.[136]

Endorsing Private Settlements

What about publicly endorsing private settlements – do judges have the power to do that? Probably not. Federal courts have limited jurisdiction; they possess only the powers given to them by the Constitution and statutes.[137] The three possible sources of power include parties' consent, legislative authorization, and courts' inherent authority.

In run-of-the-mill settlements, consent plays a prominent role in subsequent judicial involvement. For example, if parties reach a mutually agreeable deal and ask the court to embody their agreement in a stipulated judgment or consent decree, then the court would retain jurisdiction.[138] If one party breaches the agreement, the other could return to the same judge and ask for help. Both parties consented to the court's involvement, but neither needed the judge's permission to settle. By allowing a plaintiff to dismiss her action without a court's order, Rule 41(b) makes that point clearly.

This status quo is worth emphasizing: absent affirmative consent, judges have no authority to coerce or police private settlements.[139] In fact, judicial ethics allow

[133] *In re* Digitek Prods. Liab. Litig., 264 F.R.D. 249, 259 (S.D.W.Va. 2010).
[134] Judge Goodwin later changed course slightly when handling the sprawling pelvic mesh proceedings – the largest since asbestos. As of this writing, he issued show cause orders in proceedings against American Medical Systems, C. R. Bard, and Coloplast. These orders required plaintiffs who did not attend mandatory settlement conferences to show cause as to why their claims should not be dismissed with prejudice.
[135] Adinolfe v. United Tech. Corp., 768 F.3d 1161, 1168 (11th Cir. 2014).
[136] *Id. But see* Avila v. Willits Envtl. Remediation Tr. 633 F.3d 828, 834 (9th Cir. 2011) (noting that Lone Pine orders do not "skirt accepted procedure").
[137] Kokkonen v. Guardian Life Ins. Co., 511 U.S. 375, 377 (1994).
[138] *Id.* at 381.
[139] Courts have consistently held that judges may not coerce settlement, but the boundaries of that line remain hazy. Newton v. A.C. & S., Inc., 918 F.2d 1121, 129 (3d Cir. 1990); Ellen E. Deason,

judges to "encourage and seek to facilitate settlement," but state unequivocally that they "should not act in a manner that coerces any party into surrendering the right to have the controversy resolved by the courts."[140]

Of course, in mass torts, individual plaintiffs have not consented to settle; that is, after all, why dealmakers urge judges to get involved – to nudge them. Nor can lead plaintiffs' lawyers' consent to the deal suffice: these are not class actions, judges do not appoint lead lawyers according to the due process dictates of adequate representation, and there is no such thing as virtual representation.[141] Thus, leaders' consent does not bind plaintiffs.

Even if plaintiffs do not consent, Congress might legislatively empower judges to play a greater role in overseeing settlements. One possibility would be through the Federal Rules of Civil Procedure. In class actions, for instance, Congress tasks judges with monitoring settlements using Rule 23. Yet, as Third Circuit Judge Anthony Scirica explains, "[O]utside the federal rules governing class actions, there is no prescribed independent review of the structural and substantive fairness of a settlement including evaluation of attorneys' fees, potential conflicts of interest, and counsel's allocation of settlement funds among class members."[142]

Nevertheless, some judges blend several rules to create a "quasi class action."[143] While nonclass multidistrict proceedings share some characteristics with class actions, a class is either certified or not. Judges may not legitimately treat Rule 23 as a grab bag of authority from which to select helpful provisions and ignore ill-fitting constraints.[144] Doing so permits attorneys and judges to strip away constitutional due process protections that impede closure.

Without class actions on the table, judges turn to snippets of other rules, like Rule 42, which governs consolidations and allows courts to "make such orders . . . as may tend to avoid unnecessary costs or delay," and Rule 16(a)(5), which allows courts to play a role in "facilitating settlement."[145] Yet, Rule 16's advisory committee note admonishes, "[I]t is not the purpose of [this rule] to impose settlement negotiations on unwilling litigants." And "[o]f course settlement is dependent upon agreement by

---

Beyond Managerial Judges: Appropriate Roles in Settlement, 78 OHIO ST. L.J. 73, 112 (2017); Jaros & Zimmerman, *supra* note 31, at 590.

[140] CODE OF CONDUCT FOR U.S. JUDGES Canon 3A(4) cmt., http://www.uscourts.gov/judges-judgeships/code-conduct-united-states-judges#d.

[141] Taylor v. Sturgell, 128 S. Ct. 2161, 2176 (2008).

[142] Sullivan v. DB Invs., Inc., 667 F.3d 273, 336 (3d Cir. 2011).

[143] *E.g.*, In re Vioxx Prods. Liab. Litig., 574 F. Supp. 2d 606, 611–12 (E.D. La. 2008).

[144] Linda S. Mullenix, *Dubious Doctrines: The Quasi-Class Action*, 80 CINCINNATI L. REV. 389, 389 (2012).

[145] FED. R. CIV. P. 42(a); *see, e.g.*, In re Actos (Pioglitazone) Prods. Liab. Litig., No. 11-md-2299 (W.D. La. Apr. 28, 2015) (citing Rule 16(a)(5), (d), *Vioxx*, and *Propulsid* as giving the court the authority to enter orders implementing the private settlement's timeline). Rule 42, however, speaks to consolidations under that rule, not to coordinated pretrial handling under § 1407 unless the judge also orders consolidation.

the parties."[46] Likewise, Rule 42(a) allows judges to consolidate related cases to avoid cost and delay. It speaks explicitly to consolidations under that rule – not to coordinated pretrial handling under § 1407. In short, neither rule gives judges license to endorse private settlements, substitute their judgment for the plaintiffs' judgment, or goad plaintiffs into settling. Nor does combining these rules transform them into something more than the sum of their parts.

"A judge's case management remains moored to these Rules," writes Judge Clay Land. "He cannot simply do as he pleases even if doing so will result in [Rule 1's] just, speedy, and inexpensive resolution of the proceeding. To allow him to do so would make him king, not judge." And "coercing a settlement by making the alternative so dissatisfying that true choice no longer remains," Land explains, likewise "risks having the judge become a player in the proceeding instead of the umpire."[47]

When rules come up short, however, some judges turn to their own inherent authority – a lacuna in which practice and doctrine have parted ways. In practice, transferee judges such as Judges Wigenton and Hellerstein have cited their "inherent authority" or "inherent equitable authority" as authorizing them to do all manner of things, from endorsing and enforcing private settlements to cutting private attorneys' contingent fee contracts. Judges regularly summon these powers when regulatory voids appear – often for good reason. The federal rules cannot contemplate everything a trial judge must do; gaps will exist and judges need flexibility.

The trouble is that inherent authority appears to have no limits. It is guided neither by consent nor contract principles. It swells to fill whatever role it must, sacrificing transparency, predictability, and restraint in its wake.

This expansive view is likewise out of step with existing Supreme Court precedent. The Court defines "inherent powers" as those that "cannot be dispensed with … because they are necessary to the exercise of all the others."[48] Accordingly, courts can do things like discipline attorneys appearing before them and dismiss actions when plaintiffs fail to prosecute them. But, the Court explains, "Because inherent powers are shielded from direct democratic controls, they must be exercised with restraint and discretion."[49]

Inherent authority allows courts to take only those steps necessary to "permit the courts to function" and should be "used sparingly."[50] Such limits, for instance, have

---

[46] FED. R. CIV. P. 16 advisory comm. notes.

[47] Letter from the Honorable Clay D. Land, Chief U.S. District Judge, Middle Dist. of Ga., to Professor D. Theodore Rave (May 15, 2018) (on file with author).

[48] Chambers v. NASCO, Inc., 501 U.S. 32, 43 (1991); *see also* United States v. Hudson & Goodwin, 11 U.S. 32 (1812).

[49] Roadway Express, Inc. v. Piper, 447 U.S. 752, 764 (1980); *see also Chambers*, 501 U.S. at 32, 44.

[50] Young v. United States *ex rel.* Vuitton, 481 U.S. 787, 819–20 (1987) (Scalia, J., concurring); Sentis Group, Inc. v. Shell Oil Co., 559 F.3d 888, 900 (8th Cir. 2009).

prevented courts from using their inherent authority to enforce private settlement agreements that fail to reserve jurisdiction – it has not given them the freedom to mandate and administer settlements.[151] Even appellate courts require that judges use these powers "with restraint" and ensure that they comport "with procedural fairness."[152]

Professor Robert Pushaw's exhaustive research on inherent judicial authority led him to the same conclusion, "The constitutional basis of inherent authority is indispensable necessity rather than convenience, and therefore such powers should be exercised sparingly."[153] In short, Article III limits federal judges to using their enumerated powers and those that are strictly necessary for carrying out those powers.

In some ways, this stretching of authority is unsurprising, for it fits snugly into a broader trend of "slouching toward discretion," as Professor Richard Marcus puts it.[154] But discretion is not limitless. While a "judge may encourage parties . . . to settle," judicial codes of conduct forbid them from acting "in a manner that coerces any party into settlement."[155] As judges insist upon their own power to drive settlement, actively promote that settlement, impose costs on nonsettling parties, and then enforce the settlement's terms, they engage in activity that exceeds the authority that rightly belongs to them.[156]

"[E]ncouraging judges to actively enter the peace-buying negotiations runs the risk of most seductions – ultimate disappointment on the part of the seduced," concludes Judge Clay Land.[157] As Chapter 6 explores, courts stand on firmer footing when it comes to issuing merits-based rulings and policing attorneys' fees, for lawyers are officers of the court. Judges are supposed to monitor counsel. And there is ample need to do so, for attorneys are not newcomers to the art of framing clients' choices or rigging those choices to satisfy their own ends.

---

[151] Kokkonen v. Guardian Life Ins. Co., 511 U.S. 375, 377 (1994).

[152] *E.g.*, *In re* Atlantic Pipe Corp, 304 F.3d 135, 143 (1st Cir. 2002).

[153] Robert J. Pushaw Jr., *The Inherent Powers of Federal Courts and the Structural Constitution*, 86 IOWA L. REV. 735, 782 (2001).

[154] Richard L. Marcus, *Slouching Toward Discretion*, 78 NOTRE DAME L. REV. 1561, 1590–93 (2003) ("Usually a judge has no explicit authority to pass on the fairness or desirability of a settlement, but it is difficult to know when or whether judges have given effect to their substantive preferences in molding the parties' agreement or in using the procedural tools available to them to prod parties toward settlements.").

[155] MODEL CODE OF JUDICIAL CONDUCT r. 2.6(B) (2009); *see also* Judicial Conference of the U.S., *Code of Conduct for United States Judges, in* 2a GUIDE TO JUDICIARY POLICY, Canon 3(A)(4)(d).

[156] Judith Resnik, *Procedure as Contract*, 80 NOTRE DAME L. REV. 593, 645 (2005) (noting "concern about the distribution of power ought also to apply when the source of settlement pressures is the judiciary").

[157] Letter from the Honorable Clay D. Land, Chief District Judge, Middle Dist. of Ga., to Professor D. Theodore Rave (May 15, 2018) (on file with author).

5

When Multidistrict Litigation Settles into "Alternative Dispute Resolution"

Until now, commentators and judges have compared nonclass mass torts resolved through multidistrict litigation with class actions. Parallels do exist, both in the way judges manage cases and in settlement provisions. In *Actos*, for example, Judge Rebecca Doherty's decision to notify all the plaintiffs about her order on the private settlement resembled a class-action notice.[1] And remember how Judge David Herndon automatically enrolled all the gallbladder plaintiffs into the *Yasmin/Yaz* settlement?[2]

But focusing exclusively on the similarities between aggregate settlements and class actions misses the many ways in which the settlement programs mirror, and sometimes directly incorporate, alternative dispute resolution (ADR). ADR is an umbrella term for various methods of resolving disputes outside of court – mediation and arbitration are the two most common.

A mediator acts as a go-between; she has no power to rule on the merits of a dispute but facilitates discussions between the parties.[3] Arbitration, by contrast, is principally a creature of contract. Parties embed arbitration provisions in their business deals to address how they'll handle a dispute if and when one arises.

An arbitrator's decision binds the parties as a court would. Yet, arbitrators needn't follow the law precisely; they can do justice as they see fit, which leaves a great deal of wiggle room. And because arbitration is contractual, the party with the superior bargaining power who designs the deal can easily gain the upper hand. You see,

---

[1] *In re* Actos (Pioglitazone) Prods. Liab. Litig., No. 11-md-2299 (W.D. La. Apr. 28, 2015) (order regarding settlement agreement and deadlines). Class notice falls under Federal Rule of Civil Procedure 23(c).

[2] Settlement Agreement at § 1.01(A), *In re* Yasmin & Yaz (Drospirenone) Mktg., Sales Practices Prods. Liab. Litig., No. 09-md-2100 (S.D. Ill., Mar. 15, 2013); *In re* Yasmin & Yaz (Drospirenone) Mktg., Sales Practices Prods. Liab. Litig., No. 09-md-2100 (S.D. Ill., Mar. 15, 2013) (case management order 60, at 2).

[3] Some states now require parties to mediate before they will set a trial date, and in federal court the Alternative Dispute Resolution Act of 1998 requires each district to authorize, devise, and implement its own program. 28 U.S.C. §§ 651 et seq. (2012).

arbitration treats court procedures as a menu of options, allowing the contract drafter to pick and choose which ones to apply – or not. Embedding arbitration provisions in ordinary consumer and employment contracts has become a standard way for corporations to take disputes out of the courts and "resolve" them on their own terms: they can pick the arbitrator, dictate the procedures used, and select which evidence the arbitrator may consider.

Back in 1925 when Congress passed the Federal Arbitration Act, arbitration was used primarily by mutually consenting businesses for commercial transactions. Today, however, envelope stuffers, customer e-mails, and blanket notices allow arbitration's tentacles to reach their way into every aspect of consumers' lives. Although arbitration provisions must be written, they needn't be signed. So, renting a car, purchasing a cell phone, updating software, and even entering a nursing home or starting a new job can mean that you "consented" to arbitrate (not litigate) your disputes.

Until now, torts have remained relatively unblemished by arbitration. Unless you're a wrestler or ultimate fighter, you probably don't agree to get hurt. So there is no contract in which to insert an arbitration provision. And when tort victims settle, the dispute is usually over. But mass-tort settlement programs in multidistrict proceedings don't *end* disputes – they contractually move disputes out of the courts and into private resolution. That move puts ADR's menu of options back on the table.

In both *NuvaRing* and *Actos*, for instance, participating in the settlement program meant agreeing to ADR and waiving all rights to pursue relief in court.[4] And in the *Zimmer Durom Hip Cup* litigation we saw Judge Wigenton order elderly plaintiffs to participate in 18 months of mediation under that settlement program. Likewise, in *DePuy ASR*, the claims administrators sat as arbitrators under the Federal Arbitration Act; in *American Medical Systems*, all challenges and disputes over pelvic-mesh payouts went directly to JAMS, a for-profit arbitration company; and in the *Conserve Hip Implant* proceeding against Wright Medical, the court appointed a special master from JAMS to preside over the private settlement, used its "inherent authority" to give that special master the final say over any settlement appeal, and prohibited judicial review of those appeals.[5]

Why might this move into ADR be troubling? Consider consumer arbitration, for instance. The Chamber of Commerce claims that consumer arbitration is cheaper and faster, and that consumers like it.[6] But evidence shows otherwise.

---

[4]   Master Settlement Agreement at § 11.03(C), *In re* NuvaRing Prods. Liab. Litig., No. 08-md-1964 (E.D. Mo. Feb. 7, 2014); Master Settlement Agreement at § 14.03, *In re* Actos (Pioglitazone) Prods. Liab. Litig., No. 11-md-2299 (W.D. La. Apr. 28, 2015).

[5]   *In re* Wright Medical Tech., Inc. Conserve Hip Implant Prods. Liab. Litig., No. 12-md-2329 (N.D. Ga. Dec. 1, 2016) (case management order no. 5).

[6]   Lisa A. Rickard, President, *U.S. Chamber Institute for Legal Reform, Letter to the Editor, N.Y. Times*, Nov. 14, 2005.

Several years ago, the *New York Times* ran a front-page series entitled *Arbitration Everywhere, Stacking the Deck of Justice*, which illustrated the many ways in which American corporations use arbitration to take disputes out of court and deter consumers from exercising their rights. Through arbitration, corporations free themselves from class actions and small claims: assembling four years of records from arbitration companies nationwide, *The Times* found only 505 instances where consumers arbitrated a dispute for $2,500 or less.[7] "[O]nly a lunatic or a fanatic sues for $30," explained one federal judge.[8]

When *Fortune* magazine's top 100 companies bargain with each another, less than one-tenth of them choose to arbitrate.[9] Nearly all prefer court. When those same companies contract with those who have less say, sophistication, or bargaining power, however, more than three-quarters include mandatory arbitration provisions.[10] So businesses favor arbitration when it helps their bottom line – where power imbalances exist and where others' consent is weak, at best.

Many parallels exist between outright arbitration and postsettlement ADR. Just as arbitrators preside over a dispute, *claims administrators* preside over the settlement program. They interpret the agreement creating the program, review confidential guidance documents, consider evidence, and decide whether a plaintiff is eligible to receive money under the program (though she's already entered the program and dismissed her lawsuit). If she's eligible, administrators then decide how much money she's entitled to receive.

Special settlement masters may be certified arbitrators or mediators and their work varies by proceeding. Some hear appeals from parties unhappy with claims administrators' decisions while others play the role of a claims administrator in law-firm-by-law-firm inventory settlements – they calculate, allocate, divide, and distribute payments among plaintiffs. Still others resolve settlement-related disputes as they arise and bind parties to their decisions.

Regardless of their duties, however, like arbitrators, claims administrators and special settlement masters may hope to maintain and foster business by courting the insiders who select them. So, just as consumers might worry about impartiality when they must arbitrate before someone who's repeatedly paid by the companies on the

---

[7] Jessica Silver-Greenberg & Robert Gebeloff, *Arbitration Everywhere, Stacking the Deck of Justice*, N.Y. TIMES, Oct. 31, 2015, at A1.

[8] Carnegie v. Household Int'l, Inc., 376 F.3d 656, 661 (7th Cir. 2004).

[9] Theodore Eisenberg et al., *Mandatory Arbitration for Customers But Not for Peers: A Study of Arbitration Clauses in Consumer and Non-Consumer Contracts*, 92 JUDICATURE 118, 119 (2008); *see also* Theodore Eisenberg & Geoffrey P. Miller, *The Flight from Arbitration: An Empirical Study of Ex Ante Arbitration Clauses in the Contracts of Publicly Held Companies*, 56 DEPAUL L. REV. 335 (2007) (finding that large corporate firms included arbitration provisions in only 11% of their contracts with one another).

[10] Eisenberg et al., *supra* note 9, at 119.

other side, mass-tort plaintiffs may fret over whether repeat claims administrators and special settlement masters can be even-handed.

As in arbitration (and settlement more broadly), plaintiffs' settlement awards are almost always confidential. So plaintiffs in the same proceeding cannot compare notes to see whether they were treated favorably vis-à-vis their peers. And if a plaintiff recovers nothing or is dissatisfied with her award, sometimes she must "appeal" to the same claims administrator who already determined her fate. Nor can she return to court. Of the 10 proceedings with publicly available private deals, opting into 80% of them extinguished a plaintiff's lawsuit outright.

This impacts the public too. Litigation's discovery process helps dredge up information that could prove crucial to regulators. Judicial rulings create precedent, which makes the law more predictable. Trials allow community members to participate in a democratic process where the rich and the poor are viewed equally before the law. But, like arbitration, settlement programs may short circuit this public goods-generating process by sweeping important controversies under the rug.

More broadly, thinking about settlement programs as a form of ADR suggests that mass-tort "litigation" is better explained as a series of bargaining constraints designed to yield what defendants could not contract for at the outset: private dispute resolution. Litigation simply helps determine who has the upper hand in the negotiations. The fight begins over whether and where to centralize the multidistrict proceedings and which judge will preside. When an experienced MDL jurist receives the proceeding, that can signal which attorneys will occupy leadership roles, the ground rules for resolving the dispute, and the parameters for lead plaintiffs' lawyers' common-benefit fees. After all, some judges are repeat players too, and insiders are privy to their playbook.

These characteristics suggest a troubling conclusion: by implementing private dispute resolution programs once litigation begins, mass-tort defendants may be able to regain some of the advantages they enjoy in the consumer context. As defendants hash out private settlements before the court can issue any adverse substantive rulings (as nearly one-third of defendants did), they prevent judges from refining tort law in ways that could disserve their long-term interests. Unfavorable precedent acutely impacts repeat players. So, by settling, corporate defendants not only avoid adverse precedent but may also reframe litigation as a regulatory cost: tort suits are like fines, just the price of doing business – not a public condemnation that warrants change.

SETTLING WITH BLINDERS ON

Arbitral consent is frequently fictitious. As Judge Jed Rakoff lamented, "[W]hile appellate courts still pay lip service to the 'precious right' of trial by jury," so long as "the consumer is notified in some passing way," federal district courts must "enforce what everyone recognizes is a totally coerced waiver of both the right to a jury and the right of access to the courts."[11]

Although mass-tort plaintiffs must consciously sign settlement documents, they can be coerced into doing so. Chapter 2 described how 84% of the dataset's private settlements required attorneys to recommend them to all their clients and 53% insisted that lawyers withdraw from representing those who refused. Judges are of little help here, as Chapter 4 explained. They seem more inclined to assist lawyers by nudging reluctant plaintiffs into the deal than to relieve that settlement pressure.

For a moment, however, set those worries aside and picture a best-case scenario: *Vioxx* plaintiff Linda Isner was atypically situated in many ways – she had an attorney who vigorously represented her, amassed more information about her likely payout than most, and decided to enter the settlement program. Did she give her informed consent?

Here's what you need to know before answering: Linda's husband, Dr. Jeffrey Isner, was on the cutting edge of gene therapy and cardiovascular medicine. Teaching at Tufts University, he was an interventional cardiologist who founded Vascular Genetics and received a $10 million grant from federal health officials shortly before he had a heart attack while taking Vioxx.[12] Consequently, Ms. Isner was worried about whether the *Vioxx* settlement program would fully compensate her (and her three children) for her deceased husband's lost earnings.

When Ms. Isner and her attorney met with Merck's counsel, Ted Mayer, and co-lead plaintiffs' lawyer, Chris Seeger, they promised that she'd receive a full recovery "'dollar for dollar,' subject only to the global cap and the age cap on work-life expectancy." Confirming this in writing, Mayer wrote, "I hope that this is helpful to you and provides comfort that Ms. Isner will be fairly treated in the Program." Claims administrator Orran Brown confirmed, "You have Merck saying 'that is the way [the settlement] is to be read'. You have the plaintiffs' team saying 'that is the way it is to be read'. And you have BrownGreer saying 'that is the way it is to be read'. That's all you need."[13]

Of the two conditions that could limit her award, the global cap was never reached and administrators assigned Mr. Isner a retirement age of 66. But Ms. Isner's award was $3 million less than she anticipated. She argued that the retirement age should be 70 and that, because the global cap wasn't met, her point value should not be discounted based on how many people opted into the fund.

When she sued Seeger, Mayer, and BrownGreer for misrepresentation, however, they pointed out that by signing the settlement release she agreed to its terms, which

---

[11] Meyer v. Kalanick & Uber Techs., Inc., 15 Civ. 9796, 2018 WL 1166641, at *2 (S.D.N.Y. Mar. 5, 2018).

[12] Eric Nagourney, *Dr. Jeffrey Isner, 53, Creator of Cardiovascular Procedure*, N.Y. TIMES (Nov. 2, 2001), https://www.nytimes.com/2001/11/02/us/dr-jeffrey-isner-53-creator-of-cardiovascular-procedure.html.

[13] Opposition of the Plaintiff, Linda Isner, to the Motion for Summary Judgment, *In re* Vioxx Prods. Liab. Litig., No. 05-md-01657 (E.D. La. Mar. 28, 2014).

included the following: "I am entering into this release ... without being induced, pressured or influenced by, and without relying on any representation or other statement made by or on behalf of, Merck or any other person." And "I further acknowledge that I understand this release and the [master settlement agreement] and that there is no guarantee that I will receive any settlement payment or, if any settlement payment is made, the amount thereof."[14]

Judge Fallon held that by entering the program, she agreed to its terms. And under its terms, she also "agreed not to 'institute any proceeding, judicial or otherwise, against Merck, [negotiating plaintiffs' counsel] or [BrownGreer].'" Her claims "are clearly barred," Fallon ruled.[15]

Isner's story raises questions about whether plaintiffs can give informed consent when even with ideal representation they know far less about what they're agreeing to than traditional plaintiffs. Removing lawyers' heavy-handed tactics helps. But it still leaves questions about the preconsent information plaintiffs receive and the interplay with judicial settlement nudges that Chapter 4 described.

In *Vioxx*, for instance, when Merck decided to settle, Judge Fallon explained how he and the state-court judges "went over the document into the wee hours of the morning" before the parties announced it because "[t]here were some changes and some tweaking that was necessary at that time."[16] Settlement designers then appointed Judge Fallon as the deal's "chief administrator."

If a dispute arose while settling claims under the program, it went to Judge Fallon in his capacity as "a binding arbitration panel ... whose decision shall be final, binding and Non-Appealable." If warring parties couldn't agree on the rules he should use, then he would use the American Arbitration Association's Commercial Arbitration Rules.[17]

Judge Fallon thus had one foot in the private deal as an arbitrator and the other in the public dispute as an Article III judge. As a federal judge, he allowed attorneys to withdraw from representing plaintiffs who refused to settle, dismissed ethics challenges to the deal, and invoked the ire of some plaintiffs' attorneys by capping their contingent fees. As a private arbitrator, Judge Fallon's rulings on the claims were final and binding, not subject to appeal as they would be ordinarily.

Nonsettling plaintiffs claimed these dual roles made Judge Fallon appear partial.[18] "The problem," wrote Professor Judith Resnik many years ago, "is whether a judge who helps shape a proposed consent decree [or here, a settlement] can fairly

[14] Brief of Appellees Hughs Hubbard & Reed LLP, Theodore V.H. Mayer, BrownGreer PLC, and Orran L. Brown, *In re* Vioxx Prods. Liab. Litig., No. 15-31070, 2016 WL 4379268 (5th Cir. Aug. 15, 2016).

[15] *In re* Vioxx Prods. Liab. Litig., No. 05-md-01657 (E.D. La. July 2, 2014) (order & reasons, at 13).

[16] Transcript of Status Conference at 12, *In re* Vioxx Prods. Liab. Litig., No. 05-md-1657 (E.D. La. Jan. 18, 2008).

[17] Master Settlement Agreement § 8.1, *In re* Vioxx Prods. Liab. Litig., No. 05-md-1657 (E.D. La. Nov. 9, 2007) [hereinafter Vioxx Settlement].

[18] Petition for a Writ of Certiorari at 5a, *In re* Vioxx Prods. Liab. Litig., No. 10-666, 2010 WL 4717579 (U.S. Nov. 17, 2010).

adjudicate either the adequacy of the representation or the adequacy of the compromise itself."[19] At least one plaintiff, Gene Weeks (the front-end maintainer who worked for Ball Corporation), thought not. He felt his attorney pressured him into accepting the deal. He wanted out. Judge Fallon refused. Just as he did with Ms. Isner, he ruled that Mr. Weeks's decision to enroll was irrevocable.[20]

Appeals to the Fifth Circuit proved fruitless. It rejected both the argument that the settlement's terms coerced Weeks's consent and the contention that Judge Fallon's dual roles created a conflict that demanded he recuse himself.[21] As *Vioxx* plaintiff Al Pennington lamented, "[T]here must be safeguards in place to insure a fair and equitable settlement for both plaintiffs and defendants. Currently, no such safeguards exist. Those plaintiff[s] who signed on to the Vioxx settlement ... were given little or no choice but to accept the settlement."[22]

Informed Consent

Al Pennington, Gene Weeks, and Linda Isner each consented to a process, not a settlement offer. Before agreeing to that process, they lacked the information they needed to make educated settlement decisions. But once they'd agreed to the process, that consent then bound them to the resulting settlement award.

As Table A.7 shows, in 60% of the dataset's publicly available aggregate settlements, plaintiffs had little idea how much (if anything) they would recover if they "settled," or, more accurately, gave up their right to sue to enter a settlement program. In *Propulsid*, *Fosamax*, and *NuvaRing*, for example, the agreements gave plaintiffs no information about their potential recovery. Instead, news reports offered flashy settlement fund numbers – $90 million, $27 million, and $100 million. Granted, 80% of the programs such as those in *Vioxx*, *Yasmin/Yaz*, *DePuy* ASR, *Biomet*, and *Actos*, provided snippets of information like points criteria, allocation tiers, or base awards, but, as Judge Alvin Hellerstein recognized, even those numbers varied depending on how many plaintiffs opted in.

Like Al Pennington, Judge Hellerstein worried about informed consent when he pronounced the proposed settlement in the *World Trade Center* litigation unfair. Whether a plaintiff should settle was like a puzzle with missing pieces – there were "points" but no values ascribed to them. Thinking from plaintiffs' perspective, Judge Hellerstein wondered:

[19] Judith Resnik, *Judging Consent*, 1987 U. CHI. LEGAL F. 43, 97.
[20] *In re* Vioxx Prods. Liab. Litig., Case No. 05-4580, MDL No. 1657, 2010 WL 724084 (E.D. La. Feb. 18, 2010).
[21] *In re* Vioxx Prods. Liab. Litig., 412 F. Appx., 653, 653–54 (5th Cir. Dec. 17, 2010) (denying plaintiff's motion to set aside his consent to settle); *In re* Vioxx Prods. Liab. Litig., 388 F. App'x., 391, 395–97 (5th Cir. July 16, 2010).
[22] Elizabeth Chamblee Burch, *Group Consensus, Individual Consent*, 79 GEO. WASH. L. REV. 506, 514 (2010) (quoting Plaintiffs View, http://plaintiffsview.org/aboutus.html [established by Al Pennington]).

What am I getting? [I]s it worth it for me to give up my chance of getting more or losing everything? What's it going to do with my life? [Plaintiffs] don't know. Nobody in this settlement can figure it out. The points in this settlement can make a Talmudist's head or a canonical scholar's head spin and revolve 24 hours a day and still it would be hard to grasp these numbers.[23]

Plaintiffs couldn't decide in a vacuum. "I will not preside over a settlement that is based on fear or ignorance ... without people fairly being aware of what's at stake for what may be the most important decision of their lives," Judge Hellerstein concluded.[24] But, as the numbers show, he is a judicial outlier.

Informed consent is the backbone of legal ethics rules. What makes consent informed depends on the information revealed and the client's capacity to understand it.[25] Potential clients must consent to the risks of having the same attorney represent them alongside others. And, upon receiving an "aggregate settlement" offer,[26] "the lawyer must inform each [client] about all the material terms of the settlement, including what the other clients will receive."[27] According to the American Bar Association's ethics opinion, this means that clients must learn about the total settlement amount, whether other clients are participating (and, if so, how much they will get), the attorney's fees and costs, and how those costs will be shared.[28]

None of the aggregate settlements in the dataset supplied the information that Model Rule of Professional Conduct 1.8(g) requires. Yet, with the exception of the *Biomet* settlement, opting into a settlement program extinguished a plaintiff's legal claim just as a traditional settlement would. Put simply, most mass-tort plaintiffs in the dataset who entered settlement programs did so without knowing precisely what, if anything, they would receive, and they gave up their right to sue even if the settlement ultimately awarded them nothing.

Should plaintiffs' consent bind them under circumstances like these? Some claim that justice means respecting someone's freely made choice, whatever it is and regardless of whether it is objectively fair, so long as that choice doesn't impinge

[23] Transcript of Proceedings at 57, *In re* World Trade Ctr. Disaster Site Litig., No. 1:21-mc-00100-KH (S.D.N.Y. Mar. 19, 2010).

[24] *Id.* at 57–58.

[25] RESTATEMENT (THIRD) OF THE LAW GOVERNING LAWYERS § 122 cmt. c(i), d (AM. LAW INST. 2000) (discussing the role of client sophistication in informed consent); MODEL RULES OF PROF'L CONDUCT r. 1.7 cmt. 22 (AM. BAR ASS'N 2016).

[26] An aggregate settlement settles "the claims of two or more individual claimants" with interdependent claims, meaning that "the value of each claimant's claim is not based solely on individual case-by-case facts and negotiations." PRINCIPLES OF THE LAW OF AGGREGATE LITIGATION § 3.16 (AM. LAW INST. 2010) (citing Howard M. Erichson, *A Typology of Aggregate Settlements*, 80 NOTRE DAME L. REV. 1769 (2005)).

[27] MODEL RULES OF PROF'L CONDUCT r. 1.8(g) cmt. 13 (AM. BAR ASS'N 2016).

[28] ABA Formal Ethics Op. 06–438 (2006).

on others' rights.[29] From a moral standpoint, however, others argue that consent obligates only when it is the product of a well-informed person's free choice.[30] Just because someone consents to something (like a settlement) doesn't necessarily mean her consent was freely given or that the deal is fair.[31] When plaintiffs like Ms. Isner and Mr. Weeks are dissatisfied by their awards, they find themselves boxed out of the very court system that led them to this predicament in the first place. Judges shrug. A deal's a deal.

Proponents of the status quo suggest that walkaway and withdrawal provisions are must-haves for achieving closure. But settlement documents tell plaintiffs too little. Points, tiers, and evidentiary criteria pretend to equip them with the information they need, while circumventing ethical rules that prescribe a whole list of particulars required for informed consent.

These measures reflect some lawyers' and academics' creative workarounds to Rule 1.8(g). Workarounds suggest that lawyers provide allocation formulas in lieu of specifics on others' claims, ask clients to consent in advance to be bound by a majority vote, seal the walkaway percentages, and employ settlement masters or special masters to divvy up the funds. But these alternatives ensure that crucial information about the material elements of the deal or about intragroup conflicts of interest are either withheld or unknown at the decision point.

For example, the *Principles of the Law of Aggregate Litigation* suggest that an allocation formula should suffice. Plaintiffs would consent to the process rather than the amount.[32] The *Principles* likewise propose substituting a supermajority vote for individual consent. That is, if enough people vote to accept the deal, they would bind everyone – dissenters too. These new procedures could be embedded in the fine print of the attorney's retainer agreement.

On the upside, fights over how money is divvied up shift to an earlier stage where people don't yet know what they might receive and are thus operating behind a veil of ignorance. But, if past behavior indicates the future, trouble could be brewing. You see, the proposal is based on the asbestos bankruptcy provision, § 524(g), which codified the approach used for Combustion Engineering's bankruptcy.

When Combustion Engineering filed bankruptcy, its parent company hired prominent *plaintiffs'* asbestos attorney Joe Rice, to make sure the confirmation vote went smoothly.[33] Despite his ethically compromised position (he represented both the debtor and its asbestos creditors), the company promised Rice a success fee of

---

[29] *See* Anthony T. Kronman, *Contract Law and Distributive Justice*, 89 Yale L.J. 472, 478–79 (1980).

[30] John Rawls, for example, believed that we could be bound by both natural duties and voluntarily incurred obligations, but that those obligations must be construed against a backdrop of preexisting morality. John Rawls, A Theory of Justice 343 (1971).

[31] Michael J. Sandel, Liberalism and the Limits of Justice 106 (2d ed. 1998).

[32] Principles of the Law of Aggregate Litigation, § 3.17 (Am. Law Inst. 2010).

[33] Richard A. Nagareda, Mass Torts in a World of Settlement 169 (2007).

$20 million. Under the bankruptcy procedures, someone exposed to asbestos who may develop no future injury had the same vote as someone with deadly mesothelioma.[34] So Rice flooded the voting pool with weak claims to gerrymander a positive vote.[35] Attorneys could do the same thing under the *Principles* by choosing which clients to accept.

What should change then? If it's true that we must have attorney-recommendation and walkaway provisions to prevent the dreaded holdouts, and that we're going to look the other way while the strong arming occurs, then judges should allow plaintiffs to keep their tort claims alive until they accept the settlement money. Money for a claim's release, not a release in exchange for a chance at recovering something at some point in the future through an opaque process. Acting contrary to this maxim should open attorneys up to disciplinary hearings, for they will have failed to garner clients' informed consent before participating in an aggregate settlement.[36]

But some will ask: *What about the duds, the claims that administrators reject?* Defendants peg somewhere around 30% of all mass-tort plaintiffs' claims as frivolous. Some claims will be unsupported, yes, and administrators will rightfully reject them. If no good-faith basis existed for filing those lawsuits, then our system has a rule and a process for sanctioning the lawyers who brought them.[37]

Some of the claims that corporate defendants lump into this statistic, however, aren't meritless. For a variety of reasons, lead lawyers decide not to develop certain claims. And some claims fall outside of a program's compensable parameters, but lawyers must nevertheless put them into the settlement program to comply with the deal's attorney-recommendation and participation provisions. Those claims might, for instance, lack the narrow evidentiary proofs that settlement administrators require, but could have fared better in court. In *Fosamax*, for instance, the judge permitted evidence to come from either pharmacy records or physician and dental records. But the settlement designers limited proof to pharmacy records. In at least one client's case, this meant the difference between a $500 "category 1" claim and a $80,000 "category 4" case.[38]

So here's a simple idea: settlement money should be exchanged for a claim's release. Plaintiffs shouldn't dismiss their lawsuits in exchange for a gamble at a potential recovery. Settlements aren't lotto tickets. Until now, parties have always

---

[34] Lester Brickman, *Ethical Issues in Asbestos Litigation*, 33 HOFSTRA L. REV. 833, 866 (2005).

[35] NAGAREDA, *supra* note 33, at 170–73.

[36] E.g., *In re* Gatti, 356 Or. 32 (2014) (disciplining an attorney for violating ethics rules 1.8(g) and 1.7).

[37] FED. R. CIV. P. 11.

[38] While the client pushed to reclassify the claim, Merck tried to get the judge to dismiss it with three Lone Pine orders. Osborn Law, P.C.'s Response to Merck's Third Motion for a Lone Pine Order at 3, *In re* Fosamax Prods. Liab. Litig., No. 06-md-1789 (S.D.N.Y. June 18, 2014). Although the attorney staved off dismissal with a series of extensions, the record doesn't show what the plaintiff received – the ultimate settlement was confidential.

dismissed their lawsuits knowing what they'll receive when they do. Mass torts shouldn't be any different.

If plaintiffs knew that, collectively, they'd all be better off putting up with some coercive practices that force them together and push them to accept a deal, then some might be willing to tolerate an all's-well-that-ends-well approach so long as fair procedures exist to divvy up their settlement proceeds.

Settling has become such a lucrative business that it has spawned an entire support network filled with claims administrators, lien resolution groups, settlement masters, and special masters. And though their incentives vary, each is a repeat player. None works for free, only a handful receive the vast majority of the business, and, as they clamor for repeat business, the worry is that they may shade their substantive judgments accordingly. So, even if plaintiffs are willing to tolerate some attorney arm twisting and judicial nudges if they lead to a fair outcome, plaintiffs would still worry about having a biased allocation czar.

Claims Administrators and Special Settlement Masters

Chapter 3's social network included attorneys and proceedings, not settlement administrators or special settlement masters. But these actors may impact settlement design significantly. Of all the settlements within the dataset, provisions within *DePuy ASR, NuvaRing, Actos,* and *Yasmin/Yaz* closely resembled one another. Many clauses were identical. Each included the most advanced versions of attorney-withdrawal clauses, walkaway provisions, and case-census orders. The proceedings didn't all have the same leaders, though. What they shared was the claims administrator – BrownGreer, which is one of a handful of repeat administrators along with Providio and Garretson Resolution Group.[39]

On the special master front, tracking the careers of a just few could give you an extensive history of mass torts. Louisiana defense lawyer Patrick Juneau served as a special master in *Propulsid, Silicone Gel Breast Implants, Vioxx, Guidant Defibrillators, Avandia, Toyota's Unintended Acceleration,* and *Deepwater Horizon,* to name but a few. And after Judge Marina Corodemus presided over all New Jersey's *Propulsid* cases, she retired and began her own ADR law firm, serving as a special master in *DePuy ASR*, American Medical Systems' pelvic-mesh cases, and *Vioxx.* She also joined for-profit arbitration company JAMS, and teamed up with HB Litigation Conferences, which hosts mass-tort continuing education programs and

---

[39] For a visual connection between these entities, see Elizabeth Chamblee Burch & Margaret S. Williams, *Repeat Players in Multidistrict Litigation: The Social Network*, 102 CORNELL L. REV. 1445, 1503 (2017).

charges $695 per attendee. Similarly, Cathy Yanni works full-time for JAMS, and has served as a settlement master or special master in litigation over *Opioids, DePuy ASR, Ortho Evra, Zyprexa, Avandia, Gadolinium, Breast Implants, Baycol, Yasmin/ Yaz, Fen-Phen*, and a host of lawsuits against pelvic-mesh manufacturers (where she charges plaintiffs $2,000 to appeal her initial award).

These individuals and organizations do not preside over private settlements by happenstance. Negotiating lead lawyers jointly move to appoint a particular person. Professor Bryant Garth describes those selected as a "special elite group ... who provide tailor-made justice geared specifically to large business disputes." Like the *"lex mercatoria"* who served merchants' needs while making a living off of them, this system "is also a means for those with market value as high-end dispute profession-als – including judges – to cash in on that market value." Those accepted into this elite cadre, Garth explains, "must be people acceptable to the parties who are repeat players."[40]

Concerns over shading justice toward repeat players crop up all the time in arbitration. Even though the nation's largest arbitration firms, American Arbitration Association and JAMS, require arbitrators to divulge conflicts of interest, the *New York Times* reported "more than 30 arbitrators said in interviews that the pressure to rule for companies that give them business was real." "[C]ompanies can steer cases to friendly arbitrators," and "some arbitrators cultivate close ties with companies to get business," concluded the reporters.[41] One JAMS arbitrator, for instance, had 29 cases simultaneously involving the same payday lender.

Similar concerns afflict "futures representatives" in asbestos bankruptcies (those who represent people exposed to asbestos whose injuries haven't yet manifested). Like arbitrators, special masters, and claims administrators, futures representatives hope to become repeat players – "someone whom later bankruptcy courts and debtors would feel comfortable placing in a similar role again," explains Professor Richard Nagareda. To do this in the bankruptcy context, though, one must put up "just enough resistance to secure some nominal concessions" but not protest "so much as to scuttle the plan entirely," he notes. Scrapping the plan would mean that there was no fund from which that representative could get paid. So, Nagareda argues, becoming a repeat player means "pulling one's punches" and "going along to get along."[42]

Like futures representatives and arbitrators, special masters and claims administrators clamor for future business. But there's a twist: repeat players on both sides of the aisle occupy decision-making roles. And all settlement designers must agree on the person or entity selected. Special masters and claims administrators

---

[40] Bryant G. Garth, *Tilting the Justice System: From ADR as Idealistic Movement to a Segmented Market in Dispute Resolution*, 18 GA. ST. UNIV. L. REV. 927, 930, 939 (2002).

[41] Jessica Silver-Greenberg & Michael Corkery, *In Arbitration, a "Privatization of the Justice System,"* N.Y. TIMES, Nov. 1, 2015, at A1.

[42] NAGAREDA, *supra* note 33, at 177.

who favor one side outright are unlikely to be retained again. Remember, however, that what's good for defendants and plaintiffs' *lawyers* isn't always good for the *plaintiffs*. When judgment calls pit insiders against one-shot plaintiffs (or one-shot attorneys), there may be a tendency to err on the side of keeping one's future employers happy.

The same insiders administer class-action settlements too, and similar issues arise there. Whereas private deals in the MDL context cover up the bumps like shoes over bunions, mass tort class actions tend to air them – bunions and all. So, despite their unusual class status, the more transparent personal-injury claims processes in the Deepwater Horizon Oil Spill and National Football League's concussion settlement give us a glimpse into how settlement masters and claims administrators might tilt their decisions in ways that help insiders at outsiders' expense.

Deepwater Horizon

In litigation over BP's Deepwater Horizon oil spill, allegations surfaced that special master Pat Juneau's claims team showed favoritism toward the repeat players who appointed them by expediting steering committee members' clients over earlier filed claims.[43] To dig deeper, Judge Carl Barbier appointed former FBI director Louis Freeh. After investigating for two months, Freeh published a 98-page report citing "ample evidence that three attorneys worked together to corrupt a settlement process."[44]

The wrongdoing ranged. One of Juneau's employees, Lionel "Tiger" Sutton, allegedly conspired with two outside lawyers to hide around $40,000 in referral fees and then expedited an $8 million award to one of those lawyer's firms. According to Freeh, two of Juneau's employees (Sutton and his wife) worked with claims administrator BrownGreer to "promote BG's own business and financial interests within the [claims administration office] in an effort to resist and to undermine the implementation of new business practices which would control costs and eliminate inefficiencies." Other staff members said they felt like BrownGreer "was not always receptive of their concerns and was generally unaccountable."[45]

The CEO of Juneau's claims administration office also apparently tried to use his position to cultivate new business for himself. He submitted a proposal to "perform work under [BrownGreer's] supervision" in the *Chinese Drywall* litigation, which was also pending in New Orleans. BrownGreer eventually reported this submission

[43] Jason Brad Berry, *DHECC – Proof Positive of Claims Being Expedited by the PSC*, AM. ZOMBIE (Mar. 11, 2014), http://www.theamericanzombie.com/2014/03/dhecc-proof-positive-of-claims-being.html.

[44] Report of Special Master Louis J. Freeh at 8–9, *In re* Oil Spill by the Oil Rig "Deepwater Horizon" in the Gulf of Mexico, on April 20, 2010 No. 10-md-02179 (E.D. La. Sept. 6, 2013).

[45] *Id.*

to Juneau and the CEO withdrew his proposal. "Despite the clear ethical 'tone at the top' and sound written policies established by Mr. Patrick Juneau, many of his key executives and senior attorneys engaged in conduct which the Special Master finds to be improper, unethical, or not in accordance with the [claims committee's] Code of Conduct," Freeh wrote.[46]

Juneau told the *New York Times* that he "was essentially a bystander in disputes between BP and the plaintiffs' lawyers."[47] But some journalists, including the *Times* reporter, questioned this. Independent reporter Jason Berry conducted an in-depth interview with Tiger Sutton (one of Juneau's discharged attorneys). In it, Sutton explains how he'd known Juneau for years, that he'd disclosed the prior client referrals to him, and that checking on and expediting claims was his job. In short, Sutton alleges that he became Juneau's fall guy.[48]

NFL Concussion

The allegations arising out of the *NFL Concussion* settlement bear similar hallmarks of insiders' close relationships, but add third-party funders into the mix. The accusations are dramatic enough that even a soap-opera script writer might have a hard time pitching them. It all began as retired players claimed that the National Football League knew about the evidence and risks of repetitive brain injuries (such as chronic traumatic encephalopathy [CTE], Alzheimer's, Parkinson's, ALS, dementia, and death), but ignored and concealed that information from them.

What began as a typical nonclass multidistrict proceeding turned into a mass tort class action, which Judge Anita Brody (who presided over the MDL) eventually deemed fair. Our story is the tale of what happened next, how some plaintiffs' attorneys' conflicted financial interests and ties to third-party financiers may have allowed them to profit from the very delay that they were positioned to create. And how claims administrators, who are beholden to those same attorneys for future business, may have turned a blind eye.

Many retired players needed their settlement money sooner, not later. But most states' ethics rules prohibit lawyers from loaning money to clients for living expenses

---

[46] *Id.* at 8–9, 74, 85–93.

[47] Joe Nocera, *Getting Skewered in New Orleans*, N.Y. TIMES (July 19, 2013), https://www.nytimes .com/2013/07/20/opinion/nocera-getting-skewered-in-new-orleans.html.

[48] Jason Brad Berry, *DHECC – Lionel Sutton Interview Part 2 – How the "Go-to-Guy" Became the Fall Guy*, AM. ZOMBIE (May 27, 2014), http://www.theamericanzombie.com/2014/05/dhecc-lionel-sutton-interview-part-2.html. Mr. Berry has broken a number of high-profile stories. E.g., Michael Patrick Welch, *Meet the New Orleans Blogger Whose Story on Senator David Vitter's Alleged Love Child Could Derail His Campaign*, VICE (Oct. 26, 2015, 5:30 PM), https://www.vice.com/en_us/article/kwx9pe/jason-brad-berry-david-vitter-121 ("Independent journalist Jason Brad Berry has broken big stories before, but his latest might change the course of the Louisiana gubernatorial race.").

because it "gives lawyers too great a financial stake in the litigation."[49] So plaintiffs experiencing financial hardship had to go to third-party lenders who can do what attorneys can't. Financiers like Esquire Bank, Cash4Cases, LawCash, and RD Legal Funding loaned players advances on their settlement proceeds, much like tax-refund anticipation loans – all in return for substantial interest. The longer the settlement program takes to pay them, the more money financiers earn. Players will get cash advances then wait, wait some more, then pay up once they're paid.

If lawyers hold stock in those third-party funders, they may profit from bogging down players' settlement awards. The longer it takes to administer claims, the more players will seek financing. And the longer the life of the loan, the more the funder and its shareholders will profit. When claims administrators pay plaintiffs, financiers' stakes and attorneys' fees come off the top of that award. So, lawyers who partner with (or become) third-party investors could profit twice, though at some point their desire to be paid attorneys' fees will likely compete with lengthier loan periods.

A year into administering the *NFL* claims, the *Boston Globe* reported that Chris Seeger, who helped lead the proceeding and represents 20 players, "has been widely criticized for not fighting aggressively enough against the NFL over rules and moves that have negatively affected player claims" and that the settlement was "on the brink of collapse."[50] Co-class counsel Larry Coben and Gene Locks tried to get the settlement program back on track: Coben asked the court to streamline the adminis-trative process and Locks, who represented around 1,100 players, requested to be named "administrative class counsel."[51] Locks also accused the NFL of turning "the Settlement into a secret, privately litigated claim system that involves changing standards" and of "luring" BrownGreer, the Appeals Advisory Panel, and the special masters into second-guessing doctors' diagnoses.[52]

Despite support from law firms representing the most players,[53] Judge Brody denied Gene Locks's request to become administrative class counsel and take over Seeger's position. Seeger is doing "a fine job" of "protecting all Members of the Class," she wrote. In her view, Locks's involvement with "facilitating Third-Party

---

[49] MODEL RULES OF PROF'L CONDUCT r. 1.8 cmt. 10 (AM. BAR. ASS'N 2016).

[50] Bob Hohler, *Billion-Dollar NFL Concussion Settlement "On the Brink of Collapse,"* BOS. GLOBE, Mar. 30, 2018.

[51] Motion of Class Counsel the Locks Law Firm for Appointment of Administrative Class Counsel, *In re* NFL Players' Concussion Injury Litig., No. 12-md-02323 (E.D. Pa. Mar. 20, 2018); Motion of Co-Lead Class Counsel Anapol Weiss for a Hearing to Seek Court Intervention on the Processing of Certain Claims, *In re* NFL Players' Concussion Injury Litig., No. 12-md-02323 (E.D. Pa. Mar. 19, 2018).

[52] Motion of Class Counsel the Locks Law Firm for Appointment of Administrative Class Counsel, *In re* NFL Players' Concussion Injury Litig., No. 12-md-02323 (E.D. Pa. Mar. 20, 2018).

[53] Matthew Guarnaccia, *NFL Players' Firms Back Concussion Suit Settlement Counsel,* LAW360 (Apr. 4, 2018, 6:36 PM), https://www.law360.com/articles/1029760/nfl-players-firms-back-con cussion-suit-settlement-counsel.

Funding Agreements to Class members prohibited under the Settlement Agreement" doomed him.[54]

This allegation linking Locks to third-party financiers came from Chris Seeger's motion opposing Locks's request. Seeger claimed Locks was "not fit" to become administrative class counsel because in his discovery to date, "I have learned that Locks has acknowledged and signed off on at least 28 funding agreements that assigned all or part of 16 of its clients' claims." These funding agreements, Seeger explained, compound interest rates. This means that an annual rate could be "in excess of 38% for the first year" and grow "exponentially in subsequent years."[55]

Citing to the settlement, which prohibited players from assigning their claims to third parties, Judge Brody voided predatory deals with 15 third-party lenders.[56] She later ordered attorneys applying for common-benefit fees to disclose whether any of their clients entered into agreements with the banned funders. She also wanted to know about "any agreements that are similar" to those, and "any other role that you, your law firm, or any attorney associated with your law firm may have had in creating, promoting, or facilitating" those assignments.[57]

Because Seeger represented only a handful of clients who hadn't accepted funding, he responded "no" and "not applicable."[58] So too did co-lead class counsel Arnold Levin, who limited his responses to those funders on the banned list (defining them collectively as Third Party Litigation Funder). "No LSB [Levin Sedran & Berman] attorney or attorney associated with LSB has a direct or indirect association with any Third Party Litigation Funder used by Settlement Class members," he declared.[59]

But both Seeger and Levin had close ties to one of the third-party financiers that Seeger chastised Locks for allowing his clients to use. NFL players' attorney Craig Mitnick (who referred many of his cases to Gene Locks) later explained how Seeger asked him to "meet with and assist Esquire [Bank] in developing a funding program for retired players." "Craig," wrote Seeger, "I want to introduce you to a close

[54] *In re* NFL Players' Concussion Injury Litig., No. 12-md-02323 (E.D. Pa. Apr. 18, 2018) (order). In denying his request for reconsideration, Judge Brody later wrote that she had "enlisted the Locks Firm to lead the coordination of the Third-Party Funder settlement-implementation issues" and that "the Locks Firm has performed admirably in that role." *In re* NFL Players' Concussion Injury Litig., No. 12-md-02323 (E.D. Pa. July 2, 2018) (order).
[55] Declaration of Christopher A. Seeger at ¶30, *In re* NFL Players' Concussion Injury Litig., No. 12-md-02323 (E.D. Pa. Apr. 13, 2018).
[56] *In re* NFL Players' Concussion Injury Litig., No. 12-md-02323 (E.D. Pa. Dec. 8, 2017) (explanation and order).
[57] *In re* NFL Players' Concussion Injury Litig., No. 12-md-02323 (E.D. Pa. Mar. 28, 2018) (order).
[58] Declaration of Christopher A. Seeger, *In re* NFL Players' Concussion Injury Litig., No. 12-md-02323 (E.D. Pa. May 1, 2018).
[59] Declaration of Arnold Levin, *In re* NFL Players' Concussion Injury Litig., No. 12-md-02323 (E.D. Pa. Apr. 10, 2018).

friend ... who works for a bank with a special relationship to the plaintiffs' bar."[60] Seeger e-mailed Mitnick on February 13, 2015 – the same day that Seeger filed the NFL class settlement.[61]

From 2012 until May 2016, Chris Seeger sat on Esquire Bank's parent company's board of directors (Esquire Financial). Seeger's remark about the bank's "special relationship" alludes to the fact that mass-tort lawyers Russ Herman, John Morgan, and Marc Grossman helped found it and that Herman and Morgan remain on Esquire Financial's board. And despite wordsmithing his *NFL* declaration, in the *Chinese Drywall* lawsuits, Arnold Levin declared, "I personally purchased 8,000 shares of Esquire Financial Holdings, Inc. for $100,000.00 on November 30, 2012, and continue to hold this investment."[62] As we'll see in a moment, both this and his *NFL* declaration are technically accurate because Seeger never included Esquire Bank on the list of forbidden funders.

When Esquire Financial went public, it boasted about how the delays inherent in claims administration provide it with "loan and deposit opportunities." As of December 2017, "NFL loans represented $21.8 million or 85.3% of our total post-settlement loans," wrote Esquire Financial in its 10-K filing. "[O]ur post-settlement consumer loans to claimants should increase based upon recent mass tort settlements including, but not limited to, the World Trade Center Victims Compensation Fund and the NFL Concussion case."[63]

Esquire Financial flaunts its close ties to mass-tort lawyers. It brags that its advisory board members and investors "are well-known, influential market figures and active members of some of the leading litigation law firms in the nation." And it asserts, "[W]e rely heavily on our directors' and our advisory board members' extensive business and personal contacts and relationships to help establish and maintain our customer base."[64] Nowhere, however, does it disclose the names of those investors or advisory board members.

Meanwhile, the NFL claimed that "widespread fraud" infected the settlement program and asked Judge Brody to appoint a special investigator. It alleged that players' lawyers coached them on how to answer neuropsychological exams, sent them to pediatric neurologists, and submitted reports that included identical

[60] Letter to The Honorable Anita Brody from Craig Mitnick, *In re* NFL Players' Concussion Injury Litig., No. 12-md-02323 (E.D. Pa. Apr. 16, 2018).

[61] Class Counsel & the NFL Parties' Joint Submission, *In re* NFL Players' Concussion Injury Litig., No. 12-md-02323 (E.D. Pa. Feb. 13, 2015).

[62] Declaration of Arnold Levin at ¶ 6, *In re* Chinese Manufactured Drywall Prods. Liab. Litig., No. 09-md-2047 (E.D. La. June 26, 2018).

[63] Yance Law Firms Motion to Immediately Transfer Attorney Fee Qualified Settlement Fund to a Different Depository Bank, Exhibit A, *In re* Chinese Manufactured Drywall Prods. Liab. Litig., No. 09-md-2047 (E.D. La. May 18, 2018).

[64] Esquire Financial Holdings, Inc., Prospectus, June 26, 2017.

vital signs for 21 different players.[65] Gene Locks opposed the NFL's motion as "unnecessary" and worried that it would cause further delay, whereas Chris Seeger agreed that a "Special Investigator could be a valuable source of information."[66]

The retired players were caught in limbo. New England Patriots fans might remember Ronnie Lippett, a hard-hitting defensive back in the 1980s who played nine seasons and started in the Patriots' first Super Bowl. He went on to parent 26 of the most severely physically and sexually abused foster children in Massachusetts. Today, he forgets what he planned to say, stutters, and carries a spiral notebook with phone numbers, his itinerary, and his favorite Bible verses whenever he leaves home. "I know I'm not going to live that long," he said. "I'm fighting to take care of my wife and kids and grandkids after I'm gone, but I'm getting set up to fail."[67] Although a board-certified neurologist diagnosed Lippett with a qualifying injury, BrownGreer denied his claim. This was not unusual. A year after the settlement began, it had paid less than 0.6% of dementia claims.

Ronnie Lippett's lawyer, who helped initiate the proceedings, said that Lippett "is a poster child of somebody who is supposed to get a payment." But "[e]verybody is being roadblocked."[68]

Craig Mitnick's e-mails along with declarations from Steven Marks and Gene Locks explain how Chris Seeger steered cash-strapped retired players to Esquire Bank where they could receive interest-charging advances on their settlement money.[69] Mitnick's e-mails also show that Seeger and his law partner, David Buchanan, helped calculate payments to retired players.[70] And of the 32 funding

---

[65] Memorandum of Law in Support of NFL's Motion for the Appointment of a Special Investigator, *In re* NFL Players' Concussion Injury Litig., No. 12-md-02323 (E.D. Pa. Apr. 13, 2018).

[66] Response in Opposition, *In re* NFL Players' Concussion Injury Litig., No. 12-md-02323 (E.D. Pa. Apr. 27, 2018); Response of Co-Lead Class Counsel to Motion for the Appointment of Special Investigator, *In re* NFL Players' Concussion Injury Litig., No. 12-md-02323 (E.D. Pa. Apr. 27, 2018).

[67] Hohler, *supra* note 50.

[68] Bob Hohler, *Denied Benefits, Delayed Payments, and the Bureaucratic Roadblocks of the NFL's Concussion Settlement*, Bos. GLOBE (Mar. 17, 2018), https://www.bostonglobe.com/sports/pat riots/2018/03/17/denied-benefits-delayed-payments-and-bureaucratic-roadblocks-nfl-concussion-settlement/rEDWWKRygxJod2VvB74oaM/story.html; Hohler, *supra* note 50.

[69] Declaration of Gene Locks, *In re* NFL Players' Concussion Injury Litig., No. 12-md-02323 (E.D. Pa. May 1, 2018); Declaration of Steven C. Marks & Ricardo M. Martinez-Cid, *In re* NFL Players' Concussion Injury Litig., No. 12-md-02323 (E.D. Pa. May 1, 2018). Locks pointed out these ties in moving to request that Judge Brody reconsider his earlier request to become administrative class counsel. She denied that request, but withdrew her remarks about his role in third-party funding. *In re* NFL Players' Concussion Injury Litig., No. 12-md-02323-AB (E.D. Pa. July 2, 2018) (order).

[70] Peter Keating, *Documents Allege Lead Attorney in NFL Concussion Deal Did Not Disclose Conflict of Interest*, ESPN (Apr. 26, 2018), http://www.espn.com/espn/otl/story/_/id/23324920/court-documents-lay-another-ugly-allegation-nfl-concussion-deal.

agreements that Gene Locks ultimately "signed off on" (in Seeger's words), 29 were funded by Esquire Bank.[71]

Esquire Bank works hand in hand with third-party lender LawCash. Before his death in August 2018, Dennis Shields, one of Esquire Bank's founders, directors, and executive officers was also LawCash's CEO, and Ari Kornhaber moved from Law-Cash's National Marketing Director to Esquire Bank's Director of Sales.[72] When LawCash needs funding, Esquire Bank makes the loans.[73] When lawyers need money to bankroll suits, LawCash refers them to Esquire Bank: Why use your own money to fund cases? asks LawCash's website. Instead, "[Y]ou could borrow money from a third-party like Esquire bank and either write off the interest as a business expense, or ... pass along the interest to your clients, thereby getting virtually an interest-free loan."[74]

Retired NFL players used both LawCash and Esquire Bank for postsettlement loans. In August 2016, LawCash paid $1.3 million to settle Colorado Attorney General's claims that it offered "predatory interest rates."[75] And though most players' funding agreements were not publicly available, the NFL docket did include one LawCash loan. In it, LawCash charged 3.25% monthly compounded interest.[76]

A 3.25% monthly compounded interest rate sounds reasonable. But, as Seeger spelled out in objecting to Locks's motion to become administrative class counsel, monthly compounded interest can be "deceptive" and he noted some were "as high as 2.75%." He explained, "While this may seem like a low interest rate on its face the rate translates to an effective annual interest rate in excess of 38% for the first year, and grows exponentially in subsequent years." In Seeger's example, a retired player receiving a $100,000 advance with a 2.75% monthly compounded interest rate would owe the funder almost double, or $191,000, two years later and would owe more than $265,000 three years later.[77]

[71] Declaration of Gene Locks, *In re* NFL Players' Concussion Injury Litig., No. 18-md-02323 (E.D. Pa. May 1, 2018).

[72] Dennis Shields, *Esquire Bank Supports Trial Attorneys in the Fight for Justice: Most Other Banks Do the Opposite*, LawCash (May 2, 2017), https://www.lawcash.net/esquire-bank-supports-trial-attorneys-fight-justice-banks-opposite/. For fans of the Real Housewives franchise, before he died of a possible overdose in August 2018, Shields had an on–off relationship with Bethenny Frankel, who has an onscreen feud with Erika Jayne, who is married to elite lead lawyer Tom Girardi, who you might recall from the *Avandia* fee fight.

[73] Esquire Financial Holdings, Inc., Prospectus at 106, June 26, 3017.

[74] LawCash, https://www.lawcash.net/video/esquire-capital/; Complaint at 8, Hirschhorn v. LawCash, No. 13-cv-02360 (E.D.N.Y. Apr. 18, 2013).

[75] Joe Rubino, *Colorado AG Distributing More Than $2.3 Million from 2016 Lendig Settlement*, Denver Post (Jan. 23, 2018, 6:00 AM), https://www.denverpost.com/2018/01/23/colorado-predatory-lending-settlement/.

[76] Declaration of Richard S. Lewis Pursuant to the Court's Order Dated March 28, 2018, Exhibit 5, *In re* NFL Players' Concussion Injury Litig., No. 12-md-02323 (E.D. Pa. Apr. 26, 2018).

[77] Opposition of Co-Lead Class Counsel Christopher A. Seeger to Motion of the Locks Firm for Appointment of Administrative Class Counsel at 17, *In re* NFL Players' Concussion Injury Litig., No. 12-md-02323 (E.D. Pa. Apr. 13, 2018).

Indeed, the *New York Post* reported that, in other cases, LawCash charged interest rates as high as 124% and courted plaintiffs' attorneys for business. "They took me to a football game at MetLife Stadium, the Hertz suite," said lawyer Andrew Plasse. "You're talking big money: two tickets and parking. It was fantastic," he recalled.[78]

Curiously, however, neither LawCash nor Esquire Bank appeared on Seeger and Judge Brody's no-pay list, which differentiated between permissible lenders with standard loan contracts and "unscrupulous" lenders who sought to have players' settlement rights assigned to them.[79] But both the banned funders and Esquire Bank include an "assignment of rights" clause – the language that Brody's order interprets the settlement agreement to forbid. As Gene Locks argued, there is "no basis for any distinction under the Settlement Agreement between the validity of advances offered by most funders and advances offered by Esquire Bank."[80] Following Judge Brody's order, however, BrownGreer and the special masters decided that Esquire Bank's advances were permissible under the settlement agreement – the others weren't.

Consider the big picture for a moment: retired players are unhappy – the settlement program is taking too long and denying what they argue should be compensable claims.[81] As of May 21, 2018, BrownGreer had deemed only 29% of their claims payable. The other 71% were: denied (18.2%), denied after an audit (9.7%), or sent back for more information (42.5%).[82] The longer it takes to pay the awards, the more likely it is that players in need of money will turn to outfits like

[78] Shawn Cohen et al., *Inside the Cottage Industry that's Fleecing NYC Taxpayers*, NEW YORK POST (Jan. 2, 2018, 11:15 PM), https://nypost.com/2018/01/02/how-firms-are-getting-rich-on-the-surest-money-grab-in-nyc/. LawCash also allegedly flew pelvic-mesh victims to a strip mall in Florida for revision surgery to increase their lawsuit's value – and their referring attorneys' fees. Matthew Goldstein & Jessica Silver-Greenberg, *How Profiteers Lure Women into Often-Unneeded Surgery*, N.Y. TIMES (Apr. 14, 2018), https://www.nytimes.com/2018/04/14/business/vaginal-mesh-surgery-lawsuits-financing.html; Alison Frankel & Jessica Dye, *RPT-Pelvic Mesh Maker AMS Claims Women Were Lured into Needless Surgeries*, REUTERS, May 20, 2016, https://www.reuters.com/article/usa-litigation-mesh/rpt-pelvic-mesh-maker-ams-claims-women-were-lured-into-needless-surgeries-idUSL2N18H0WV. Later complaints allege that LawCash is part of "a deep-running conspiracy to turn a potentially defective medical product into a cash cow for a wide range of people including lawyers, doctors, and investors." But not for victims. First Amended Complaint, Plummer v. McSweeny, 18-cv-00063 (E.D. Ark. Feb. 7, 2018).

[79] Co-lead Class Counsel's Memorandum in Support of Motion to (1) Direct Claims Administrator to Withhold Any Portions of Class Member Monetary Awards Purported Owed to Certain Lenders and Claims Service Providers and (2) Direct Disclosure to the Claims Administrator of Existence of Class Member Agreements with All Third Parties, *In re* NFL Players' Concussion Injury Litig., No. 12-md-02323 (E.D. Pa. Oct. 23, 2017).

[80] Motion for Reconsideration, *In re* NFL Players' Concussion Injury Litig., No. 12-md-02323 (E.D. Pa. May 1, 2018). The LawCash funding agreement on the NFL docket does not contain an assignment of rights clause.

[81] Dom Cosentino, *What It's Like to Navigate the NFL's Concussion Settlement Hellscape*, DEADSPIN (May 9, 2018, 9:32 AM), https://deadspin.com/what-its-like-to-navigate-the-nfls-con cussion-settlemen-1825471309.

[82] NFL Concussion Settlement, Monetary Award Claims Report, May 21, 2018; NFL Concussion Settlement, Summary of Registrations and Claims Submitted, May 21, 2018.

Esquire Bank and LawCash. Administrative delay means more loans with longer life spans, both of which benefit funders. Lawyers who own stock in Esquire Financial or other financiers may profit from that delay too.

That lawyers have found ways to cash in on the lengthy claims process is troubling in and of itself even if their loyalties aren't divided. But when dealmakers sit on a third-party funder's board (like Esquire Financial) while crafting a settlement program's terms, alarm bells should sound. And when third-party funders face scrutiny but are exempted based on what appears to be their special relationship with the plaintiffs' bar and the attorneys in leadership positions, judges should consider how the appearance of impropriety (or actual impropriety) affects the proceeding and whether it warrants leadership changes.

In short, Esquire Bank may not be just a clever end run around the prohibition on attorney lending – it may allow attorneys to profit from the slowdowns that they're positioned to create. And because Esquire Financial's stock is publicly traded, even corporate defendants, their lawyers, and claims administrators could profit from prolonging plaintiffs' awards.

Chinese Drywall

Chris Seeger, Arnold Levin, and Russ Herman are also among the leaders in the *Chinese Drywall* litigation, where plaintiffs alleged that Chinese drywall emitted sulfur gases and caused respiratory ailments. BrownGreer is also administering that settlement and Esquire Bank holds the money for attorneys' fees in a qualified settlement fund. Russ Herman and Arnold Levin co-chair the Fee Allocation Committee.

Remember that Levin owns 8,000 shares of Esquire Financial stock. And Russ Herman owns 62,412 shares, allegedly valued at $1.4 million, as do several of his family members, including his son Steve Herman who helped lead *Deepwater Horizon*.[83] (You may recall Russ Herman from his key role in engineering the *Propulsid* settlements.)

All these seemingly unrelated facts came together in Tucker Yance's request that Judge Fallon take *Chinese Drywall's* attorneys' fee funds out of Esquire Bank. Yance cited "inexplicable delays in the Fee Committee Recommendation process," Esquire Bank's "incredibly small size," and "its multi-faceted conflicts of interest" as reasons for the move.

---

[83] Declaration of Russ M. Herman at 13, *In re* Chinese Manufactured Drywall Prods. Liab. Litig., No. 09-md-2047 (E.D. La. June 27, 2018); Yance Law Firm's Memorandum in Support of Motion to Immediately Transfer Attorney Fee Qualified Settlement Fund to a Different Depository Bank at 4, *In re* Chinese Manufactured Drywall Prods. Liab. Litig., No. 09-md-2047 (E.D. La. May 18, 2018); Interview by Jason Bass Barry with Russ Herman, Senior Partner of Herman, Herman & Katz, in New Orleans, La. (June 29, 2018).

Yance, along with others, alleges that Esquire Bank's total deposits ($448.4 million) pale when compared with even mid-sized regional banks like Iberia Bank ($21.4 billion), and that the *Chinese Drywall* attorneys' fees that Esquire Bank holds constitute 44% of its total deposits.[84] In other words, paying fees might empty the bank's reserve. "Esquire Bank appears to have paid a near zero interest rate" on the $200 million qualified settlement fund despite holding it for more than four years, Yance argues. By comparison, the Treasury Bill rate on a five-year T-Bill averaged 1.5% during the same period. For lawyers' fees, that meant the difference between $87,000 and $2 million.[85]

In response, Herman explained that he'd disclosed his and other leaders' affiliation with Esquire Bank to Judge Fallon. "I've been at this a long time," he said, "I've never been accused of any sort of ethical problem. Neither has Arnold Levin. And ya know, I'm from New Orleans, if I wanna listen to a philosopher, it's Bo Dollis," he continued. "Big Chief, Bo Dollis, who says, if you don't like what the Big Chief say I-ko- I-ko un day. So, if they don't like what Judge Fallon says, they can go I-ko un-day, whatever the heck that means."[86]

What it all *seems* to mean is this: Russ Herman and Arnold Levin allegedly kept Esquire Bank afloat by waylaying the fee-allocation process in *Chinese Drywall*. While it retained those fees, Esquire Bank paid out extremely low interest rates – .019% annually. Meanwhile, it loaned money (that money?) to NFL players at a 9% annual interest rate.[87] Although the attorneys continue to battle over *Chinese Drywall* fees, Judge Fallon transferred the money from Esquire Bank to the court registry "until further notice."[88]

Chinese Drywall, NFL Concussion, and *Deepwater Horizon* are but a few examples of a systemic problem. Free market incentives can reward plaintiffs' attorneys for tinkering with claims administration, and special masters and claims administrators for slanting decisions in a particular way or expediting some claims over others. Just as market incentives tempt plaintiff and defense attorneys to negotiate lead plaintiffs' lawyers' common-benefit fees in ways that are mutually advantageous, special masters and claims administrators can get in on the game too.

---

[84] Yance Law Firm's Motion to Immediately Transfer Attorney Fee Qualified Settlement Fund to a Different Depository Bank, *In re* Chinese Manufactured Drywall Prods. Liab. Litig., No. 09-md-2047 (E.D. La. May 18, 2018).

[85] *Id.*

[86] Interview by Jason Bass Barry with Russ Herman, Senior Partner of Herman, Herman & Katz, in New Orleans La. (June 29, 2018); Declaration of Russ M. Herman, *In re* Chinese Manufactured Drywall Prods. Liab. Litig., No. 09-md-2047 (E.D. La. June 27, 2018).

[87] Herman's response, however, says "No QSF funds have been used for collateral for loans." Declaration of Russ M. Herman at 14, *In re* Chinese Manufactured Drywall Prods. Liab. Litig., No. 09-md-2047 (E.D. La. June 27, 2018). The Esquire Bank financing agreements on file in the *NFL Concussion* litigation did not use monthly compounding like LawCash's agreements did.

[88] *In re* Chinese Manufactured Drywall Prods. Liab. Litig., No. 09-md-2047 (E.D. La. June 12, 2018) (order).

They are able to do so because the system favors settlement and few checks on that bargaining process exist.

The webs of infrastructure engulfing the mass-tort industry – from television advertisers and lead generators to those that fund revision surgery to those that act like payday lenders for cash-strapped plaintiffs – are entrenched, convoluted, and often subject to very little oversight. There is no way to demonstrate with any certainty how these industries and their occasionally cozy relationships with the lawyers who recommend and use them may affect mass litigation. Similarly, there is no way to suss out how claims administrators and special masters' biases may manifest – presiding over private settlements is a confidential enterprise.

Because they were all publicity magnets and certified class actions, however, the *Chinese Drywall, NFL Concussion,* and *Deepwater Horizon* proceedings unearthed some connections that typically remain buried in private mass-tort settlements. They illuminate ties that raise questions about tilted justice and conflicted interests. And they show that there are few true neutrals – everyone has a stake of some sort. Claims administrators and special settlement masters need attorneys to designate them. Perhaps that means biting their tongues and going along to get future work. Funders rely on lawyers for business (and some lawyers get into the funding business). Repeat players inhabit every corner of the mass-tort world. And they are all connected.

The tangled incentives in *Chinese Drywall, NFL Concussion,* and *Deepwater Horizon* appear not to be a few isolated instances, but the tip of an iceberg. For example, *Chinese Drywall* isn't Esquire Bank's only qualified settlement fund. Just within the dataset, it held qualified settlement funds in *Fresenius GranuFlo, Tylenol, Avandia, Chantix, Yasmin/Yaz,* and *Biomet.* And Esquire Bank isn't alone in its cozy ties to plaintiffs' lawyers. Perry Weitz and Arthur Luxenberg, co-founding members of Weitz & Luxenberg (one of the nation's largest mass-tort plaintiffs' firms) are on the board of Counsel Financial Services, another litigation funder.

When all these ties come to light courtesy of class-action objectors in mass torts that hold that unique class status, what should we make of private global and inventory settlements that aren't transparent and have no outlet for dissent? It's likely that those settlements are every bit as messy. Yet, they lack meaningful safety valves for speaking out when things heat up. In *Vioxx* and most other private settlement programs, few disputes pop up in the courts – not because they don't exist, but because special masters are poised to quietly resolve them through arbitration.

PRIVACY VERSUS EQUAL TREATMENT

As we have seen, plaintiffs have little idea what they're getting in exchange for giving up their suit when they enter into a settlement program. When their claims are denied or they're awarded less than they expected, many have no idea why. Some claims administrators give no reasoned explanation and some settlements explicitly forbid them from doing so. Even if reasoned opinions existed, the confidential nature of other plaintiffs' awards keeps them from knowing whether they're being treated fairly vis-à-vis everyone else or whether administrators favor insider attorneys' clients over others.

As Table A.7 shows, few of the publicly available private settlements within the dataset indicated whether claims administrators would explain their decisions and, if so, what details they would provide. In *Vioxx*, claimants received their point allocation and in *Fosamax*, they received a category allocation letter. But in *Propulsid*, where only 0.6% of plaintiffs recovered any money through the strict doctor-reviewed claims process, plaintiffs had no idea why the panel of doctors denied their claim. When they asked about it so they could decide whether to request that the panel reconsider, they got nowhere. Johnson & Johnson's counsel Tom Campion insisted the panel write only "approved" or "denied." "[T]he medical panel," he argued, "is the Supreme Court as far as this is concerned. They don't have to justify their positions."[89] Of course, the actual Supreme Court justifies its positions routinely.

Contrast *Propulsid*, a nonclass mass tort, with *Sulzer Inter-Op Hip Prothesis*, a mass tort class action: like most of the private deals in the dataset, *Sulzer* class members had to release their claims without knowing whether they would recover. Yet, if they were unhappy with their ultimate award, their dissatisfaction wasn't shielded in secrecy. They had five chances to perfect their claim and, as the administrator explained, after each review "the claims administrator, or the party-approved special master, was required to explain in writing the reason for any benefit denial."[90] When class members appealed, the appeals, the responses, and all the objections, reasons, and rulings appeared on Judge O'Malley's public docket. For those deciding whether to appeal, this transparency gave them a yardstick to measure whether they were being treated fairly as compared with one another.

As Judge Nancy Gertner observed, "Meaningful access to justice, a judge who will look deeply into your case and issue a reasoned decision, not just a single word 'denied,' [is] also critical."[91] When claims administrators decline to give reasoned opinions and judges encourage plaintiffs to enter settlement programs that admit or deny their claims without explanation, they contribute further to a process that already leaves plaintiffs searching for answers.

---

[89] Transcript of Status Conference at 9, *In re* Propulsid Prods. Liab. Litig., No. 00-md-01355 (E.D. La. Sept. 27, 2007).

[90] Cullen D. Seltzer, *Lessons Learned from Implementing a Class Action Settlement*, 8 MASS TORTS No. 3, 2010, at 14, 15.

[91] Judge Nancy Gertner (Ret.), *Opinions I Should Have Written*, 110 Nw. L. REV. 423, 431 (2016).

SELF-CONTAINED APPEALS

Given how little plaintiffs may know about why administrators denied or reduced their claim, they may appeal in hopes of faring better. But something else may be going on too. To figure out why litigants appeal in civil cases, Professor Scott Barclay interviewed a random sample of 1,103 losing litigants (622 of whom appealed). Their answers revealed that their primary motivator wasn't losing – it was a desire to be treated fairly. Appellants felt like the trial court hadn't heard them, hadn't listened to their arguments.[92]

When things don't go your way in court, appealing allows you take the decision away from those who got it wrong and put the matter into other decision makers' hands. While appellants will have to produce the record and may need to overcome difficult review standards like abuse of discretion, appeals give dissatisfied parties a second chance. But when that "appeal" is part of a private settlement program rather than the judicial system, that second chance looks more like the odds in Vegas.

Imagine that the litigation process afforded you few, if any, opportunities to participate in your own suit. Your lawyer tells you there's a settlement on the table, one that you have a chance of qualifying for. You should take it, she says. Even though it's a private deal, it has a judicial imprimatur (recall that 64.7% of judges in the dataset appointed the private claims administrators and special settlement masters). This seems like a chance to interact directly with what feels like the court system.

After you dismiss your lawsuit with prejudice and submit your medical records and paperwork, however, your claim is denied outright – perhaps with no explanation. If you were a *Propulsid* plaintiff, you'd be out of luck, for no appeals process existed. But most programs weren't that draconian. Instead, as Table A.7 shows, special settlement masters can often review claims administrators' eligibility and allocation decisions.

So, if the administrator places you in the wrong tier, which halves your expected recovery, you could invoke the internal appeals process. But your objection might go to the same person who decided your fate initially, something akin to a motion for reconsideration in court. Or it might be "appealed" to one of the many repeat players dependent on lead plaintiff and defense attorneys for more business. Or it might be a hybrid of the two, as in *Actos*.

In litigation over diabetes drug Actos, plaintiffs who opted into the settlement program had their claims extinguished. If BrownGreer decided that they didn't qualify for recovery, they could ask it to reconsider, but that decision was final,

[92] Scott Barclay, An Appealing Act: Why People Appeal in Civil Cases 84, 119–22 (1999); see also Gillian K. Hadfield, *Framing the Choice Between Cash and the Courthouse Experiences with the 9/11 Victim Compensation Fund*, 3 Law & Soc'y Rev. 645 (2008).

binding, and nonappealable.[93] Deficient claims packages went before an eligibility committee comprised of the lead plaintiff and defense lawyers. Appeals thereafter went to a special master as did disputes over points, settlement terms, and whether someone qualified for the extraordinary injury fund. Just like an arbitrator, the special master's decisions were final and binding.

Other programs deter appeals by imposing barriers, but do not limit them outright. For instance, in the *Zimmer Durom Hip Cup* settlement, if a plaintiff disputed her eligibility or award, she had to split the costs of mandatory mediation with Zimmer, and Zimmer got to choose the date and location.[94] In both the *Pradaxa* and *Yasmin/Yaz* gallbladder programs, the losing party on appeal had to pay $300 or $500 in costs, respectively.[95] And in *DePuy ASR*, appeals initially went to the same claims processor. Special masters heard second appeals but had their hands tied by an abuse of discretion standard.

Other programs relied on judges but turned them into arbitrators. As we saw in *Vioxx*, settlement designers tapped Judge Eldon Fallon to serve as its chief administrator. And in *Fosamax*, Magistrate Judge James Francis served as the general special master. Neither settlement allowed appellants to return to the public court system, however. Instead, programs constrained judges' authority by dictating what evidence claims administrators could hear and what the standard of proof would be. When appeals came before the judicial arbitrator, those constraints remained in place. And judicial arbitrators' decisions were final and binding, not appealable as they would have been if they'd been decided under the judge's public authority.

It's possible, of course, that appeals matter less in settlement programs than in litigation. On one hand, because dealmakers have already agreed about things like what evidence to accept and what the parameters for a compensable claim should be, there may be fewer errors to correct. But on the other, mass-tort plaintiffs lack the typical information that ordinary litigants have before they settle such as whether they've met the eligibility criteria and how much money they will receive. And sometimes the rules of the road change midstream. Like legislatures, settlement designers can't contemplate all ambiguities in advance. As the class claims administrator in *Sulzer Inter-Op Hip Prosthesis* explained, administrators adopted more than 30 procedures to address open-ended questions.[96]

[93] Master Settlement Agreement at §§ 2.05, 2.06, *In re* Actos (Pioglitazone) Prods. Liab. Litig., No. 11-md-2299 (W.D. La. Apr. 28, 2015) [hereinafter Actos Settlement].

[94] U.S. Durom Cup Settlement Program Agreement § IV.A, *In re* Zimmer Durom Hip Cup Prods. Liab. Litig., No. 09-cv-04414 (D.N.J. Feb. 11, 2016) [hereinafter Zimmer Durom Settlement].

[95] *In re* Pradaxa (Dabigatran Etexilate) Prods. Liab. Litig., No. 12-md-02385 (S.D. Ill. Oct. 21, 2014) (CMO No. 86); Settlement Agreement at § 5.03(F), *In re* Yasmin & Yaz (Drospirenone) Mktg., Sales Practices Prods. Liab. Litig., No. 09-md-2100 (S.D. Ill., Mar. 15, 2013) [hereinafter Yaz Gallbladder Settlement].

[96] Seltzer, *supra* note 90, at 15.

If Professor Barclay is right that plaintiffs appeal because they feel that the court hadn't heard them or listened to their arguments, and if my concern about special masters and claims vendors tilting justice to satisfy their employers is accurate, then appeals are inevitable. But the internal nature of those appeals may not appease plaintiffs.

Of course, making these claims with any empirical authority is impossible – the confidential process sees to it that such complaints rarely, if ever, surface publicly. So, even just raw "appellate" numbers for claims programs are difficult to come by. Those that are available show a range: In *Fosamax*, only 38 of some 1,050 plaintiffs appealed (3.6%); in *Vioxx*, Lyhn Greer of BrownGreer reported that "[a]round 15 percent ultimately get appealed to us or then on to the special master"; and in *NuvaRing*, some 1,100 of the first 3,704 plaintiffs – nearly 30% – appealed.[97]

But the *NFL Concussion* litigation gives us an anecdotal peek into what is typically a closed-door process. Because of its unique status as a mass-tort multidistrict proceeding that Judge Brody certified as a settlement class action, objections appear on the record.

After the designers inked the deal, the terms seemed to change. Co-lead class counsel Larry Coben argued the claims process "has evolved into a thicket of privately litigated, changing standards."[98] Nor did the appellate process provide relief: "[E]ach claim, each appeal is being administratively adjudicated in complete secrecy," plaintiffs' attorney Lance Lubel explained. So, while confidentiality was important, appeals were "analogous to blind stare decisis" and class members' claims were "being measured against an unpublished benchmark."[99]

This opaque process can lead plaintiffs to wonder whether they're being treated fairly when compared with others. It can prompt questions about whether some receive better deals for reasons unrelated to their actual damages or causation. Worrying over the "lack of transparency," Larry Coben asked, "what other retired player and his family have been waiting a year and have been given the same run-around?"[100]

Apparently, quite a few. "More than half of all claims have been placed into audit or denied, thereby causing interminable delay and preventing payments," wrote

---

[97] Transcript of Status Hearing at 9, *In re* NuvaRing Prods. Liab. Litig., No. 08-md-01964 (E.D. Mo. Sept. 8, 2015); *In re* Fosamax Prods. Liab. Litig., No. 06-md-1789 (S.D.N.Y. Dec. 18, 2014) (order scheduling oral arguments for master settlement agreement eligibility/allocation appeals); Transcript of Status Conference at 10, *In re* Vioxx Prods. Liab. Litig., No. 05-md-1657 (E.D. La. Oct. 23, 2009).

[98] Motion of Co-Lead Class Counsel Anapol Weiss for a Hearing to Seek Court Intervention on the Processing of Certain Claims at 8, *In re* NFL Players' Concussion Injury Litig., No. 12-md-02323 (E.D. Pa. Mar. 19, 2018).

[99] Memorandum in Support of Movants' Joinder in the Motion of Class Counsel, the Locks Law Firm, for Appointment of Administrative Class Counsel, *In re* NFL Players' Concussion Injury Litig., No. 12-md-02323 (E.D. Pa. Mar. 3, 2018).

[100] Motion of Co-Lead Class Counsel Anapol Weiss for a Hearing to Seek Court Intervention on the Processing of Certain Claims at 8, *In re* NFL Players' Concussion Injury Litig., No. 12-md-02323 (E.D. Pa. Mar. 19, 2018).

Gene Locks. The settlement, he argued, not only suffered from the issues that Lubel and Coben identified but also from "a black hole of audits, alleged deficiencies, anonymous opinions, denials, appeals, remands, [and] technical squabbles over what a valid diagnosis might be."[101] Building on the theme, the Yerrid Law Firm argued that BrownGreer was improperly conducting ex parte interviews with players' doctors, "preventing the Court from hearing the voices of the players," and refusing to provide information about the number of awards it made to show that it hadn't exceeded its audit authority.[102]

The internal appeals process was arbitrary, too, argued plaintiffs' attorney Wendy Fleishman. In challenging the special master's decision to reverse one of her client's awards, she explained that her client had already passed through three rigorous claims hurdles – the claims administrator's initial review, the Advisory Physician's Panel's internal review, and a full audit by the claims administrator. The special master, however, relied upon and adopted advice from an undisclosed Appeals Advisory Panel and "reversed the twice-approved award without any explanation." Asking Judge Brody to vacate the special master's ruling, Fleishman argued that the "Court should not set a precedent of claims being determined behind closed doors with no way of knowing how the determination was made or who made it."[103]

All these objections are unique. Because this mass tort proceeded as a certified class, each objection appears on the court's docket for Judge Brody to decide. When MDLs conclude in private settlement programs, however, these grievances remain in the shadows. They are privately resolved before a claims administrator or special master.

Research on justice systems around the world consistently demonstrates that people want a few key things when it comes to resolving their disputes: adversarial procedures that give them the opportunity to present arguments and evidence before a neutral third-party, assurances that the procedures used do not favor one side over the other, and mechanisms to correct error such as appellate review, precedential constraints, judicial codes of conduct, and even impeachment.[104]

But, as we've seen, these procedural-justice values are often forgotten when it comes to mass torts. The concerns that Lance Lubel, Larry Coben, and Wendy

---

[101] Motion of Class Counsel, The Locks Law Firm, for Appointment of Administrative Class Counsel, *In re* NFL Players' Concussion Injury Litig., No. 12-md-02323 (E.D. Pa. Mar. 20, 2018).

[102] The Yerrid Law Firm's Reply to the Response by the Claims Administrator, *In re* NFL Players' Concussion Injury Litig., No. 12-md-02323 (E.D. Pa. Mar. 23, 2018).

[103] Objection to the Special Master's May 31, 2018 Ruling, *In re* NFL Players' Concussion Injury Litig., No. 12-md-02323 (E.D. Pa. June 21, 2018). Judge Brody remanded the matter back to the special master and requested that he explain his determination. *In re* NFL Players' Concussion Injury Litig., No. 12-md-02323 (E.D. Pa. July 19, 2018) (order).

[104] Elizabeth Chamblee Burch, *Procedural Justice in Nonclass Aggregation*, 44 WAKE FOREST L. REV. 1 (2009).

Fleishman raised are likely the same ones that arise daily in private settlements, for administering claims "behind closed doors" is precisely what they do.

COMMUNITY DISENGAGEMENT

Closing the courthouse doors isn't just a problem for the litigants inside. Private settlements and their embedded ADR provisions substitute for jury trials. "We've been co-opted as partners in ADR at no cost to the litigants. And the taxpayer foots the bill," writes Judge Clay Land. But the Constitution "clearly contemplates that our court shall 'decide' cases and controversies, and that 'factual disputes' shall be decided by a jury," he argues.[105]

Trials remain the most public aspect of our civil justice system, but they are steadily disappearing.[106] "The jury has essentially vanished," surmises Professor Suja Thomas.[107] As Table A.5 shows, only 44% of judges within the dataset held bellwether trials before the first settlement. And even when they occur, a handful of bellwethers give the public only a glimpse into the facts. There are often thousands of other plaintiffs in a proceeding who may share little in common with the bellwether plaintiffs.

To be sure, conducting some bellwether trials is better than no trials at all. But bellwether trials unfold before a single judge in front of jurors from a single place. Plaintiffs, however, hail from all corners of the country.

Jury trials are meant to bring communities' diverse perspectives and norms to bear on fact-finding. And even communities within a single state can vary dramatically. Given the plurality of viewpoints and experiences within our country, it is no surprise that jurors may approach the adjudicative and deliberative process differently even with regard to the same product.[108] As debates over marijuana, immigration, and gun control illustrate, communities fall along a broad spectrum when it comes to moral views and social values. So, holding more bellwethers before members of the same community doesn't cure the legitimacy problem.

"In cases that do not concern technical legal questions, but rather people's values and sense of reasonableness, people are going to differ," writes Professor Alexandra Lahav. "The jury right," she explains, "recognizes that reasonable minds can interpret facts differently from one another and asks for consensus from a group

[105] Judge Clay D. Land, *Lamentations of a Trial Judge*, Remarks to the Columbus Inn of Court (Jan. 28, 2015) (on file with author).

[106] E.g., Marc Galanter, *The Vanishing Trial: An Examination of Trials and Related Matters in Federal Courts*, 93 YALE L.J. 1073 (1984); David Luban, *Settlements and the Erosion of the Public Realm*, 83 GEO. L.J. 2619 (1995); Judith Resnik, *Courts: In and Out of Sight, Site, and Cite*, 53 VILL. L. REV. 771 (2008).

[107] SUJA A. THOMAS, THE MISSING AMERICAN JURY 2 (2016).

[108] See Dan M. Kahan, David A. Hoffman & Donald Braman, *Whose Eyes Are You Going to Believe? Scott v. Harris and the Perils of Cognitive Illiberalism*, 122 HARV. L. REV. 837, 864–81 (2009); Cass R. Sunstein, *Rights and Their Critics*, 70 NOTRE DAME L. REV. 727, 745 (1995).

intended to be representative of the local population."[109] That is what legitimizes the outcomes.

The legitimacy that comes from a closeness with the people the system serves can't be manufactured. That refrain echoes throughout states' and counties' fights to keep their opioid cases local and out of the federal multidistrict proceeding. Houston, Texas's county attorney put it simply: "We believe that our judge, our county, our juries in Harris County not only have the right, but that they should be the ones to decide the fate of this lawsuit. This is where it happened."[110] Houston is not alone – more than a dozen states and Native American tribes have fought to keep their opioid lawsuits local. As the attorney representing Hopkins County, Texas, explained, "Time will tell whether Hopkins County is served well enough by little old me and my co-counsel. But we believe that Hopkins County's claims should be decided in Hopkins County."[111]

Centralizing cases using multidistrict litigation "is a significant departure from our traditional notion of dispensing justice using 'local' citizens (jurors) and 'local' judges," explains Judge Land. "Historically, this decentralized model not only helped establish 'standards of conduct' in our tort system, but its 'closeness' to the people was designed to give it legitimacy," he writes.[112] As he watched products liability cases swept away, he lamented, "I sense something is lost when Mrs. Smith, who is injured by ingesting a drug in Columbus, Georgia, does not have the opportunity to tell her story here at home but must be relegated to 'Plaintiff number X' in some settlement grid in a faraway courthouse by a faceless judge."[113]

"When people think that group authorities represent their values, they identify and cooperate with them," explains procedural-justice scholar Professor Tom Tyler.[114] Transferee judges in far off locales, however, may hold less sway.[115]

Local trials may also improve the relationship between a case's merits and its outcome. They unearth state law differences and prompt the judges most familiar with those laws to apply them to factual variations. As negotiating parties factor new

---

[109] ALEXANDRA LAHAV, IN PRAISE OF LITIGATION 99 (2017).

[110] Andrew Joseph, *Why Houston and Other Cities Want Nothing to Do with the Massive National Opioid Lawsuit*, STAT NEWS (Mar. 27, 2018), https://www.statnews.com/2018/03/27/houston-national-opioid-lawsuit/.

[111] *Id.*

[112] Letter from The Honorable Clay D. Land, U.S. Dist. Judge Middle Dist. of Ga., to Professor Francis E. McGovern, Duke Law School (Oct. 29, 2010) (on file with author).

[113] *Id.*

[114] Jason Sunshine & Tom Tyler, *Moral Solidarity, Identification with the Community, and the Importance of Procedural Justice: The Police as Prototypical Representatives of a Group's Moral Values*, 66 SOC. PSYCHOL. Q. 153, 154 (2003).

[115] *See generally* CASS R. SUNSTEIN ET AL., ARE JUDGES POLITICAL? AN EMPIRICAL ANALYSIS OF THE FEDERAL JUDICIARY 17–46 (2006) (suggesting that there are systematic differences in decision-making patterns among federal appeals judges appointed by Democratic or Republican presidents).

information into global or inventory settlements, they can better price and categorize awards by keying them to substantive law.[116]

Juries can likewise "function as a much needed check on the judicial branch," argues Professor Lahav. "[J]uries do not answer to judges, nor do their futures depend on being in the judge's good graces" as a lawyer's livelihood does, she observes.[117] This provides what Alexander Hamilton dubbed a "double security" in *The Federalist Papers*. "[I]t will readily be perceived that this complicated agency tends to preserve the purity of both institutions. By increasing the obstacles to success it discourages attempts to seduce the integrity of either," Hamilton writes.[118]

Juries don't just legitimize outcomes and monitor judges – they can be transformative for those who participate in them. "There are very few other opportunities for a random citizen to play such an integral role in democracy," writes Judge Land. "The skeptics will scoff at such observations as sentimental patriotic nonsense. But I have seen it – initially reluctant jurors who after their service was done described it as one of the best experiences they ever had."[119]

Despite these upsides, local jury trials have their critics, especially in high-volume mass torts. Though there are different variants, these critiques boil down to two primary objections: first, jury trials are inefficient. Judges should streamline the proceedings, ignore most substantive differences, and seek ways to apply a single law. There are differing opinions about how to do this, of course – conduct a few bellwether trials, massage choice-of-law principles, delay substantive rulings for an imaginary remand, or encourage settlements that sweep differences under the rug. All share a noble but flawed desire to make complex cases easier to handle.[120]

The second objection is that people who have suffered from similar injuries nationwide should be treated similarly across the board.[121] The fortuity of where they live or were harmed shouldn't matter and their claims shouldn't be decided by fickle jurors. The flip side of this argument is that corporations shouldn't have to cater to the state with the country's strictest laws when manufacturing and marketing its products. In short, applying different laws is unfair.

---

[116] *Cf.* Eldon E. Fallon, Jeremy T. Grabill & Robart Pitard Wynne, *Bellwether Trials in Multidistrict Litigation*, 82 TUL. L. REV. 2323, 2342 (2008) ("By allowing juries an initial opportunity to [match medical conditions with compensation payouts] on an ad hoc, case-by-case basis, bellwether trials essentially supply counsel with 'raw' data around which a more fair and equitable grid-based compensation system can ultimately be constructed.").

[117] LAHAV, *supra* note 109, at 103–4 (2017).

[118] THE FEDERALIST No. 83, at 564 (Alexander Hamilton) (Jacob E. Cooke Ed., 1961).

[119] Judge Clay D. Land, Lamentations of a Trial Judge, Remarks to the Columbus Inn of Court, Jan. 28, 2015 (on file with author).

[120] *E.g.*, *In re* Agent Orange Prod. Liab. Litig., 580 F. Supp. 690 (E.D.N.Y. 1984); COMPLEX LITIGATION PROJECT § 6.01 (AM. LAW INST. Proposed Final Draft, Apr. 5, 1993); Freidrich K. Junger, *Mass Disasters and the Conflict of Laws*, 1989 U. ILL. L. REV. 105, 126.

[121] Junger, *supra* note 120, at 122.

Taking each criticism in turn, first, administrative ease shouldn't justify altering individual rights. Otherwise, court procedures could change legislative actions in undemocratic ways – a practice forbidden by the Rules Enabling Act.[122] Choosing and applying state law is, as former Stanford Law Dean Larry Kramer puts it, "part of the process of defining the parties' rights." Substantive law "should not change simply because, as a matter of administrative convenience and efficiency, we have combined many claims into one proceeding," he argues.[123]

That's not to say that individual actions are better – they aren't. But it's not so black and white as that. As I suggest in Chapter 6, remands offer ways to promote pretrial efficiency while preserving litigants' ability to demand trial. And should remands occur, home districts can still coordinate suits "without the need to rewrite anyone's substantive rights," Professor Kramer explains.[124]

The second objection, that people nationwide with similar harms should be treated the same, intuitively appeals to our fairness principles. But the idea that applying different laws is unfair suffers from three main weaknesses. First, there is no nationwide federal tort law. To date, tort law lies firmly within the states' province. And under the Constitution, powers not delegated to the federal government "are reserved to the states."[125] So, even if we rightly care about plaintiffs receiving equal treatment under the law, which law?

State legislatures can disagree over which rights to value and how to implement them. There's nothing unfair about reaching conflicting outcomes so long as substantive differences explain them. "Such differences are what a federal system is all about," Professor Kramer notes.[126] The quest for parity cannot mean watering down a hodgepodge of substantive variations, applying that distilled version, and dubbing it fair. To do so would be inconsistent with state sovereignty principles that lie at the very heart of federalism.

Second, corporations have wormed their way into every aspect of our lives. Pharmaceutical companies send representatives to our doctors' offices, ship drugs to our local pharmacies, and use our home televisions to convince us of our ailments – and how they can fix them. Interacting with us nets a benefit for them – revenue. And that contact with us, in our home state, is the primary focus of the Supreme Court's personal-jurisdiction jurisprudence.

For courts to exercise their power over a corporate defendant and adjudicate a claim against it, they examine the corporation's in-state activities. After the Supreme

---

[122] 28 U.S.C. § 2072 (2012) (allowing the Supreme Court to prescribe general rules of practice and procedure but cautioning that those rules "shall not abridge, enlarge or modify any substantive right").

[123] Larry Kramer, *Choice of Law in Complex Litigation*, 71 N.Y.U. L. REV. 547, 549 (1996).

[124] *Id.* at 587.

[125] U.S. CONST. amend. X.

[126] Kramer, *supra* note 123, at 579; Robert A. Sedler, *The Complex Litigation Project's Proposal for Federally-Mandated Choice of Law in Mass Torts Cases: Another Assault on State Sovereignty*, 54 LA. L. REV. 1085, 1086 (1994).

Court's opinion in *Bristol-Myers Squibb*, courts must also seek "a connection between the forum and the specific claims at issue."[127] This means that plaintiffs cannot pick a random state in which to sue. But the corollary is that when corporations target us at home and profit from doing so, they cannot then shrug off an obligation to defend themselves there. Nor can they legitimately claim that it's unfair to be judged by those juries or to have that state's laws apply to them.

Finally, jurors can be as wise as judges. "The unpredictability claim is particularly easy to dismiss outright," writes Professor Lahav, "because there is little evidence that juries are more unpredictable than legal professionals." In fact, "Judges and juries agree on liability about 80 percent of the time." Where differences do arise, they reflect pluralism and conflicting worldviews.[128]

Because juries necessarily include more than one person, they can also incorporate the value of dissent. Summarizing her decades of work on juries, Berkeley psychology professor Charlan Nemeth notes that when jurors must reach unanimous results, dissenters "improved the quality of the discussion and the decision-making process." "[P]articipants considered more evidence and more ways of explaining that evidence" instead of rushing to judgment.[129] In a nutshell then, the judicial system should be seeking ways to foster, not stifle, local jury trials.

LITIGATION AS CONTRACT BARGAINING

By understanding what we give up in the name of efficiency and situating private settlements as an outcropping of the ADR movement we can better understand multidistrict proceedings as setting up a series of bargaining constraints. It is the next generation of what Professor Judith Resnik labeled "procedure as contract" over a decade ago.[130] Instead of contracting for ADR *before* disputes arise as Professor Resnik described, however, private settlements are the backend equivalent. They're designed to accomplish what defendants couldn't do without a contract before the dispute began: move claims into arbitration.

Pretrial litigation simply allows the parties to duel over the bargaining advantages. Fights over whether and where to centralize the proceedings and which judge will hear the case often dictate which attorneys will occupy leadership positions, the ground rules for resolving the suits, and the parameters for lead plaintiffs' lawyers' common-benefit fees.

Framing litigation as a prelude to ADR through settlement places plaintiffs' consent – not judicial rulings – as the primary legitimizing mechanism. But, as Chapters 2 and 4 described, plaintiffs' own attorneys and sometimes the judges steer

---

[127] Bristol-Myers Squibb Co. v. Superior Court, 137 S. Ct. 1773, 1781 (2017).
[128] LAHAV, *supra* note 109, at 101–2.
[129] CHARLAN NEMETH, IN DEFENSE OF TROUBLEMAKERS 110–11 (2018).
[130] Judith Resnik, *Procedure as Contract*, 80 NOTRE DAME L. REV. 593 (2005).

these choices, hog-tying plaintiffs' freedom to decide. They then use procedural maneuvers to wrangle the holdouts. As this chapter has illustrated, once plaintiffs enter the settlement program, they may encounter overt or hidden biases in an entirely new set of repeat players. But the insular nature of "appeals" may afford them little relief.

When parties co-opt a public system for their private bargaining needs, the whole structure shifts. Some judges see their jobs as ushering parties toward a contractual resolution – not trial. Getting rid of time-consuming jury trials for all but a few bellwether cases means greater efficiency. But the costs are steep too: fewer opportunities for public judgments, less transparency, fewer procedural safeguards, and, quite possibly, less fairness.

Litigation-as-contract-bargaining can also barter away the rule of law. As merits rulings diminish, so does precedent. This not only undermines important civic values like democratic participation and accountability, but the lingering ambiguity makes complying with the law tough for diligent corporations. Put bluntly, putting dispute resolution on the front burner risks failing to articulate, define, and enforce our public values.[131]

If we reframe that system to better align with its civic-minded purpose, we would see that it primarily supplies a forum in which parties can vindicate their legal rights. Assisting in the exchange that follows is secondary. But thinking in these terms raises two big questions.

First, it recognizes that plaintiffs may bargain with defendants for money or reforms. But as plaintiffs' consent becomes less meaningful and less informed as the system's need for efficiency increases, it also suggests that court-facilitated and judicially endorsed settlements have some obligation to procedurally safeguard those deals. How can courts do this legitimately?

Second, mass-tort multidistrict litigation is a species of ordinary tort law. It grows within a judicial system where plaintiffs expect to participate, tell their stories, and control their lawsuits. Yet, when a corporation allegedly harms many people in similar ways, those foundational values look more like the bygone days of a Norman Rockwell painting. The scarcity of judicial resources, the widespread demise of jury trials, the national reach of corporations, and the need to capture some pretrial efficiencies suggest that a return to those days is not only unfeasible but also unwise. So, if we can't resurrect individual suits and those procedural values, how can we modernize them?

We now begin to tackle those questions.

---

[131] Luban, *supra* note 106, at 2634–40.

6

Reforming Multidistrict Litigation

When an enterprising reporter asked why he robbed banks, Willie Sutton, one of the most notorious gangsters of the 1930s, supposedly said, "Because that's where the money is." As we've seen, a great deal of money changes hands in mass torts too. And there are many modern-day Suttons looking to cash in. Stopping them might help, but it'd be a little like pulling up a few crabgrass patches in a field of weeds – another one's bound to pop up. Point is, the issues I've identified in previous chapters are systemic, not episodic. No one person or segment is to blame. Finding ways to align attorneys' self-interest and paydays with litigants' substantive and procedural fairness is crucial.

The previous chapters have described cracks in the system, failings in need of fixes. The problems are complex, deep rooted, integrated, and multifaceted. Anyone who promises a silver bullet or quick fix is peddling snake oil. Like all complex dynamic systems, tweaking one aspect will produce reverberations and unintended consequences elsewhere. You can't squeeze a half-inflated balloon and expect the rest to remain stationary. But that's not to say that we can't do better. We can and should. Still, as this chapter moves from the descriptive to the proscriptive, I can promise you only a start, not a cure-all.

Think about the tort system as an old car for a moment. It's not a perfect analogy, but the idea is that it was built to transport a few people from here to there just as our tort system was designed to resolve individual suits. But it needs to carry a great deal more people now. Replacing the engine isn't going to cut it. The top gets removed, chairs get packed in, and, after a while, it looks like an old jalopy rigged with stadium seating. Our system needs a multifaceted rebuild. We've tried to retrofit a justice system designed for individuals to serve the many. The conversion's been less than ideal. And though we might be better off scrapping the whole thing and buying a train, that kind of overhaul is probably unrealistic.

Just as you might have a hard time trusting some auto mechanics, class actions and the vast literature on principals and agents have taught us that attorneys can wield their expertise and control to serve their own interests at their clients' expense. And under the current structure, no one is well situated to police them.

In theory, *clients* might monitor, much as they do in individual suits. But they tend to be legally unsophisticated – that's why they hire a lawyer, after all. Plus, attorneys often represent hundreds of clients, making tailored communication and informed consent difficult. And, whether they like it or not, clients mostly follow their lawyers' advice.

While bar complaints might help target unscrupulous lawyers, attorney malpractice claims rarely make it out of the starting gate. As Chapter 3 described, doctrinal confusion over ethical obligations in aggregate settlements and over what duties leaders owe nonclient plaintiffs undermines malpractice's enforcement threat. Plus, lead lawyers angle for favorable treatment by removing the claims from state to federal court where they then ask the Panel for a transfer to the same judge who empowered them.

Even if they are not in a leadership role in a particular proceeding, most *plaintiffs' attorneys* play the long game. So, even though they are knowledgeable, assertive, and ambitious, if they want a shot at entering "the club," their calculated response to procedural inadequacies and ethical lapses may be to bite their tongues. Objecting in the face of judicially sanctioned cooperative norms and powerful repeat players can derail their dreams and impact their wallets. Lead lawyers have the power to control access to judges, inflict costs on dissenters, and reward cooperators. They distribute common-benefit work to allies, serve on common-benefit fee-allocation committees, and report uncooperative behavior to the judge – carrots and sticks, in other words.

Because plaintiffs' attorneys currently have little incentive to dissent, *judges* may know only what leaders want them to know. Unless they have ruled on the proceeding's merits, they are likely to suffer from information deficits. Plus, six-month reports, embedded norms, and the lure of new complex assignments pressure and reward judges for settling their cases.

Of course, courts might revive plenary *class actions* and let judges act as a fiduciary for absent class members. Although settlement class actions display many of the same problems as their nonclass brethren,[1] courts could certify a defendant's uniform conduct toward plaintiffs as an *issue class*.[2] Whether this leads to a better substantive outcome is impossible to say without more data. And while there are plenty of examples of class-action abuse, there are ready-made procedures for judicial oversight, dissent, and appeals.

---

[1] Howard M. Erichson, *What MDL and Class Actions Have in Common*, 70 VAND. L. REV. EN BANC 29 (2017); Howard M. Erichson, *The Problem of Settlement Class Actions*, 82 GEO. WASH. L. REV. 951 (2014).

[2] Elizabeth Chamblee Burch, *Constructing Issue Classes*, 101 VA. L. REV. 1855, 1871–90 (2015).

Though judges appear increasingly comfortable with issue classes, plaintiffs' lawyers rarely propose them; if they lose the issue-class trial, then issue preclusion prevents them from relitigating. And, even if they win (unless the win prompts the defendant to settle), there is still no fund from which leaders can collect their common-benefit fees.

Finally, looking outside the traditional litigation context, *third-party financiers* – if they made substantial changes – might monitor lead lawyers. Chapter 5 painted a dismal picture of financiers as having cozy relationships with plaintiffs' attorneys. But, as with issue classes, if funders disclosed their origins and contracts in camera to judges and tweaked their business model, potential exists.

Here's what I mean: assume plaintiffs could assign a financier a stake in their lawsuit as the contingent fee does now. In exchange, the financier funds the suit on a nonrecourse basis and pays attorneys a billable-hour rate plus some small percentage of the recovery as a bonus. As funders compete for plaintiffs' business, the market becomes more efficient. Like institutional lead plaintiffs in securities class actions, financiers could become super stakeholders who are better suited to challenge corporate defendants pound for pound and monitor their attorneys in the same way defendants supervise theirs.[3]

In this revamped capacity, third-party financiers might help manage principal-agent problems by unbundling attorneys' conflicting roles as investors and advisors. They too would become repeat players. Just as the NAACP, ACLU, and unions counteract the typical disadvantages one-shot plaintiffs face by aggregating interests and resources, a third-party financier could monitor and discipline lawyers by ending relationships with certain law firms and overseeing spending. The more difficult and worrisome question, however, is whether financiers would turn into toll collectors who extract additional rents from plaintiffs.[4]

Although both issue classes and third-party financing hold promise, my focus here is on crafting better practices, better procedures – retrofitting the old car, in other words. Now that we've looked under the hood, it's easier to diagnose the problems: information barriers for judges, a rush to settlement, and an overemphasis on cooperation. As substantial research across a variety of disciplines has shown, authentic dissent and competition can work hand in hand to combat these problems.

In the few mass tort class actions that we've examined like *NFL Concussion* and *Sulzer Inter-Op Hip Prosthesis*, both formal and informal objections have proven ready sources of dissent. As plaintiffs' lawyer Elizabeth Cabraser and Professor Samuel Issacharoff argue, "Independent groups of counsel provide a more engaged

---

[3]   Elizabeth Chamblee Burch, *Financiers as Monitors in Aggregate Litigation*, 87 N.Y.U. L. Rev. 1273, 1291–1300 (2012).

[4]   Samuel Issacharoff, *Litigation Funding and the Problem of Agency Cost in Representative Actions*, 63 DePaul L. Rev. 561, 581 (2014).

form of class counsel monitoring than either court oversight or unrepresented class members making a yes or no decision on a settlement offer." And when tort victims file their own suits, "[C]entralization would make it more likely that they will avail themselves of social media to follow the progression of their claims," they explain.[5]

But what's the best way to incorporate dissent and competition into *nonclass* multidistrict proceedings? Rules? Legislation? Common-law practices? Recently, both Congress and the Federal Rules Advisory Committee have taken an interest in tinkering with multidistrict litigation, opening up the possibility of top-down reforms. But past congressional proposals largely missed the mark by overlooking some of the actual problems and overstating issues tied to monied special interest groups like Big Pharma.[6] With little understanding of the system's complexities, positive attributes, and shortcomings, proposed legislation has attempted to tie transferee judges' hands in ham-handed ways.[7]

The federal rules process is better balanced and informed. Top-down reforms through rulemaking could help overcome the inherent biases and idiosyncrasies that judicially implemented changes would face. Formal rulemaking can also avoid the ad hoc nature of common-law reform.

Although transferee judges emphasize that every proceeding is different, as we have seen, patterns do exist. And certain changes could benefit from uniformity. Requiring that judges hew to Rule 23(g)'s adequate-representation requirements when appointing nonclass lead lawyers and tying leaders' common-benefit fees to plaintiffs' actual outcomes (as opposed to a fund's sticker price) are two such examples.

But there are downsides to top-down modifications too. Attorneys in this elite bar have proven adaptive, resilient, and likely to withstand change. Indeed, as Professor Amalia Kessler has shown in her exhaustive history, attorney gamesmanship has been around since the late 1600s.[8] Thus, the broader lesson is that improving MDL should not depend exclusively on top-down or external reforms, but on using procedural adjustments to encourage plaintiffs' lawyers to compete and dissent when needed. After all, they are the ones with the most information and the most at stake. If we can get the incentives right, then we could harness an equally adaptive power that already exists within the system – the repeat players.

[5] Elizabeth J. Cabraser & Samuel Issacharoff, *The Participatory Class Action*, 92 N.Y.U. L. Rev. 846, 864 (2017).

[6] H.R. 985, 115th Cong. (as passed by the House Mar. 7, 2017); Letter from Elizabeth Chamblee Burch, Charles H. Kirbo Chair of Law, Univ. of Ga. Sch. of Law, to James J. Park, Chief Counsel, Democratic Staff, Subcomm. on the Constitution & Civil Justice, Comm. on the Judiciary for the U.S. House of Representatives (Feb. 13, 2017), http://lawprofessors.typepad .com/files/final-comments-on-fairness-in-class-action-litigation-act.pdf.

[7] Elizabeth Chamblee Burch & Myriam Gilles, *Congress's Judicial Mistrust*, 45 Prod. Safety & Liab. Rep. (BNA) No. 14, at 340 (Apr. 3, 2017).

[8] Amalia Kessler, Inventing American Exceptionalism: The Origins of American Adversarial Legal Culture, 1800–1877 (2017).

This chapter builds opportunities for dissent and competition into the fabric of nonclass proceedings and incentivizes lawyers to use them. But doing so relies on judges. Educating judges and encouraging them to select leaders through a competitive process, tie leaders' fees to the benefits they confer on plaintiffs, open the courthouse doors to hear about those benefits (or not) directly from the plaintiffs, and remand those litigants who don't want to settle can allow the vibrant rivalries within the plaintiffs' bar to see to it that dissent and competition flourish. As attorneys object and compete, they are likely to divulge new information, thereby equipping judges with pieces of the puzzle that they currently lack. In short, this chapter explains how arming judges with procedures that better align plaintiffs' attorneys' self-interest with their clients' best interest equips courts to hold parties accountable even without legislation or rulemaking.

NUDGING LAWYERS, NOT PLAINTIFFS

Before we consider the nuts and bolts of these changes, it's helpful to briefly revisit the judicial role and mind-set. As we saw in Chapter 1, the fact that most cases settle seems to encourage judges to view that as the end goal rather than the by-product of vigorous adjudication and risk aversion. Chapter 4 then described the ways in which judges promoted settlement – facilitating discussions, publicly endorsing the deals, and imposing evidentiary burdens on nonsettling plaintiffs, for example.

Transferee judges find it hard to resist dealmakers' pleas for orders promoting their private settlements. After all, it's rare that adversaries agree on something. Yet, judicial assistance bears the hallmark of an imprimatur without any rigorous scrutiny as to whether the deal is fair, reasonable, and adequate. Plus, the legal basis for "approving" private settlements is thin, at best.

Judges stand on firmer footing when it comes to issuing merits-based rulings and policing attorneys' fees, for lawyers are officers of the court. Judges are supposed to monitor attorneys. And there is ample need to do so, for as we learned in Chapter 2, attorneys are not newcomers to the art of framing clients' choices or rigging those choices to satisfy their own ends.

As Professors Charles Silver and Geoffrey Miller argue, "[J]udges have compromised their independence, created unnecessary conflicts of interest, intimidated attorneys, turned a blind eye to ethically dubious behavior, and weakened plaintiffs' lawyers' incentives to serve clients well."[9] Perhaps. But there is ample blame to go around, for judicial acts are often urged by the negotiating parties.

So, although judges may contribute to a systemic problem, they can be an integral part of the solution too. Most care about achieving justice, but they may lack neutral guidance and impartial information. In other contexts, judges have welcomed

---

[9]   Charles Silver & Geoffrey P. Miller, *The Quasi-Class Action Method of Managing Multi-District Litigations: Problems and a Proposal*, 63 VAND. L. REV. 107, 111 (2010).

training on how to overcome their own biases and have been receptive to critiques and new methods.[10]

Accordingly, judges should nudge lead lawyers – not plaintiffs – in two ways. First, as later parts of this chapter argue, by tying lead lawyers' common-benefit fees to the benefit those attorneys actually confer on plaintiffs, judges can incentivize loyal representation. As we shall see, this tempts even repeat players with a powerful carrot and provides judges with a valid but limited toehold for reviewing private settlements. Second, as this section explores, by issuing reasoned opinions on merits-related motions, judges can send signals about a proceeding's strength.

"No judge worthy of his office wants merely to dispose of cases as if he were working on an assembly line," Judge Alvin B. Rubin once quipped.[11] In lieu of a settlement factory, deciding disputed motions and publishing opinions not only informs parties about the case's merits but also enhances transparency before leaders negotiate settlements behind closed doors.

As Judge Clay Land acknowledges, "[I]f private parties wish to opt out of the system and settle their dispute along the way; that is fine. And a trial judge has no business discouraging them." But "the trial judge, who first and foremost has a responsibility to the law, should not be *focused* on that option, or worse active in *pushing* that option. The trial judge should be managing the case toward trial – the place where our founders thought the ultimate resolution should occur."[12] Continuing, Judge Land notes, "[W]e as judges can take a fundamental step of asking ourselves each time we make decisions regarding the management of our cases: how does this facilitate the movement of this case *toward trial*; rather than: how does this increase the chances that this will get the case off my docket."[13]

In presiding over multidistrict proceedings alleging that Johnson & Johnson's unit, Mentor Corp., defectively designed, manufactured, and marketed ObTape to women, Judge Land put his philosophy into action, illustrating how a trial-oriented approach might work.

Instead of treating urinary incontinence (a common side effect of giving birth or having a hysterectomy), ObTape apparently made things worse by perforating some recipients' internal organs and causing infections and abscesses. As Judge Land concludes, "Mentor's scientists and doctors warned its executives of these issues, and yet Mentor continued to sell the product over their objections."[14] More than 850 women sued in federal court.

---

[10] Terry A. Maroney, *Response, Why Choose? A Response to Rachlinski, Wistrich, & Guthrie's "Heart versus Head: Do Judges Follow the Law or Follow Their Feelings?,"* 93 Tex. L. Rev. See Also 317, 318–19 (2015).

[11] Alvin B. Rubin, *Views from the Lower Court*, 23 UCLA L. Rev. 448, 453 (1976).

[12] Judge Clay D. Land, Lamentations of a Trial Judge, Remarks to the Columbus Inn of Court (Jan. 28, 2015) (on file with author).

[13] *Id.*

[14] *In re* Mentor Corp. ObTape Transobturator Sling Prods. Liab. Litig., MDL No. 08-md-2004, Case No. 12-cv-176 (M.D. Ga. Oct. 20, 2016) (order at 4).

Rather than putting the cases on track to settle, Judge Land's initial order gave leaders eight months to complete discovery in Phase I cases.[15] He eventually consolidated three cases for a jury trial. On the fifth day of trial, however, plaintiffs' counsel, Henry Garrard, told Judge Land that he'd reached a confidential deal with Johnson & Johnson that covered all his cases in the proceeding – leaving only 12 pending cases at the time.[16] Because none of them originated in the Middle District of Georgia, Judge Land planned to remand them for trial after he'd completed the pretrial proceedings.

As more cases flooded into the docket, however, Judge Land scheduled more trials. Mentor Corp. won a bellwether trial in 2013 and settled another one.[17] In early 2015, Johnson & Johnson settled more than 100 cases even as parties set additional bellwethers. Ever the trial-oriented judge, Judge Land remarked, "Despite my best efforts, I just can't get these cases to go to trial. We set them down, and Mr. Lewis [Mentor's lawyer] picks them off."[18] After Mentor settled yet another bellwether case, plaintiffs eventually won a $4.4 million verdict – though, per statute, Judge Land had to reduce punitive damages to $2 million.[19]

Settling plaintiffs' lawyers did ask Judge Land to deem their settlement a "qualified settlement fund" and approve the fund's trustee, a process required by the Internal Revenue Service.[20] Qualified settlement funds allow defendants to pay settlement proceeds into a fund (releasing them from further liability) and instill an independent trustee to handle the proceeds as a trust. You might think that this all looks the same from the plaintiffs' perspective, but there are key differences: a bank, not an arbitrator, administered the trust; the document heading is "Declaration of Trust" not "Pretrial Order X Appointing So and So as Special Master;" the trust came to be *after* plaintiffs chose to settle; and no nudges like Lone Pine orders or attorney withdrawals preceded or followed it. So, although Judge Land appointed the trustee and formally approved the qualified settlement fund, this was a ministerial task that differed from the settlement approvals in *Vioxx*, *Pradaxa*, *Zimmer Durom Hip Cup*, and *Yasmin/Yaz*, for instance.

Along the way, Judge Land decided more than 100 summary judgment motions, tried three bellwether trials, and made numerous evidentiary rulings – but didn't

---

[15] *In re* Mentor Corp. ObTape Transobturator Sling Prods. Liab. Litig., No. 08-md-2004 (M.D. Ga. Jan. 27, 2009) (discovery, scheduling, and case management order).

[16] *In re* Mentor Corp. ObTape Transobturator Sling Prods. Liab. Litig., No. 08-md-2004 (M.D. Ga. Sept. 9, 2010) (order).

[17] Caroline Simson, *Judge Selects 6 Bellwether Contenders in Vaginal Sling MDL*, Law360 (Jan. 22, 2015, 1:21 PM), https://www.law360.com/articles/613833/judge-selects-6-bellwether-con tenders-in-vaginal-sling-mdl.

[18] Transcript of Proceedings at 8, *In re* Mentor Corp. ObTape Transobturator Sling Prods. Liab. Litig., No. 08-md-2004 (M.D. Ga. Nov. 23, 2015).

[19] *In re* Mentor Corp. ObTape Transobturator Sling Prods. Liab. Litig., MDL No. 08-md-2004, Case No. 12-cv-176 (M.D. Ga. Oct. 20, 2016) (order).

[20] 26 U.S.C. § 468B (2012).

issue a single Lone Pine or census order.[21] To dispense with frivolous claims, he put plaintiffs' lawyers on notice that if their cases lacked a good-faith basis for continuing through summary judgment he would require them to show cause as to why he shouldn't impose sanctions.[22] A month later, in October 2016, he told the Panel that the multidistrict proceeding had run its course, requested that it stop transferring new cases to him, and began remanding cases to their home courts.[23]

As Judge Land's handiwork indicates, the ready-made rules judges use in routine cases, the ones that rely on the rationalistic processes that have long legitimized the judiciary, might just be sophisticated enough for multidistrict proceedings.[24] While larger proceedings might require that judges break them into different tracts to pay careful attention to adequate representation, group-specific issues, and proof, there seems to be little need to reinvent the wheel, to treat multidistrict litigation as a different species than routine civil cases.

Engaging with motions to dismiss for failing to state a claim, *Daubert* criteria to test experts, motions in limine to assess pretrial evidence, summary judgment motions to suss out whether disputes over important facts exist, discovery disputes, and even bellwether trials provide judges ample opportunity to reason through a proceeding's merits publicly. Yale professor Owen Fiss puts it plainly, "Only after hearing witnesses, examining the relevant documents, and sorting out the truth of the lawyers' claims about the facts and law does a judge have a basis to declare what justice requires: to determine whether the law has been violated and if so, what remedy should be imposed."[25]

To be sure, changing the way judges approach these proceedings is but one piece of a multifaceted makeover. Even judges who engage with the merits through traditional means may face information barriers. Judges cannot raise merits-related motions on their own. And even if they signaled that they would not bless or enforce a private deal without first digging into the suit, once that requirement is known, repeat players can adapt. After they've adjusted, motion practice may reveal nothing new; rather, it may simply affect the timing and the nature of when actors divulge the same information.

---

[21] *In re* Mentor Corp. ObTape Transobturator Sling Prods. Liab. Litig., No. 08-md-2004 (M.D. Ga. Oct. 18, 2016) (order).

[22] *In re* Mentor Corp. ObTape Transobturator Sling Prods. Liab. Litig., No. 08-md-2004 (M.D. Ga. Sept. 7, 2016) (order).

[23] *In re* Mentor Corp. ObTape Transobturator Sling Prods. Liab. Litig., No. 08-md-2004 (M.D. Ga. Oct. 18, 2016) (order).

[24] This is not necessarily at odds with others who have advocated for judges to play a role in encouraging parties to exchange information and develop the facts supporting their positions. *See, e.g.,* Jaime Dodge, *Facilitative Judging: Organizational Design in Mass-Multidistrict Litigation,* 64 EMORY L.J. 329, 351 (2014); David M. Jaros & Adam S. Zimmerman, *Judging Aggregate Settlement,* 94 WASH. U. L. REV. 545, 598–99 (2017).

[25] Owen M. Fiss, *The History of an Idea,* 78 FORDHAM L. REV. 1273, 1278 (2009).

By changing the way they appoint and compensate leaders and handle remands, however, judges can build in additional safeguards by encouraging plaintiffs' lawyers to compete, dissent, and divulge hidden information. Judges may be the last line of defense, but if they aren't armed with the facts, they are handicapped. Incentivizing those who hold that information – other plaintiffs' attorneys – to disclose it, wield it to their clients' benefit, and hold leaders accountable is critical.

INCENTIVIZING ATTORNEY LOYALTY

As we saw in Chapter 3, allowing lawyers to coronate their own leaders can promote back-scratching deals, create ineffective committees, and encourage undisclosed fee-sharing arrangements that may perversely affect settlement incentives. To ward off the old mafia-movie scene that Lance Cooper described, judges must take the reins on selecting lead lawyers. It's not as easy as deferring to attorneys' own consensus picks, but employing truly competitive processes is important.

Why? Consensus numbs competition. Consumers and clients alike tend to fare better in competitive markets. When law firms compete, they can distinguish themselves based on price, expertise, specialization, and results. Competition can thus act as an antidote to corruption by rewarding attorneys' loyalty to clients, reducing unnecessary spending, and bringing conflicted interests to light.[26]

Timing, Criteria, and Mechanics

Instituting a competitive application process and conducting a selection hearing are good first steps. Hearings can introduce nonrepeat players to the court, increase transparency, and help prevent echo chambers. But, to select leaders, judges need relevant information – not the undulating accolades and irrelevant tidbits that some lawyers include. In applying to lead *GM*, for instance, attorney Dan Becnel noted that his son "recently spent two weeks in China with First Lady Michelle Obama and was in charge of coordinating the Seventieth Anniversary of the Normandy Landings for the President of the United States."[27] But Becnel's *son* wasn't applying for a leadership position – he was, and this had no bearing on his own qualifications.

In lieu of soliciting freewheeling applications, judges should tailor forms for specific positions and request pertinent data points. For example, it's helpful for judges to know applicants' involvement with past (and concurrent) proceedings including their leadership roles, work performed, the type of proceeding, the overall outcomes, their clients' outcomes, and their common-benefit fee requests versus their common-benefit recovery. For the proceeding at hand, applicants should

---

[26] Scott E. Page, Diversity and Complexity 214–17 (2011).

[27] Daniel E. Becnel Jr. Leadership Application at 1, *In re* Gen. Motors LLC Ignition Switch Litig., No. 14-md-2543 (S.D.N.Y. July 9, 2014).

identify the injuries and claims of their firm's current clients, likely conflicts that will arise among the plaintiffs, financing arrangements (in chambers), and any relationships they or their firm have with third-party vendors or third-party funders.[28]

If done appropriately, allowing attorneys to vet each other can supplement applications and unearth new information. But if judges require lawyers to object on the record or in open court, they may learn little.[29] As Chapter 3 explored, once an heir apparent emerges, conditions become ripe for conformity and informational cascades. The mass-tort bar is small. Speaking out against the consensus group may mean being excluded from common-benefit work once that group takes power. So, others are more likely to withhold privately held information, fall in line behind the emerging consensus, and simply echo that sentiment.[30]

Soliciting objections needn't sully or imperil lawyers' reputations, however. If judges appoint a magistrate judge or special master to oversee leadership selection, then lawyers can air their preferences and grievances confidentially to her and perhaps the judge's career clerks.[31] The clerks and the magistrate or special master can speak with applicants privately, assimilate and evaluate applications, raise the substance of any objections with the applicant, and then recommend a slate to the judge.[32] The judge can then treat the final appointment as a confirmation hearing.[33]

Appointing temporary counsel and giving the litigation a few months to develop before selecting leaders may give judges a better idea as to the potential fault lines between plaintiffs. Waiting can also expand the pool of available leaders. Empirical data from the Federal Judicial Center demonstrates that highly specialized repeat players appear earlier in multidistrict proceedings than do other attorneys. Elite insiders appear an average of 73 days after transfer. Repeat players with fewer appearances arrive after 333 days and, on average, other attorneys appear 419 days posttransfer.[34]

---

[28] For a sample leadership application form see Elizabeth Chamblee Burch, *Monopolies in Multidistrict Litigation*, 70 VAND. L. REV. 67, 162–63 (2017).

[29] E.g., *In re* Oil Spill by the Oil Rig "Deepwater Horizon" in the Gulf of Mexico, on Apr. 20, 2010, No. 10-md-2179 (E.D. La. Aug. 10, 2010) (pretrial order no. 1, setting initial conference).

[30] CASS R. SUNSTEIN, WHY SOCIETIES NEED DISSENT 23–24, 68–69 (2005); CASS R. SUNSTEIN, GOING TO EXTREMES: HOW LIKE MINDS UNITE AND DIVIDE 90–93 (2009) [hereinafter SUNSTEIN, GOING TO EXTREMES].

[31] Judge David Proctor has used this procedure. Special Master's Rule 23 Report Recommending Interim Plaintiff Leadership Counsel, *In re* Blue Cross Blue Shield Antitrust Litig., No. 2:13-cv-20000-RDP (N.D. Ala. Apr. 10, 2013). Should due process objections arise to this approach, anonymizing the critiques could help. CHARLAN NEMETH, IN DEFENSE OF TROUBLEMAKERS: THE POWER OF DISSENT IN LIFE AND BUSINESS 37 (2018).

[32] For detailed information on this interview and screening process as well as sample forms see, Burch, *supra* note 28 at 137–38, 162–64.

[33] E.g., Transcript of Evidentiary Hearing, *In re* Blue Cross Blue Shield Antitrust Litig., No. 2:13-cv-20000-RDP (N.D. Ala. Apr. 25, 2013).

[34] Margaret S. Williams, Emery G. Lee III & Catherine R. Borden, *Repeat Players in Federal Multidistrict Litigation*, 5 J. TORT L. 141 (2014).

When significant divisions exist between plaintiffs within a proceeding, those groups should have their own representative. In the words of the American Law Institute, which are grounded in the Supreme Court's opinion in *Amchem Products, Inc. v. Windsor*, structural conflicts of interest arise when there's a danger that counsel "might skew [the litigation] systematically" to favor some plaintiffs over others "on grounds aside from reasoned evaluation of their respective claims or . . . disfavor claimants generally vis-à-vis the lawyers themselves."[35] Put differently, if lumping claims or plaintiffs together creates a risk that counsel will trade one group to gain favorable treatment for another, then each group deserves its own attorney. Adequate representation depends less on good faith ideals and more on harder edged notions of self-interest.[36]

For instance, in *Ortiz v. Fibreboard Corp.*, the Court required separate representatives for those exposed to asbestos before and after 1959 – when Fibreboard's insurance policy expired. Why? Insurance made some claims more valuable than others.[37] Requiring separate representatives when claims have different values makes sense, reasoned the Second Circuit. "The rationale is simple: how can the value of any subgroup of claims be properly assessed without independent counsel pressing its most compelling case?" "It is for this reason," the court continued, that including "impartial mediators and institutional plaintiffs does not compensate for the absence of [separate] representation." Those neutrals "safeguarded the negotiation process," but "no one advanced the strongest arguments in favor of [a particular category of claims'] recovery."[38]

The judges in both *NFL Concussion* and *Deepwater Horizon* implied the opposite, however. They reasoned that separate representatives were less necessary if court-appointed neutrals facilitated the deals. Special masters may smooth the path toward settlement, but as the Second Circuit recognized, they're a poor substitute for separate representation. Special masters aim to finalize a deal to please the judge and thereby ensure future business for themselves. They fear that dividing plaintiffs into subgroups and ensuring that they have someone to speak on their behalf during negotiations will create insurmountable rifts, balkanize the process, and jeopardize settlements. As Professor Morris Ratner recognizes, however, the "choice is not between zero and an infinite number, as the Balkanization metaphor suggests."[39]

[35] PRINCIPLES OF THE LAW OF AGGREGATE LITIGATION § 2.07(a)(1)(B) (AM. LAW INST. 2010); Amchem Prods., Inc. v. Windsor, 521 U.S. 591, 627 (1997); *see also* Samuel Issacharoff & Richard A. Nagareda, *Class Settlements under Attack*, 156 PENN. L. REV. 1649, 1677–1701 (2008). Separate representation matters less in certain leadership positions, like liaison counsel. Liaison counsel disseminates information and acts more as a conduit than a decision maker. But adequate representation is critically important in conducting discovery, choosing bell-wether cases, and negotiating settlement.

[36] *See, e.g.*, Gen. Tel. Co. v. Falcon, 457 U.S. 147, 156–57 (1982).

[37] 527 U.S. 815, 857 (1999).

[38] *In re* Literary Works in Elec. Databases Copyright Litig., 654 F.3d 242, 253 (2d Cir. 2011).

[39] Morris A. Ratner, *Class Conflicts*, 92 WASH. L. REV. 785, 829–36 (2017).

What the Balkanization worry really boils down to is a concern about giving those marginalized by the process a voice. But, as I'll explain shortly, dissenters are invaluable. They should be prized for the information they generate and the divergent thinking they stimulate, not closeted. For now, however, the thing to remember is that without a lawyer whose economic interests are tied to theirs, some plaintiffs' claims may be undeveloped and some may be inadequately represented.

In sum, early in the proceedings, it may be impossible to predict where these important fault lines will lie. And, once they're appointed, leaders have little incentive to raise conflicts on their own – doing so could drive wedges between their own clients. The judge isn't much help at that point either, for she may simply know too little.

The cure isn't to take an ostrich-like stance, it's to encourage individual attorneys who have first-hand knowledge to use it. There's no incentive to do so now. But imagine if those lawyers could get a coveted leadership spot by raising critical conflicts.

How might this work? Judges could issue an order that creates a presumption in favor of removing lead lawyers who create or ignore structural conflicts and replacing them with the attorney who successfully raised and demonstrated the conflict.[40] To be sure, the challenger would need the requisite experience and funding, but the idea is to spur those with the most knowledge to speak up.

The judge's response to a successful challenge will vary, of course. If the leaders have harmed the plaintiffs to further their own self-interest, then it would make sense to begin from a clean slate. If some leaders negotiated side deals for their own clients, have no clients left in the proceedings, or litigated in a way that systematic-ally biases nonclients for reasons unrelated to their claims' merits,[41] then the judge should replace those attorneys.[42] If plaintiffs have materially different claims or circumstances such that unified representation would pose a conflict, then judges might add the challenger to the leadership roster to separately represent those plaintiffs' interests.[43]

---

[40] Richard A. Nagareda, *Administering Adequacy in Class Representation*, 82 Tex. L. Rev. 287, 347–63 (2003); *see also* Judith Resnik, *Money Matters: Judicial Market Interventions Creating Subsidies and Awarding Fees and Costs in Individual and Aggregate Litigation*, 148 Penn. L. Rev. 2119, 2127 (2000) ("[J]udges will have to pay for process, by funding subclass represen-tatives, objectors, independent evaluators, or court employees to generate information and to organize the claimants effected in a manner that serves the civil justice system goals of resolving disputes equitably.").

[41] The latecomer provisions in the *DePuy ASR* settlements provide one such example. *See supra* notes 66–69 in Chapter 2 and accompanying text.

[42] *See* John C. Coffee Jr., *Class Action Accountability: Reconciling Exit, Voice, and Loyalty in Representative Litigation*, 100 Colum. L. Rev. 370, 388 (2008); Samuel Issacharoff, *Govern-ance and Legitimacy in the Law of Class Actions*, 1999 Sup. Ct. Rev. 337, 385; Richard G. Stuhan & Sean P. Costello, *Robbing Peter to Pay Paul: The Conflict of Interest Problem in Sibling Class Actions*, 21 Geo. J. Legal Ethics 1195, 1213–14 (2008).

[43] Burch, *supra* note 28, at 143–45.

Although the execution differs, the proposal harmonizes with what some judges do already. In *Zyprexa*, for example, after the original steering committee negotiated a deal, Judge Jack Weinstein appointed a new plaintiffs' steering committee for nonsettling plaintiffs.[44] And in *Vioxx*, after the settlement, Judge Eldon Fallon appointed additional counsel to the plaintiffs' steering committee for those who were ineligible or unenrolled.[45]

Encouraging challengers and replacing leaders as necessary is, however, different than the one-year "term" limits that some judges have imposed. Although continual reassessment motivates lawyers to keep working hard, it also makes them principally beholden to the judge. Leaders shouldn't fear replacement for vigorously representing plaintiffs nor should they be tempted to curry judicial favor at plaintiffs' expense. So, instead of term limits, if leaders or nonleaders notice neglect or discover new information, they can request that the judge add or substitute counsel as needed.

Building the Best Team: Members' Attributes

As they consider applications, judges and special masters should aim to compile the best team – not the best individual lawyers. In doing so, they should keep size and skills in mind. As to size, even though some circumstances will demand larger groups, empirical studies consistently show that from a decision-making standpoint, groups with five or six members are optimal.[46] As to skills, the goal is to appoint a small, cognitively diverse group whose members possess different information, knowledge, and tools. Just as teams of doctors need skeptics to make accurate diagnoses and successful corporate boards require assertive members that don't kowtow to the CEO,[47] leadership groups in multidistrict litigation need lawyers with mixed perspectives who aren't afraid to openly disagree.

Judges are accustomed to seeking team players with deep war chests who are mass-tort experts. Expertise is important, but it can leave gaps. For instance, appointing lawyers with the most mass-tort experience may net a group with a great deal of procedural expertise but could exclude the non-MDL attorney who spent years cracking open the case. Similarly, some attorneys have excellent reputations as negotiators. But a negotiating team without a seasoned trial lawyer doesn't pose a credible threat to the defendant. Point is, teams need people with a diverse array of knowledge, skills, perception, and training. So the best leadership group for any proceeding is unlikely to be a collection of the most grizzled mass-tort lawyers.

---

[44] *In re* Zyprexa Prods. Liab. Litig., 467 F. Supp. 2d 256, 261–62 (E.D.N.Y. 2006).
[45] *In re* Vioxx Prods. Liab. Litig., No. 05-md-1657 (E.D. La. Jan. 8, 2010) (pretrial order no. 45A).
[46] Susan A. Wheelan, *Group Size, Group Development, and Group Productivity*, 40 SMALL GROUP RES. 247, 257–58 (2009, No. 2).
[47] SUNSTEIN, GOING TO EXTREMES *supra* note 30, at 147–48; Jeffrey A. Sonnenfeld, *What Makes Boards Great*, 80 HARV. BUS. REV., Sept. 2002, at 106.

It's not that experience isn't important – it is – it's just not the *only* thing that's important.

Think of it this way: when homogenous minds approach a problem in the same manner, they are likely to get stuck at the same point.[48] But a group with members who have unique tools and skills, and who frame the problem differently, might solve it in a way that no one else considered. Once one person fixes it, the whole group can move forward.

Still, even heterogenous groups can lose that edge as they interact over time, for their thinking may converge.[49] Newcomers, however, "may be a rich source of ideas for improving group performance," explain psychologists, because newcomers "lack strong personal ties to other members that inhibit their willingness to challenge group orthodoxy," aren't already "committed to the group's task strategy," and "bring fresh perspectives gained in other groups."[50]

These are the ideas at the heart of Scott Page's work on cognitive diversity and group decisions.[51] Page is a professor of complex systems, political science, and economics. His models are scientific, nuanced, and mathematically based. But here's the *"Reader's Digest"* version.

Cognitive diversity is a bit different than what typically comes to mind when we hear the word "diversity." There has, for instance, been a recent push for judges to appoint more women and minorities to leadership positions. But gender, race, age, physical abilities, economic status, and sexual orientation are all types of *identity* (or descriptive) diversity. *Cognitive* diversity, by contrast, considers whether people have diverse knowledge and expertise stemming from training, experiences, and, yes, identity.[52] Identity can play a role by creating experiential differences that prompt contrasting analytic tools to develop. Yet physical characteristics alone may tell us little.[53]

As Page explains, "[B]y mapping people into identity groups . . . we lump a recent immigrant from Nairobi, Kenya, a grandson of a sharecropper from the Mississippi delta, and the daughter of a dentist from Barrington, Illinois, into the same category: African Americans." We also "place the granddaughter of a miner from Copper Harbor, Michigan, a son of Gloria Vanderbilt (that would be Anderson Cooper),

---

[48] Scott E. Page, The Difference: How the Power of Diversity Creates Better Groups, Firms, Schools, and Societies 157 (paperback ed., 2007).

[49] *Id.*

[50] John M. Levine & Hoon-Seok Choi, *Minority Influence in Interacting Groups: The Impact of Newcomers, in* Rebels in Groups 73, 78 (Jolanda Jetten & Matthew J. Hornsey eds., 2011).

[51] Page has made these ideas accessible in his most recent book. Scott E. Page, The Diversity Bonus (2017).

[52] Page, *supra* note 48, at 7–8, 302–12; Elizabeth Mannix & Margaret A. Neale, *What Differences Make a Difference? The Promise and Reality of Diverse Teams in Organizations*, 6 Am. Psychol. Soc'y 31, 41–42 (2005).

[53] Abby L. Mello & Lisa A. Delise, *Cognitive Diversity to Team Outcomes: The Roles of Cohesion and Conflict Management*, 46 Small Group Res. 204, 204–5 (2015).

and a recently married former au pair from Lithuania into the box labeled non-Hispanic white." But each lump, if disaggregated, would prove cognitively diverse.[54] Likewise, as Berkeley psychology professor Charlan Nemeth notes, simply aggregating a mix of genders, races, and ethnicities "does not ensure diversity of perspective."[55]

Normative claims about representation, fairness, and social legitimacy may well dictate a need for more identity diversity among lead lawyers. The thrust is that those who represent heterogeneous groups ought to reflect the group's makeup.[56] After all, women are more than half of the U.S. population and 35% of the legal profession.[57] Of the top 50 repeat players within the dataset, however, only 11 were women.[58] Yet, a number of mass torts, such as those over transvaginal mesh and birth control like Mirena, Yaz/Yasmin, Essure, and NuvaRing, pertain principally to women.

Plaintiffs' attorney Alyson Oliver put it simply in her request to help lead *Mirena*, "Similar to the apparent disconcert of having an all-female leadership team on a testicular implant case, I think that it remains of both strategic and symbolic importance to voice my concerns on the lack of gender-related representation on the leadership of this inherently female litigation."[59] Judge Cathy Seibel agreed, noting that including female leaders was "important."[60]

But diversity proponents frequently advance a second proposition: diversity improves outcomes. This claim needs a great deal of fleshing out. What kind of diversity improves outcomes? When, how, and under what conditions should we see such gains?

As it turns out, leveraging diversity's benefits isn't as simple as assembling a slapdash group of different looking people. Some studies even suggest that when

[54] PAGE, *supra* note 48, at 363–64.
[55] NEMETH, *supra* note 31, at 169.
[56] Christina L. Boyd, Lee Epstein & Andrew D. Martin, *Untangling the Causal Effects of Sex on Judging*, 54 AM. J. POL. SCI. 389, 390 (2010) (citing Charles Cameron & Craig Cummings, *Diversity and Judicial Decision Making: Evidence from Affirmative Action and Cases in the Federal Courts of Appeals, 1971–1999* (paper presented at the Crafting and Operating Institutions Conference, 2003)).
[57] AM. BAR ASS'N, A CURRENT GLANCE AT WOMEN IN THE LAW 2 (2017), https://www.american bar.org/content/dam/aba/administrative/women/a-current-glance-at-women-in-the-law-jan-2018.authcheckdam.pdf.
[58] Other studies reflect these differences as well. One showed that women were far less likely to occupy top leadership positions, holding only 15% of those spots across all multidistrict proceedings from 2011 to 2016. DANA ALVARÉ, VYING FOR LEAD IN THE "BOYS' CLUB": UNDERSTANDING THE GENDER GAP IN MULTIDISTRICT LITIGATION LEADERSHIP APPOINTMENTS (2017), https://www2.law.temple.edu/csj/publication/mdl-study/. Lower-level leadership positions fared little better, with only 19% women. Although it's impossible to say without surveys allowing leaders to self-identify, minorities appear to fare worse still.
[59] Letter from Alyson Oliver to the Honorable Cathy Seibel, *In re* Mirena IUD Prods. Liab. Litig., No. 13-md-2434 (S.D.N.Y. May 10, 2013).
[60] Stephanie Francis Ward, *Women Should Be among Lead Lawyers in IUD Case, Federal Judge Says*, A.B.A. J. (May 20, 2013, 7:00 PM), http://www.abajournal.com/news/article/iud_litiga tion_needs_some_women_as_lead_lawyers_says_federal_judge/.

people perceive themselves as belonging to opposing groups they may tune each other out; those with privately held information may be less inclined to divulge it for fear of being mocked or socially ostracized.[61] There is little to be gained from a situation like that.

Research on judges vividly illustrates this point. Summarizing and analyzing the studies to date, Professors Christina Boyd, Lee Epstein, and Andrew Martin concluded, "[T]he presence of women in the federal appellate judiciary rarely has an appreciable empirical effect on judicial outcomes. Rarely, though is not never."[62] As Alyson Oliver's comment suggested, gender can matter where gender itself is an issue, such as in employment-discrimination and sexual-harassment cases. In one study, for instance, the mere presence of a single female appellate court judge on a three-judge panel increased female plaintiffs' success rate in sex-discrimination cases.[63]

To answer the earlier questions as to how diversity improves outcomes, however, *cognitive* diversity in groups can create "bonuses" when group members perform disjunctive, nonroutine, thought-provoking tasks.[64] In other words, intellectually challenging assignments that require only one good idea for everyone to move forward – not making copies or conducting document review. Reviewing documents is a conjunctive task: one missed, critical document can pose setbacks for the entire team, so each member must perform well for the group to succeed. Disjunctive tasks, however, are those in which only one person needs to propose a winning strategy or idea for everyone to move forward. Deciphering the best legal strategy, identifying successful negotiating tactics, and selecting which issues to appeal would all be good examples.

As best they can then, judges should strive to compile cognitively diverse leadership teams by seeking members whose knowledge, skills, information, and tools differ.[65] Although soliciting and assessing the relevant information I identified earlier gets judges closer to the mark, assembling a cognitively diverse group is not an exact science. It involves a bit of guesswork. Even if it didn't, the danger persists that lead counsel may silo individual team members, that the conditions for collaborating might deteriorate, and that all the potential upside may be lost.

---

[61] Marie-Élène Roberge & Rolf van Dick, *Recognizing the Benefits of Diversity: When and How Does Diversity Increase Group Performance?*, 20 Hum. Resource Mgmt. Rev. 295, 297 (2010) (citing studies).

[62] Boyd et al., *supra* note 56, at 54.

[63] Jenifer L. Peresie, *Female Judges Matter: Gender and Collegial Decisionmaking in the Federal Appellate Courts*, 114 Yale L.J. 1759 (2005).

[64] Page, *supra* note 48, at xiv–xv, 325–27; Gayle W. Hill, *Group versus Individual Performance: Are N + 1 Heads Better Than One?*, 91 Psychol. Bull. 517, 533 (1982).

[65] These criteria are linked to adequate representation and thus avoid the constitutional challenge that Justice Alito raised to race and gender-based appointments in class actions. Martin v. Blessing, 571 U.S. 1040 (2013).

Adequate Representation Depends on Dissent and Outsiders

The key – as uncomfortable and irritating as it may be – is to prize dissent, to permit and embrace it at every turn. In a culture that has placed cooperation and consensus on a pedestal, preaching the need for dissent may sound heretical. But it's crucial.

In any other situation we might label people who don't go along with the majority as "rogues," "obstacles," "holdouts," or "troublemakers." When they appear on committees in experimental settings, others relegate them to menial tasks.[66] But these outliers are exactly the people that judges and lead lawyers need to heed – not shun – in mass torts. As I spell out in the pages that follow, dissenters add value in three ways: (1) they unravel the power of consensus and subject it to questioning; (2) they stimulate divergent thinking even when they are wrong; and (3) they may introduce (and prompt others to divulge) new information.

First, majorities are powerful: study after study shows that people conform, even when the majority is wrong. Some think that the truth lies in numbers. Mostly, we want to fit in, or at least not stick out. As we saw in Chapter 3, lead and nonlead attorneys are unlikely to speak up when they spot problems if doing so pits them against everyone else. Maybe it's a cascade effect, maybe some think it won't make any difference, or maybe they fear financial repercussions, ostracization, or ridicule. Whatever the reason, as psychology professor Charlan Nemeth explains, "Silence then becomes part of the power of the majority." But, she continues, "Just one person challenging the consensus can break that power and increase our ability to think independently and resist moving to erroneous judgments."[67]

Second, similar to the benefits of cognitive diversity, dissenters can prompt us to think about things in different ways. A variety of experimental studies on juries show that when there's a dissenter present and jurors must deliberate until they reach a consensus, they consider more evidence, explanations, and alternative possibilities.[68] And when Supreme Court justices dissent, the majority opinion reveals more integrative complexity. In other words, the majority considers and evaluates more positions and trade-offs.[69] Put simply, dissent staves off a rush to judgment, prompts majorities to seek multiple problem-solving strategies, stimulates original thinking, and can encourage more creative solutions to emerge.[70]

---

[66] Stanley Schachter, *Deviation, Rejection, and Communication*, 46 J. ABNORMAL & Soc. PSY-
CHOL. 190 (1951).

[67] NEMETH, *supra* note 31, at 29–31, 39.

[68] Charlan Nemeth, *Jury Trials: Psychology and the Law*, in 14 ADVANCES IN EXPERIMENTAL
SOCIAL PSYCHOLOGY, 309 (Leonard Berkowitz ed., 1981).

[69] Deborah H. Gruenfeld, *Status, Ideology, and Integrative Complexity on the US Supreme Court:
Rethinking the Politics of Political Decision Making*, 68 J. PERSONALITY & Soc. PYSCHOL. 5
(1995).

[70] Charlan J. Nemeth & Jack A. Goncalo, *Rogues and Heroes: Finding Value in Dissent*, in
REBELS IN GROUPS: DISSENT, DEVIANCE, DIFFERENCE, AND DEFIANCE 17, 22 (Jolanda Jetten &
Matthew J. Hornsey eds., 2010); Stefan Schulz-Hardt et al., *Dissent as a Facilitator: Individual-*

Third, dissent can reveal new information. In general, when we think we're right (and who doesn't?), we look for information that confirms our own position. Yet, oddly enough, when the majority disagrees with us, we tend to seek information that *supports* the majority. As Professor Nemeth explains, we "seek and analyze information selectively, in ways that justify [the majority] perspective." So, without realizing it, we "become complicit in our own brainwashing."[71] According to psychologist Robert Cialdiani, this strikes at the heart of social proof: "Usually, when a lot of people are doing something, it is the right thing to do." So, he explains, "[W]hen people are uncertain, they are more likely to use others' actions to decide how they themselves should act."[72]

This herd mentality leads cattle to slaughter, people into cults, multidistrict lawyers into ethical blunders, and multidistrict plaintiffs into deals that may not be in their best interest. Dissent, however, can be an antidote. When confronted with dissent, we widen our search for information. "[I]t stimulates our thinking so that we look at multiple sides of the issue, detect new solutions, and even think in more original ways," says Professor Nemeth.[73]

As plaintiffs' aims and preferences vary, dissenters can challenge the status quo and inject previously undisclosed information into the discussion. Still, it helps to be specific about who's in charge of raising concerns on behalf of certain plaintiffs. This is where subgrouping for structural conflicts can help tremendously. When groups fail to elicit and use all the information that each member holds privately, it's often because no one sees themselves as the designated expert.[74]

Dissent is healthy, but it isn't always welcomed. As Chapter 1 described, all the regular stakeholders – judges, plaintiffs' leaders, defendants and their lawyers – favor settlement. Objectors can disrupt or slow down the end game. They're not the prized "team players." But they play a critical and genuine role.

Of course, not all conflict is productive. I suspect we've each encountered contrarians, cantankerous folks who disagree just to be disagreeable. There are some contrarians who achieve their reputation because they consistently point out errors all around. These mavericks may be killjoys, but if they are disclosing accurate information that's been suppressed, others should listen.[75] But when fights break out over routine tasks like reviewing discovery materials and producing documents, it

and Group-Level Effects on Creativity and Performance, in THE PSYCHOLOGY OF CONFLICT MANAGEMENT IN ORGANIZATIONS 149, 150–54, 162–63 (Carsten K. W. De Dreu & Michele J. Gelfand eds., 2008).
[71] NEMETH, *supra* note 31, at 88; Charlan Nemeth & John Rogers, *Dissent and the Search for Information*, 35 BRITISH J. SOC. PSYCHOL. 35, 67–76 (1996).
[72] ROBERT B. CIALDINI, INFLUENCE: THE PSYCHOLOGY OF PERSUASION 116, 140 (2007).
[73] NEMETH, *supra* note 31, at 107.
[74] Garold Stasser & William Titus, *Hidden Profiles: A Brief History*, 14 PSYCHOL. INQUIRY 304, 310 (2003).
[75] *Id.* at 303, 311.

helps no one.[76] Interpersonal conflicts likewise distract group members from their jobs. Instead of focusing on the task at hand, they think about increasing their own power, rousing their supporters, or threatening their enemies.[77]

The goal isn't to empower this bunch. It's to foster dissent over nonroutine, substantive tasks like which legal theories are best suited for class certification, what strategy will defeat a motion to dismiss or a motion for summary judgment, and whether a settlement offer is fair for all plaintiffs. By welcoming conflict from insiders and outsiders on critical issues like these and opening the docket to supplemental briefing or disagreement, judges can harness dissent's value: more information, divergent thinking, and adequate representation.[78] In her handling of both the *Avandia* and *Zoloft* proceedings, for instance, Judge Cynthia Rufe permitted any attorney who didn't agree with the steering committee's nonadministrative stipulations to object.[79] If dissent becomes valued rather than shunned and dissenters are rewarded rather than snubbed, more lawyers are likely to weigh in.

Dissent can come from two sources: (1) cognitively diverse leaders who represent subgroups with structurally conflicting interests and (2) outsiders, the bevy of non-lead lawyers on the sidelines who have much to lose or gain for their clients. Just as organizations hire external consultants to suggest improvements and challenge the status quo, outsiders can poke the bear a bit without disrupting the hierarchical powers that be. Unlike insiders whose reputations and livelihoods are at stake, sidelined attorneys may be willing to raise issues that insiders either can't see or are afraid to voice.[80]

When marginalized attorneys object and share new information, their actions support adequate representation's aims. After all, having someone represent you means that she will dissent on your behalf when your interests are threatened, state your position to the group and, if that fails, to the judge. Dissenters can thus act as a fail-safe for adequate representation – not a substitute. When leaders' actions result in dismissing a plaintiff's claim or affect her case's value, adequate representation demands that someone at the decision-making table first present the most compelling case for her (or someone like her).

---

[76] *See* Karen A. Jehn, *A Multimethod Examination of the Benefits and Detriments of Intragroup Conflict*, 40 Admin. Sci. Q. 256, 275–76 (1995).

[77] Karen A. Jehn, *A Qualitative Analysis of Conflict Types and Dimensions in Organizational Groups*, 42 Admin. Sci. Q. 530, 531 (Sept. 1997); Jehn, *supra* note 76, at 275–76.

[78] Nemeth & Goncalo, *supra* note 70, at 17, 27–28.

[79] *In re* Avandia Mktg., Sales Practices & Prods. Liab. Litig., No. 07-md-01871 (E.D. Pa. Feb. 28, 2008) (case management order no. 1); *In re* Zoloft (Sertraline Hydrochloride) Prods. Liab. Litig., No. 12-md-2342 (E.D. Pa. May 4, 2012) (pretrial order no. 1).

[80] Page, *supra* note 48, at 344; Ulrich Klocke, *How to Improve Decision Making in Small Groups: Effects of Dissent and Training Interventions*, 38 Small Group Res. 437, 437–38, 460–62 (2007).

TYING COMMON-BENEFIT FEES TO PLAINTIFFS' OUTCOMES

Judges have other tools at their disposal as well. One of the most powerful is the ability to award common-benefit fees. By tying leaders' common-benefit fees to the benefit they confer on plaintiffs – not the sticker price of a settlement fund – judges can nudge them to loyally represent plaintiffs. As this section explains, linking fees to benefits using quantum-meruit principles checks self-dealing even for repeat players and realigns common-benefit fees with basic contingent-fee principles: the better plaintiffs fare, the better leadership fares. Quantum meruit likewise provides judges with a valid but limited basis to review private settlements and hear about the settlement's benefits (and drawbacks) from the plaintiffs.

The Quantum-Meruit Theory

No uniform positive law exists for judges to award leaders a common-benefit fee. So they have cannibalized class-action law's common-fund doctrine, contract principles, ethics, and equity, while ignoring the constraints of each. Each isolated theory fails to fully explain fee awards. And though they appear to create a seamless façade when combined, this doctrinal patchwork lacks coherence, uniformity, and predictability.

As we saw in Chapter 2, the uncertainty surrounding these misappropriated theories encourages lawyers to contract around judicial common-benefit orders by embedding fee provisions within settlements. And instead of chastising lawyers for self-dealing or holding them in contempt of court for undermining previous judicial orders, judges appear to accept these moves. After all, contractual consent provides a safe harbor amid a choppy sea of borrowed doctrine.

But lead lawyers exist because the judge appointed them, not because plaintiffs or their attorneys selected them. Therein lies the rub: judicially appointed lead lawyers should have the judge set their fees through a transparent process. Leaders shouldn't be allowed to slip backdoor trades with the defendant into a settlement. Instead, judicially created common-benefit funds should be judicially administered and subject to appeal – not hidden in settlements or shielded by sealed fee petitions.[81]

What piecemeal doctrine lacks, equity provides using quantum meruit. Quantum meruit implies a recovery goal – how much is merited – not a specific cause of action. Yet, it lies at the heart of each of the theories judges have invoked in the past to stitch together compensation awards – contract, restitution, and equity.[82]

---

[81] E.g., *In re* DePuy ASR Hip Implant Prods. Liab. Litig., No. 10-md-02197 (N.D. Ohio Mar. 7, 2016) (sealed order no. 18 granting 1036 sealed motion to transfer & release funds filed by plaintiffs' liaison counsel).

[82] Elizabeth Chamblee Burch, *Judging Multidistrict Litigation*, 90 N.Y.U. L. REV. 71, 102–6 (2015).

Quantum meruit also accommodates the uniqueness of common-benefit fees, which essentially divvy up contingent fees (the 30% or so that lawyers charge in their retainer agreement) between individually retained attorneys and lead lawyers. This makes common-benefit fees quintessentially different from common-fund awards, which award the equivalent of the *entire* contingent fee, not just a portion of it.[83] So what may seem like a small 6% tax on a fund "means that the [individual] attorney is likely losing 20% of a 30% contingent fee (6/30)," explains Professor William Rubenstein. If we're thinking in terms of taxes, Rubenstein points out that this 20%–30% tax on an individual lawyer's fee is "significantly (33%) higher than the highest federal capital gains tax (15%) and roughly half the highest federal income tax rate (39.6%)."[84]

It makes sense then to treat common-benefit assessments like other situations in which attorneys divide fees among themselves. If no fee agreement exists, or a lawyer voluntarily withdraws for good cause, or attorneys fight about how to share fees, or clients fire contingent-fee attorneys or local counsel without cause, judges must decide who gets what. In doing so, they universally turn to quantum meruit.

As the *Restatement (Third) of the Law Governing Lawyers* observes, counsel has a right to recover "a fair fee in quantum meruit" when "a client and lawyer have not made a valid contract providing for another measure of compensation."[85] In multidistrict litigation, even though the client contracts with her chosen attorney, she typically has no agreement with the lead lawyers. Rather, the situation is more like a forced referral or sale, where the individual's attorney must fork her clients over to the lead lawyers who bundle and pursue some aspects of those claims jointly. So, even though quantum meruit isn't a perfect fit – it's a theory of equitable recovery as opposed to a legal right – it aligns with attorneys' fees jurisprudence more generally.

Given its mixed lineage in contract, equity, common-benefit funds, and attorneys' fees, the law surrounding quantum-meruit awards is muddled, to say the least. Although lead lawyers plainly have the burden of establishing their fee's reasonableness and hence the value they conferred, values can fluctuate depending on the cases cited.

Thus, getting the precedent right is important. Relying on cases in which attorneys failed to contract in advance with clients, for instance, would miss the mark. Those circumstances result in conservative fees and do not capture the uniqueness of multidistrict litigation committees.[86] Similarly, standards used to assess fees under fee-shifting statutes have different public-policy goals in mind and run the risk of being too generous. Instead, leadership committees are most

[83] William B. Rubenstein, *On What a "Common Benefit Fee" Is, Is Not, and Should Be*, CLASS ACTION ATT'Y FEE DIG. Mar. 2009, at 87, 89.

[84] 5 WILLIAM RUBENSTEIN, ET AL., NEWBERG ON CLASS ACTIONS § 15.116 (5th ed. 2013).

[85] RESTATEMENT (THIRD) OF THE LAW GOVERNING LAWYERS § 39 (AM. LAW INST. 2000).

[86] *See id.* at § 39 cmt. c.

analogous to a situation in which the client employs her chosen attorney and that attorney, in turn, relies on (in effect, employs) lead lawyers.

Applying Quantum Meruit to Common Benefit

Assessing fair value for common-benefit fees depends on factors like lead lawyers' opportunity costs, financial risks, billing practices (whether hourly billing or contingent fees), work and time spent, the proceeding's stage at settlement (e.g., does the settlement come before detailed discovery or merits-related motions), the amount of work the individual plaintiffs' chosen attorneys contributed to the outcome, and, most importantly, the plaintiffs' ultimate success.[87] Consequently, judges must evaluate lead attorneys' work and risk over time – not employ a flat percentage-of-the-fund tax when the suit begins. That could over- or undercompensate later on.

Rather than tying their fees to plaintiffs' benefits, however, lead lawyers push courts to base fees on the total amount of the fund – awarded or not. Their typically unopposed motions misleadingly cite the Supreme Court's decision in *Boeing Co. v. Van Gemert* as support.[88] But there's a crucial difference between *Boeing*, a class action, and nonclass MDL: in *Boeing*, all class members had to do to get their settlement money was prove they were class members. That made them the "equitable owners" of their award.[89] The money doesn't come so easily for mass-tort plaintiffs. They aren't automatically entitled to anything when they enter a settlement program – they must overcome significant evidentiary hurdles first.

Perhaps that seems like lawyerly semantics, but it's a critical difference. It means that the entire unjust-enrichment theory that *Boeing* relies on must shift. In *Boeing*, class members would receive a windfall if they got paid but didn't compensate class counsel for helping them recover. Class members would, in other words, be unjustly enriched.[90]

---

[87] Johnson v. Ga. Highway Exp., Inc., 488 F.2d 714, 717 (5th Cir. 1974) (assessing time spent on a case); Ackermann v. Levine, 610 F. Supp. 633 (S.D.N.Y. 1985), *aff'd in part, rev'd in part*, 788 F.2d 830 (2d Cir. 1986) (examining specific services rendered); Richardson v. Parish of Jefferson, 727 So. 2d 705 (La. Ct. App. 1999); Hiscott & Robinson v. King, 626 A.2d 1235 (Pa. Ct. App. 1993) (considering an attorney's hourly billing rate); 520 E. 72nd Commercial Corp. v. 520 E. 72nd Owners Corp., 591 F. Supp. 728, 739 (S.D.N.Y. 1988), *aff'd without op.*, 872 F.2d 1021 (2d Cir. 1989); *In re* Hall, 415 B.R. 911, 923 (Bankr. M.D. Ga. 2009) (citing Lewis v. Smith, 618 S.E.2d 32, 35–36 (Ga. Ct. App. 2005)); Restatement (Third) of the Law Governing Lawyers § 39 cmt. c (Am. Law Inst. 2000); Joseph M. Perillo, *The Law of Lawyers' Contracts Is Different*, 67 Fordham L. Rev. 443, 448 (1998); Lester Brickman, *Setting the Fee When the Client Discharges a Contingent Fee Attorney*, 41 Emory L.J. 367, 392–93 (1992); Burch, *supra* note 82, at 130–31 (citing a variety of cases that further develop this theory).

[88] 444 U.S. 472 (1980); *e.g.*, Memorandum in Support of Motion for Distribution of Attorney's Fees at 5 and Exhibit B (Re: MDL Settlement Program II), *In re* Propulsid Prods. Liab. Litig., No. 00-md-1355 (E.D. La. Aug. 1, 2012).

[89] *Boeing*, 444 U.S. at 480–82.

[90] *Id.* at 478.

In mass-tort settlement programs,[91] however, funds aren't just ripe for the claiming: plaintiffs must typically surrender their right to sue in court to enter the program and provide claims administrators with evidence linking their injury to the product. When they enter the program, most don't know what, if anything, they will recover. So, hashing out a settlement program doesn't mean that plaintiffs have received a windfall in the way the *Boeing* class members did. While negotiating a claims-resolution process that may compensate plaintiffs based on identifiable medical criteria is a start, long-standing restitution principles still demand a link between plaintiffs' ultimate recovery and attorneys' fees.[92] Without that link, results like those in *Propulsid* (where leadership's fees – $27 million – grossly outpaced claimants' collective recovery – $6.5 million) are possible.

This well-founded fear that fees will dwarf plaintiffs' recovery is the same one that animated Congress to change class-action coupon settlements. Before 2005, class counsel could gin up hefty fees for themselves by exchanging class members' rights for worthless coupons (sometimes even coupons for the same product that ripped members off in the first place).[93] If class members used them at all, it brought business back to the corporate defendant. At the same time, class counsel lined their pockets by pegging their fees to the settlement's "value" – the coupons' collective face value, whether class members redeemed the coupons or not. After Congress passed the Class Action Fairness Act, judges had to calculate class counsel's fees based on the value of coupons consumers *used*, not consumers' potential savings.[94]

Common-benefit fees necessitate a similar shift.[95] Without connecting fees to real benefits, leaders have negotiated high settlement fund numbers and anchored their fee requests to that illusory value, but have then capitulated to defendants' demands for stringent claims-resolution criteria, reversionary clauses, or both. Using quantum-meruit principles, however, cuts through the ruse and thereby deters these practices.

Moving Fees from Theory to Practice

As the current piecemeal approach illustrates, courts have exercised substantial latitude when it comes to awarding common-benefit fees. As Professor Rubenstein observes, "[T]he law concerning the substantive right to a common benefit fee and the procedures for establishing that fee are both notably sparse."[96] While that

---

[91] This applies to mass torts resolved through global settlements and class actions, like *Sulzer* and *NFL Concussion*.

[92] Charles Silver, *A Restitutionary Theory of Attorneys' Fees in Class Actions*, 76 Cornell L. Rev. 656, 663–66 (1991).

[93] S. Rep. 109-14, 151 Cong., 119 Stat. 4 (2005) (enacted).

[94] 28 U.S.C. § 1712 (2012).

[95] *See* Principles of the Law of Aggregate Litigation § 3.13 cmt. a (Am. Law Inst. 2010) (discussing issues with fees that are not tied to the actual value of class members' claims).

[96] 5 Rubenstein et al., *supra* note 84, at § 15.115.

flexibility has hurt predictability in the past, it does pave the way for judges to implement changes that attorneys can count on as a proceeding begins.

By their nature, quantum-meruit awards entail evaluating the results obtained and the objective benefit to clients. But that doesn't mean that judges must wait until the end to think about fees. On the contrary, issuing an initial order holding back a portion of attorneys' fees generated from early settlements and disbursing interim payments to reimburse counsel for certain litigation costs may be necessary. But without putting the appropriate caveats in place, the worry is that the arbitrary holdback percentage will become an anchor, prompting leaders to expect at least that much.

In addition to letting leaders know what to expect down the road, judges should appoint a certified public accountant to audit monthly billing sheets and spot billing outliers early on.[97] As a proceeding draws to a close, using a magistrate judge or special master to propose fee allocations based on the accountant's work can alleviate the fears that arise when judges designate lawyer-led fee-allocation committees.[98] Judicial adjuncts can help stymie fee fights and alleviate the concern that leaders will financially sanction dissenters.

Of course, the devil is in the details. So, how should special masters and, ultimately, judges set percentages and calculate fees? Common-benefit fees have several components. In a moment, I'll introduce a formula that judges can use, but, if you're like me and a bit math adverse, it's helpful to understand each piece first. (If equations really give you fits, the text following Table 6.1 should make this section easier to digest.) As you might imagine, altering just one component can dramatically change lawyers' incentives and behavior:

- h = *hours* a lead lawyer spends working for all plaintiffs, not individual clients;
- w = an attorney's billable-hour rate or "*work*" rate;
- wh = billable hours (hours $*$ rate) – for leaders, the billable hours that count for common-benefit fee purposes are only those spent working on behalf of the group as a whole, not individual clients;
- c = litigation *costs* (depositions, experts, etc.);
- a = *administrative* costs for the claims process (claims administrators, special settlement masters, etc.);

---

[97] E.g., *In re* Vioxx Prods. Liab. Litig., No. 05-md-1657 (E.D. La. Apr. 8, 2005) (pretrial order 6).

[98] E.g., *In re* Blue Cross Blue Shield Antitrust Litig., No. 2:13-cv-20000-RDP (N.D. Ala. May 31, 2013) (order regarding protocols for plaintiffs' counsel time and expense submissions) (using a special master to compile and submit billing expenses on a monthly basis); *see also In re* Blue Cross Blue Shield Antitrust Litig., No. 2:13-cv-20000-RDP (N.D. Ala. June 10, 2014) (order regarding nonwaiver of work product doctrine protection and attorney-client privilege as a result of the submission of plaintiffs' common benefit time and expense records to the special master and the court).

- g = *gross recovery*, the amount of the entire settlement fund, its "sticker price," which includes any "separately" negotiated fee;[99]
- u = *unrecovered funds*, money in the fund that does not go to plaintiffs; it might revert to the defendant or be awarded using cy pres (funds that go to a third party, such as a charity);
- n = *net recovery*, the gross recovery minus litigation and administrative costs, minus unrecovered funds;
- x = court-awarded percentage of the net recovery (n), not a percentage of the gross recovery;
- i = the contractual percentage of *individually* retained plaintiffs' attorneys' (IRPA) contingent fees.

Common-benefit awards should be based on two components: (1) leaders' reasonable litigation and administrative costs, which should be subtracted from the gross recovery and (2) a percentage of plaintiffs' net recovery. Plaintiffs' net recovery (before attorneys' fees) would be:

$$g - (c + a) - u = n$$

Subtracting litigation and administrative costs as well as the unrecovered funds before calculating attorneys' fees immediately eliminates *Propulsid*'s concerns. There, leaders' outsized fees dwarfed plaintiffs' recovery, and the remaining money went to third-party charities and Canadian victims, or reverted to Johnson & Johnson.

Common-benefit fees would then be calculated as: $x(n)$. And presumably, attorneys would want leadership positions so long as their common-benefit fees ($x(n)$) are greater than or equal to their billable hours (wh). The formula for individually retained attorneys' fees, which tend to contractually award contingency lawyers some percentage of a plaintiff's net recovery less leaders' common-benefit fee would then be:

$$i(n) - x(n) \text{ or } (i - x)n$$

Finally, plaintiffs' actual award, the amount received, would be their gross recovery minus litigation and administrative costs (thereby creating the net recovery) minus attorneys' fees (IRPA fees minus common-benefit fees):[100]

$$g - (c + a) = n$$

$$n - [(i - x)n + x(n)] = \text{plaintiffs' final award}$$

---

[99] As Judge Brody explained in quoting Professor Rubenstein, it makes no sense to think about fees apart from recovery, instead "fees must be considered a component of the class's relief." The same principle holds true in calculating the gross recovery in nonclass cases. *In re* NFL Players' Concussion Injury Litig., No. 12-md-2323 (E.D. Pa. Apr. 4, 2018) (memorandum on fees at n.2).

[100] This assumes that there are no liens (Medicare, Medicaid, insurance, third-party financing, etc.) on plaintiffs' award.

Let's consider a basic example.[101] Suppose leaders worked 750 hours at a $200/hour rate.[102] That work yielded a gross recovery of $2,475,000, but it cost those lawyers $75,000 in litigation expenses and $700,000 to administer all the claims. (For simplicity, I assume that leaders incur all costs, but any costs that individual counsel incur would likewise be subtracted from a plaintiff's gross recovery before any fees are calculated.[103] I also assume that leaders will be paid for their work on behalf of individual clients under the "IRPA fees.") All the funds go to the plaintiffs and none revert to the defendant or go to cy pres. The judge awards 3% in common-benefit fees. And individually retained attorneys' contingent-fee contracts all call for 30% of plaintiffs' net recovery. Awards would be calculated like this:

$$n = \$2,475,000 - 775,000 - 0 = \$1,700,000$$
$$wh = 200^* 750 = 150,000$$
$$\text{common-benefit fees} = .03(1,700,000) = \$51,000$$
$$\text{IRPA fees} = .30(1,700,000) - 51,000 = \$459,000$$
$$\text{Total attorneys' fees} = \$510,000$$

$$\text{Plaintiffs' final award} = n - [(i - x)n + x(n)]$$
$$1,700,000 - [(.30 - .30)1,700,000 + .03(1,700,000)]$$

$$\text{Or, } 1,700,000 - (459,000 + 51,000) = \$1,190,000 \text{ plaintiffs' final award}$$

$$\text{In sum, } 2,475,000 \text{ (gross recovery)} - 775,000 \text{ (costs)}$$
$$-510,000 \text{ (total attorneys' fees)} = \$1,190,000$$

Under this hypothetical, leaders would be in the red ($.03(1,700,000) - 150,000 = -\$99,000$). Administrative costs were about 31% of the entire fund, leaders' billable hours were high, the x percentage doesn't consider leaders' efforts versus individual attorneys' efforts, and the common-benefit amount doesn't reflect the contingent fees leaders would receive for their individual clients (IRPA fees).

But we want to encourage lawyers to play socially useful roles in bringing dangerous products to light. So, in a moment, I'll explain how leaders can easily profit under this quantum-meruit approach and improve plaintiffs' outcomes too. First, however, let's compare quantum meruit with the "status quo."

The "status quo" is a moving target with judges calculating fees in myriad ways. Using the same numbers from our earlier hypothetical (and not the actual numbers

[101] This example is adapted from Jay Tidmarsh, *Cy Pres and the Optimal Class Action*, 82 GEO. WASH. L. REV. 767, 790 (2014).

[102] Attorneys' hourly rates will fluctuate based on geography, experience, and proceeding. For instance, Judge Fallon designated an hourly rate of $443.29 for *Vioxx* leaders and noted that the court had "previously used a range of $300 to $400 per hour for members of a Plaintiffs' Steering Committee and $100 to $200 per hour for associates." *In re* Vioxx Prods. Liab. Litig., 760 F. Supp. 2d 640, 660 (E.D. La. 2010).

[103] Most contingent-fee agreements require clients to pay the law firm a percentage of the net recovery, where a net recovery is the total recovery minus expenses.

from the proceeding), consider the method used in *Vioxx* where courts award leaders a percentage of the gross recovery to compensate them for fees and costs.[104]

In *Vioxx*, Judge Fallon capped the total amount of attorneys' fees at 32% of the gross recovery (it would be 30% in our scenario). He awarded leaders 6.5% of that gross recovery (3% in our hypothetical). He then subtracted those common-benefit fees from individually retained attorneys' awards to create plaintiffs' net recovery. Finally, per the settlement agreement, he subtracted costs from the plaintiffs' net recovery.[105] Using this methodology, but plugging in our hypothetical numbers for comparison purposes, plaintiffs would receive:

$$(i(g) - x(g)) = n$$
$$n - (c + a) = \text{plaintiffs' final award}$$

Using the same numbers as before, the calculations would look like this:

$$\text{Common-benefit fees} = .03(2,475,000) = \$74,250$$

$$\text{IRPA fees} = (.30(2,475,000)) - (.03(2,475,000)) = \$668,250$$

$$\text{Total attorneys' fees} = .30(2,475,000) = \$742,500$$

$$\text{Plaintiffs' net recovery} = 2,475,000 - 742,500 = 1,732,500$$

$$\text{Plaintiffs' final award} = \$1,732,500 \text{ (net)} - 775,000 \text{ (costs)} = \$957,500$$

Finally, consider one additional popular variant for awarding common-benefit fees. As Professor Rubenstein's expert report in *NFL Concussion* explained, common-benefit fees and expenses could be extracted from the gross recovery, IRPA fees extracted from the subsequent net recovery, then IRPA costs extracted thereafter. At this more granular level, let us assume that leaders spent $700,000 to develop and administer the claims and that plaintiffs' individual attorneys spent $75,000 in costs. Under this approach, plaintiffs would receive:

$$g - (x(g) + a) = n$$

$$n - i(n) - c = \text{plaintiffs' final award}$$

$$\text{Common-benefit fees and expenses} = (.03(2,475,000)) + 700,000 = \$774,250$$

$$\text{Plaintiffs' net recovery} = 2,475,000 - 774,250 = \$1,700,750$$

$$\text{IRPA fees} = .30(1,700,750) = \$510,225$$

$$\text{Plaintiffs' final award} = 1,700,750 - 510,225 - 75,000 = \$1,115,525$$

---

[104] 5 RUBENSTEIN et al., *supra* note 84, at § 15.115 ("Most commonly, the common benefit fee is an assessment on the gross settlement value").

[105] *In re* Vioxx Prods. Liab. Litig., 760 F. Supp. 2d 640 (E.D. La. 2010); *In re* Vioxx Prods. Liab. Litig., No. 05-md-1657 (E.D. La. Sept. 11, 2013) (pretrial order 51A). For the subsequent *NFL Concussion* example, see Expert Report of Professor William B. Rubenstein at 12 n.41, *In re NFL Players' Concussion Injury Litig.*, No. 12-md-2323 (E.D. Pa. Dec. 11, 2017).

TABLE 6.1 *Comparing fee award methods*

	Quantum-Meruit Method (Percentage of Plaintiffs' Net Recovery)	Method 1 (*Vioxx* Derivative)	Method 2 (*NFL* report Derivative)
Gross Recovery (*g*)	2,475,000	2,475,000	2,475,000
Litigation Costs (*c*)	75,000	75,000	75,000
Administrative Costs (*a*)	700,000	700,000	700,000
Common-Benefit Percentage (*x*)	3% $x(n)$	3% $x(g)$	3% $x(g)$
IRPA Percentage (*i*)	30% $i(n)$	30% $i(g) - x(g)$	30% $i(g - x(g))$
Total Attorneys' Fees	$510,000	$742,500	$584,475
Common-Benefit Fees	$51,000 (10% of total fees)	$74,250 (10% of total fees)	$74,250 (12% of total fees)
Costs Reimbursed	All costs attributed to leaders and subtracted from g before fees calculated $g - (c + a) = n$	All costs attributed to leaders and taken from *n*, after fees are subtracted	*a* costs attributed to leaders and subtracted after $x(g)$; *c* costs attributed to IRPAs and subtracted from *n*
IRPA Fees	$459,000	$668,250	$510,225
Net Recovery (*n*)	$1,700,000 $g - (c + a) - u = n$	$1,732,500 $g - i(g) = n$	$1,700,750 $g - (x(g) + a) = n$
Formula for Plaintiffs' Award	$n - [(i - x)n + x(n)]$	$n - (c + a))$	$n - i(n) - c$
Plaintiffs Final Award	$1,190,000	$957,500	$1,115,525

As Table 6.1 shows by using the same hypothetical numbers to compare these methods, plaintiffs fare best under quantum meruit. Breaking fees down into their component parts illustrates how using quantum meruit (basing common-benefit fees on plaintiffs' net recovery, in other words) aligns leaders' interests with plaintiffs' outcomes and alleviates some of the problems identified in earlier chapters:

First, it gives judges a limited but legitimate basis to review private settlements. As Chapter 4 explored, judges may overstep their authority when they publicly endorse private deals. But quantum-meruit awards require that judges assess the results obtained and plaintiffs' objective benefit. In other words, whether leaders' efforts paid off for those they represent.

So, while judges lack the authority to endorse a settlement, they do have the power to reward or penalize lead lawyers through awarding fees. Although this settlement review would be more tailored than class settlement review under Rule

23(e), assessing plaintiffs' benefits in the fee context creates a strong disincentive toward self-dealing, overreaching, or collusion.

Second, tying common-benefit fees to plaintiffs' outcomes opens the door for judges to hear about those benefits (or the lack thereof) first hand from plaintiffs. In other words, holding hearings on common-benefit fees gives plaintiffs an opportunity to voice their concerns to the judge. As later parts of this chapter examine in more detail, for attorneys' and plaintiffs' sake alike, there is no need to wait until a deal has been finalized to receive that input.

Third, this quantum-meruit approach encourages fiscal responsibility. Including costs and expenses in plaintiffs' gross recovery and basing fees on that inflated amount encourages lawyers to spend freely. They receive a percentage of the fund's bloated sticker price that comes from high costs. Subtracting and reimbursing reasonable costs out of plaintiffs' gross recovery first, then awarding leaders a percentage of plaintiffs' net recovery thereafter promotes fiscal responsibility.

Claims administrators are expensive and their payment structures vary. They might be paid from the fund, by defense counsel, or out of plaintiffs' counsel's fee. Some offer tiered pricing based on how quickly lawyers agree to select them, some give discounts if counsel relies on a variety of their services (such as lien resolution and electronic document services). Others cap their amounts at a certain percentage of the gross recovery. Like any other cost, judges should consider these expenses as part of the gross recovery and subtract them before awarding fees. Doing so focuses leaders on getting plaintiffs the best deal, not on which administrator courts them or which pricing structure makes the fund appear larger.

Similarly, because document review can generate billable time, law firms may be less likely to outsource it to a cheaper legal process vendor.[106] Under the proposed model, however, outsourcing this task to a reliable vendor could drive down billable hours and increase both leaders' profit and plaintiffs' net recovery.

Tying leaders' fees to plaintiffs' net recovery rewards them for the benefit they bestow. It thus aligns common-benefit fees with the restitution theories that justify them. Because leaders don't get paid until plaintiffs do, this change encourages them to streamline and simplify the claims process, expedite payouts, and maximize plaintiffs' total recovery as well as each plaintiff's award.[107]

Fourth, leaders who bill a great deal of hours and invest heavily in the case but don't benefit plaintiffs will not be rewarded. Lead lawyers must demonstrate that their guidance and efforts paid off. In *Propulsid*, for example, leaders may have invested substantial time and fronted tremendous costs, but they recovered little money for their clients. The very nature of contingent work is that it will sometimes be unsuccessful.

---

[106] Morris A. Ratner & William B. Rubenstein, *Profit for Costs*, 63 DePaul L. Rev. 587, 603–4 (2014).

[107] If the fund remains open for years, as the *NFL Concussion* settlement does, then periodically making interim attorneys' fee awards based on the plaintiffs' payouts as of a particular date would make sense.

Conversely, when leaders benefit plaintiffs enormously, judges should not be shy about awarding them substantial fees. Lawyers tend to think of contingent-fee cases as a portfolio of risk. Litigation's risks and rewards cannot be measured by a single proceeding. Diversifying cases diversifies risk, which means that the winning cases not only finance their own costs but the costs of the losing cases as well. It is this insurance-like dimension that judges may sometimes fail to appreciate.[108]

Fifth, in lieu of an arbitrary percentage of the fund based on past proceedings' arbitrary percentages, the quantum-meruit approach requires leaders to demonstrate the benefit they conferred through a final accounting; objectors bear the burden of showing otherwise. In assessing plaintiffs' benefit, judges should require lead lawyers applying for fees to submit an accounting.[109] The accounting should describe the benefits leadership conferred on plaintiffs, how administrators allocated the settlement funds, the number of plaintiffs who submitted claims, the number who recovered within each category or tier, and the average recovery amount in each category or tier. Where available, leaders should likewise compare information about settlement values and verdicts obtained *outside* the multidistrict proceeding with the deal they negotiated.

Accountings should also include data on billable hours and attorneys' rates. Billable hours consider typical lodestar questions about what constitutes a reasonable hourly rate and a reasonable number of hours to spend on a particular task. Of course, what's reasonable often depends on who you ask. It's no surprise then that lodestar methods have come under attack; lawyers can exaggerate both hours and rates. Plus, the multipliers courts have used are hazy and sometimes arbitrary.[110] Still, the basic idea here is that billable hours may give judges some insight into what percentage of individually retained attorneys' fees is fair to allot to leaders. This is where certified public accountants who have been monitoring leaders' monthly billing can become invaluable.

Accounting for firms' hours helps to reward efficiency and ensure that they aren't duplicating tasks. In the *Anthem Data Breach* litigation, for example, Judge Lucy Koh questioned why 26 law firms representing the named plaintiff would need to then subcontract with another 27 firms. "I would not have appointed you had I known you

---

[108] HERBERT M. KRITZER, RISKS, REPUTATIONS, AND REWARDS: CONTINGENCY FEE LEGAL PRACTICE IN THE UNITED STATES 10–18 (2004); Jonathan T. Molot, *How U.S. Procedure Skews Tort Law Incentives*, 73 IND. L. J. 59, 82 (1997); Richard W. Painter, *Litigating on a Contingency: A Monopoly of Champions or a Market for Champerty?*, 71 CHI.-KENT L. REV. 625, 678–80 (1995).

[109] *See* PRINCIPLES OF THE LAW OF AGGREGATE LITIGATION § 3.13(e) (AM. LAW INST. 2010) (proposing a similar accounting for class counsel's attorneys' fees).

[110] Charles Silver, *Unloading the Lodestar: Toward a New Fee Award Procedure*, 70 TEX. L. REV. 865 (1992).

were going to pile on 53 law firms," she admonished.[111] "It would be helpful to get a sense of who did what and when, just delve a little deeper on those categories."[112]

As Judge Koh suggests, delving deeper should be routine.[113] Accounts should then be available to the plaintiffs and their individual attorneys so that they can respond. A transparent accounting, the information it unearths, and adversarial vetting allows judges to fine-tune fee awards.[114] It discourages attorneys from padding their hours and seeking reimbursement for private jets and first-class airfare. It likewise enables judges to base their common-benefit percentage on concrete information from the case before them rather than the arbitrary percentages from past proceedings.

Table 6.2 illustrates how reducing costs and considering information from leaders' final accounting should affect fees under a quantum-meruit approach. As you can see, it is flexible enough to accommodate a variety of circumstances. It rewards leaders for reducing litigation and administrative costs, and affords judges the flexibility to compensate greater effort by leaders or individually retained attorneys as the circumstances warrant.

Finally, the quantum-meruit approach allows judges to tailor fees for dissimilarly situated plaintiffs. After attorneys submit accounts and objectors vet them, judges should customize common-benefit fee percentages to match plaintiffs' actual recovery. Judges needn't make individual determinations for each plaintiff; instead, they could place them into presumptive categories based on whether the case is pending in state or federal court, individual counsel's efforts, whether individual counsel relied on leaders' discovery or negotiation efforts, how the settlement classified a plaintiff's injury, and so forth. Leaders may benefit different plaintiffs to different degrees. So, judges can refine percentages accordingly. Here are some examples:

First, objections from a particular tier of plaintiffs might prompt group-specific adjustments. This encourages attorneys to put forward the best possible case for "lower tier" plaintiffs with less severe injuries. Even if they don't receive substantial compensation, a settlement might allow them to return if more severe injuries developed later,

---

[111] Transcript of Proceedings at 22, *In re* Anthem, Inc. Data Breach Litig., No. 15-md-02617 (N.D. Cal. Feb. 1, 2018).

[112] Bonnie Eslinger, *Anthem Breach Attys' $38M Fee Ask "Overreach," Judge Says*, Law360 (June 14, 2018, 10:41 PM), https://www.law360.com/articles/1053987/anthem-breach-attys-38m-fee-ask-overreach-judge-says.

[113] As Professor Judith Resnik argues, "To ensure the integrity of their own efforts, judges will have to breach the old civil justice system etiquette of minimal inquiry about financial arrangements among lawyers." Resnik, *supra* note 40, at 2127.

[114] Of course, to the extent that this accounting includes plaintiffs' personal information, then that should remain confidential and under seal. Transparency is important here, however, and unless there is an exceptional and compelling reason, information should not be filed under seal. Even when it is filed under seal, nonpersonal information should be made available to plaintiffs and their individual counsel. Others' recoveries and injury types (or categories) can be made known without personally identifying information attached.

TABLE 6.2 *Tailoring the quantum-meruit approach to different scenarios*

	Quantum-Meruit Approach Using the Same Example as Table 6.1	Leaders Reducing Costs	Leaders Reducing Cost and Judges Recognizing IRPA Windfall	IRPA Efforts High, Leaders Efforts Low
Gross Recovery (g)	$2,475,000	$2,475,000	$2,475,000	$2,475,000
Leaders Hours (h)	750	750	750	200
Leaders' Rate (w)	200	200	200	200
Litigation Costs (c)	$75,000	$55,000	$55,000	$75,000
Administrative Costs (a)	$700,000	$450,000	$450,000	$700,000
IRPA Hours (h)	20	20	20	500
IRPA Rate (w)	200	200	200	200
Common-Benefit Percentage $x(n)$	3%	3%	15%	3%
IRPA Percentage $i(n)$	30%	30%	30%	30%
IRPA Fees $i(n) - x(n)$	$459,000	$531,900	$295,500	$459,000
Common-Benefit Fees	$51,000	$59,100	$295,500	$51,000
Leaders' Incentive	–$99,000	–$90,000	$145,500	$11,000
$x(n) > wh$	51,000< 150,000	59,100< 150,000	295,500> 150,000	51,000> 40,000
Total Attorneys' Fees	$510,000	$591,000	$591,000	$510,000
Net Recovery (n) $g - (c + a) = n$	$1,700,000	$1,970,000	$1,970,000	$1,700,000
Plaintiffs' Final Award $n - [(i - x)n + x(n)]$	$1,190,000	$1,379,000	$1,379,000	$1,190,000

for example.[115] Reducing fees doesn't cure inadequate representation, but it does prevent leaders from profiting from a group they've disserved.

Second, as the third column of Table 6.2 indicates, free-riding attorneys who do little more than file cases, wait for lead lawyers to negotiate a proposed settlement, and then collect their fee, should pay substantially more in common-benefit fees. Likewise, so long as leaders confer some material benefit on pro se litigants, they should pay too.

Third, if state-court plaintiffs' counsel consistently negotiates higher settlements for her clients without the federal leaders' efforts (as the fourth column of Table 6.2 illustrates), the judge might lower the common-benefit percentage across the board. Of course, many factors come into play here. Leaders can't pick and choose who gets swept into the federal proceeding in the same way that individual counsel can

---

[115] Although contingent fees from their own clients may still spur leaders to maximize payouts in particular tiers, some leaders have few clients.

screen her clients. Some cases will inevitably have stronger evidence linking plaintiffs' injuries to a product than others. Or, state lawyers may rely on the multidistrict litigation's common work product to produce the results. The point, however, is that higher settlements outside the centralized proceeding should trigger closer judicial scrutiny.

State Courts as Competitive Checks

As this nuanced approach suggests, quantum meruit can motivate lawyers to compete in state court. Chapter 2 explained how lead lawyers have gone to great lengths to ensure that state-court plaintiffs pay common-benefit fees. Leaders' concern is somewhat understandable: state-court lawyers might simply sit back and wait for them to negotiate a deal. Avoiding common-benefit fees would unjustly enrich idle lawyers.

But courts are using a hammer when they need a chisel – awarding a flat common-benefit percentage is too blunt a tool. It doesn't distinguish between an attorney with all her cases in the multidistrict proceeding and objectors like Tom Girardi. (Girardi, you may recall, represented 25 federal *Avandia* plaintiffs and roughly 4,000 state-court plaintiffs. He invested substantial money in developing his clients' claims, settled them for more money than leaders negotiated, but was taxed for all 4,025.) Nor does it adapt for the lawyer who has litigated exclusively in state court without any help from the federal leaders and is ready for trial but has clients who opt for the global settlement. And it doesn't increase taxes on counsel who do little besides recommend that their clients accept the deal leaders negotiated.

A flat tax thus deters competition. Why spend money conducting discovery, deposing witnesses, hiring experts, and trying cases when the transferee judge will slice 20%–30% off your contingent fee?

The status quo also discourages state-court lawyers from uncovering information about claims' diverse values. States can differ over parties' rights, and respecting those differences is central to federalism.[116] But global settlements are expertly designed to reduce outcome variance. They may thus provide less money to people in states that permit idiosyncratic claims such as loss of consortium, emotional distress, fear of disease, or medical monitoring.

Nuance is necessary both to serve fairness principles and encourage state-court markets to function as rival regimes. On the front end, if state-court litigants want to access federal leaders' work product, then transferee judges should customize participation agreements. While contract principles are ill-suited for attorneys litigating in the transferee court who have no choice but to

---

[116] Larry Kramer, *Choice of Law in Complex Litigation*, 71 N.Y.U. L. REV. 547, 579 (1996).

accept, tiered pricing packages (like digital photography bundles, for example) would allow state-court attorneys to contract with the federal leadership based on their discovery needs.

On the back end, as some courts have done,[117] judges should award common-benefit fees to state-court counsel who add value to the federal suit by objecting to practices that threaten adequate representation or trying state-court cases, for example. This encourages counsel to invest in state suits and bring to light state-specific information that informs settlement awards.

EMPOWERING THE MASSES

Chapter 5 described how mass-tort litigation has inched away from its tort-law origins. Now it resembles an elaborate bargain toward a contractual settlement process where the system and some lawyers treat plaintiffs like commodities and trade their rights for money in a business transaction. But plaintiffs are people, not widgets in a warehouse or inventories of cattle. Reframing the public justice system as one that primarily vindicates victims' legal rights and secondarily assists in their exchange recognizes that plaintiffs may bargain with defendants for money or reforms. But it also suggests that plaintiffs should have a meaningful say in this arrangement.

"I never saw a single plaintiff appear before me," lamented Judge Jack Weinstein, who presided over *Zyprexa*.[118] Yet, the vast research on procedural justice demonstrates that when people go to court, they want the chance to participate and tell their side of the story to a neutral authority. In torts, this gives people some control over matters that seem to have gotten away from them; it allows them input into deeply personal decisions – matters that affect their health, safety, and financial well-being. They then want those authorities to decide matters by applying consistent legal principles to their case."[119]

Aggregating plaintiffs can have a big upside: when injuries are widespread but expensive to prove, it provides court access. And for corporations accused of wrong-doing, it minimizes litigation costs. Deposing an employee once instead of hundreds of times keeps businesses running.

But, as procedural-justice values suggest, there is a costly downside to aggre-gating too. People get lost in the shuffle. Plaintiffs' inability to participate and exert even a modicum of control over their claims means they may be less satisfied with the process and view the system as less legitimate. Judge Weinstein

---

[117] *In re* Vioxx Prods. Liab. Litig., No. 05-md-01657 (E.D. La. Aug. 9, 2011) (order and reasons allocating common benefit fees, at 31).

[118] Alexandra Lahav, In Praise of Litigation 90 (2017).

[119] Tom R. Tyler, *The Psychology of Aggregation: Promise and Potential Pitfalls*, 64 DePaul L. Rev. 711, 714 (2015).

recognizes the conundrum: "How can we provide each plaintiff and each defendant with the benefits of a system in mass torts that treats him or her as an individual person? How can each person obtain the respect that his or her individuality and personal needs should command in an egalitarian democracy such as ours?"[120]

As Judge Weinstein's questions reflect, these are real people with actual lives that statistics alone cannot capture. And they want a say. Take the parents of 24-year-old Erika Langhart, for example. The day before Thanksgiving in 2011, Erika was getting ready to fly home. At almost six feet tall, lanky, and athletic, she planned to attend Georgetown Law School the next year. But none of that happened. Instead, her boyfriend found her writhing on the floor of her apartment, struggling to breathe. When the EMT called her mother, he asked, "was your daughter using birth control?" "Yes, NuvaRing," her mom answered. "I thought so because she's having a pulmonary embolism," replied the EMT.[121] After having two heart attacks in the ambulance, Erika died on Thanksgiving Day.

Like many other deals, the *NuvaRing* settlement required 95% of plaintiffs to opt in. "This settlement agreement, orchestrated by Merck and the attorneys on both sides, driven by their own greed, has all but eliminated the chance for Merck to be taken to trial," said Erika's father. "Shame on them." Erika's mother concurred, "We would rather, quite frankly, die than take blood money from Merck," she said, "we will not settle."

Formal studies on medical-malpractice victims echo the Langharts. The subjects of Professor Tamara Relis's research led her to conclude that litigation is "not about the money!" That sentiment "was a common theme throughout virtually all plaintiffs' discourse," she observed.[122] Likewise, in interviewing the September 11 plaintiffs, Professor Gillian Hadfield found that "litigation represents more to some potential litigants than a means to satisfying private material ends; it represents principled participation in a process that is constitutive of a community."[123] So, while some plaintiffs will need money first and foremost, others want information, accountability, judgments of wrongdoing, and to do something that promotes change.

The Langharts' lawyer, Hunter Shkolnik, represented hundreds of *NuvaRing* plaintiffs and praised the deal as a "good opportunity" for them, but said the settlement's 95% plaintiff-participation demand wouldn't affect people like the

---

[120] JACK B. WEINSTEIN, INDIVIDUAL JUSTICE IN MASS TORT LITIGATION: THE EFFECT OF CLASS ACTIONS, CONSOLIDATIONS, AND OTHER MULTIPARTY DEVICES 3 (1995).

[121] Jonas Karlsson & Marie Brenner, *Danger in the Ring*, VANITY FAIR'S HIVE (Dec. 12, 2013), https://www.vanityfair.com/news/politics/2014/01/nuvaring-lethal-contraceptive-trial.

[122] Tamara Relis, *"It's Not about the Money!": A Theory on Misconceptions of Plaintiffs' Litigation Aims*, 68 U. PITT. L. REV. 701, 721 (2007).

[123] Gillian K. Hadfield, *Framing the Choice between Cash and the Courthouse: Experiences with the 9/11 Victim Compensation Fund*, 42 LAW & SOCIETY REV. 645, 649 (2008).

Langharts.[124] A year later, however, the Langharts claimed that their lawyers "abandoned them when they refused the settlement," leaving them "to defend themselves against one of the largest U.S. drugmakers."[125]

A year after a San Francisco court dismissed the Langharts' suit, Erika's mother, Karen, took her own life. "All Karen wanted was these people to be held accountable," said Erika's father. "It was never about the money, we just wanted a court date where we could stand in front of representatives of Merck and tell them what they had done to us and what they're still doing to young women."[126]

As studies by Relis and Hadfield demonstrate, the Langharts aren't alone. For instance, after the tissue around her mesh died due to gangrene, *Kugel Mesh* plaintiff Trudy Thomas went into respiratory failure, spent six weeks in the hospital with a perforated bowel, and had to have her gangrene-riddled gallbladder removed. "I'm getting bills by the millions from Medicare they want me to pay back. I've had 17 surgeries after Kugel mesh and it's all Kugel mesh related," Thomas explained.[127] Although C. R. Bard settled approximately 2,600 cases for $184 million in 2011, most of the $70,000-per-plaintiff average would go to Medicaid, Medicare, and insurance liens.[128] Thomas didn't want to settle, "I said right away I'm not taking it, I want to go to trial." Her law firm, she complains, consistently urges her to take the settlement even though it would not cover her medical bills.[129]

Mass-tort plaintiffs need an outlet. Some feel victimized not only by the defendant but also by the process and by the very people who are supposed to advocate for them.

As the rest of this section explores, there are several ways that the system can accommodate these needs. First, plaintiffs might form their own groups, which give them internal participation opportunities and allow them to designate a spokesperson to voice their concerns. Second, as the last section discussed, to determine common-benefit fees and whether leaders' actions helped plaintiffs, transferee judges can open the courthouse doors to hear directly from those affected. But for those who don't want to settle like Trudy Thomas and the Langharts, this doesn't help them much. So, third, allowing lawsuits to play out in state courts and remanding cases to their courts of origin once discovery on common questions

[124] Chase Olivarius-McAlister, *Parents Turn Down $100M Settlement*, DURANGO HERALD (Feb. 16, 2014, 4:28 PM), https://durangoherald.com/articles/68885.
[125] Peter Marcus, *NuvaRing Lawsuit Is Dismissed*, DURANGO HERALD (Sept. 28, 2015, 9:55 PM), https://durangoherald.com/articles/96002.
[126] Ann Butler & Shane Benjamin, *Karen Langhart Sends Nearly 40 Packages to Friends Before Taking Her Own Life*, DURANGO HERALD (Jan. 12, 2016, 5:01 PM), https://durangoherald.com/articles/100188-karen-langhart-sends-nearly-40-packages-to-friends-before-taking-her-own-life.
[127] Jane Akre, *Trudy Thomas: Suffering in Silence and Financially after Kugel Mesh Settlement*, MESH MED. DEVICE NEWSDESK (Aug. 19, 2012), https://www.meshmedicaldevicenewsdesk.com/trudy-thomas-suffering-in-silence-and-financially-after-kugel-mesh-settlement/.
[128] Bibeka Shrestha, *Bard Offers $184M to Settle Hernia Patch Suits*, LAW360 (July 1, 2011, 3:24 PM), https://www.law360.com/articles/255403/bard-offers-184m-to-settle-hernia-patch-suits.
[129] Akre, *supra* note 127.

has completed (or leaders have negotiated a global deal) would give plaintiffs more control over their cases. Although trials are rare across all civil cases, remands place those who truly desire their day in court in a better position to demand it – or at least to try to get the answers they want.

Plaintiff Groups

No one chooses to be injured by a drug or product. But when the same thing injures people in comparable ways, it changes them, changes their stories, and ties them together in a way that they never chose, nor would ever choose. It becomes part of their identity. Procedures can serve as a means for uniting these plaintiffs, plugging their individual stories into a collective narrative, making sense of that narrative as a community, reasoning together about the right thing to do, and pursuing that end collectively.[130]

Some groups predate lawsuits such as labor unions in the asbestos litigation, support groups in the tainted blood products litigation, and veterans' groups in *Agent Orange*. After local disasters, affected communities might form committees. For instance, two weeks after a coal company's dam burst in West Virginia and unleashed a flood of black waste water, The Buffalo Creek Citizens Committee materialized, elected representatives, and sought legal counsel.[131]

Groups can transcend geographic boundaries and form as a result of the litigation too. In the *DES* litigation over synthetic estrogen that caused cancer in the daughters of women who ingested the drug during pregnancy, female plaintiffs had little physical interaction, but nevertheless coalesced over their shared suffering from reproductive organ problems. [132] And the Asbestos Victims of America, the Dalkon Shield victims' organizations, and the Silicone Gel Breast Implant groups are just a handful of other examples.[133]

Today, the Internet and social media make it easier than ever for plaintiffs to communicate, build support networks, and share information. There are sites for pelvic-mesh victims, Vioxx users, Essure plaintiffs, and retired NFL players.

As the mass-tort system treats plaintiffs as a collective, they may begin seeing each other that way as well. "The key point for the legal system," explains Yale professor Tom Tyler, "is that when people define themselves as members of a group, they are more likely to respond to collective injustice by taking organized, group based-action."[134] For instance, in California's *Stringfellow Acid Pits* toxic-tort litigation, a

---

[130] Elizabeth Chamblee Burch, *Litigating Together: Social, Moral, and Legal Obligations*, 91 B.U. L. REV. 87 (2011).

[131] GERALD M. STERN, THE BUFFALO CREEK DISASTER 6–7 (1976).

[132] WEINSTEIN, *supra* note 120, at 47.

[133] Byron G. Stier, *Resolving the Class Action Crisis: Mass Tort Litigation as Network*, UTAH L. REV. (2005) 863, 919–21.

[134] Tyler, *supra* note 119, at 732.

single group of 4,000 people – the Concerned Neighbors in Action – formed out of other community organizations and created a charter that governed members' litigation and settlement activities. The plaintiffs even developed constitutional procedures for approving a settlement offer, which included using a separate judge to decide whether the offer was fair.[135]

If some plaintiffs begin to think *"we're all in this together,"* and start to see themselves as a group, then that identity can play a role in shaping members' participation expectations. Voice opportunities in group governance can sometimes serve as a stand-in for formal procedures.[136] As the *Stringfellow Acid Pits* litigation demonstrated, group processes can embody basic democratic ideals, giving members opportunities to argue, bargain, and "vote" about what path to take. When plaintiffs feel marginalized, they can designate a spokesperson of their own to air their concerns – whether it's to the judge, the lawyers, or the media.

Collectively, plaintiffs can impact settlements too. Walkaway thresholds in both global and inventory deals are designed to give defendants closure. But they're a double-edged sword. When plaintiffs unite in protest, walkaway provisions give them leverage to bust the deal and send a powerful message of resistance without saying a word.[137]

Common-Benefit Fee Hearings

"Opening up the settlement review process to plaintiffs – for example, by holding a settlement hearing and inviting objectors to come forward as in Rule 23 class actions – would be a more radical step," writes Stanford professor Deborah Hensler. But that step wouldn't be too onerous because, as she explains, "[G]lobal settlements often require publicity campaigns to assure that a threshold agreement percent specified in the settlement is met."[138]

Although Chapter 4 described how judges likely lack the authority to endorse private settlements, awarding common-benefit fees according to quantum-meruit principles provides an "in." Because common-benefit fees are grounded in restitution principles, tying those fees to plaintiffs' outcomes allows judges to hear about those benefits – or the lack thereof – directly from the plaintiffs. And there is no need to wait until a settlement program concludes to receive that input. On the contrary, informal opportunities for plaintiffs to participate and give feedback should come

---

[135] Jack Hitt, *Toxic Dreams: A California Town Finds Meaning in an Acid Pit*, HARPER'S BAZAAR, July 1995, at 62.

[136] Tyler, *supra* note 119, at 734–35.

[137] D. Theodore Rave, *Closure Provisions in MDL Settlements*, 85 FORDHAM L. REV. 2175, 2181 (2017).

[138] Deborah R. Hensler, *No Need to Panic: The Multi-District Litigation Process Needs Improvement Not Demolition*, 4, https://www.law.gwu.edu/sites/g/files/zaxdzs2351/f/downloads/Deborah-Hensler-MDL-Paper.pdf.

early and often. Leaders can provide electronic avenues for plaintiffs to communicate not only with them but also with each other. Centralizing communication prevents misinformation and rumors, gives plaintiffs an outlet, and provides leaders insight into plaintiffs' needs and concerns.

"Communication is instantaneous and cheap, if not free – courtesy of the internet, email, Facebook, Twitter, and forms of electronic discourse as yet unimaged," write plaintiffs' attorney Elizabeth Cabraser and Professor Samuel Issacharoff.[139] Plaintiffs could participate in hearings by video or telephone. Or, as Judges Alvin Hellerstein and Jack Weinstein did in the *September 11, Agent Orange,* and *DES* cases, judges could hold town hall meetings. Either way, the aim is to provide a forum for plaintiffs and their individual lawyers to react to the settlement offer's terms, seek clarity about what those terms mean, understand how the claims administration process is supposed to work, and decide whether to consent to a deal with as much information as possible in hand.

Opening the courtroom doors to voices that not only lend support but also inject new information and dissent is critical to fostering legitimacy and reaching the best possible outcome. As psychologists Charlan Nemeth and Jack Goncalo – two of the world's leading experts on group decisions – explain, minority views are critical "not because they may be correct but because *even when they are wrong* they stimulate thinking that on balance leads to better decisions. It stops the rush to judgment by providing a counter to the majority view."[140]

When people raise contrary perspectives, everyone begins to look for more information and facts. This "task" conflict (disagreements over the settlement's substantive terms) can prompt groups to critically evaluate the information that emerges and give judges and litigants alike insight into a settlement's pros and cons.[141]

Of course, some might argue that allowing any judicial review insults autonomous agents. But just because plaintiffs have the right to enter into these deals doesn't mean that judges should compensate leaders for creating them. On the contrary, tying lead lawyers' common-benefit fees to the outcome they helped produce can maintain a delicate balance: it preserves the parties' decision-making autonomy on the one hand, and promotes procedural fairness and institutional integrity on the other. As Professor Tom Tyler concludes, "[W]hen an injury is widespread or when there is a sense that the offender behaved unethically, the failure to have a hearing can be damaging to the courts, the law, and the government."[142]

---

[139] Elizabeth J. Cabraser & Samuel Issacharoff, *The Participatory Class Action*, 92 N.Y.U. L. Rev. 846, 854 (2017).

[140] Nemeth & Goncalo, *supra* note 70, at 23.

[141] On types of conflict, see Karen A. Jehn, *A Qualitative Analysis of Conflict Types and Dimensions in Organizational Groups*, 42 Admin. Sci. Q. 530, 531, 551 (Sept. 1997).

[142] Tyler, *supra* note 119, at 719.

REMANDING CASES AS EXIT OPPORTUNITIES

Plaintiffs' lawyers tout trial as their most valuable bargaining chip. But multidistrict litigation cripples that threat for all but a few bellwether cases. When Congress enacted § 1407, the legislative history explained that "trial in the originating district is generally preferable from the standpoint of the parties and witnesses."[143] So Congress limited MDL to *pretrial* proceedings.[144] On the surface at least, the idea was to centralize for efficiency but remand to "maximize the litigant's traditional privileges of selecting where, when and how to enforce his substantive rights or assert his defenses while minimizing possible undue complexity from multiparty jury trials."[145]

As Dr. David Foscue discovered, however, remands are as scarce as hen's teeth. In March 2012, Foscue, a family doctor from Warren, Arkansas, sued Zimmer over his faulty hip cup. Over the course of the next five years, he asked the court to remand his case multiple times. Each time, Judge Susan Wigenton said that he had not satisfied various procedural hurdles – he hadn't sought the court's leave and he hadn't conferred with defense counsel. After jumping through those hoops, she denied his request again "[b]ecause the Global Settlement Program is still ongoing, any request to remand individual actions to state court is premature."[146] Of course, Dr. Foscue wasn't trying to get back to *state* court, he was trying to return to the Western District of Arkansas.

Pleading with the Panel, which has the authority to remand cases, resulted in a collective shrug: "we consistently have accorded great weight to the transferee judge's determination," it explained. Judge Wigenton "is in the best position to determine the future course of this and the other actions before her" and she "recently considered – and rejected – the *Foscue* plaintiffs' request for a suggestion of remand," the Panel wrote.[147]

Transferee judges tend to hold on to their cases with an iron grip. As Judge Eduardo Robreno, who handled the asbestos multidistrict litigation and actively encourages remand, explained, "As a matter of judicial culture, remanding cases is viewed as an acknowledgement that the MDL judge has failed to resolve the

---

[143] S. REP. No. 90–454, at 5 (1967).

[144] 28 U.S.C. § 1407 (2012).

[145] Report of the Coordinating Committee on Multiple Litigation Recommending New Section 1407, Title 28 (Mar. 2, 1965), *reprinted in In re* Plumbing Fixture Cases, 298 F. Supp. 484, 499 (J.P.M.L. 1968). The remand rate has always been quite low and the notes surrounding the bill indicate that the Coordinating Committee may have been paying lip service to trials while pushing for transferee judges to close the proceedings.

[146] *In re* Zimmer Durom Hip Cup Prods. Liab. Litig. No. 09-cv-4414 (D.N.J. Sept. 5, 2017) (order); *In re* Zimmer Durom Hip Cup Prods. Liab. Litig. No. 09-cv-4414 (D.N.J. May 1, 2018) (order).

[147] *In re* Zimmer Durom Hip Cup Prods. Liab. Litig. MDL No. 2158, Case No. 09-cv-4414 (J.P.M.L. June 8, 2018) (order denying remand).

case."[148] As if to prove the point, in overseeing the *Gadolinium-Based Contrast Dye* litigation, Judge Dan Polster warned the parties, "no one can try their way out of this MDL"; if someone has a handful of cases, "the costs are prohibitive." "[R]emanding the case accomplishes nothing. It will go to a Judge who has little or no context or background, who will probably put this case at the bottom of his or her pile and it will just sit there," Polster argued.[149]

But the plaintiffs' lawyers appearing before Judge Polster disagreed. "[W]e have an excellent trial packet that is ready to be used in any case by any attorney in the United States," explained steering committee member Howard Nations. "We also have a core group of PSC attorneys who are perfectly willing to go in and assist in any trial we get in any court," so "they will not be left alone." Presentations by Nations and several others requesting remand "set[] forth the problems that we have when we don't have trial settings," explained plaintiffs' attorney Peter Weinberger.[150]

Limiting plaintiffs' freedom to select their forum, sending them to a place that would ordinarily lack personal jurisdiction over them, and retaining their cases indefinitely such that returning home for trial is a near impossibility raises constitutional questions. In *Phillips Petroleum Co. v. Shutts*, the Supreme Court addressed whether absent members of an opt-out class action had to have minimum contacts with the forum state. No, it held. Because the class member can opt out, her choice to stay means that she consents to the forum.[151] But, as Professor Patrick Woolley points out, how can a court that lacks personal jurisdiction over you require you to do anything? The short answer is that it can't. *Shutts* makes sense only if what binds the absent plaintiffs to the judgment is adequate representation – not consent.[152]

So, what binds plaintiffs to transferee courts' judgments? Not minimum contacts. Nothing in § 1407 confers nationwide jurisdiction on transferee judges, despite what some of them seem to think.[153] Not consent, for plaintiffs' transfer is forced and they cannot opt out. And not adequate representation because judges don't appoint leaders based on those requirements.

---

[148] Eduardo C. Robreno, *The Federal Asbestos Product Liability Multidistrict Litigation (MDL-875): Black Hole or New Paradigm?*, 23 WIDENER L. J. 97, 144 (2013).

[149] Transcript of Proceedings at 9–11, 15, *In re* Gadolinium-Based Contrast Agents Prods. Liab. Litig., No. 08-gd-50000 (N.D. Ohio May 2, 2011). Judge Polster presided over hundreds of remanded asbestos cases from the Eastern District of Pennsylvania but apparently none of them went to trial.

[150] *Id.*

[151] 472 U.S. 797, 813 (1985).

[152] Patrick Woolley, *Collateral Attack and the Role of Adequate Representation in Class Suits for Money Damages*, 58 KAN. L. REV. 917, 970 (2010).

[153] *E.g.*, *In re* Agent Orange Prods. Liab. Litig., 996 F.2d 1425, 1432 (2d Cir. 1993); *In re* Agent Orange Prods. Liab. Litig., 818 F.2d 145, 163 (2d Cir. 1987); Andrew D. Bradt & D. Theodore Rave, *Aggregation on Defendants' Terms: Bristol-Myers Squibb and the Federalization of Mass-Tort Litigation*, 59 B.C. L. REV. 1252, 1294–96 (2018).

What makes the transferee court's exercise of power constitutional is that the *transferor* court could properly exercise personal jurisdiction over both the plaintiff and the defendant. And, because the suit returns for trial, all's well that ends well. But as the possibility of remand moves from convenient fiction to virtual impossibility, it puts transferee judges' ability to constitutionally bind plaintiffs in peril.

Remand Is Rare

Transferee judges rarely remand cases. Statistics from across all types of multidistrict proceedings show that since the Panel's inception in 1968, it has centralized more than 500,000 civil actions. But it has remanded only around 3% of those.[154]

Oftentimes, no one but the plaintiffs and sometimes their individual attorneys want cases to go home. As Chapter 1 explained, the key stakeholders – plaintiffs' lead lawyers, defense attorneys, and the judge – all prefer to settle within the centralized proceeding. Remands threaten defendants' ability to gain closure, leaders' common-benefit fees rely on shakier precedent, and transferee judges face the stigma of failure that Judge Robreno identifies. So, judges do their best to hold on to the proceedings.[155]

Some judges even threaten remand to drive settlements. "Unless a settlement has been reached, the Court's first order suggesting remand will be entered," warned Judge John Keenan in the *Fosamax* litigation.[156] Of course, most civil cases settle and both routine cases and multidistrict proceedings settle at about the same rate. But as Judge William Young suggested, the settlement culture "is nowhere more prevalent than in MDL."[157]

Current procedures reinforce transferee judges' stranglehold. Technically, all transferee judges can do is suggest that the Panel remand a case, and, on the books at least, parties may make remand requests directly to the Panel.[158] But Dr. Foscue's request in *Zimmer* was hardly an anomaly: the Panel appears never to have remanded a case without the transferee judge's blessing.[159] Even though judges lobby for multidistrict assignments, as a matter of practice, the Panel refuses to "look

[154] Judicial Panel on Multidistrict Litigation – Judicial Business 2017, Table S-20, http://www.uscourts.gov/sites/default/files/jb_s20_0930.2017.pdf.

[155] Elizabeth Chamblee Burch, *Remanding Multidistrict Litigation*, 75 La. L. Rev. 399, 419 (2014). Early on transferee judges even transferred cases to themselves for trial under § 1404(a). But, relying on the plain language of § 1407, the Supreme Court held that they have "no such authority." Lexecon, Inc. v. Milberg Weiss Bershad Hynes & Lerach, 523 U.S. 26, 28 (1998).

[156] *In re* Fosamax Prods. Liab. Litig., No. 06-md-1789 (S.D.N.Y. Oct. 3, 2013) (order).

[157] DeLaventura v. Columbia Acorn Tr., 417 F. Supp. 2d 147, 150 (D. Mass. 2006).

[158] Rules of Procedure of the Judicial Panel on Multidistrict Litigation, Rule 10.1(b), 277 F.R.D. 480 (2010).

[159] Burch, *supra* note 155, at 418.

over the shoulders of [its] transferee judges" for fear of "severely compromis[ing] [its] ability to attract [them]."[160]

Appellate practices further reinforce this single-gatekeeper system. If appellate courts review the Panel's remand decisions at all, it is only upon an extraordinary writ of mandamus, and then subject to a clear error standard, both of which insulate the Panel's decisions from reversal.[161] Even cases that make it to the appellate level have little hope of remand. Appellate courts have allowed transferee judges to hold on to cases "even if common issues are present only in relation to cases that have already terminated."[162]

Yet, as Table A.6 illustrates, some cases do find their way back. What happens to them? Although it is still too early to track most of the cases within the dataset, researchers at the Federal Judicial Center delved into products-liability proceedings from 1992 to 2013 (the period that immediately precedes this book's dataset). They found that judges remanded 1% of asbestos cases and 6% of all other products-liability cases. But all those other cases really boiled down to just five proceedings, which accounted for 89% of that 6%.

Upon their return home, only 2% of remanded cases went to trial – 27 jury verdicts, 2 bench trials, and 1 directed verdict. At least 50% of them settled, probably more. The rest were voluntarily dismissed (15%) or subject to some other form of dismissal (18%), which surely includes some settlements too. Finally, around 5% concluded with a dispositive pretrial motion, likely a summary judgment that focused on an individual's specific causation or a motion to dismiss based on statutes of limitation.[163]

Episodic Remands

Retaining cases to spur unwilling plaintiffs to settle can spark a host of concerns. Plaintiffs can no longer adjudicate their issues before a judge and jury close to home. Private global settlements tend to dilute differences among state laws and give appellate courts few chances to fix errors unless parties petition to appeal merits-based rulings along the way. And if jury trials take place, those bellwethers may occur nowhere near affected communities.

To be sure, centralizing pretrial processes is efficient and efficiency can foster justice. But episodically remanding blocks of cases at key points doesn't nullify efficiency. It strikes a better balance between efficiency and procedural justice,

---

[160] John G. Heyburn II & Francis E. McGovern, *Evaluating and Improving the MDL Process*, 38 Litig., Spring 2012, at 27, 31. Yet, as Chapter 1 described, 70% of federal judges who haven't presided over a multidistrict proceeding would like to and 80% of those who had would like another one.

[161] 28 U.S.C. § 1407(e) (2012).

[162] *In re* Wilson, 451 F.3d 161, 170 (3d Cir. 2006).

[163] Catherine R. Borden, Emery G. Lee III & Margaret S. Williams, *Centripetal Forces: Multidistrict Litigation and Its Parts*, 75 La. L. Rev. 425, 448–50 (2014).

litigant autonomy, states' rights, and democratic participation.[164] So, remanding cases doesn't "accomplish nothing," as Judge Polster suggested.

In fact, when Professor Francis McGovern interviewed a cross-section of 90 attorneys involved in multidistrict proceedings, he concluded that many lawyers "simply want out and want a way to express their frustration without alienating the judge." "The palpable frustration of some counsel came through vividly in the interviews," he wrote.[165] Periodic remands at key points determined early in the proceedings provide that relief.

Remand benchmarks will vary by proceeding, but here are three things to consider in crafting them. First, if the steering committee decides that they will not develop certain claims and those claims would not benefit from coordinated discovery, then those cases should return home. Committees decide which claims to work up for a variety of reasons ranging from the ease of proving a causal connection to the claim's economic worth.

Using fact sheets to identify and remand plaintiffs that fall outside the committee's choices would protect those in the litigation's shadow from experiencing inadequate representation and unnecessary delay. Similarly, a block of plaintiffs might demonstrate that they were inappropriately centralized, are no longer benefitting from the committee's work, or that only case-specific discovery remains. If they want to advance their claims outside of the centralized proceeding, judges should return them to their court of origin.

Second, once coordinated discovery concludes, parties should decide which cases to remand before certain case-specific summary judgment motions occur. As the Third Circuit recognized in *Fosamax*, summary judgment presents "a deeper problem" because a "mass tort MDL is not a class action." While some "legal issues may apply in every case," explained the judges, "merits questions that are predicated on the existence or nonexistence of historical facts unique to each Plaintiff … generally are not amenable to across the board resolution." In short, streamlining the proceedings "cannot override the Plaintiffs' basic trial rights," ruled the Third Circuit.[166]

Third, if leaders negotiate a global settlement, then judges should remand non-settling plaintiffs.[167] This dislodges leaders' omnipotent power and vests control in individual counsel's hands. It also undermines the settlement vortex, which forces plaintiffs to choose between settling or risking dismissal. Remanding puts the

---

[164] Although I've argued for remands in the past, I cannot claim credit for the idea of episodic remands. Several professors and attorneys raised and elaborated upon it during an American Association of Justice meeting in May 2018. If memory serves, contributors included Samuel Issacharoff, Howard Erichson, and Tobi Millrood. The kernel of the idea is also included in the Memorandum from AAJ's MDL Working Group to Judge Robert Dow and Members of the MDL Subcommittee (Feb. 22, 2018).

[165] Heyburn & McGovern, *supra* note 160, at 31.

[166] *In re* Fosamax (Alendronate Sodium) Prods. Liab. Litig., 852 F.3d 268, 302 (3d Cir. 2017).

[167] Burch, *supra* note 28, at 152–54.

possibility of trials back on the table, but, as the statistics show, that doesn't mean more trials will necessarily occur. Instead, it allows plaintiffs to negotiate on a retail rather than wholesale basis and opens the door to a secondary market for representation.

In *Biomet*, for example, after Judge Miller closed the multidistrict proceedings, an attorney sent an e-mail to a listserv of products-liability lawyers requesting that they refer those cases to him: "Some attorneys are under the impression that there isn't a strong case to make against Biomet. We strongly disagree," wrote Ilyas Sayeg. "For many years now, we have litigated these cases outside of the MDL in state courts across the country. Our independence from the discovery limitations in the MDL have allowed us to conduct *extensive* fact as well as expert discovery," he explained. "We believe these are excellent cases and are prepared to take them to trial."[168] Litigating these cases individually or in smaller groups also allows defendants to use motions to dismiss and motions for summary judgment to combat weaker claims, which can no longer hide within the crowd.

If a mass exodus occurs after a global deal, that can signal something is amiss. Envision securities class actions for a moment. There, opting out has become de rigueur. The more class members vote with their feet, the stronger the message becomes that the deal is unattractive.[169] Within the dataset, remember that nearly one-third of the aggregate settlements came before any merits-related rulings. While early deals can save time and costs, common discovery may remain and plaintiffs may lack a sense as to their claim's strengths and weaknesses. Judges should not only probe these questions during common-benefit fee hearings, but they should also consider leaders' ability to continue to lead. After all, judges should not expect leaders who have settled their cases to soldier on, nor should the plaintiffs want them to.

Remanding blocks of cases at key benchmarks maintains the upside of centralizing, but it also counterbalances aggregating's traditional downsides. Here's what I mean:

First, remands can give plaintiffs control and voice opportunities. An escape hatch offers plaintiffs the chance to strike out on their own or form more cohesive groups outside the central proceeding. Smaller groups can preserve plaintiffs' forum choice, safeguard defendants' right to assert individual affirmative defenses, and exclude unique claims that are most likely to be disserved by a leadership that caters to the majority.

"We have worked long and hard to get these [*Prempro*] cases to trial," attorney Zoe Littlepage remarked. "The law firms that are left after these settlements are eager to see that every woman gets her day in court."[170] If faced with an

---

[168] Posting of Ilyas Sayeg, lsayeg@mctlawyers.com to American Association of Justice's Products Liability Listserver (Sept. 20, 2018) (on file with author).

[169] John C. Coffee, Jr., *Accountability and Competition in Securities Class Actions: Why "Exit" Works Better Than "Voice,"* 30 CARDOZO L. REV. 407, 425–29 (2008).

[170] Jef Feeley, *Pfizer Paid $896 Million in Prempro Settlements*, BLOOMBERG, June 19, 2012.

unsatisfactory settlement offer, remand allows plaintiffs like Littlepage's clients to pursue their suits in their chosen fora.[171] But remands also pressure lead lawyers to negotiate the best deal possible for plaintiffs of every type because common-benefit fees become much harder to recover postremand.[172]

Second, remands can correct judicial error by building in redundancy. As we have seen, few appellate opportunities exist in multidistrict litigation. But when state substantive laws lie at the heart of the dispute, the remedy need not be an interlocutory appeal that delays the entire proceeding. Remanding and coordinating federal cases on a statewide basis would build judicial redundancy into the process.[173]

The law-of-the-case doctrine permits judges to revisit their rulings if circumstances change or where "the initial decision was clearly erroneous and would make a manifest injustice."[174] So, even though transferor judges should not routinely revisit pretrial rulings, they may have to expand, modify, or vacate certain orders affecting trial. Plus, because some transferee judges refuse to rule on summary judgment motions that implicate state laws, remand offers parties an opportunity to air substantive disputes, proceed toward trial, and appeal – if warranted.

Third, remanding cases can relieve the substantive burdens caused by aggregating state-law claims with minimal commonality. When transferee judges consider state-law claims from around the country, they are confronted with sticky choice-of-law questions. As they are the first to admit, they are not experts on applying other states' laws.[175] When issues are state-specific and do not affect the corpus of cases, transferor judges are best equipped to decide them.[176] Remanding likewise allows them to consider whether statewide class actions are appropriate.

In this way, remands can alleviate some of the tension between multidistrict litigation and basic federalism principles. As Professor Larry Kramer observed, when states differ about what parties' rights should be, those differences "are not a 'cost' of

---

[171] This may affect counsel and plaintiffs' decision of where to sue, for many of them currently file directly in the transferee court after consolidation. Andrew D. Bradt, *The Shortest Distance: Direct Filing and Choice of Law in Multidistrict Litigation*, 88 NOTRE DAME L. REV. 759, 763 (2012).

[172] Burch, *supra* note 2, at 1906–16.

[173] On the benefits of judicial redundancy, see Robert M. Cover, *The Uses of Jurisdictional Redundancy: Interest, Ideology, and Innovation*, 22 WM. & MARY L. REV. 639, 646–57 (1981); Alexandra D. Lahav, *Recovering the Social Value of Jurisdictional Redundancy*, 82 TUL. L. REV. 2369 (2008).

[174] Christianson v. Colt Indus. Operating Corp., 486 U.S. 800, 816 (1988).

[175] *E.g., In re* Activated Carbon-Based Clothing Mktg. & Sales Practices Litig., 840 F. Supp. 2d 1193, 1199 (D. Minn. 2012).

[176] *E.g., In re* Bisphenol-A (BPA) Polycarbonate Plastic Prods. Liab. Litig., 276 F.R.D. 336, 347 (W.D. Mo. 2011); *In re* Light Cigarettes Mktg. Sales Practices Litig., 832 F. Supp. 2d 74 (D. Me. 2011).

the system. They are its object, something to be embraced and affirmatively valued."[77]

Fourth, remanded cases that proceed to trial allow diverse communities to partici-pate in fact finding and democracy. As Chapter 5 explained, the decline in civil trials can undermine democratic values and rob nationwide citizens of the chance to engage in fact finding. Bellwether trials in one judicial district simply cannot provide an outlet for those perspectives or profit from the "second-order diversity" that they would create.

Second-order diversity is generated when many different kinds of groups exist, but their members lack internal diversity. Ideologies and goals differ across, not within, the groups. As Yale Law Dean Heather Gerken explains, "second-order diversity provides a richer, more textured view" of decision-making bodies by "reveal[ing] the full democratic spectrum," making minority views visible, and "showcas[ing] div-ision and dissent *within* groups."[178] Although the low trial rate for all civil cases suggests that remand alone will not revitalize jury trials, it is a small step in the right direction.

As was the case with appointing leaders according to adequate-representation metrics, fostering dissent, compensating leaders using quantum meruit, and provid-ing voice opportunities to plaintiffs, transferee judges could implement episodic suggestions of remand on their own. But it must not come out of the blue. Instead, it should be part and parcel of a well-orchestrated pretrial package that ensures predictable escape hatches. Alternatively, to achieve uniformity, the Panel could institute this check unilaterally by simply amending its own Rule 10.1(b).[179] After all, it (not the transferee judge) has the power to remand. Amending Rule 16 of the Federal Rules of Civil Procedure would also do the trick. Like reworking the Panel's rules, changing Rule 16 could provide uniformity but with the built-in flexibility of tailoring the pretrial schedule to a proceeding's uniqueness.

---

[177] Kramer, *supra* note 116, at 579.
[178] Heather K. Gerken, *Second-Order Diversity*, 118 HARV. L. REV. 1101, 1104, 1172–73 (2005).
[179] Rules of Procedure of the Judicial Panel on Multidistrict Litigation, Rule 10.1(b), 277 F.R.D. 480 (2011).

Conclusion

Brooke Melton (*GM*), Michelle Pfeleger (*Yasmin/Yaz*), Linda Isner (*Vioxx*), Gene Weeks (*Vioxx*), Trudy Thomas (*Kugel Mesh*), Erika Langhart (*NuvaRing*), and David Foscue (*Zimmer*) are but a handful of the faces behind multidistrict litigation statistics. Stories like theirs lurk within many of the more than 312,500 actions included in this book's dataset. In each case, it would be easy to pin blame on the lawyers, the FDA, the company, or the doctors. But targeting only one paints an incomplete picture and misses the point: there are problems with each that affect, reflect, and amplify failings elsewhere.

It's true that for the judicial system to act as a reliable failsafe, plaintiffs-side lead lawyers' financial incentives must align with the plaintiffs' interests and checks and balances must exist. But when we consider the system as a whole, beginning with product development and marketing, it's clear that plaintiffs' lawyers don't have a monopoly on misaligned incentives.

For instance, according to former FDA official Madris Tomes, from 2002 until the end of 2017, some 30,000 women reported side effects from Bayer's permanent birth control, Essure. She concluded that, "[T]he benefit risk profile touted by Bayer simply didn't jibe with the data that was pouring into the FDA from both patients and physicians."[1] But when Bayer pulled Essure from the U.S. market in the summer of 2018, it claimed its decision "is based on a decline in U.S. sales" and that "[t]he safety and efficacy of Essure have not changed."[2] But those declining sales surely had something to do with lawsuits from 16,000 women (and their estates) who alleged that Essure caused death and perforated their fallopian tubes and uteruses. And that decline could be linked to a 36,000-member-strong Facebook

---

[1] Sheila Kaplan, *Bayer Will Stop Selling the Troubled Essure Birth Control Implants*, N.Y. TIMES (July 20, 2018), https://www.nytimes.com/2018/07/20/health/bayer-essure-birth-control.html.

[2] Kevin Kelleher, *Bayer Says It Will Halt Sales of Essure Birth-Control Implant*, FORTUNE (July 20, 2018), http://fortune.com/2018/07/20/bayer-sales-essure-birth-control-implant/.

group called "Essure Problems," the FDA's order requiring that Bayer label Essure with the risk that it could travel to the abdomen or pelvic cavity, and the FDA's threat of civil and criminal penalties if Bayer didn't limit Essure sales to medical practices that agreed to inform patients of its risks.

Bayer, as you might remember, has also faced suits over Yasmin and Yaz as well as its Mirena birth control. It withdrew its anticholesterol drug Baycol from the market in 2001 amidst claims that it broke down muscle fibers. And it recently acquired Monsanto, the same company that makes the weed killer, Roundup. In August 2018, a jury awarded Dewayne Johnson, a school groundskeeper, $289 million when he linked Roundup to his non-Hodgkin's lymphoma. (More than 800 other people have sued Monsanto over Roundup too.[3])

Like Bayer, other pharmaceutical and manufacturing giants battle multiple mass torts. Take Johnson & Johnson, for instance. Plaintiffs allege that its baby powder and shower-to-shower body powder cause ovarian cancer and contain asbestos, its blood thinner Xarelto has no antidote (like Pradaxa), its type-2 diabetes drug Invokana increases the risk of lower-body amputations, its vaginal mesh (Ethicon and Gynecare) perforates organs, its schizophrenia drug Risperdal can cause heart attacks and strokes, and its hip implants (DePuy Pinnacle and DePuy ASR) loosen prematurely and cause metal poisoning.

Lawsuits against companies like Bayer and Johnson & Johnson face mixed success in court and the corporations rarely admit to any wrongdoing (though they sometimes pay billions of dollars to settle claims). Yet, the discovery and trial process can sometimes reveal unsettling internal cost-benefit analyses that prize profit over patients. Consider, for example, the suits against Johnson & Johnson's unit, DePuy Orthopaedics, over the DePuy ASR (articular surface replacement) hip implant.

In 2005, DePuy's internal projections indicated that the implant would fail in 40% of the 93,000 patients worldwide within five years – more than eight times the failure rate for other hip implants.[4] Plus, when recipients moved, the metal-on-metal design shed cobalt and chromium debris into their hip joint's surrounding tissue and bone.

Company documents revealed that DePuy's own consulting surgeons flagged the design flaw early on and suggested a redesign. "My thoughts would be that DePuy should at least de-emphasize the A.S.R. cup while the clinical results are studied," consultant Dr. William Griffin explained.[5] But a redesign wasn't cost effective and the company was busy promoting the device as a new breakthrough. Consultants'

---

[3] Holly Yan, *Jurors Give $289 Million to a Man They Say Got Cancer from Monsanto's Roundup Weedkiller*, CNN (Aug. 11, 2018, 9:28 PM), https://www.cnn.com/2018/08/10/health/monsanto-johnson-trial-verdict/index.html..

[4] Barry Meier, *During Trial, New Details Emerge about Hip Maker*, N.Y. Times, Jan. 30, 2013, at B2.

[5] *Id.*

pleas were ignored.[6] "It is like playing Russian roulette," explained one orthopedic surgeon.[7] Rather than listen to those warnings, however, DePuy's officials blamed the high failure rates on the surgeons who implanted them – not on any design flaw.

Four years after launching the product, DePuy executive Raphael Pascaud conceded, "The issue seen with A.S.R. and XL today, over five years post-launch, [is] most likely linked to the inherent design of the product and that is something we should recognize."[8] After the FDA asked the company for more safety data in 2009, it decided to phase out the device and sell off its inventory. DePuy eventually recalled the ASR implant in mid-2010, but not before pain and permanent injuries prompted more than 8,000 lawsuits. (The company continued to sell the hips in non-U.S. markets, however, and didn't recall the devices in India until August 2018. Even then, a DePuy spokesperson said that the recall "doesn't imply that the product is 'faulty.'"[9])

Problems like this arise because pharmaceutical companies are responsible to shareholders and need to demonstrate profits. This may lead them to rush drugs and devices to market, ignore internal caution lights, and continue to offer them in countries with less oversight. Unfortunately, we have few protections to prevent them from doing so. Doctors are on the front lines, but they may not always be a reliable prophylactic. They may have incentives to overtreat or too little time to advise patients on the risks and benefits of the treatments they prescribe. And even in a perfect doctor-patient relationship, physicians must still rely on the adverse warnings that drug companies give them – they can't consider risks that aren't disclosed.

The FDA cannot act as a reliable failsafe, either: it regulates everything from tainted spinach to medical devices, pharmaceutical drugs, and pet food. It's not omniscient, it doesn't have unlimited resources, and its officials can be tempted by more lucrative jobs in the private sector that they regulate. So-called revolving doors may entice leniency and even faithful regulators must depend on the very entities they regulate for the information they need to perform their jobs. That the FDA sometimes acts only after entrepreneurial private lawyers point out problems and uncover information through discovery should not come as a surprise. As Professor John Coffee concluded in his careful treatment of plaintiffs' attorneys as "private attorneys general," "private enforcement of law through entrepreneurial litigation does litigate complex cases well (probably better than more resource-

[6] Barry Meier, *J.&J. Loses First Case Over Faulty Hip Implant*, N.Y. Times, Mar. 8, 2013, at B1.
[7] Barry Meier & Janet Roberts, *Hip Implant Complaints Surge, Even as the Dangers Are Studied*, N.Y. Times, Aug. 22, 2011, at A1.
[8] Meier, *supra* note 4.
[9] Teena Thacker, *Voluntary Recall Doesn't Imply Hip Implant Was Faulty, Says J&J*, MINT, Aug. 30, 2018.

constrained public enforcers can do) but is persistently misdirected by the tendency of plaintiff's attorneys to settle cases in their own interest."[10]

Plaintiffs' lawyers are the last line of defense. But corporate tort-reform efforts have aimed to breach this wall by making these cases less lucrative and procedurally harder for plaintiffs' lawyers to bring. As early victims of the GM ignition switch defect found when punitive damage caps made it too costly for lawyers in Wisconsin to take their cases, "successful" corporate lobbying efforts take a human toll. When some cases nevertheless manage to surface, corporate defendants may then try to exploit the misaligned incentives between plaintiffs' lawyers and their clients.

Johnson & Johnson and the lead plaintiffs' lawyers in *DePuy ASR* struck a deal in 2013 and another one in 2015. As Chapter 2 mentioned, those settlements required attorneys with a case in the multidistrict proceeding to "register" all their clients regardless of where (or even whether) the case was pending. Then attorneys had to use their "best efforts" to enroll all their clients. If the special master thought a law firm didn't comply with those requirements in good faith, DePuy could expel that law firm or attorney's other clients from the deal.[11] (When clients can't settle, their attorneys don't get paid either.) So, lawyers didn't have to withdraw from representing nonsettling clients, but they still had to nudge them to accept.

By designing settlement programs like those in *DePuy ASR*, corporations can rope in as many plaintiffs as possible by dangling the promise of increased common-benefit fees for lead plaintiffs' lawyers and paydays for compliant individual counsel. Clauses in the *DePuy ASR* deals said that consenting to settle also meant consenting to the MDL judge's orders, which included his common-benefit-fee order. By bargaining with the defendant then, leaders expanded their turf and taxed formerly out-of-reach state-court plaintiffs 5% in common-benefit fees and 1% in costs.[12]

All leaders had to do to get that substantial bump (the first settlement alone was reported at $2.5 billion, 5% of which would be $125 million) was convince 94% of all plaintiffs to abandon their lawsuits and enter into a settlement program that may or may not compensate them. In the program, claims administrators sat as arbitrators under the Federal Arbitration Act and issued final, binding, and nonappealable decisions. If the claims administrator decided not to determine an issue for some reason, then it went to one of three "special masters," who were all arbitrators from the for-profit arbitration company, JAMS.[13]

---

[10] John C. Coffee, Jr., Entrepreneurial Litigation: Its Rise, Fall, and Future 219 (2015).

[11] Settlement Agreement, art. 17, *In re* DePuy Orthopaedics, Inc. Hip Implant Prods. Liab. Litig., No. 10-md-2197 (N.D. Ohio Nov. 9, 2013) [hereinafter 2013 DePuy ASR Settlement]; 2015 ASR Settlement Agreement, art. 17, *In re* DePuy Orthopaedics, Inc. Hip Implant Prods. Liab. Litig., No. 10-md-2197 (N.D. Ohio Mar. 2, 2015) [hereinafter 2015 DePuy ASR Settlement].

[12] 2013 DePuy ASR Settlement, *supra* note 11, at § 4.1.8; 2015 DePuy ASR Settlement, *supra* note 11, at § 4.1.8.

[13] 2013 DePuy ASR Settlement, *supra* note 11, at art. 14; 2015 DePuy ASR Settlement, *supra* note 11, at art. 15.

Steven Skikos, one of the plaintiffs' lead lawyers, said, "[W]e did all of this by consent. There were no cram down orders in any of the settlements. There was no outmaneuvering to get these settlements done."[14] Some plaintiffs felt differently, however. Commenting on the deal, hip-implant recipient Van Fleming, a retired mortgage loan officer from Greenville, North Carolina, said, "I don't think it is fair at all." Celeste Laney, a patient and former occupational therapist, concurred: "I'm not taking it, it's a joke."[15] And the *New York Times* reported that "some patients contend that the deal's real winners are Johnson & Johnson and the plaintiffs' lawyers," but that plaintiffs "may have few alternatives" to accepting it because "[t]hey are unlikely to see a courtroom for years, if ever."[16]

Ninety-nine percent of eligible plaintiffs enrolled. Susan Sharko, Johnson & Johnson's lawyer, deemed the program "an overwhelming success."[17] Whatever plaintiffs did or didn't recover remains confidential, and plaintiffs' leaders filed all their common-benefit fee requests under seal. Judicial orders on those fees remain sealed as well.[18]

Tweaking one aspect of the system cannot mend every break. I can't promise you a cure-all. But encouraging plaintiffs' lawyers to faithfully represent their clients and to compete and dissent can have ripple effects. In 1972, MIT mathematician and meteorologist Edward Lorenz provocatively asked, "Does the flap of a butterfly's wings in Brazil set off a tornado in Texas?"[19] His point was that in complex systems (think ecosystems, cities, stock markets, and yes, multidistrict proceedings), a small variance in initial conditions could have unpredictable, profound, and widely divergent effects. Small changes, in other words, can set off chain reactions that result in big impacts.[20]

Chapter 3 demonstrated a tight network between multidistrict litigation's insiders – lawyers, judges, and defendants. They adapt through feedback and their connections produce effects beyond their one-on-one interactions. Introducing changes that capitalize on these connections may have far greater impact than trying to work against the grain by imposing top-down legislative reforms. Those reforms may temporarily disrupt the system, but insiders will quickly adapt. Far better to harness the equally adaptive powers of competition and dissent.

[14] Transcript of Open Court Conference Proceedings at 11, *In re* DePuy Orthopaedics, Inc. Hip Implant Prods. Liab. Litig., No. 10-md-2197 (N.D. Ohio Nov. 10, 2016).
[15] Barry Meier, *Frustration from a Deal on Flawed Hip Implants*, N.Y. TIMES, Nov. 25, 2013, at B1.
[16] *Id.*
[17] Transcript of Open Court Conference Proceedings at 8–9, *In re* DePuy Orthopaedics, Inc. Hip Implant Prods. Liab. Litig., No. 10-md-2197 (N.D. Ohio Nov. 10, 2016).
[18] *E.g., In re* DePuy Orthopaedics, Inc. Hip Implant Prods. Liab. Litig., No. 10-md-2197 (N.D. Ohio Mar. 24, 2017) (sealed orders no. 30–34 transfer & release funds filed by plaintiffs' liaison counsel).
[19] Jamie L. Vernon, *Understanding the Butterfly Effect*, 105 AM. SCIENTIST 130 (2017).
[20] *See* JOHN H. MILLER & SCOTT E. PAGE, COMPLEX ADAPTIVE SYSTEMS: AN INTRODUCTION TO COMPUTATIONAL MODELS OF SOCIAL LIFE 221 (2007).

In Chapter 6, we explored the ways in which basic economic principles might reinvigorate competition among plaintiffs' lawyers while opening up channels for plaintiffs and their individual counsel to dissent. As judges consider who to appoint to lucrative plaintiffs' leadership positions, they should *reject consensus slates, empower a cognitively diverse group,* and *designate attorneys representing differently situated clients to advocate for them and those like them.* Allowing those who weren't selected to *join or replace leaders* who fail to recognize and address important conflicts of interest can galvanize those on the outskirts to police conflicts that may arise as litigation progresses. Successful challenges can put those lawyers in the saddle. Not only do they gain a seat at the decision-making table, but they're in a position to receive common-benefit fees too. So, instead of staying mum, ingratiating themselves with the leaders, and playing the long game in hopes of receiving common-benefit work and future leadership roles, individual lawyers may compete.

As leaders survey the litigation landscape and decide which claims to develop – or not – outsiders can also raise information about which plaintiffs are unlikely to benefit from coordinated discovery so that judges can remand them early on. *Episodic remands* allow individual attorneys to control their clients' cases again and free them from having to pay common-benefit fees for work that does little for their clients. When combined, remanding cases and allowing dissenters to question whether leaders fairly represent plaintiffs with differently situated claims (or claims that fall on the margins) can maximize the payoffs for objecting.

Then, once a deal is on the table, why not *open up the courthouse doors* to facilitate a conversation about it? If the settlement program is truly private, then leaders could hold a question and answer forum among their constituents – plaintiffs and their lawyers. Plaintiffs could call in or participate through a web-based service. Either way, people like Van Fleming and Celeste Laney, who were unhappy with the *DePuy ASR* settlement, should have opportunities to voice their concerns. Plaintiffs are hungry for updates and information. When they don't have formal chances to discuss a deal, they will find their own outlets. Pelvic mesh victims, for instance, have held their own webinars, created newsletters, and joined online groups to complain about not only the defendants but also the way their attorneys treat them.[21]

Using *quantum-meruit principles* to tie leaders' common-benefit fees to plaintiffs' actual results (and not a fund's misleadingly high amount) encourages leaders to communicate with plaintiffs, to explain how the deal works, what the pitfalls and risks of trial may be, and how the settlement program is likely to compensate them. Quantum-meruit principles can also invigorate state-court competition by rewarding

---

[21] E.g., MESH NEWS DESK, https://www.meshmedicaldevicenewsdesk.com; We Are Mesh Survivors, https://www.facebook.com/WeAreMeshSurvivors/; The Mesh Warrior, https://www.facebook.com/themeshwarrior/; TRUTH IN MEDICINE, http://www.truthinmedicine.us.com/; LANA KEETON, http://www.lanakeeton.com/plaintiffpoweredlaw.htm; MESH ANGELS, http://www.meshangels.com.

state lawyers whose efforts help all plaintiffs and by replacing flat percentage taxes with tailored pricing packages for state litigants who want to access some (but not all) common-benefit work.

Linking leaders' common-benefit fees to plaintiffs' outcomes creates less incentive to deceive participants about a settlement program's potential benefits. But as long as corporate defendants continue using walkaway provisions like the 94% in *DePuy ASR*'s settlements, attorneys will still have reasons to push plaintiffs into the program.

This is where a stronger judicial devotion to *ethics rules* should kick in. Most of the publicly available private deals within the dataset did not disclose enough information for plaintiffs to provide informed consent before dismissing their lawsuit and entering into a settlement program. As I argued in Chapter 5, voluntary dismissals should be exchanged for settlement money, not a chance at future recovery. When lawyers lure clients into relinquishing their lawsuits without knowing everything that Model Rule of Professional Conduct 1.8(g) demands, then judges should be prepared to refer attorneys to the appropriate bar association for disciplinary procedures.

Finally, what about the claims that remain postsettlement? The people who aren't eligible for the settlement program and those who don't want to settle? In other words, what should happen to people who find themselves in the same predicament as the 4,000 *DePuy ASR* plaintiffs who weren't eligible to settle?

The answer will depend, in part, on leaders' presettlement efforts. When settlements occur early and cover all or most of the leaders' clients, those leaders have no economic motive to continue investing time and money into the proceeding. Yet, discovery on common issues surely remains. So, judges should *appoint new leadership* and ensure that ample common-benefit funds exist to finance their efforts. If, however, leaders took all the key depositions and made trial packets available as Howard Nations argued was the case in the *Gadolinium* litigation, then only case-specific discovery may be left. *Remanding* those plaintiffs to their home court puts them back in the driver's seat. Their individual attorney can negotiate a settlement that suits them better or threaten to take the case to trial.

Lawyers and corporate executives alike respond to economic incentives. Paying plaintiffs' lead lawyers based on client results discourages them from accepting deals with illusory benefits. The shift may mean that leaders have to test the waters a bit more to achieve the paychecks they prefer. But trying cases and bringing or fighting merits-related motions can expose new information. If that information reveals that some claims lack merit, dismissing them provides an important check for defendants and ensures that those claims don't dilute the compensation available for other plaintiffs. *Testing the merits* may also mean that corporations have to pay more to settle egregious suits. If businesses begin factoring this possibility into their cost-benefit analysis early on, perhaps they will be less inclined to ignore internal warning signs like those that Johnson & Johnson received from its own consultants.

Sadly, there is almost always a mass tort de jour – recent headlines include Essure, opioids, and talc. But incentives within multidistrict litigation tend to skew toward insiders' self-interest, not the public interest or the plaintiffs' interests. Left unchecked, self-interest can takeover. And there are no checks. There is thus an urgent need to look beyond a singular focus on the lawyers, the defendants, or the judge, and to improve the mass-tort system and its inhabitants as a whole. For a system that serves as the last line of defense for hundreds of thousands of plaintiffs, the status quo is unacceptable. Plaintiffs aren't commodities on an assembly line or inventory in a lawyer's filing cabinet – they're people like us.

APPENDIX

Data Collection

Researchers have long suspected that repeat players dominate leadership roles in aggregate litigation. To determine whether repeat players existed in multidistrict litigation and, if so, to what extent, I began collecting data on plaintiffs-side leadership appointments in the summer of 2013. Gathering that data entailed pulling docket information from Bloomberg Law, identifying the relevant judicial orders, and creating a database with the names of all judicially appointed lead plaintiffs' attorneys in all electronically accessible products-liability and sales-practice proceedings pending on the MDL docket as of May 14, 2013 (72 cases).

I found that repeat players did exist and were quite prevalent.[1] Over the next year, I documented defense-side leadership appointments in the same proceedings by repeating the previous process. I was also able to obtain information that had not previously been electronically available on the *Blood Products* litigation, which expanded the initial dataset to 73 proceedings.

Given that the 73 proceedings in my dataset were all pending in May 2013, the majority of those litigations have now concluded. As Figure A.1 illustrates, as of May 2018, parties settled 34 of those 73 proceedings through global or inventory settlements (nonclass settlements),[2] 20 through class-action settlements, 1 through individual settlements, and 1 through bankruptcy. Defendants successfully used *Daubert* motions, summary judgment, or arbitration to resolve 12 proceedings,[3] and parties are actively litigating the remaining 5 proceedings. These numbers

---

[1] That initial research appears in Elizabeth Chamblee Burch, *Judging Multidistrict Litigation*, 90 N.Y.U. L. Rev. 71, 95–98 (2015).

[2] Despite global or inventory settlements resolving most of the cases within these proceedings, as Table A.1 indicates, some proceedings remain open. In those, cases that haven't settled remain pending and postresolution issues persist.

[3] There were some individual settlements and successful trials even in some of the proceedings that I coded as "defense" victories. Those cases did not have massive settlements, however, and were principally resolved by a successful defense motion.

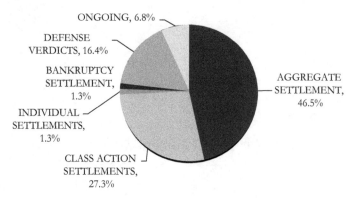

FIGURE A.1 Resolutions within the dataset of multidistrict products-liability and sales-practice proceedings

exclude the asbestos litigation's inventory settlements because early docket entries were not electronically available for that proceeding. Including it would increase the number of nonclass settlements from 34 to 35.

Again, excluding the asbestos litigation's inventory settlements because early docket entries were not electronically available, I collected and analyzed all of the nonclass settlements that were publicly available in those 34 proceedings by using Bloomberg Law, PACER, court websites dedicated to particular proceedings, SEC filings, and news and litigation reports. Ten of the 34 nonclass proceedings concluded with publicly available "private" settlements. And three of those 10 proceedings yielded 2 settlements each for a total of 13 settlements.[4]

In analyzing those 13 publicly available private settlements, I looked for indicia of advantages that repeat players might enjoy that one-shotters do not. Accordingly, I identified provisions that one might argue principally benefit the lead lawyers or the defendants, and not necessarily the plaintiffs. I focused my inquiry on four main types of provisions: (1) those that induce claimants to settle and thereby generate closure for defendants; (2) those compensating lead lawyers; (3) those that allow unclaimed funds to revert to the defendant; and (4) those that deter new lawsuits from being filed. I also analyzed the accompanying lead lawyers' common-benefit fee awards and identified the attorneys in leadership roles who had the authority to negotiate and design the settlements.

Next, I began to consider what role transferee judges play in prompting and enforcing these "private" aggregate settlements. To that end, I collected judicial orders and analyzed a number of variables relating to the judge's role in the 34 proceedings

---

[4] One of the 13 settlements, the one in the pelvic-mesh proceeding against American Medical Systems, is a partial settlement. It covers only the plaintiffs representd by one law firm, so it is unclear whether that settlement is representative of others in that litigation.

that concluded in nonclass aggregate settlements.[5] Once again, I gathered information from the MDL docket sheets on Bloomberg Law, decisions on Westlaw, websites dedicated to a particular proceeding, and news and litigation reports.

As indicia of a transferee judge's traditional role in the adversarial system, I identified litigation events that proceduralists characterize as merits-related inquiries: issuing orders on summary judgment, *Daubert* motions, and class certification, as well as conducting bellwether trials. To the extent possible, using the centralized MDL docket and media reports (such as Law360 and BNA's Class Action Litigation Report), I determined whether these rulings (or trials) occurred before the earliest known settlement date. I then searched for information about the range of variables that might suggest a deviation from judges' traditional "hands-off" approach to private settlement such as approving private settlements, appointing claims administrators or settlement masters, overseeing the settlement's administration, and issuing orders that enforce the private settlement's terms (case census orders, Lone Pine orders, and orders allowing attorneys to withdraw from nonsettling clients).

While working with the settlements, I noticed a number of parallels with arbitration. To explore this further, I first identified arbitration's hallmark characteristics. Because they are creatures of contract, arbitrations inevitably vary. But most include final, binding decisions; choice-of-law clauses; confidentiality provisions; provisions that circumscribe evidentiary submissions as well as appellate rights; and summary decisions without reasons. Accordingly, I determined whether these variables were present in the 13 publicly available "private" aggregate settlements.

Finally, to research malpractice actions against repeat players arising out of their involvement in the 34 proceedings ending in private aggregate settlements, research assistants searched Bloomberg Law's dockets by entering all or a unique portion of the law firm's name as a defendant. They then combed through the results to identify which cases included malpractice claims. After identifying malpractice actions, they then pulled the complaints and noted whether the action stemmed from the law firm's involvement in 1 of the 34 proceedings ending in private aggregate settlements. They repeated this process for all plaintiffs-side law firms that were involved in 3 or more of the 73 multidistrict proceedings in the dataset.

On the whole, this dataset should provide a representative sample for several reasons. First, products-liability and sales-practice proceedings constitute more than one-third of all multidistrict proceedings. And looking beyond the simple count of multidistrict *proceedings* to the actual number of *actions* contained in each shows that products-liability cases comprise up to 95% of all pending multidistrict actions. Second, examining pending cases on a certain date includes data from nonclass cases coordinated over 22 years and settled over a 14-year span – from 2004 to 2018.

---

[5] Because the book focuses on the practices and norms that develop outside of directly authorized judicial supervision under established class-action principles, I limited my analysis to the 34 proceedings concluding in nonclass settlements.

Third, although the number of publicly available private settlements was relatively small (10 of the 34 proceedings concluding in private aggregate settlements), the proceedings in which those settlements occurred collectively included 64,107 federal actions. Each "action" means a civil action, which is triggered by filing a complaint. Each complaint, however, can contain hundreds of plaintiffs. Plaintiffs' attorneys file consolidated complaints to avoid paying filing fees for each plaintiff. Moreover, the 64,107 doesn't include the thousands of related state-court cases resolved through the same settlements. Nor does it include a tally of the claimants' cases resolved under the deal who never filed a lawsuit (attorneys often wait as long as they can before filing so that they can watch the strategy unfold in various jurisdictions). This means that the actual number of *plaintiffs* is impossible to count and that there are likely to be far more plaintiffs than the number of actions reflects. So, even though the number of publicly available private deals was somewhat small, analyzing these deals should nevertheless provide some critical insights.

When viewed collectively, this information should give an accurate sense of how federal courts in the United States handle mass torts. The scope of the data suggests that the results may be generalizable outside the realm of products liability (and indeed the results are consistent with past work), but I cannot say with certainty that my findings are true across all proceeding types, or even for all products-liability proceedings for all time. Nonetheless, the importance of products-liability proceedings to the larger world of civil litigation suggests this is an appropriate starting place.

Data Analysis

TABLE A.1 Dataset proceedings, dispositions, and repeat player percentages

This table includes the outcomes (as of May 2018) of the 73 products-liability and sales-practice cases that were pending on the MDL docket as of May 14, 2013, organized by the date of the first reported settlement or, if no settlement, grouped by the outcome and centralization date. The proceedings with publicly available private settlements are in bold.

MDL No.	MDL Name	Centralization Date	First Settlement Date or Disposition	Year MDL Terminated (as of 8/15/18)	Class-Action Settlement	Publicly Available	Total Actions[6]	Percentage of Plaintiff-Side Repeat Players in Leadership
875	Asbestos	7/29/91	1980s	—	No	No	192,000	16% (2/12)
986	Factor VII or IX Concentrate Blood Prods.	12/7/1993	5/8/1997	2013	Yes	Yes	309	15% (2/13)
1203	Diet Drugs	1/6/1998	1/3/2002	2016	Yes	Yes	20,195	15% (2/13)
1355	**Propulsid**	**8/7/2000**	**4/30/2004**	**2013**	No	**Yes**	**474**	**90% (10/11)**
1431	Baycol	12/18/01	6/30/2005	—	No	No	9,107	68% (15/22)
1657	**Vioxx**	**2/16/2005**	**11/9/2007**	—	No	**Yes**	**10,313**	**50% (14/28)**
1742	Ortho Evra	3/1/2006	10/13/2008	2015	No	No	1,572	71% (15/21)
1836	Mirapex Prods. Liab. Litig.	6/22/2007	1/29/2009	—	No	No	441	100% (1 firm)
1909	Gadolinium Contrast Dyes	2/27/2008	4/15/2009	2015	No	No	574	72% (13/18)
1845	ConAgra Peanut Butter	6/17/2007	5/29/2009	2015	No	No	377	26% (5/19)
1763	Human Tissue	6/13/2007	1/30/2010	2014	No	No	249	33% (2/6)
2004	Mentor Corp. ObTape	12/3/08	6/8/2010	2018	No	No	263	66% (4/6)
1928	Trasylol	4/7/2008	7/6/2010	2015	No	No	1,834	62.5% (10/16)
1871	Avandia	6/11/2007	7/26/2010	—	No	No	5,299	79% (19/24)
1967	Bisphenol-A Polycarbonate Plastic	8/13/2008	1/3/2011	2013	Yes	Yes	38	22% (2/9)

1953	Heparin	9/23/2016	2/1/2011	2016	No	No	574	57% (12/21)
1873	FEMA	10/24/2007	3/14/2011	2013	Yes	Yes	4,828	18% (2/11)
1842	Kugel Mesh Hernia Patch	6/22/2007	7/1/2011	2017	No	No	2,224	75% (9/12)
2188	Apple iPhone 4 Mktg. & Sales Practices	10/8/2010	1/1/2012	2013	Yes	Yes	18	0% (0/4)
2179	Deepwater Horizon	8/10/2010	4/18/2012	—	Yes	Yes	1,165	36% (7/19)
2308	Sketchers Toning Shoe	12/19/11	5/02/2012	—	Yes	Yes	56	80% (4/5)
2023	Bayer Corp. Combination Aspirin	4/14/2009	5/16/2012	2013	Yes	Yes	13	50% (6/12)
1507	Prempro	3/4/2003	6/8/2012	2015	No	No	9,760	12.5% (3/24)
2047	Chinese Drywall	1/13/10	6/14/2012	—	Yes	Yes	356	70.5% (12/17)
1958	Zurn Pex Plumbing	8/21/2008	10/15/2012	2013	Yes	Yes	15	70% (7/10)
2284	Imprelis Herbicide	10/20/2011	10/19/2012	2018	Yes	Yes	131	60% (3/5)
1943	Levaquin	6/13/2008	10/30/2012	2017	No	No	1,983	62.5% (5/8)
2223	Navistar 6.0 Diesel Engine	4/13/2011	11/1/2012	2013	Yes	Yes	39	44% (8/18)
2151	Toyota Motor Corp. Unintended Acceleration	4/9/2010	12/26/2012	—	Yes	Yes	410	40.9% (9/22)
2092	Chantix (Varenicline)	10/1/2009	1/15/2013	2015	No	No	3,014	75% (12/16)
2100	**Yasmin and Yaz**	10/1/2009	3/15/2013	—	No	**Yes**	11,098	**89% (17/19)**
2372	Watson Fentanyl Patch	8/15/2014	6/4/2013	2014	No	No	31	0% (0/8)
2233	Porsche Plastic Coolant Tubes	5/23/2011	7/26/2013	2014	Yes	Yes	8	7% (1/13)
2197	**DePuy ASR Hip Implant**	12/3/2010	11/11/2013	—	No	**Yes**	1,236	**80% (25/31)**
1789	**Fosamax**	11/21/2011	12/9/2013	2018	No	**Yes**	1,119	**66% (8/12)**
2325	**American Medical Systems**[7]	2/7/12	4/30/2013	—	No	**Semi**	6,094	**100% (62/62)**[8]
2008	Land Rover LR3 Tire Wear	2/23/09	5/30/2013	2013	Yes	Yes	9	66% (4/6)

(continued)

TABLE A.1 (continued)

MDL No.	MDL Name	Centralization Date	First Settlement Date or Disposition	Year MDL Terminated (as of 8/15/18)	Class-Action Settlement	Publicly Available	Total Actions[6]	Percentage of Plaintiff-Side Repeat Players in Leadership
2391	**Biomet Magnum Hip Implant**	10/2/2012	**1/31/2014**	—	No	**Yes**	308	**58% (14/24)**
1964	**NuvaRing**	8/22/2008	**2/7/2014**	—	**No**	**Yes**	**1,232**	**35% (6/17)**
1629	Neurontin	10/26/2004	5/30/2014	2015	Yes	Yes	253	50% (4/8)
2385	Pradaxa	8/8/2012	8/13/2014	—	No	No	689	70% (19/27)
2387	Coloplast Corp. Pelvic Support Systems	8/6/2012	9/22/2014	—	No	No	2,674	100% (3/3)
2333	MI Windows & Doors	4/23/12	12/24/2014	2015	Yes	Yes	14	46% (6/13)
2419	New England Compounding Pharmacy[9]	2/12/2013	2/13/2015	—	Bank.	Yes	172	42.8% (3/7)
2283	Building Materials Corp. of Am.	10/11/11	4/22/2015	2014	Yes	Yes	13	69% (9/13)
2299	**Actos (Pioglitazone)**	12/29/2011	**4/29/2015**	—	**No**	**Yes**	**1,585**	**68% (18/22)**
2316	Ford Motor Co Spark Plug and 3-Valve Engine	2/8/2012	6/19/2015	2016	Yes	Yes	5	83% (5/6)
2187	C. R. Bard, Inc. Pelvic Repair System	6/12/2010	6/23/2015	—	No	No	15,701	100% (62/62)
2326	Boston Scientific Corp. Pelvic Repair System	2/7/2012	12/7/2015	—	No	No	25,662	100% (62/62)
2327	Ethicon, Inc. Pelvic Repair System	2/7/2012	1/27/2016	—	No	No	40,397	100% (62/62)

2001	Whirlpool Corp. Front-Loading Washer	9/26/2008		2016	Yes	Yes	11	61.5% (8/13)
2158	**Zimmer Durom Hip Cup**	**6/9/2010**	05/2016	–	**No**	**Yes**	**732**	**100% (3/3)**
2428	Fresenius GranuFlo/NaturaLyte Dialysate	12/12/2012	8/3/2016	–	No	No	4,370	64.7% (11/17)
2329	Wright Medical Conserve Hip Implant	2/8/2012	11/1/2016	–	No	No	641	11% (1/9)
2436	Tylenol	4/1/2013	2/10/2017	–	No	No	233	75% (6/8)
2272	Zimmer NexGen Knee Implant	8/8/2011	02/12/2018	–	No	No	1,741	89% (17/19)
1626	Accutane	11/01/2004	Some individual settlements; summary judgment for defendant	2016	No	No	124	46% (12/26)
1687	Ford Motor Co. E-350 Van	6/16/2005	Claims dismissed after certification was denied	2013	No	No	5	18% (2/11)
1760	Aredia and Zometa	4/18/2006	Individual settlements, summary judgment motions granted for defense, remands ongoing	2014	No	No	480	28.5% (2/7)
1718	Ford Motor Co. Speed Control Deactivation Switch	8/9/2006	Some individual settlements; summary judgment granted for defendant	2013	No	No	135	0% (0/9)
2045	Apple iPhone 3G	6/15/2009	Granted motion to compel arbitration	2014	No	No	13	13.6% (3/22)
2051	Denture Cream	6/9/2009	Dispositive *Daubert* motion granted	2016	No	No	223	58% (7/12)
1736	Celexa and Lexapro	8/19/2009	Individual settlements, remaining cases remanded	2013	No	No	43	20% (1/5)
2172	Toyota Motor Corp. Hybrid Brake	8/17/2010	Summary judgment granted for defense	2013	No	No	14	20% (1/5)

(continued)

TABLE A.1 (continued)

MDL No.	MDL Name	Centralization Date	First Settlement Date or Disposition	Year MDL Terminated (as of 8/15/18)	Class-Action Settlement	Publicly Available	Total Actions[6]	Percentage of Plaintiff-Side Repeat Players in Leadership
2226	Darvocet, Darvon and Propoxyphene	8/16/2011	Summary judgment granted for defense	2016	No	No	272	50% (7/14)
2342	Zoloft (Sertraline Hydrochloride)	4/17/2012	Summary judgment granted for defense	2018	No	No	339	81% (13/16)
2404	Nexium (Esomeprazole)	12/6/2012	Summary judgment granted for defense	2016	No	No	55	100% (1/1)
2434	Mirena IUD	3/29/2013	Summary judgment granted for defense	–	No	No	1,776	52.9% (9/17)
2104	IKO Roofing Shingle	12/3/2009	Pending	–	–	–	19	62.5% (5/8)
2243	Fosamax (Alendronate Sodium)	2/3/2012	Pending	–	–	–	1,257	66.6% (8/12)
2244	DePuy Pinnacle	2/8/2012	Pending	–	–	–	9,903	40% (14/35)
2331	Propecia (Finasteride)	4/16/2012	Pending	–	–	–	1,178	73% (11/15)
2418	Plavix	2/1/2013	Pending	–	–	–	347	100% (1/1) (interim counsel)

[6] As described in the preceding text, an "action" is a civil action, the filing of a complaint. There can be hundreds of plaintiffs included in a single complaint. So, the number of actions is unlikely to reflect news reports about the number of plaintiffs.

[7] This settlement was included as an exhibit to a Securities and Exchange Commission filing; some confidential parts of it were redacted. The agreement is between American Medical Systems and Freese & Goss, PLLC and Matthews & Associates.

[8] The judge handling pelvic-mesh proceedings appointed the same 62 attorneys as lead lawyers in four out of the five multidistrict proceedings within the dataset (two pelvic mesh proceedings began after May 2013 and are not included here).

[9] New England Compounding Pharmacy is in the midst of bankruptcy proceedings, so the settlement is a bankruptcy trust.

TABLE A.2 *High-level repeat player defense firms with five or more leadership appearances*

Defense Law Firm	Attorney MDL Appearances	Multidistrict Proceedings
Venable LLP	23	Fosamax (MDL 1789)
		Mirapex
		Propecia (Finasteride)
		Nexium (Esomeprazole)
Williams & Connolly LLP	13	Prempro
		Vioxx
		Chantix
		Nexium (Esomeprazole)
Bryan Cave LLP	12	Ford Motor Co. E-350 Van (No. II)
		Fosamax (MDL 1789)
		Bisphenol-A (BPA) Polycarbonate Plastics
		Propecia (Finasteride)
		Pradaxa (Dabigatran Etexilate)
Butler Snow LLP	12	Fosamax (MDL 1789)
		Ethicon, Inc. Pelvic Repair Sys.
		Propecia (Finasteride)
		Tylenol (Acetaminophen) Marketing
Ulmer & Berne LLP	12	Celexa and Lexapro
		Yasmin and Yaz (Drospirenone) Marketing
		Darvocet, Darvon and Propoxyphene
		Watson Fentanyl Patch
Covington & Burling LLP	10	Accutane (Isotrentinoin)
		Fosamax (MDL 1789)
		Pradaxa (Dabigatran Etexilate)
		Nexium (Esomeprazole)
Tucker Ellis LLP	10	OrthoEvra
		DePuy Orthopaedics Inc., ASR Hip Implant
		Propecia (Finasteride)
		Coloplast Corp. Pelvic Support Sys.
		New England Compounding Pharmacy, Inc.
Fulbright & Jaworski LLP	9	Fosamax (MDL 1789)
		Denture Cream
		Coloplast Corp. Pelvic Support Sys.
		New England Compounding Pharmacy, Inc.
McGuire Woods LLP	7	ConAgra Peanut Butter
		New England Compounding Pharmacy, Inc.

(continued)

TABLE A.2 (*continued*)

Defense Law Firm	Attorney MDL Appearances	Multidistrict Proceedings
Skadden, Arps, Slate, Meagher & Flom LLP	7	Toyota Motor Corp. Unintended Acceleration Darvocet, Darvon and Propoxyphene DePuy Orthopaedics, Inc., Pinnacle Hip Implant New England Compounding Pharmacy, Inc.
Baker & Daniels LLP	6	Zimmer Durom Hip Cup Zimmer Nexgen Knee Implant
Ice Miller LLP	6	Accutane (Isotrentinoin) Darvocet, Darvon and Propoxyphene
Jones Day	6	Mentor Corp. ObTape Transobuturator Sling Nexium (Esomeprazole)
Nelson Mullins Riley & Scarborough LLP	6	FEMA Trailer Formaldehyde C. R. Bard, Inc., Pelvic Repair System Boston Scientific Corp Pelvic Repair Sys. Whirlpool Corp. Front-Loading Washer
Reed Smith	6	Mirapex Kugel Mesh Hernia Patch Fosamax (Alendronate Sodium) (No. II) NuvaRing American Medical Systems Inc., Pelvic Repair Sys.
Drinker Biddle & Reath LLP	5	OrthoEvra Levaquin DePuy Orthopaedics Inc., ASR Hip Implant Tylenol (Acetaminophen) Marketing Propulsid
Halleland Lewis Nilan & Johnson	5	Mirapex Levaquin Baycol
McDermott, Will, & Emery	5	Diet Drugs (Phentermine/Fenfluramine/Dexfenfluramine) Methyl Tertiary Butyl Ether (MTBE) IKO Roofing Shingle
Wheeler Trig O'Donnell LLP	5	Gadolinium Contrast Dyes Whirlpool Corp. Front-Loading Washer

TABLE A.3 Repeat plaintiffs' attorneys participation in publicly available private nonclass settlements

This table includes a list of the highest level repeat player plaintiffs' attorneys (based on their number of appearances within the dataset) and whether they participated in any of the 10 multidistrict proceedings that resulted in a publicly available nonclass settlement.

Attorney	Total No. Leadership Appearances	Total No. MDL Appearances	Propulsid	Vioxx	Yasmin/Yaz	DePuy ASR	Fosamax (1789)	Biomet	NuvaRing	Actos	American Medical Systems	Zimmer Durom Hip Cup
Arsenault, Richard	21	18	Yes	Yes	No	Yes	No	Yes	Yes	Yes	Yes	No
Seeger, Christopher	21	16	Yes	Yes	Yes	Yes	Yes	No	No	Yes	No	Yes
Nast, Dianne	19	14	No	Yes	Yes	No	No	No	No	Yes	Yes	No
Becnel Jr., Daniel	14	14	Yes	No	No	No	No	No	No	No	No	No
Parker, Jerrold	11	11	No	Yes	Yes	Yes	No	No	No	Yes	Yes	No
Robinson Jr., Mark	14	10	No	No	No	Yes	No	No	No	Yes	No	No
Conroy, Jayne	12	10	No	No	No	No	No	No	No	Yes	Yes	No
Parfitt, Michelle	11	10	No	No	No	No	Yes	No	No	No	Yes	No
Levin, Arnold	15	9	Yes	Yes	Yes	No	No	No	No	No	Yes	No
London, Michael	14	9	No	No	Yes	Yes	No	No	No	No	No	No
Thompson III, Fred	12	8	No	No	No	Yes	No	Yes	No	Yes	No	No
Lanier, W. Mark	11	8	No	No	No	No	No	No	No	Yes	No	No
Shkolnik, Hunter	9	8	No	No	No	No	No	No	Yes	No	Yes	No
Crump, Martin	8	8	No	No	No	No	No	No	No	No	Yes	No
Restaino, John	10	7	No	No	No	No	No	No	No	No	Yes	No
Cartmell, Thomas	8	7	No	No	No	No	No	No	No	No	Yes	No

(continued)

Attorney	Total No. Leadership Appearances	Total No. MDL Appearances	Propulsid	Vioxx	Yasmin/Yaz	DePuy ASR	Fosamax (1789)	Biomet	NuvaRing	Actos	American Medical Systems	Zimmer Durom Hip Cup
Flowers, Peter	8	7	No	No	No	No	No	Yes	No	No	Yes	No
DeBartolomeo, A. J.	7	7	No	No	Yes	No	No	No	No	Yes	Yes	No
Flaherty, Yvonne	7	7	No	No	No	No	No	No	Yes	No	Yes	No
Osborne, Joseph	7	7	No	No	No	No	No	Yes	No	No	Yes	No
Dugan II, James	7	7	No	Yes	No	No	Yes	No	No	No	No	No
Matthews, David	7	7	No	No	No	No	No	No	No	No	Yes	No
Meadow, Richard	7	6	No	Yes	Yes	No	No	No	No	No	Yes	No
Cabraser, Elizabeth	10	6	No	No	No	No	No	No	No	No	No	No
Aylstock, Bryan	9	6	No	No	No	No	No	No	No	No	Yes	No
Zonies, Joseph	7	6	No	No	No	No	No	No	No	No	Yes	No
Anapol, Thomas	7	6	No	No	No	Yes	No	Yes	No	No	Yes	No
Salim, Robert	7	6	No	No	No	No	No	No	No	No	Yes	No
Abrams, Rachel	6	6	No	No	No	No	No	No	No	No	Yes	No
Blizzard, Edward	6	6	No	No	No	Yes	No	No	No	No	Yes	No
Oliver, Alyson	6	6	No	No	No	No	No	No	No	No	Yes	No
Monsour, Doug	6	6	No	No	No	No	No	No	No	No	Yes	No
Climaco, John	6	6	No	No	No	No	No	Yes	No	No	No	No
Placitella, Christopher	6	6	No	No	No	Yes	No	No	No	No	Yes	No
Garrard III, Henry	11	5	No	No	No	No	No	No	No	No	Yes	No
Denton, Roger	9	5	No	Yes	No	No	No	No	Yes	No	No	No
Chaffin, Eric	7	5	No	No	No	No	No	No	No	No	Yes	No

Name												
Love, Scott	7	5	No	No	No	No	No	No	No	No	Yes	No
Potts, Derek	7	5	No	No	No	No	No	No	No	No	Yes	No
Burnett Jr., Riley	6	5	No	No	No	No	No	No	No	No	Yes	No
Mueller, Mark	6	5	No	No	No	No	No	No	No	No	No	No
Alonso, Andres	6	5	No	No	Yes	Yes	No	No	No	No	Yes	No
Clarke, Clayton	6	5	No	No	No	No	No	No	No	No	Yes	No
Grand, Jeff	6	5	No	No	Yes	No	No	No	No	No	Yes	No
Papantonio, J. Michael	6	5	Yes	Yes	No	No	No	No	No	No	No	No
Barrios, Dawn	6	5	Yes	Yes	No	No	No	No	No	Yes	No	No
Copeland, Erin	5	5	No	No	No	No	No	No	No	No	Yes	No
Goetz, Michael	5	5	No	No	No	No	No	No	No	No	Yes	No
Hauer, Stacy	5	5	No	No	No	No	No	Yes	No	No	Yes	No
Maniatis, Victoria	5	5	No	No	No	No	No	No	No	No	Yes	No
Miller, Michael	5	5	No	No	No	No	No	No	No	No	Yes	No
Robins III, Bill	5	5	No	No	No	No	No	Yes	No	No	Yes	No
Saunders, Joseph	5	5	No	No	No	No	No	No	No	No	Yes	No
Skikos, Steven	6	4	No	No	Yes	Yes	No	No	No	No	No	No
Bell, Harry	5	4	No	No	No	No	No	No	No	No	Yes	No

TABLE A.4 *Common-benefit fee practices, fee awards,*

MDL Information								Common-Benefit Fees
MDL No.	MDL Name	Nonclass Settlement Publicly Available	Common-Fund Holdback Increased Midstream	Initial Percentage of Fees/Costs	Final Percentages of Fees/Costs	Escalating Percentages Based on Timing of Consent	Fee Aspects Negotiated with Defendant?	
1355	Propulsid	Yes, I & II	No	6%	6%	No	Yes, directly	
1431	Baycol	No	No	6%	6% (4/2)	No	Confidential settlement	
1507	Prempro	No	No	5% federal; 3% state	5% federal; 3% state	No	Confidential settlement	
1657	Vioxx	Yes	Yes	3% (2/1)	6.5%	Yes	Yes	
1742	Ortho Evra	No	Yes	3%	6 to 8%	Yes	Confidential settlement	
1763	Human Tissue	No	No	6% federal; 4% state	6% federal; 4% state	No	Confidential settlement	
2243	Fosamax	Yes	No	9%	9%	Yes	Yes	
1836	Mirapex	No	Unknown	Unknown	Unknown	Unknown	Confidential settlement	
1842	Kugel Mesh Hernia Patch	No	No	12% (8/4)	12% (8/4)	No	Confidential settlement	
1845	ConAgra Peanut Butter	No	No	4%	4%	No	Confidential settlement	
1871	Avandia	No	No	7%	7% (4/3)	No	Confidential settlement	

and plaintiff recovery in private, aggregate settlements in the dataset

State-Court Attorneys Taxed for Common Benefit?	Common-Benefit Fee and Cost Awards	Fee Objections on MDL Docket	Plaintiffs' Recovery, if Known	
			Percent of Claimants Who Recovered	Aggregate Amount of Recovery
Yes, if state-court judge orders or counsel agrees, and using settlement agreement	$27,026,449	No	0.6% (37 of 6,012)	$6,521,482.74
Yes, using court order	Sealed	No	Kept confidential	Kept confidential
Yes, using participation agreement	$77,768,733	Yes	Kept confidential	Kept confidential
Yes, using participation agreement and settlement agreement	$356,054,692	Yes	65.9% (32,886 of 49,893)	$4,353,152,064
Yes, using participation agreement	$41,081,123	Yes	15% (state); 5% (federal)	$68,717,843.00 (partial)
Yes, using participation agreement (could exclude state cases with a promise not to use common-work product in them)	Only partial information available	No	Kept confidential	Kept confidential
Yes, using participation agreement and settlement agreement	$2,459,475.00	No	Kept confidential	Kept confidential. $27,327,500 1,100 "resolved"
No order available	Unknown	No	No information available	No information available
Yes, using participation agreement and jurisdiction over defendant	$11,004,673	Yes	Kept confidential	Kept confidential
Yes, if counsel consents or if plaintiff received a tangible benefit	$266,052.21	Yes	Kept confidential	Kept confidential
Yes, using participation agreement	$153,800,000	Yes	Kept confidential	Kept confidential

(continued)

TABLE A.4 (*continued*)

MDL Information					Common-Benefit Fees		
MDL No.	MDL Name	Nonclass Settlement Publicly Available	Common-Fund Holdback Increased Midstream	Initial Percentage of Fees/Costs	Final Percentages of Fees/Costs	Escalating Percentages Based on Timing of Consent	Fee Aspects Negotiated with Defendant?
1909	Gadolinium Contrast Dyes	No	No	6% (5/1)	6% (5/1)	Yes[10]	Confidential settlement
1928	Trasylol	No	No	6%	6%	No	Confidential settlement
1943	Levaquin	No	Yes	Undetermined	9.5%	No	Confidential settlement
1953	Heparin	No	No	6% (3/3)	6% (3/3)	Yes	Confidential settlement
1964	NuvaRing	Yes	Yes	8% (5/3)	15.5% (11/4.5)	No	No
2004	Mentor Corp. ObTape	No	No	5%	5% (3/2)	No	Confidential settlement
2092	Chantix (Varenicline)	No	Yes	6%	7% (4/3)	Yes	Confidential settlement
2100	Yasmin and Yaz	Yes, I & II	Yes	6% (4/2)	11% (9/2) for ATE; 6% (4/2) for gallbladder	Yes	Yes
2158	Zimmer Durom Hip Cup	Yes	No	4% (2/2) Federal P's only	4% (2/2) State and federal P's	No	Yes
2187	C. R. Bard, Inc. Pelvic Repair Sys.	No	No	5%	5%	Yes[10]	Confidential settlements

State-Court Attorneys Taxed for Common Benefit?	Common-Benefit Fee and Cost Awards	Fee Objections on MDL Docket	Plaintiffs' Recovery, if Known	
			Percent of Claimants Who Recovered	Aggregate Amount of Recovery
Yes, using participation agreement	Sealed	No	Kept confidential	Kept confidential
Yes, using participation agreement	$1,323,202	Yes	Kept confidential	Kept confidential
Yes, using court order	Sealed	No	Kept confidential	Kept confidential
Yes, using participation agreement	Sealed	No	Kept confidential	Kept confidential
Yes, using order claiming jurisdiction over attorneys	$13,939,817	Yes, one	42% (1,556 of 3,704 as of Sept. 9, 2015)	Unknown. Fund amount: $100,000,000
Yes, using participation agreement	$908,868.34	No	Kept confidential	Kept confidential
Yes, using participation agreement, or by benefitting from MDL work product	Sealed	No	Kept confidential	Kept confidential
Yes, using participation agreement and settlement agreement	$83,447,010 (partial amount, will increase as VTE cases settle)	Yes	Partial info: Gallbladder 1,386 approved out of 1,410; total pending - 7,205 as of 9/29/14	Partial info: VTE cases - $1,800,000,000 for 9,185 claimants; Gallbladder cases – 59% paid as of 4/20/15
Yes, using settlement agreement and court order requiring all plaintiffs to participate in settlement	$3,230,137 first disbursement	Yes	Kept confidential	Kept confidential
Yes, using participation agreement, by seeking compensation, or benefiting from PSC's work	Not yet awarded	Unknown[11]	Kept Confidential	Kept Confidential

(continued)

TABLE A.4 (*continued*)

MDL No.	MDL Name	Nonclass Settlement Publicly Available	Common-Fund Holdback Increased Midstream	Initial Percentage of Fees/Costs	Final Percentages of Fees/Costs	Escalating Percentages Based on Timing of Consent	Fee Aspects Negotiated with Defendant?
2197	DePuy ASR Hip Implant	Yes, I & II	Yes	4% (3/1)	6% (5/1)	Yes	Yes
2272	Zimmer NexGen Knee Implant	No	No	None set	8% (5/3)	No	Confidential settlement
2299	Actos (Pioglitazone)	Yes	No	None set	8.6%	No	Yes
2325	American Medical Systems Pelvic Repair	Semi	No	5%	5%	Yes[10]	Partially confidential settlements
2326	Boston Scientific Corp. Pelvic Repair Sys.	No	No	5%	5%	Yes[10]	Confidential settlements
2327	Ethicon, Inc. Pelvic Repair	No	No	5%	5%	Yes[10]	Confidential settlements
2329	Wright Medical Conserve Hip Implant	No	No	7% (3.5/3.5)	7%	No	Confidential settlements
2373	Watson Fentanyl Patch	No	No order	No order	No order	No order	Confidential settlement

| | | | Plaintiffs' Recovery, if Known | |
State-Court Attorneys Taxed for Common Benefit?	Common-Benefit Fee and Cost Awards	Fee Objections on MDL Docket	Percent of Claimants Who Recovered	Aggregate Amount of Recovery
Yes, using settlement agreement subjecting them to the court's fee order	Sealed	Yes, one initially	Sealed	Sealed
Yes, using participation agreement or by using common benefit work	Not yet awarded	No	Kept confidential	Not yet awarded
Yes, court order covered payments made by defendants to any plaintiff participating in settlement	$25,000,000 withheld[12]	No	Kept confidential	Kept confidential
Yes, using participation agreement, by seeking compensation, or benefiting from PSC's work	Not yet awarded	Unknown	Kept confidential	Kept confidential
Yes, using participation agreement, by seeking compensation, or benefiting from PSC's work	Not yet awarded	Unknown	Kept confidential	Kept confidential
Yes, using participation agreement, by seeking compensation, or benefiting from PSC's work	Not yet awarded	Unknown	Kept confidential	Kept confidential
No, state cases expressly excluded by court	$11,900,000	No	Kept confidential	Kept confidential
No common benefit order – cases brought by one law firm	No order (most claims brought by one firm)	No	Kept confidential	Kept confidential

(*continued*)

TABLE A.4 (*continued*)

	MDL Information					Common-Benefit Fees	
MDL No.	MDL Name	Nonclass Settlement Publicly Available	Common-Fund Holdback Increased Midstream	Initial Percentage of Fees/Costs	Final Percentages of Fees/Costs	Escalating Percentages Based on Timing of Consent	Fee Aspects Negotiated with Defendant?
2391	Biomet Magnum Hip Implant	Yes	No	6% (5/1)	3.99%	No	Yes, directly
2385	Pradaxa	No	No	6%	6% (4/2)	Yes	Kept confidential
2387	Coloplast Corp. Pelvic Support Sys.	No	No	5%	5%	Yes[10]	Kept confidential
2428	Fresenius Granuflo/ Naturalyte	No	Yes	9% (7/2)	11% (7/4)	No	Confidential settlement
2436	Tylenol	No	Yes	10% (8/2)	19% (10/9)	No	Yes, fees paid by D
Total: 34 MDLs			26.4% Yes	6.2% avg.	7.28% avg.	41.1% Yes	Of those proceeding with publicly available settlements 90% negotiated fees with defendant (9 of 10)

---

[10] Escalating percentages were not specified in the order, but the judge noted that attorneys who did not sign participation agreements may be subject to increased assessments.

[11] Judge Goodwin presides over seven technically separate pelvic-mesh proceedings; some objections are filed in one proceeding, but pertain to all. None appeared on this proceeding's docket as of May 2018, but as this book was in press, several objections appeared as to fees in January of 2019.

[12] *In re* Actos (Pioglitazone) Prods. Liab. Litig., No. 11-md-2299 (W.D. La. Sept. 1, 2015) (case management order: holdback order, at 5).

State-Court Attorneys Taxed for Common Benefit?	Common-Benefit Fee and Cost Awards	Fee Objections on MDL Docket	Plaintiffs' Recovery, if Known	
			Percent of Claimants Who Recovered	Aggregate Amount of Recovery
Yes, by signing motion or seeking compensation, and by settlement agreement	$6,849,250	No	Kept confidential	$144,365,980 for 1,837 of 2,765 (66%) claimants
Yes, by seeking compensation	$26,000,000	Yes	96.8% (4,444 of 4,590; 9 categories of payouts)	$650,000,000 for 4,444 claimants
Yes, using participation agreement	Not yet awarded	Unknown	Kept confidential	Kept confidential
Yes, using participation agreement or by benefitting from the common benefit work	$15,870,491	Yes, by state attorneys' general	Kept confidential	Kept confidential
Yes, using participation agreement	Submitted in camera	No	Kept confidential	Kept confidential
97% taxed state court attorneys in some form; 80% of proceedings with publicly available settlements (8 of 10) did so by negotiating with defendants		**38% Yes**		

TABLE A.5 *Transferee judges' role in private,*

MDL Number	MDL Name	Aggregate Settlement(s) Publicly Available	Summary Judgment Rulings on MDL Docket	Daubert Rulings on MDL Docket	Class Certification Rulings on MDL Docket	Bellwether Trials Held in MDL	Approving Private Settlement	Appointing Claims Administrator or Settlement Master
		MDL Information for Nonclass, Aggregate Settlements	**Traditional Judicial Role in Ruling on Merits-Related Motions Presettlement**					
1355	Propulsid	Yes, I & II	Yes	Yes	Yes	Yes	Yes	Yes
1431	Baycol	No°	No*	No*	No*	No	No	Yes
1507	Prempro	No°	Yes	Yes	Yes	Yes	No	No
1657	Vioxx	Yes	Yes	Yes	Yes	Yes	Yes	Yes
1742	Ortho Evra	No	No*	No	No	No	Unknown	Yes
1763	Human Tissue	No	Yes	Yes	No*	No	No	No
1789	Fosamax	Yes	Yes	Yes	Yes	Yes	Yes	Yes
1836	Mirapex	No°	Yes	Yes	No	Yes	No	No
1842	Kugel Mesh	No°	Yes	Yes	No	Yes	No	Yes

aggregate settlements within the dataset

Transferee Judge's Role in Private Settlement Approval and Administration	Judicial Role in Settlement Enforcement		
Settlement Oversight	Case "Census" Orders	Lone Pine/Show Cause Orders	Allowing Attorneys to Withdraw from Nonsettling Clients
• Accepts jurisdiction over enrollees • Terminates noncompliant claim submissions • Receives regular updates • Authorized awards to Canadian program and to charitable organizations • Ordered unclaimed funds to revert to defendant	No	No	Yes
• Court created settlement/mediation program • Court allocates special master's payment and provides immunity from testimony and suit	No	Yes	No
None	No	No	No
• Judge served as settlement's chief administrator, issued final and nonappealable arbitration decisions that bound special master • Accepts jurisdiction over enrollees • Commented on adequacy of settlement amount	Yes	Yes	Yes
• Held settlement conferences • Issued sealed orders for administering settlements • Appointed special settlement master	No	Yes	No
• Mediated a global settlement • Dismissed claims covered by the settlement with prejudice	No	Yes	No
• Judge served as settlement's general special master and heard all settlement "appeals" • Appointed special settlement master to promote settlement • Appointed magistrate judge as special master to hear settlement appeals and settlement disputes • Appointed allocation special master as final arbiter • Issued eligibility and categorization guidelines	No	Yes	Yes
None. Magistrate judge conducted settlement conferences	No	No	No
• Judicially ordered plaintiff fact sheets • Ordered in-court monthly settlement conferences • Judicially created claims categories for individual settlement values	No	Yes	Yes

(continued)

TABLE A.5 *(continued)*

MDL Number	MDL Name	Aggregate Settlement(s) Publicly Available	Summary Judgment Rulings on MDL Docket	Daubert Rulings on MDL Docket	Class Certification Rulings on MDL Docket	Bellwether Trials Held in MDL	Approving Private Settlement	Appointing Claims Administrator or Settlement Master
		MDL Information for Nonclass, Aggregate Settlements	**Traditional Judicial Role in Ruling on Merits-Related Motions Presettlement**					
1845	ConAgra Peanut Butter	No°	No*	No*	Yes	No	No	No
1871	Avandia	No°	No*	No*	No*	No	Yes	Yes
1909	Gadolinium Contrast Dyes	No°	No*	No*	No	No*	No	Unknown
1928	Trasylol	No°	Yes	Yes	Yes	No	No	No
1943	Levaquin	No°	Yes	Yes	No	Yes	Yes	Yes
1953	Heparin	No°	Yes	Yes	No	No	Yes	Unknown
1964	NuvaRing	Yes	Yes	Yes	Yes	No	Yes	Yes

Transferee Judge's Role in Private Settlement Approval and Administration	Judicial Role in Settlement Enforcement		
Settlement Oversight	*Case "Census" Orders*	*Lone Pine/Show Cause Orders*	*Allowing Attorneys to Withdraw from Nonsettling Clients*
• Appointed special masters for confidential settlement • Sealed settlement agreement and releases			
None. Requested status reports on settlement's progress	No	Yes	Yes
• Appointed settlement master and special master to be paid by parties; duties permitted conducting settlement negotiations, communicating with parties ex parte, sanctioning parties, and conducting evidentiary hearings • Approved special masters' fees • Appointed fund administrators as part of qualified settlement funds • Ordered simultaneous mediation and trial dates for nonsettling cases • Suspended litigation pending settlement conclusion	No	Yes	Yes
• Issued sealed orders for administering settlements • Ordered in-court settlement conferences • Ordered mediation and appointed JAMS mediator	Yes	Yes	No
• Approved settlements only for decedents' estates pursuant to state law	No	Yes	Yes
• Ordered in-court settlement conferences • Appointed special settlement master and provided master with final, binding, and nonappealable authority to create settlement allocation protocol and allocate settlement awards • Allocated settlement funds under seal	No	Yes	Yes
• Appointed sitting federal judge as mediator • Issued sealed orders approving settlements	Yes	Yes	No
• Appointed retired federal judge as mediator • Ordered notice of the settlement sent to all plaintiffs • Imposed settlement deadlines and dismissed noncompliant claims • Appointed retired state court judge as special master for settlement disputes • Receives recommendations from settlement special master on motions to dismiss	Yes	Yes	No

(continued)

TABLE A.5 *(continued)*

MDL Number	MDL Name	Aggregate Settlement(s) Publicly Available	Summary Judgment Rulings on MDL Docket	Daubert Rulings on MDL Docket	Class Certification Rulings on MDL Docket	Bellwether Trials Held in MDL	Approving Private Settlement	Appointing Claims Administrator or Settlement Master
		MDL Information for Nonclass, Aggregate Settlements	Traditional Judicial Role in Ruling on Merits-Related Motions Presettlement					
2004	Mentor Corp. ObTape	No	Yes	Yes	No	Yes	No	No
2011	Zimmer NexGen Knee Implant	No	Yes	Yes	No	Yes	No	No
2092	Chantix	No°	Yes	Yes	No	No	No	No
2100	Yasmin and Yaz	Yes, I & II	No*	Yes	Yes	No	Yes	Yes
2158	Zimmer Durom Hip Cup	Yes	Yes	Yes	No	Yes	Yes	No
2197	C. R. Bard, Inc. Pelvic Repair Systems	No°	Yes	Yes	No	Yes	Yes	Yes

Transferee Judge's Role in Private Settlement Approval and Administration — *Settlement Oversight*	Judicial Role in Settlement Enforcement		
	Case "Census" Orders	Lone Pine/Show Cause Orders	Allowing Attorneys to Withdraw from Nonsettling Clients
• Appointed settlement special master to monitor common benefit fund • Appointed fund administrators as part of qualified settlement funds	No	No	No
• Stayed the proceedings • Ordered all plaintiffs and their counsel to coordinate and consult with lead lawyers on resolving their cases under the settlement • Ordered monthly updates on finalizing the settlement	Yes	Yes	Yes
• Ordered nonsettling plaintiffs to mediate	No	Yes	No
• Conducted in-chambers, sealed conference to discuss settlement • Imposed settlement deadlines through court orders, with settlement attached to orders • Ordered MDL gallbladder plaintiffs automatically enrolled in and bound by the nonclass settlement unless they opted out • Appointed special masters to preside over settlement, police deadlines, hear settlement appeals • Accepted jurisdiction over enrollees • Dismissed noncompliant cases	Yes	Yes	No
• Heard oral argument on the proposed settlement process as a quasi-fairness hearing • Ordered all plaintiffs to participate in the settlement, comply with the settlement deadlines, or face dismissal; participating in the settlement meant that counsel had to register all clients (state or federal court, filed or unfiled cases) and submit those claims to the settlement's mediation process; • Stayed litigation pending the conclusion of the settlement/court imposed mediation	Yes	Not yet	Not yet
• Issued orders appointing special settlement masters to administer settlements, allocate payments, mediate settlement disputes, arbitrate insurance and third-party disputes, communicate with parties ex parte, and serve as the final and binding arbitrator on all claimant appeals	Yes	Yes	No

(continued)

TABLE A.5 (*continued*)

MDL Number	MDL Name	Aggregate Settlement(s) Publicly Available	Summary Judgment Rulings on MDL Docket	Daubert Rulings on MDL Docket	Class Certification Rulings on MDL Docket	Bellwether Trials Held in MDL	Approving Private Settlement	Appointing Claims Administrator or Settlement Master
		MDL Information for Nonclass, Aggregate Settlements	**Traditional Judicial Role in Ruling on Merits-Related Motions Presettlement**					
2197	DePuy ASR Hip Implant	Yes, I & II	No	No	No	No	Yes	Yes
2299	Actos	Yes	Yes	Yes	No	Yes	Yes	Yes
2325	American Medical Sys. Pelvic Repair	Semi°	No	No	No	No	Yes	Yes
2326	Boston Scientific Pelvic Repair	No°	Yes	Yes	No	Yes	Yes	Yes
2327	Ethicon, Inc. Pelvic Repair	No°	Yes	Yes	No	Yes	No	Yes

Transferee Judge's Role in Private Settlement Approval and Administration		Judicial Role in Settlement Enforcement		
	Settlement Oversight	*Case "Census" Orders*	*Lone Pine/Show Cause Orders*	*Allowing Attorneys to Withdraw from Nonsettling Clients*
	• Required special settlement masters to report to the court quarterly • Court approves special settlement master's payment			
	• Sealed orders administering settlements and motions for qualified settlement funds • Appointed settlement oversight committee to build consensus and oversee settlement program in state and federal court • Appointed settlement escrow agent for common benefit funds • Enforced settlement deadlines	Yes	No	Yes
	• Stayed discovery pending the completion of the settlement program • Ordered notice of the settlement sent to all plaintiffs • Imposed settlement deadlines and dismissed noncompliant claims • Appointed special masters and claims administrators to preside over settlement, police deadlines, hear settlement appeals • Accepted jurisdiction over enrollees	Yes	No	Yes
	• Issued orders appointing special settlement masters to administer settlements, allocate payments, mediate settlement disputes, arbitrate insurance and third-party disputes, and communicate with parties ex parte • Required special settlement masters to report to the court quarterly • Court approves special settlement master's payment	No	Yes	No
	• Issued orders appointing special settlement masters to administer settlements, allocate payments, mediate settlement disputes, arbitrate insurance and third-party disputes, communicate with parties ex parte, and serve as the final and binding arbitrator on all claimant appeals • Required special settlement masters to report to the court quarterly • Court approves special settlement master's payment	No	No	No
	• Issued orders appointing special settlement masters to administer settlements, allocate payments, mediate settlement disputes, arbitrate insurance and third-party disputes, communicate with parties ex parte, and serve as the final and binding arbitrator on all claimant appeals • Required special settlement masters to report to the court quarterly • Court approves special settlement master's payment	No	No	No

(continued)

TABLE A.5 (*continued*)

MDL Number	MDL Name	Aggregate Settlement(s) Publicly Available	Summary Judgment Rulings on MDL Docket	Daubert Rulings on MDL Docket	Class Certification Rulings on MDL Docket	Bellwether Trials Held in MDL	Approving Private Settlement	Appointing Claims Administrator or Settlement Master
		MDL Information for Nonclass, Aggregate Settlements	Traditional Judicial Role in Ruling on Merits-Related Motions Presettlement					
2329	Wright Medical Conserve Hip Implant	No	Yes	Yes	No	Yes	No	Yes
2372	Watson Fentanyl Patch	Noᵒ	No	No	No	No	Yes	Unknown
2385	Pradaxa	No	No	No	No	No	Yes	Yes
2387	Coloplast Corp. Pelvic Repair	Noᵒ	No	No	No	No	Yes	Yes
2391	Biomet Magnum Hip Implant	Yes	No*	No	No	No	Yes	Yes

Transferee Judge's Role in Private Settlement Approval and Administration		Judicial Role in Settlement Enforcement		
Settlement Oversight		*Case "Census" Orders*	*Lone Pine/Show Cause Orders*	*Allowing Attorneys to Withdraw from Nonsettling Clients*
• Court appointed special master from JAMS to preside over private settlement • JAMS special master hears all appeals, and decision is final and binding • Claims administrator and special master can speak with parties ex parte • Ordered claims administrator and special master to file monthly court reports		No	No	No
• Issued sealed orders approving settlements		No	No	No
• Supervised mediation, appointed a negotiation committee, and appointed a special master to negotiate and implement a master settlement agreement • Stayed litigation to facilitate settlement completion • Imposed settlement deadlines through court orders • Appointed fund administrators as part of qualified settlement fund • Commented on adequacy of settlement amount • Ordered claims administrator and special master to attend court's monthly status conferences and provide detailed settlement status reports • Ordered payment allocations under the settlement		Yes	Yes	No
• Issued sealed orders appointing special masters to administer settlements, allocate payments, mediate settlement disputes, arbitrate insurance and third-party disputes, communicate with parties ex parte, and serve as the final and binding arbitrator on all claimant appeals • Required special masters to report to the court quarterly		No	Yes	No
• Entered settlement agreement into court's docket • Stayed responsive pleadings until the settlement process concluded • Ordered settlement deadlines		No	Yes	No

(continued)

TABLE A.5 (*continued*)

MDL Information for Nonclass, Aggregate Settlements			Traditional Judicial Role in Ruling on Merits-Related Motions Presettlement					
MDL Number	MDL Name	Aggregate Settlement(s) Publicly Available	Summary Judgment Rulings on MDL Docket	Daubert Rulings on MDL Docket	Class Certification Rulings on MDL Docket	Bellwether Trials Held in MDL	Approving Private Settlement	Appointing Claims Administrator or Settlement Master
2428	Fresenius Granuflo/ Naturalyte	No	No	Yes	No	No*	No	Yes
2436	Tylenol	No	Yes	Yes	No	No	No	Yes
Totals 34 proceedings			61.7% yes; 38.2% no	67.6% yes; 32% no	23.5% yes; 76.4% no	44% yes; 55.8% no	52.9% yes; 47% no or unknown	64.7% yes; 35% no or unknown

° Denotes inventory settlements and subsequent data refers to the date of the first known inventory settlement.

* Denotes a ruling (or trial) after the first settlement occurred.

Transferee Judge's Role in Private Settlement Approval and Administration		Judicial Role in Settlement Enforcement		
	Settlement Oversight	*Case "Census" Orders*	*Lone Pine/Show Cause Orders*	*Allowing Attorneys to Withdraw from Nonsettling Clients*
• Appointed lien administrator • Sent settlement disputes to mediation in accord with settlement				
• Appointed settlement special master with authority to create, approve, and distribute settlement funds; resolve settlement disputes; preside over postsettlement allocations; communicate ex parte with the court; resolve appeals from compensation awards • Reviewed settlement special master's rulings on a clear error standard of review as opposed to the default de novo standard in FRCP 53 • Settlement special master must provide the court with status updates on the settlement program • Imposed and extended private settlement's opt-in deadlines		No (done by D)	Yes	No
• Appointed magistrate judge as special settlement master who would oversee private settlement allocation • Appointed a qualified settlement administrator		Yes	Yes	Yes
		35% yes; 64.7% no	67.6% yes; 32% no	35% yes; 64.7% no

TABLE A.6 Pre- and Postsettlement judicial orders in dataset proceedings ending in private, aggregate settlements

MDL Information for Nonclass, Aggregate Settlements			Presettlement Information			Postsettlement Orders				
MDL No.	MDL Name	First Settlement Date	Plaintiffs' Fact Sheets First Ordered	No. of Days to Comply with Fact Sheet Request	Expert Reports Required	Census Order	Lone Pine/ Show Cause Orders	No. of Days to Produce Expert Report (from Lone Pine Order)	Stay of Proceedings	Remands
1355	Propulsid	4/30/2004	1/31/01	45 days	No	None	None	N/A	None	None
1431	Baycol	6/30/2005	3/4/02	45 days	No	None	3/18/04	81–134 days depending on transfer date and phase	2/14/05	05/09/07 1 case only
1657	Vioxx	11/9/2007	8/16/05	60–75 days with 20 days to cure	No	11/9/07	11/9/07	45 days after census, others vary based on tolling agreements	11/9/07	periodic remands
1742	Ortho Evra	10/13/2008	6/27/06	45–60 days	No	None	3/10/09	52–83 days depending on label and negotiation stage	None	None
1836	Mirapex	2/29/2009	9/5/07	45–90 days depending on wave, 30 days to cure	No	None	None	N/A	8/8/11; 6/20/11 Individual cases	None thus far; case ongoing

1909	Gadolinium Contrast Dyes	4/15/2009	6/16/08	35–45 days	No	1/26/12 3/1/13	2/28/13	Not requested	None	1 case only
1845	ConAgra Peanut Butter	5/29/2009	10/23/07	60 days	No	None	8/16/10	Not requested	1/27/10 (4 cases)	5/9/11–3/20/ 15 11 cases
1763	Human Tissue	1/30/2010	10/16/06	30–60 days	No	None	12/8/09	38 days	3/3/08	5/20/09–10/ 7/12 3 cases
1871	Avandia	6/01/2010	6/9/08	60 days	No	None	11/15/10	60 to 150 days to serve physician certification depending on filing or tolling agreement.	9/22/10	None thus far; case ongoing
2004	Mentor Corp. ObTape	6/8/2010	11/22/11	30–90 days	No	None	None	N/A	None	7/25/11 beginning of periodic remands
1928	Trasylol	7/6/2010	5/22/08	60–90 days	No	5/11/11; 5/16/12; 5/23/11; 5/23/12	None	5/11/11 and 5/16/12 Ps who failed to provide a case-specific expert report according to 4/26/11 order, have 10 days to cure	None	None

(continued)

TABLE A.6 (continued)

	MDL Information for Nonclass, Aggregate Settlements		Presettlement Information					Postsettlement Orders			
MDL No.	MDL Name	First Settlement Date	Plaintiffs' Fact Sheets First Ordered	No. of Days to Comply with Fact Sheet Request	Expert Reports Required	Census Order	Lone Pine/ Show Cause Orders	No. of Days to Produce Expert Report (from Lone Pine Order)	Stay of Proceedings	Remands
1842	Kugel Mesh Hernia Patch	7/1/2011	12/6/07; 1/30/08 (amended)	90 days with 45 days to cure	No	None	5/22/12 9/16/14 1/6/15	30 days to provide medical reports and supporting evidence, 30 days to cure deficiency	06/09/11	11/26/12; 11/14/16 9 cases
1953	Heparin	12/1/2011	10/21/08	60 days	No	5/10/12	11/24/10 11/30/10 12/23/10	190–120 days to produce evidence to overcome summary judgment	None	None
1507	Prempro	6/8/2012	04/13/04	60–90 days	No	None	None	N/A	None	Multiple suggested remands beginning 2/23/10; 399 cases

1943	Levaquin	10/30/2012	2/20/09	24–90 days depending on phase	No	None	10/11/13	Not Requested	None	Multiple suggested remands beginning 4/24/13; 66 cases
2092	Chantix (Varenicline)	1/15/2013	2/24/10	60 days	No	None	3/12/13	Ps transferred to MDL on or after 2/28/13 shall serve a case-specific expert report within 30 days of filing complaint	None	None
2100	Yasmin and Yaz (Drospirenone)	3/15/2013	3/3/10	45 days	No	8/3/15 10/5/15	3/15/13 8/3/15	60–120 days depending on transfer date.	8/3/15	None thus far; case ongoing
2372	Watson Fentanyl Patch	6/4/2013	04/23/13 scheduling order for unsettled cases	PFS not specifically ordered	No	None	None	N/A	None	None
2197	DePuy ASR Hip Implant	11/1/2013	9/26/11	90–120 days depending on surgery and transfer	No	11/22/13	None	N/A	None	11/1/11; 11/3/11; 3 actions; case ongoing

(continued)

TABLE A.6 (continued)

			Presettlement Information				Postsettlement Orders			
MDL Information for Nonclass, Aggregate Settlements										
MDL No.	MDL Name	First Settlement Date	Plaintiffs' Fact Sheets First Ordered	No. of Days to Comply with Fact Sheet Request	Expert Reports Required	Census Order	Lone Pine/ Show Cause Orders	No. of Days to Produce Expert Report (from Lone Pine Order)	Stay of Proceedings	Remands
1789	Fosamax	12/9/2013	11/1/06, modified 12/18/06; 11/20/12 presettlement Lone Pine	60 days, 30 days to cure	Yes, per 11/20/12 Ps with certain injuries had 92–198 days to produce case-specific expert	None	7/30/14	86 days	1/21/14 (Court stays remand order)	None
2325	American Medical Systems	4/30/2013	10/4/12; 2/28/13 (forms)	18–60 days depending on discovery pool and wave	No	None	None but mandatory conf on 12/11/18 for unresolved cases	N/A	None	7/3/14 3/3/17
2391	Biomet M2a Magnum Hip Implant	1/31/2014	3/25/13	90 days	No	None	12/14/16; 12/15/16	104–124 days depending on injury and whether pro se	2/14/14	None

262

1964	NuvaRing	2/7/2014	11/7/08	60–75 days depending on transfer and answer	No	10/8/13 1/29/14	2/7/14	30–45 days, with 30 days to cure	5/29/14 staying proceedings until 7/30/14. 8/1/14, lifting stay for non-settling Ps	Multiple suggested remands beginning 11/1/16; 10/19/16; 10/2/17; 6/22/18 (12 cases)
2385	Pradaxa	5/28/2014	10/29/12	45–60 days with 14 days to cure	No	5/29/14	5/29/14	15 days from the opt-in deadline to produce records; 30 days from opt-in deadline to produce generic and case-specific expert reports; 20 days to cure	5/20/14	None
2387	Coloplast Corp. Pelvic Support Sys.	9/22/2014	6/21/16	24–74 days depending on wave	No	None	12/16/18	N/A	No, staged discovery based on wave	None
2327	Ethicon, Inc. Pelvic Repair	3/10/2015	3/6/13	17–60 days depending on wave	No	None	None	N/A	None	None

(continued)

TABLE A.6 (continued)

MDL No.	MDL Name	Presettlement Information					Postsettlement Orders			
		First Settlement Date	Plaintiffs' Fact Sheets First Ordered	No. of Days to Comply with Fact Sheet Request	Expert Reports Required	Census Order	Lone Pine/ Show Cause Orders	No. of Days to Produce Expert Report (from Lone Pine Order)	Stay of Proceedings	Remands
2299	Actos (Pioglitazone)	4/29/2015	7/9/12	45–75 days depending on wave	No	4/28/15	None	N/A	5/1/15	09/19/17 1 case, proceedings ongoing
2187	C. R. Bard, Inc. Pelvic Repair Sys.	6/23/2015	6/7/11 (later amendments)	60–135 days depending on filing and transfer date; 20 days to cure	No	12/31/13	11/9/18	N/A	None	Proceedings ongoing, some case-specific remands
2326	Boston Scientific Corp. Pelvic Repair Sys.	12/7/2015	10/4/12 (3/6/13 – PTO_39)	15–60 days depending on discovery pool and wave	No	None	None	N/A	None	4/28/15
2158	Zimmer Durom Hip Cup	2/11/2016	2/1/13	Parties shall respond to Fact Sheets w/in 45 days of service	No	5/13/16	Not yet	N/A	5/13/16	None thus far; case ongoing

2428	Fresenius Granuflo/ Naturalyte	8/3/2016	12/06/13	45–87 days depending on medical charts and clinic; 30 days to cure	No	12/8/14 by D	01/26/17	62 days	None	None
2272	Zimmer NexGen Knee Implant	2/6/2018	12/23/11	70–93 days; 30 days to cure	No	10/11/17	1/15/18	60–90 days	2/12/18	9/17/14; 9/29/14; 2/13/12; case ongoing 03/08/18; 06/22/18
2329	Wright Medical Conserve Hip Implant	11/1/2016	5/23/12	90 days	No	No	No	N/A	No	
2436	Tylenol	2/10/2017	6/20/13	60 days	No	2/22/17	2/22/17	30 days from opt-in deadline	3/10/14	Proceedings ongoing

TABLE A.7 *Claims administration in publicly available,*

MDL Number	MDL Name	Submitted Claims Extinguished	Recovery Amount Known at Time of Entrance into Settlement Program	Confidential Awards	Evidentiary Proofs	Summary Decisions Decisions without Reasons
1355	Propulsid (two settlements)	Yes	No	Yes	Yes	Yes
1657	Vioxx	Yes	Point sheet provided	Yes	Yes	Point sheet provided
2243	Fosamax	Yes	Allocation formula	Yes	Yes	Category allocation letter
2100	Yasmin and Yaz (two settlements)	Yes	Tiers; base points known	No	Yes	Unknown
2197	DePuy ASR Hip Implant (two settlements)	Yes	Base awards known	Yes	Yes	Unknown
2325	American Medical Systems (semipublic)	Yes	Yes, mostly	Yes	Yes	Unknown
2391	Biomet Magnum Hip Implant	No	Base award	Yes	Yes	Unknown

nonclass aggregate settlements within the dataset

Settlement Claims Appeals Process	Arbitration-Like Provision for Disputes Arising Out of Agreement	Choice of Law Provision	Forum Selection Clause	Common-Benefit Attorneys' Fees
• None, final award	No	No	No	Yes
• Internal appeal from gate committee to special master who issues final, nonappealable award • Transferee judge sat as binding arbitrator	Yes, judge sat as binding arbitration panel	Yes	Yes	Yes
• Transferee court's magistrate judge determined final, binding, nonappealable settlement "appeals" by sitting as a general special master	Yes, judge resolves all disputes as general special master	Yes	No	Yes
• Claims administrators' initial decisions subject to reconsideration requests, then that decision may be appealed to the special master appointed by transferee judge • Special master's decisions are final and nonappealable • Losing party on appeal must pay $500 in costs	No	Yes	No	Yes
• Claims administrators sit as arbitrators under the Federal Arbitration Act and issue final, binding, nonappealable decisions • Noneligible applicants may appeal their status to the special master who reviews under an abuse of discretion standard • Awards initially appealed to same claims processor then to special masters using an abuse of discretion standard	Yes	Yes	Yes	Yes
• All challenges and disputes submitted to JAMS arbitration	Yes	Yes	No	No
• All challenges and disputes submitted to mediation, those not resolved in mediation remanded pursuant to court order	No, mediation	Yes	No	Yes

(continued)

TABLE A.7 *(continued)*

MDL Number	MDL Name	Submitted Claims Extinguished	Recovery Amount Known at Time of Entrance into Settlement Program	Confidential Awards	Evidentiary Proofs	Summary Decisions Decisions without Reasons
1964	NuvaRing	Yes	No	No	Yes	Unknown
2158	Zimmer Durom Hip Cup	After award	Yes	Yes	Yes	Unknown
2299	Actos (Pioglitazone)	Yes	Points matrix	No	Yes	Unknown

Settlement Claims Appeals Process	Arbitration-Like Provision for Disputes Arising Out of Agreement	Choice of Law Provision	Forum Selection Clause	Common-Benefit Attorneys' Fees
• Settlement's special master (retired state court judge) decided appeals; decisions were final, binding, nonappealable	Yes, special master resolves all disputes in final, binding way	Yes	No	No
• If eligibility or award amount is disputed, claimant must participate in and split the costs of mandatory mediation with the date and location set by the defendant	No, mandatory mediation and stay of litigation in state and federal courts	Yes	No	Yes
• Appeal of enrollment status made to same claims administrator who determined that original status and is then final, binding, and nonappealable • Claims package deficiencies may be appealed to eligibility committee, then to special master whose decision is final, binding and nonappealable	Yes, special master resolves all disputes in final, binding way	Yes	No	Yes

Index

CPSIA information can be obtained
at www.ICGtesting.com
Printed in the USA
LVHW031950060521
686706LV00018B/913

9 781108 404211